BIBLICAL THEOLOGY

J. Christiaan Beker

BIBLICAL THEOLOGY

Problems and Perspectives

In Honor of J. Christiaan Beker

EDITED BY
STEVEN J. KRAFTCHICK,
CHARLES D. MYERS, JR.,
AND
BEN C. OLLENBURGER

Abingdon Press
NASHVILLE

BIBLICAL THEOLOGY: PROBLEMS AND PERSPECTIVES

Copyright © 1995 by Abingdon Press

This book is printed on recycled, acid-free paper.

Library of Congress Cataloging-in-Publication Data

Biblical theology : problems and perspectives / edited by Steven J.
 Kraftchick, Charles D. Myers, Jr., and Ben C. Ollenburger.
     p. cm.
   "In honor of J. Christiaan Beker."
   Includes bibliographical references (p.   ).
 ISBN 0-687-03386-1 (alk. paper)
 1. Bible—Theology.   2. Bible—Theology—History of doctrines.
 3. Theology, Practical.   I. Beker, Johan Christiaan, 1924–   .
 II. Kraftchick, Steven John.   III. Myers, Charles Davison.
 IV. Ollenburger, Ben C.
 BS543.B523   1995
 230—dc20   95-9004
                                                                 CIP

Scripture quotations, unless otherwise indicated, are from the New Revised Standard Version Bible, copyright © 1989, by the Division of Christian Education of the National Council of the Churches of Christ in the United States of America.

Scripture quotations noted RSV are from the Revised Standard Version of the Bible, copyright 1946, 1952, 1971 by the Division of Christian Education of the National Council of the Churches of Christ in the USA. Used by permission.

Quotations noted TANAKH are from *The TANAKH: The New JPS Translation According to the Traditional Hebrew Text.* Copyright © 1985 by the Jewish Publication Society. Used by permission.

Permission has been granted by *Interpretation* for the use of excerpts from "The Relevance of Biblical Interpretation" by H. H. Rowley and "The Peril of Archaizing Ourselves" by Henry J. Cadbury.

Excerpts from "Wanted: A Biblical Theology," by Paul Minear, and "Creation and Human Creativity," by E. David Willis-Watkins are used by permission of *Theology Today.*

Excerpts from "The Crisis in Biblical Scholarship," by Luke T. Johnson are used by permission of the *Commonweal* Foundation.

Excerpts from "A Still Small Voice . . . Said, What Are You Doing Here?" by William Irwin are used by permission of Scholars Press.

95 96 97 98 99 00 01 02 03 04 — 10 9 8 7 6 5 4 3 2 1

MANUFACTURED IN THE UNITED STATES OF AMERICA

CONTENTS

PART THREE: PROPOSALS FOR BIBLICAL THEOLOGY

Old Testament

New Testament

PART FOUR: BIBLICAL THEOLOGY AND
THEOLOGICAL PRACTICE

INTRODUCTION

W hat *is* biblical theology? The essays gathered here to honor the work of Johann Christiaan Beker may be read as responding to that question. As anyone who has considered that question knows, no easy answer is forthcoming, and a number of difficulties arise with any answer. Some of the contributors to this volume chose to address the question directly. Others responded to it more indirectly by interpreting particular biblical texts or investigating concomitant hermeneutical, theological, and historical issues. All of the essays presented in this volume are attempts to relate biblical investigations to contemporary understandings; that is, to treat both the present and past with respect and integrity. Among the many dimensions of Chris Beker's work this concern stands as a central feature. We hope that these essays will reflect the stimulus of Beker's thought, as well as the hope for genuine conversation that has marked his relationship to us as friend, colleague, and teacher.

At points in its history, biblical theology has attempted to discover within the Bible, or in one of its Testaments, an archimedean point; a theme or subject matter that could serve as the universal factor within the particular and diverse material.[1] Even the best of these attempts have been only partially successful. Either they have tended toward abstraction, or they have drawn from some selected texts a concept or theme, or even a theology, that in the end had to be imposed on the remaining texts. Notoriously, these "remaining texts" eventually asserted themselves in ways that exposed the proffered unity to be what it was: an imposition.

To be sure, this exposure is not simply the result of textual self-assertion. By themselves, texts are relatively powerless and patient of sundry impositions. But texts are never entirely by themselves; they appear only in the company of readers. Here they appear in the company of critical interpreters. In such suspicious company, biblical texts have resisted, and have asserted themselves against the various unifying schemes proposed as impositions on them. No such scheme is proposed by the authors of this volume. Their differing approaches to biblical theology are, in important respects, a reflection of the irreducible diversity of the biblical material itself. This raises a second set of issues: the theological and social commitments of the interpreter always and everywhere affect the interpretation of the texts under consideration. Such a factor is not the result of unrecognized prejudice but is inherent in the interpretive enterprise itself.

In one form or another all of the essays do propose, assume, or in some cases display, a particular conception of biblical theology. However, even though they share this characteristic they do not, in most respects, share the *same* conception. Here one of the salient issues in biblical theology arises, for example, recognizing how the concept is being defined and enacted. Through their different approaches and views of the identity of biblical theology, these essays help to focus on the complexity of finding coherence among diverse texts and among diverse approaches to the task.

It may seem that these irreducible diversities would make theology, and especially biblical theology, impossible. If no unitary scheme can comprehend the Bible's diversity except by coercively reducing it, what has biblical theology to do? This returns us to our initial question: What *is* biblical theology? The preceding remarks have already pointed in the direction of one answer since they have suggested that biblical theology is a kind of *activity,* and especially a *critical* activity. Indeed, this has always been the case, even when biblical theologians have sought to draw from the Bible a unifying scheme and have then imposed that scheme on pliable, nonresistant texts. A quick review of some of this history makes the case.

In the seventeenth century, biblical theology became a tool critically engaged with the defense of Protestant orthodoxy against its Roman Catholic opponents. In the next century, the opposition had changed, and now biblical theology emerged as pietist criticism of the very same Protestant orthodoxy. In each case, but in different directions, biblical theology was a critical activity directed against prevailing attempts to define the Bible's unity; and in each case the objects of that criticism were the dogmatic theological schemes that muted biblical texts. Eventually a form of rationalism succeeded this pietism, and while it developed its own insights, it still preserved and enhanced biblical theology's critical nature. An example is the pure rationalist Jacob von Ammon, who, in his early years, conceived biblical theology as a critical enterprise that would refine dogmatic theology's claims on Christian belief.

That biblical theology, critically conducted, should reform Protestant dogmatic theology was the guiding conviction of Ammon's contemporary, Johann Philipp Gabler, usually considered the founder of biblical theology. Gabler warranted this consideration largely due to his rigorously historical-critical approach to the Bible as well as his commitments to the reliability of rationalist commitments. Gabler was not the first to practice historical criticism of the Bible. However, he was the first to harness a rigorous historical criticism to biblical theology, and the first to distinguish biblical theology, on just this basis, from dogmatic theology. While Gabler and the biblical theologians immediately following him were intensely occupied with dogmatic theology and, that is to say, with Christian belief and practice, Gabler came to be interpreted as providing biblical theology a particular mandate: namely, to pursue biblical theology in a thoroughly historical manner.

This full commitment to the avenues of historical-critical analyses marks Gabler's efforts from those of his predecessors. Otherwise, perhaps Luther or Zwingli or Calvin could be considered the founder of biblical theology.[2] Indeed, centuries earlier, Thomas Aquinas had proceeded in similar fashion, revising his systematic theological statements on the basis of his ongoing study of the Bible.[3] Even so, it cannot be denied that the Protestant reformers, despite differences among them, were more radical than their predecessors in returning *ad fontes*—"to the sources"—a motto of the Renaissance.

Neither can it be denied that, as is perhaps especially true of Luther, this gave their theology a more biblical or exegetical cast than was the case before them. Still, the reformers stood in some continuity with the past, but in a significant *dis*continuity with the course the future took a little less than three centuries later. Gabler is an emblem of this future, and he serves as biblical theology's founder, because the historical criticism he employed has remained dominant in biblical studies until the present, regardless of its many refinements over two centuries.

Gabler's immediate successors, most notably W. M. L. de Wette, gave sustained attention to the problems of historical understanding, and thus to what must be involved in a properly historical biblical theology.[4] De Wette managed to hold together an impressive variety of things: his biblical theology included a sophisticated anthropology and historiography, drawn from theological and especially philosophical sources; it included both Testaments of the Christian Bible; and in its 1831 edition, it was issued together with his dogmatic theology.[5] Despite the breadth of its scope and synthetic nature, subsequent generations of biblical theologians came to view precisely this kind of integration as impeding the fulfillment of, or even betraying, Gabler's mandate.

On their view, to be thoroughly historical and hence "trustworthy," biblical theology had to achieve absolute independence from dogmatic or systematic theology. This meant that it must employ the best critical-historical methods, and must employ them objectively with no control from dogmatic or ecclesial allegiances about outcome. Beyond this methodological independence it also must treat the Old and New Testaments in independence of each other, otherwise the religious commitments of one would unduly influence the reading of the other. However, this independence could only be relative from the NT's side, because the NT refers explicitly to the Old. Even so, the NT emerged within a Hellenistic culture vastly different from the ancient "oriental" world of the OT.

These became the defining issues in producing and evaluating a biblical theology. In arriving at these conclusions and others like them, biblical scholars were not simply mistaken. And they could claim, with a degree of legitimacy, to be fulfilling Gabler's mandate. Yet, over time, it became increasingly unclear why this was a mandate for *biblical theology*. Having produced such a work of historical analysis, one was left with the problem of clarifying its use and relationship to other critical endeavors. Gabler seemed to be the founder of something that had no point, except to justify the historical-critical investigation of Israel's *or* early Christianity's religious history. Hermann Gunkel and William Wrede argued just this way.[6] If they are right, then biblical theology faces another problem in addition to the Bible's diverse particularity: the biblical texts are irreducibly diverse artifacts of antique cultures and societies.

More important, the historical-critical methods that helped us to achieve this insight seem to leave us with the conclusions that Gunkel and Wrede drew; any theological unity found among these documents could not arise from historical investigations but would be something fashioned for theological or philosophical reasons. It should be noted, however, that Gunkel considered historical-critical exegesis to be eminently theological; he took theology to be concerned with religion, not with doctrine or dogmatic theology.[7] In that respect, Gunkel continued the tradition of biblical theology's critical relation to dogmatics. Similarly, a contemporary disciple of Wrede, Heiki Räisänen, envisions an essentially critical theological task for NT exegesis, which is to expose "strained application" of the texts and their "misuse" in theology.[8] If only obliquely, Gunkel and Wrede provoke questions about the very nature of theology and about the proper theological use of the biblical texts.

Contrary to their own intentions, Gunkel and Wrede, serving as representative figures, exposed an entirely new front for biblical theology's critical attention. Historically, that attention was directed to Christian dogmatic theology, which biblical theology sought variously to support, to reform, or (in the case of pietism) to replace, on behalf of Christian faith and practice.[9] But if, as Gunkel and Wrede suggest, the historical-critical methods leave biblical theology able only to describe disparate religious histories or discrete texts and traditions, and at most to exercise a veto on certain uses of the texts, then perhaps those methods themselves must become the object of biblical theology's critical attention.[10] Critical attention, however, need not mean rejection. It can mean—to recall de Wette—reflection on the nature or practice of historical understanding, and thus on the ends toward which historical methods are employed. Earlier in this century, and on the basis of this kind of reflection, Gerhard von Rad demonstrated the theological potential of a history-of-traditions approach to the Old Testament.[11] Rudolf Bultmann took this kind of reflection much farther in his *Theology of the New Testament,* and in an astonishing variety of studies accompanying it.[12]

Not surprisingly, critics from both ends of the theological spectrum have pointed out various shortcomings, or even dead ends, in the programs of Bultmann and von Rad. But in their respective fields these two interpreters provoked the widest-ranging hermeneutical, theological, and methodological questions. Indeed, they helped to open once again a space for the most basic questions about biblical theology, particularly those pertaining to contemporary meaning.

Of course neither von Rad nor Bultmann could foresee the more recent revolution in intellectual ethos, which denies to any method, to any interpretive procedure and its underlying theory, their claims to self-evidence and universality. To put it another way, and positively, our current intellectual climate exposes all interpretations and interpretive practices to the particular and socially located interests, and to the values and objectives, that guide them. This revolution provides an even deeper challenge to the activity of biblical theology because now not only is there a question about the relationship of the material to itself, nor to the viability of historical-critical methods, but also to the grounding of interpretation as an exercise of discovery. Claims of normativity, authority, and completeness are debated not just in terms of adequacy of investigation but in terms of their intrinsic legitimacy.

This does not leave particular kinds of interpretation, including historical-critical ones, without prospect of justification, but it does challenge them to provide such arguments. It requires, therefore, that they be able to justify themselves—to hold themselves accountable—without recourse to assumptions held implicitly to be self-evident. Indeed, the very values and objectives, or the moral commitments, whose ineluctable presence in every act of interpretation undermines pretensions of self-evidence and absoluteness, may be called on to play a legitimate role in justifying the choice, or the use, of a particular interpretive approach or method.

Certain types of feminist interpretation are cases in point. The objective of such types of interpretation which seek "to eliminate women's subordination and marginalization," together with the values and commitments funding that objective, play a role in justifying feminist interpretive strategies, methods, and theories.[13] The intensity, rigor, and integrity of such interpretations are neither less nor more than those of historical-critical inquiries, but the grounds and objectives are certainly different. Hence, the goals and forms of a biblical theology following such modes of discussion will necessarily take shapes that differ from their historical-critical alternatives. As they differ in preference and objective they provide needed challenge and critique of the hegemony of the historical-critical traditions.

However, all objectives, values, and commitments—these, too, may require justification—no particular instance of them can claim self-evidence. Justification, in this sense, is forever incomplete and thoroughly complex, because it constantly responds to challenges, innovations, and experience; and because there is no final and fixed external point whose self-evidence or universality secures the ground on which justification may rest. Inevitably, at least for now, justification is intersubjective and, hence, a communal affair. It goes on in—but also between and among—communities of discourse whose rhetorical practices not only depend on and shape shared values and commitments, but also disclose them and their intersubjective grounds.

11

Biblical theology is a case in point. As noted above, in the course of its history it has struggled to justify itself, to hold itself accountable to different communities whose values, commitments, and rhetorical practices are not simply identical.[14] We can illustrate the differences between two such communities with reference to God, or the use of the term "God." In an examination of several biblical narratives, Cheryl Exum observes that "the deity" is, "after all, a character within the narrative."[15] No one could dispute this, and it is assumed in biblical scholarship. Yet it is also the case that some communities refer to God as more than just a character *within* the narrative, even while (diversely) appealing to the narrative in order to show what they mean by "God" and how properly to refer to God. For some such communities, to borrow Thomas Tracy's terms, God is story-bound but not story-relative; for them, "God is a possible subject of predication connected with the field of reference to which we ourselves belong."[16] Here are different rhetorical practices embedded in different communities of discourse. Biblical theology, on one understanding, tries to negotiate the differences.

Here biblical theology can function once more in the role of critic, bringing into conversation the various communities and their individual privileged values and commitments. That the Bible and communities of faith refer to what the latter confess as the same God does not supply biblical theology with the unifying scheme it has sometimes sought. The diversity among the Bible's references to and depictions of God, and the diverse theologies in which they are embedded, are part of what generate biblical theology; they are a part of its problem.[17] But biblical theology has a stake in considering, and taking seriously, *why* and *for whom* it matters, whether "it" be a particular issue or biblical theology itself. Compatible with this understanding is Brevard Childs's claim that the question is not whether biblical theology will go on—it will and does go on, publicly, at least every Sunday—but what kind of theology it will be.[18]

In its more recent history, though not without exceptions, biblical theology has become more modest about what it can achieve, less concerned to guard its independence from other disciplines and communities, and open to a broader range of strategies and methods. Old issues remain, such as the relation(s) between the Old and New Testaments, the problem(s) of faith and history, and the theological centering of a text or an author's thought. But new issues have arisen, along with proposals for resolving or eliminating the old ones; issues about the means and goals of interpretation and the social and political commitments of interpretive communities complicate an already intricate task. In its more modest vein, biblical theology views these issues less as problems, all of which it must solve, than as the horizons of its ongoing work. In turn, this makes the question "What *is* biblical theology?" less urgent and at the same time perhaps more important.

Biblical theology is what biblical theologians do, and the reasons they offer for doing it. We hope that this book will make a contribution to both. Should *that* occur, no one will be happier than the one whom this volume wishes to honor.

PART ONE

THE BIBLE
AND THEOLOGY
IN CHURCH HISTORY

Chapter One / BIBLICAL THEOLOGY IN THE PATRISTIC PERIOD: THE LOGOS DOCTRINE AS A "PHYSIOLOGICAL" INTERPRETATION OF SCRIPTURE

Kathleen McVey

From the perspective of the history of doctrine the essential problem of the early Church was to enunciate what we would call a biblical theology. In the words of J. N. D. Kelly:

> The doctrine of one God, the Father and creator, formed the background and indisputable premiss of the Church's faith. Inherited from Judaism, it was her bulwark against pagan polytheism, Gnostic emanationism and Marcionite dualism. The problem for theology was to integrate with it, intellectually, the fresh data of the specifically Christian revelation. Reduced to their simplest, these were the convictions that God had made Himself known in the Person of Jesus, the Messiah, raising Him from the dead and offering salvation to men through Him, and that He had poured out His Holy Spirit upon the Church. Even at the New Testament stage ideas about Christ's pre-existence and creative role were beginning to take shape, and a profound, if often obscure, awareness of the activity of the Spirit in the Church was emerging. No steps had been taken so far, however, to work all these complex elements into a coherent whole. The Church had to wait for more than three hundred years for a final synthesis, for not until the council of Constantinople (381) was the formula of one God existing in three co-equal Persons formally ratified. Tentative theories, however, some more and some less satisfactory, were propounded in the preceding centuries.[1]

With the benefit of hindsight we can readily concur with this statement as a description of what the early Christian writers achieved as theologians. Before they could begin to articulate the issues in the terms used by a modern historian of doctrine, however, two prior questions had to be resolved: First, it had to be determined exactly what constituted the Bible—for example, what books were to be included, the problem of the canon—and what were acceptable parameters for its interpretation.[2] Second, theology, understood as a systematic approach to religious belief, had virtually to be invented. Returning to Kelly's

15

statement, it is important to ask why these disparate materials needed intellectual integration. In the post-Patristic age, Christian theology having been born, this may seem a frivolous question. It is taken for granted that a major religion needs to articulate a theology or theologies to achieve intellectual viability. But there was no such assumption underlying the Hebrew Bible, the New Testament, or their composite, the Christian Bible. They include a variety of literarily and theologically disparate materials whose underlying unity has been a subject of scholarly discussion and debate. Likewise, traditional religions such as the polytheism of the Greco-Roman world had no such theology—at least not in their original forms.

It was the Greek philosophers who invented the word *theologia* and thus they also began to invent the enterprise of theology, understood as "the science of things divine."[3] So in response to questions posed subsequent to the rise of Greek philosophy and brought to their attention by figures such as Marcion and Valentinus, Justin and the other Greek apologists, and Philo, Clement, and Origen of Alexandria, Christians began to create a theology. That is, they began to systematize their beliefs and to bring them into a confrontation with reason as well as with a variety of philosophical, historical, and rhetorical canons of truth. Closely connected with this development was the introduction of nonliteral modes of scriptural exegesis.

The process was complex and unpremeditated.[4] The extant Christian writings from the first centuries include compositions in Greek, Latin, Syriac, and Coptic, and they represent attempts to come to terms with a complicated array of religious traditions as well as a variety of philosophical schools. They encompass a plethora of literary genres: gospels, letters, psalms, testaments, and acts of apostles excluded from the canonical scripture; acts and passions of martyrs; apologies; scholia and commentaries on scripture; homilies, catenae, Church orders, creeds, and hymns; treatises arguing for a given theological view against its perceived opponents.[5] In many instances we know little or nothing of the author's identity and specific historical context other than what the internal evidence of the surviving documents happens to divulge or what fourth-century writers such as Eusebius, Jerome, or Epiphanius tell us. Perhaps the sole element common to all these authors is their implicit or explicit claim to base their views on scripture.

As it would, then, be an overwhelming task to attempt a synthesis of the biblical theology of the early Church, I propose instead to explore some of the background for a single issue that straddles the line between theology and biblical interpretation, the Logos theology of the second-century Greek apologists. Ultimately an essential ingredient of the Nicene formulation of the Trinity, this doctrine is commonly and rightly related to the development of Middle and Neo-Platonic understandings of the Logos. I will argue here that it is also to be understood as an aspect of the type of Stoic allegorical exegesis known in antiquity as physical allegory or "physiologizing." This perspective will shed some light on the essential linkage of allegorical interpretation with philosophical concerns within the larger setting of Greco-Roman antiquity. Thus, with Kelly, we will see the Christian writers as propounding "tentative theories . . . some more and some less satisfactory" on the way to the Nicene formulation—a matter of interest to the Christian theologian and historian of doctrine. But we will also see them more as they probably saw themselves—as proponents of a religion capable of providing answers for the intellectual and cultural concerns of their own time.

It is well known that the Stoics adopted allegorical interpretation of the earliest Greek literature to avoid the problems that literal reading of Homer and Hesiod caused for a more sophisticated age. It is equally familiar to modern students of the Bible that the nonliteral modes of interpretation devised by the Stoics and rhetoricians made their way into Christian biblical interpretation.[6] Pépin distinguishes three different types of allegory used by the Stoics and subsequently adopted by others in the Hellenistic period: "l'allégorie physique, qui voit dans les dieux et les héros d'Homère une représentation des éléments de l'universe; l'allégorie psychologique, qui en fait des dispositions de l'âme; l'allégorie morale, selon laquelle ils figurent des vertus ou des vices."[7] Hellenistic allegorical interpretation answered many different needs. For those embarrassed by the sexual and other antics of anthropomorphic deities, moral allegory proffered moral lessons as the true meaning of the problematic aspects of the traditional mythology. For the philosophically sophisticated, psychological allegory provided more satisfactory explanations based on theories of the inner workings of the human mind. Physical allegory provided food for thought for those whose interests had shifted toward the protoscientific questions of cosmology and cosmogony.[8] Although theoretically distinct, however, the three types of allegory sometimes overlap and may also serve more than one purpose. So, for example, physical allegory was often applied to the sexual relations of the gods, thus dealing with ethical problems as well as other intellectual challenges unmet by the literal reading. This type, the physical or physiological, such as cosmological or cosmogonic, interpretation of Greek myth, especially as used by the Stoics and by Philo, provides insight into variations in the trinitarian formulations of the Greek Christian apologists. This will be the focus of the balance of this paper. At this point of our argument it will be useful to provide a brief account of Stoic cosmogony and its general role in Chrysippus's reading of Homer and Hesiod.[9]

Basic Principles of Stoic Cosmogony and Cosmology and Their Application by Chrysippus to Greek Myth[10]

The monistic system of the Stoics begins with a single material substance *ousia*, "a finite natural continuum," which has two "aspects" or principles *(archai).*[11] The first is the active principle *(to poioun)* and is also known as the word *(ho logos)*, or god *(ho theos)*, as well as "creative fire" *(to pyr teknikon);* the second is the passive *(to paschon)*, known also as "inert" or "unqualified matter" *(he apoios hylē)* and as chaos or darkness *(to chaos)* or as water *(to hydor).*[12] When the logos as creative fire acts upon the inert matter construed as moisture (= Phase one),[13] the cosmos as a differentiated and ordered being is generated (= Phase two) in a manner which owes as much to Aristotelian notions of biological reproduction as to the pre-Socratic philosophers.[14] From this action the four elements are produced and arranged in "spherical tiers": earth, water, air and fire.[15] The result is a cosmic embryo.[16] The thoroughgoing application of this biological metaphor to the cosmos is the central concern and vital innovation of Stoic cosmology and cosmogony.[17] The production and arrangement of elements in the cosmic embryo is understood differently by Zeno, Cleanthes, and Chrysippus. Most important for our purposes is Chrysippus's modification of Zeno's scheme. Whereas Zeno supposed that first the earth settled out from the liquid, then the air evaporated from the water, and then some of the air changed by rarification to fire, Chrysippus modified the sequence so that *aithēr* rather than fire is produced at the end of the second stage.[18] Whereas Zeno seems to have supposed the production of compounds and further individuation of beings in the cosmos took place through a growth process governed by "nature" *(physis)* defined as "a craftsmanlike fire, proceeding methodically to genesis" *(pyr technikon hodo badizon eis genesin),*[19] Chrysippus introduced a new entity, the spirit *(pneuma),* to continue the generative action of the logos (= Phase three).[20] Closely related to Logos, thus virtually another principle, the spirit is also a sort of fifth body emerging from the *aithēr* to bring the fiery principle of life to the sublunar world.[21] Heavenly bodies and vegetable, animal, and human forms of life are understood to have come into existence through similar processes of generation. Once in existence and located in the environment to which each is suited, they are governed by the same nature that created them and guides them toward the purpose for which they were brought into existence. Thus the familiar Stoic notions of the beauty of the cosmic order, of providence and the linking of the two through astrology are closely related to the common origin of the entire cosmos.

For Chrysippus the spirit is present in the world in a manner analogous to the wind or breath in the human body.[22] In addition, although the cosmic spirit permeates the cosmos, as in the case of the human spirit in the human body, it has a center of consciousness and decision *(hegemonikon)* identified with the purest part of the *aithēr.*[23] In its role as permeating the cosmos as the human spirit permeates the body, the cosmic spirit gives life and movement to the cosmos by providing a tension *(tonos)* which holds all existents in inherent relation to one another.[24] The well-known Stoic concept of cosmic sympathy *(sympatheia)* is thus clearly rooted in this "cosmobiology," the understanding of the cosmos as a huge living being.[25]

Just as the elements and subsequently the rest of the world and its inhabitants have come into existence, they are destined to pass out of existence.[26] On the biological model this may be seen both as cosmic death and as cosmic reproduction.[27] In the periodic cosmic conflagration (*ekpyrōsis*), the cosmos reproduces itself by the same fiery generative process by which it first came into existence. The cycle will repeat itself exactly without limit.

Both the pre-Socratic philosophers and the mythology of Homer and Hesiod were interpreted, especially by Chrysippus, in a harmonizing manner to show the compatibility of Stoic cosmogony with these earliest Greek literary traditions.[28] Thus the Ionians, especially Heraclitus, along with Homer and Hesiod, were seen as effectively Stoics "before their time."[29] On the one hand, the Ionian cosmogonies were treated as fundamentally the same as their Stoic counterparts. On the other hand, the anthropomorphic deities of Homer and Hesiod were physiologized— that is, interpreted as actually symbolic of natural forces. Stories of divine copulation and reproduction were readily harmonized with the Stoic cosmobiology.[30] In many respects Hesiod's *Theogony* had provided this basic insight, but the Stoic use of Platonic and Aristotelian philosophical notions vastly increased the philosophical cohesion and credibility of the system.

Alternate Allegories of Cosmic Origin Among the Physiologists: Sexual Union with Hera vs. Parthenogenetic Production of Athena

Of the many couplings and births recounted in Hesiod's *Theogony*, we will focus on two that were of particular importance to the physiological interpreters. One, the union of Zeus with Hera is the usual sort from which children are born after gestation in their mother. In the other, the same god's union with Metis and the subsequent birth of Athena, Zeus usurps to some degree the birthing capacity of the female.

Hesiod gives a straightforward account of the marriage of Zeus to Hera: "Last of all he made Hera his fertile wife, and she bore Hebe and Ares and Eilethyia, sharing intimacy with the king of gods and men."[31] Chrysippus, however, offers as its deeper meaning a complex physical allegory which corresponds to the first phase of the cosmogony as described above. Thus, we begin with the solitary Mind (*monos ho nous*), distributed evenly throughout the "enormous place (*topon amēchanon*)." As the entirety *[to holos]* Mind emits a lightning flash, transforming himself to a milder form of fire, a fiery air (*aera purōdē*, for example, *aithēr*) before uniting with the passive aspect of *ousia*. This union is represented allegorically by the union of Zeus and Hera. After the union Mind produces a seed of the universe (*tēn pāsan autou pantos gonēn . . . hen sperma tou pantos*), which is the wet substance now permeated by himself and thus able to be shaped and ordered by him.[32]

19

The other essential locus for cosmogonic allegory in Hesiod is Athena's conception and birth, described in two passages of the *Theogony:*

> Zeus as king of the gods made Metis his first wife, the wisest among gods and mortal men. But when she was about to give birth to the pale-eyed goddess Athene, he tricked her deceitfully with cunning words and put her away in his belly *(nēdyn)* on the advice of Earth and starry heaven. They advised him in this way so that no other of the gods, the eternal fathers, should have the royal station instead of Zeus. For from Metis [Resource, Cunning] it was destined that clever children should be born; first a pale-eyed daughter, Tritogeneia, with courage and sound counsel equal to her father's, and then a son she was to bear, king of gods and men, one proud of heart. But Zeus put her away in his belly *(nēdyn)* first, so that the goddess could advise him of what was good or bad.[33]

A few verses later Hesiod returns to Athena's birth. In the intervening lines, Zeus had acquired six more wives in succession as well as numerous children, the last being Hera and her children as described in the passage quoted above. The birth of Athena, although a consequence of his first union with Metis, now appears to be his accomplishment alone, reflecting the fact that the tale of Zeus' giving birth to Athena from his head existed independently prior to its incorporation into Hesiod's narrative:[34]

> And he himself, out of his head, gave birth to the pale-eyed Tritogeneia, the fearsome rouser of the fray, leader of armies, the lady Atrytone, whose pleasure is in war and the clamour of battle; while Hera, furying and quarreling with her husband, without sharing intimacy gave birth to the renowned Hephaestus, who is endowed with skills beyond all the Celestials.[35]

In the context of Hesiod's text as it stands, the two passages concerning Metis and Athena can be reconciled by assuming that Metis remains within him and is forgotten as Zeus first marries his other wives and now performs the function of the mother by bringing Athena forth from his head.

A fragment quoted by Chrysippus and preserved by Galen demonstrates both that the earlier version of Athena's birth from Zeus without Metis was still known and that differing physical allegories had developed on the basis of the two versions of her birth. In a discussion about the location of the governing faculty of the soul *(to hegemonikon tēs psychēs),* Chrysippus says that those who hold that it is in the head base their view on Athena's coming from the head of Zeus, since she is counsel or wisdom *(mētin ousan)* and prudence, practical wisdom, or thought *(phronēsin),* "otherwise wisdom and thought would not arise in the head, if the ruling part is not in it."[36] But he himself holds that it is in the heart *(stēthesi)* since that is where Zeus stowed away Metis before Athena's birth through his head. In support of his view he adduces not only the two segments of Hesiod's *Theogony* but also nineteen additional lines from another poem of

Hesiod. The additional material presents Zeus's intercourse with Metis as motivated by retaliation for Hera's angry and solitary production of Hephaestus as well as by fear of being superseded by a more powerful son to be born of Metis. More importantly for Chrysippus's allegory the precise location of Metis within Zeus is given fuller description:

> He seized her with his hands and placed her in his belly *(egkattheto nēdyn)*,
> fearing that she might give birth to something more powerful than the thunder-bolt.
> For this reason the high-throned son of Cronos, who dwells in the aether,
> swallowed her suddenly. And straightway she was big with *(kysato)* Pallas Athena,
> to whom the father of men and gods gave birth *(etikte)*
> through the top of his head *(par koryphen)* on the banks of the river Trito;
> but Metis lay hidden in Zeus' inner organs,
> *(Metis d' aute Zēnos hupo splagchnois lelathyia esto,)*
> she the mother of Athena, doer of just deeds,
> wisest of gods and mortal men.[37]

To understand all this properly, Chrysippus argues, we should think of the notion that "people swallow the things that are said, and . . . that they are stored in the belly *(eis tēn koilian)*." When "wisdom *(phronēsis)* and art in practical matters *(peri tōn kata ton bion technē)*," which Metis represents, have been swallowed by us in this sense, they are brought forth "by speech through the mouth by way of the head *(dia tou stomatos kata tēn kephalēn)*." Thus the allegorical interpretation of the tale does not contradict the Stoic view that the center of reasoning and conscience is in the heart not the head. Chrysippus's remarks show clearly that two anthropologies and two notions of human physiology were at stake in the allegorization of the myth. Those who located the human mind in the head used only the notion that Athena had emerged from the head of Zeus as their basis. Chrysippus, by contrast, considered the mind to be located anatomically in the heart and to emerge, so to speak, by the agency of the voice exiting the body through the mouth, thus merely moving from the lower parts in the direction of the crown of the head rather than exiting through the crown of the head, as Hesiod's precise wording would demand.[38]

Galen's own views, stated at the beginning of his treatise show that the issue continued to be important in the second century CE. He himself favored a threefold distribution of human motivating powers, locating them in three different body parts. He claimed that his own views were rooted in Hippocrates and Plato as opposed to Chrysippus's views based on Aristotle and Theophrastus:

> It was my purpose at the beginning to inquire about the powers that govern us *(ton dioikouson hēmas dynameōn)*, whether they all have the heart as their only source *(ek tēs kardias monēs hormōntai)*, as Aristotle and Theophrastus supposed,

21

or whether it is better to posit three sources *(treis archas)* for them, as Hippocrates and Plato believed. But since Chrysippus disputed with the ancients not only about the sources but also about the powers themselves and did not admit the existence of either the spirited *(thymoeidē)* or the desiderative *(epithymētikēn)* [power], I decided that I must first examine his view and then return to my original plan, which was to show that the brain, the heart, and the liver *(egkephalos te kai kardia kai hēpar)* are the sources of the powers that govern us *(archai tōn dioikouson hēmas dynameōn eisin)*.[39]

Given the "cosmobiology" of the Stoics, differing understandings of human anatomy correspond to differing cosmologies as well. So each of the versions of Athena's birth also provided a basis for the Logos doctrine of the Stoic cosmogony. The allegory for the simpler version is reported by Justin: "They say Athena is the daughter of Zeus not from intercourse but, since they knew that God, having conceived (for example, having thought, *ennoēthenta*), made the cosmos through the Word *(dia logou),* so they say that the first Thought *(tēn protēn ennoian)* is Athena."[40] But this allegory conflicts with the traditional Stoic notion that the center of human consciousness is located not in the head but in the heart. The application of that anatomical view to the cosmic level had resulted in the location of the cosmic *hēgemonikon* in the earth.[41] The allegory based on the more complex version of the myth, as endorsed by Chrysippus, resolves the conflict. Without altering the traditional location of the human center of consciousness, the allegory of the birth of Athena can be applied to the bringing forth of the cosmic *pneuma* from the *aithēr.* Further, his version of the allegory corresponds precisely to the "two-stage" version of the Logos doctrine, beloved of the Stoic rhetoricians. Just as Metis remains within Zeus while Athena emerges, the eternally present *logos endiathetos* remains present in God while the *logos prophorikos* emerges to perform the work of ordering the cosmos.[42] This version of the allegory is attested in a fragment preserved in the Pseudo-Clementine literature:

> By his own heat, therefore, Zeus—that is, the seething substance *(zeousa ousia)*—evaporates the remainder of the underlying moisture, the very strong and divine spirit *(pneuma)* which they called Metis. When it has come to the top *(kata koryphēs)* of the aether and been absorbed *(synpothen)* by it, just like moisture mixed with heat *(hōsper hygron thermō migen),* having made the ever-moving pulsation, it gave birth to sagacity *(genna tēn sunesin),* which they call Pallas from this pulsation *(pallesthai),* this being the most craftsmanlike wisdom *(technikōtatēn ousan phronēsin)* by which the aetherial craftsman *(ho aitherios technitēs)* crafted the entire cosmos *(ton panta etechnēsato kosmon).*[43]

So it is clear that the marriage of Zeus and Hera, on the one hand, and the longer and shorter versions of Athena's begetting and birth, on the other, offered myths which were variously suited to the physical allegories of the Stoics and their imitators. Since competing theories of human anatomy and corresponding theories of cosmogony and cosmology were based on these myths, the choice of words that evoked one or another of them was fraught with importance. It follows that Jewish and Christian writers had to choose their words carefully as they appropriated the philosophical concepts of their contemporaries.

The Greek Apologists and the Birth of the Logos and Sophia

As is well known, the Greek apologists of the second century adopted the Stoic notion of the "two-stage Logos."[44] It is also generally accepted that in this they have followed the lead of Philo of Alexandria.[45] Theophilus provides the clearest evidence that he knew the Stoic technical terminology of *logos endiathetos* and *logos prophorikos*.[46] He also provides a vivid image of its anthropomorphic roots in his statement that, "having his own Logos innate in His own bowels, God generated him by the aid of his own Sophia, vomiting him forth before the universe."[47] The inconsistency and uniqueness of his designation of the roles of the Logos and Sophia of God have also been noted.[48] In the passage just quoted, Logos and Sophia seem to be distinct entities. A few lines later they appear to be identical with each other and with the Spirit: "this Logos . . . being spirit of God *(pneuma theou)* and Beginning *(archē)* and Sophia and Power of the Most High, came down into the prophets."[49] Again, elsewhere Sophia and Logos appear to be distinct from one another, yet both agents of God's creating power,[50] and now one, now the other, is identified with the Spirit.[51] Although Logos appears to take the role of *logos prophorikos* creating the cosmos once he has been "vomited forth" from the "bowels" of God while Sophia apparently remains within as *logos endiathetos,* Theophilus does not maintain this usage with consistency.[52]

The other apologists also betray some confusion and inconsistency in their proto-Trinitarianism. For example, Justin sometimes distinguishes, sometimes identifies, the "prophetic spirit" and the Logos, allowing both to function as preexistent Christ.[53] Athenagoras uses Logos and "prophetic spirit" similarly to Justin.[54] In using Prov 8:22-31 to establish the preexistence of the Logos, Justin and Athenagoras implicitly identify Logos with the personified Wisdom.[55] But only Theophilus allows Sophia to stand over against the Logos as a distinct entity rather than being absorbed implicitly or explicitly as a title for the Logos. Justin probably offers the explanation for this when he ridicules the notion of a feminine "First Thought" which he ascribes to the pagan allegorists: "And similarly with malicious intent they say Athena is the daughter of Zeus not from intercourse but, since they know that God, having conceived, made the cosmos through the Word, so they say that the first Thought is Athena—which we consider to be quite laughable, alleging that the image of Thought is the shape of females."[56]

Although Grant garnered an impressive array of parallels to Theophilus's "inelegant metaphor" for the generation of the Logos (and Sophia), he did not find in them a satisfactory explanation of the apologist's choice of words.[57] Curry argued that Theophilus's phrase echoed a fragment of Hesiod, and that the Christian apologist was writing a theogony to counteract his.[58] Thus he concluded that Theophilus has only the Greek poet in mind, not Ps 44:2 of the LXX or Ps 109:3 of the LXX, as Grant had suggested.[59] The Hesiodic fragment to which Theophilus alluded is the same one that Chrysippus interpreted and that Galen quoted in taking issue with that Stoic interpretation.[60] I have argued elsewhere that Theophilus's apology in its entirety is a refutation not of the *Theogony* itself but rather of its reinterpretation by Chrysippus. Thus it is an argument against the physiological allegorization of Hesiod by the later Stoics. In opposition to their reading, Theophilus proposed to read the same philosophical notions out of the Bible.[61] Applying this general approach to the case of the apologist's teaching on the generation and birth of the Logos, it is most plausible that he has Pss 44:2 and 109:3 in mind as providing the best ancient literary basis for the Logos doctrine—better than Hesiod's versions of Athena's birth. His echoing of *Exēreyxato* from Psalm 44 with *exēreyxamenos* would be as deliberate as his echoing of Hesiod's *hypo splagchnois* with *en tois idiois splagchnois.*[62] I conclude, then, that Theophilus introduced his unusual anthropomorphism not, as Curry argued, in a fairly clumsy effort to persuade his pagan friend, but because he had fallen heir to a tradition of Stoic interpretation of the Hebrew Bible that had not been demythologized to the same degree as Justin's.

If this reconstruction is correct, there should be traces of "physiologizing" the birth of Wisdom in Hellenistic Judaism as well. Rather than efforts to bolster the authority of Homer or Hesiod these would be ostensibly interpretations of biblical texts meant to show that Hebrew Scripture was the best basis for Stoic physical allegory. They would constitute a portion of the polemics on behalf of "barbarian wisdom" partially extant in the surviving Hellenistic literature.[63] Such works would be recognizable by the remnants of pagan myth still clinging to the philosophical interpretations without any foundation in the scriptural passages supposedly being interpreted. Philo provides some evidence that there was in fact a broader movement to interpret Hebrew Scripture in this manner.

Philo on the Conception and Birth of the Divine Wisdom

Philo interprets some biblical passages pertaining to the divine Wisdom in a manner that suggests the influence of the Stoic "physiologists."[64] He was familiar with this type of interpretation, espoused by the "physical men" *(physikoi andres)* among his contemporaries.[65] Although he refers not to the deities of Greek myth but only to their philosophical representations,[66] he provides examples corresponding to each of the two types of birth imagery we have seen in Stoic physiological allegory: heterosexual intercourse, conception, and birth, on the one hand; male parthenogenetic birth, on the other. The first type of interpretation is found in an aside in his comments on the nonliteral meaning of "father and mother" in Deut 21:18-21. Since he understands Prov 8:22 as stating that Wisdom is the means by which God brought the rest of creation into existence, he quotes that verse to affirm his view that Wisdom is the Mother of the creation, while God is its Father:

> Now the names of father and mother are common, but their force differs. For we would immediately and rightly say that the craftsman who made this universe *(ton goun tode to pan ergasamenon dēmiourgon)* was at the same time the father of the one that came to exist *(tou gegonoto)*, and its mother the Knowledge of [her] Maker uniting with whom,—not as a human [does]— God begot creation *(tēn tou pepoiēkotos epistēmēn, hē synōn ho theos ouch hōs anthrōpos espeire genesin)*. She, then, having received the seeds of God, gave birth with powerful birthpangs to the one and only beloved perceptible son, this cosmos *(de paradexamenē ta tou theou spermata telesphoris ōdisi ton monon kai agapēton aisthēton huion apekuēse, tonde ton kosmon)*. Thus was introduced by one of those from the divine chorus Wisdom, speaking this way, "God possessed me *(ektēsato me)* the very first of his works, and before eternity He established me." For it was necessary that all things insofar as they came into existence be younger than the mother and nurse of the universe *(tēs mētros kai tithēnēs tōn holōn panth' hōsa eis genesin ēlthen einai neōtera)*.[67]

This passage itself is clearly cosmogonic: God is Father *(patēr)* and Maker *(dēmiourgos)* of the cosmos, which is the sole beloved son *(monos kai agapētos huios* as well as *gegonotos)*, Wisdom *(sophia* and *epistēmē)* is Mother *(mētēr)* and nurse *(tithēnē)*. Cosmogony is not, however, Philo's major concern in the treatise at hand. His focus shifts quickly to the ethical consequences of this fatherhood and motherhood and remains there for the rest of the treatise. Yet his elaborate allegory of parenthood, in which father is understood as right reason *(orthos logos)* and mother as education *(paideia)*, is founded in the cosmological roles of "the parents of the universe *(tous men dē tou pantos goneis)*" as he has explained them here.[68]

In another passage Philo seems to have in mind the Stoic cosmogonic allegory based on the birth of the virgin goddess, Athena. Thus he argues that Bethuel ought to be understood as the Hebrew equivalent of Wisdom:

> It is wisdom's name *(sophias de onoma)* that the holy oracles proclaim by "Bethuel," a name meaning in our speech "Daughter of God *(thygatēr theou)*"; yea, a true-born

and ever-virgin daughter *(gnēsia ge thygatēr kai aeiparthenos),* who, by reason alike of her own modesty and of the glory of Him that begot her *(tou gennēsantos),* hath obtained a nature free from every defiling touch.[69]

Behind this interpretation of Gen 28:2 is again the speech of Wisdom in Prov 8:22-31, now read with emphasis on the wording of verse 25 *(gennā me)* to conclude that Wisdom not only antedated the rest of the creation, but that she is also appropriately to be called the daughter begotten by God. Elsewhere Philo is content to treat the speech as simply affirming the pre-existence of Wisdom.[70]

We might suppose that Philo has become entangled in his elaborate web of allegory, carelessly identifying Wisdom at times as the consort of God and mother of creation at others as the daughter of God. But both are rooted in Prov 8:22-31, the image of mother more in the twenty-second verse, that of daughter more in the twenty-fifth. As if to signal his awareness of the apparent contradiction, in one passage he bestows both metaphors on Wisdom simultaneously: "And who is to be considered the daughter of God but Wisdom, who is the first-born mother of all things and most of all of those who are greatly purified in soul."[71] It seems that here the male parthenogenetic model has begun to take over the marriage model of conception and birth. Indeed, Philo characterizes Wisdom even as father, and he is clearly uneasy with the possibility that an inference of inferiority will be drawn from the female personification.[72] Thus he anticipates the New Testament writers and the Christian apologists in replacing Sophia by Logos. An important factor in this shift must be the more direct influence of Plato's *Timaeus,* seen not only in Philo's *de opificio mundi* but also in other works, where instead of mother or daughter, Wisdom is the archetype according to which God constructed the cosmos.[73]

Without pretending to offer a comprehensive view of Philo's understanding of the Logos, we can nevertheless suggest that the passages discussed here, with their overt reproductive imagery, constitute the remnants of the Logos doctrine of the "physiologists" among his Alexandrian Jewish predecessors. Philo himself may have been primarily responsible for turning the Jewish and subsequently the Christian interpreters toward a more Platonic style of allegory, one further removed from Greek mythology. This substantially demythologized form of Logos theology was used by Justin and Athenagoras. Although Theophilus wrote approximately two decades after Justin, there is no evidence that he knew the work of the earlier apologist, nor is it clear that he knew Philo's corpus. Instead he must have used writings from a Hellenistic Jewish exegetical tradition which had remained closer to its Stoic roots. Thus he was led to describe the generation and birth of the Logos by God through Sophia in terms more similar to the generation and birth of Athena by Zeus through Metis.

Conclusions

Variations in the incunabula of trinitarian doctrine in the apologists reveal a great deal about the intellectual and cultural environment of second-century Christians. The unusual features of Theophilus of Antioch's teaching and their resonance with a lesser strand in Philo's understanding of the Logos provide insight into the exegesis of the Hellenistic Jewish "physiologists" who anticipated Philo. In attempting to bridge the gap between Jew and Greek these writers had aggressively espoused the superiority of the "barbarian wisdom" of the Hebrew Bible over the earliest Greek writings trumpeted by their Stoic contemporaries. At the same time they were quietly, perhaps to a degree unconsciously, adopting many of the Stoic doctrines. The same is true of Theophilus.

The odd features of his trinitarian expressions are not, then, careless or less sophisticated formulations. Galen's posthumous dispute with Chrysippus and the latter's previous argument against other "physiologists" show that the various mythological formulations of the birth of Wisdom or the Logos had anatomical, anthropological, and cosmological implications. In specifying that "God generated his own Logos by Sophia vomiting him forth from his bowels," Theophilus was not showing unforgivable indelicacy and foolish ignorance. Nor was he displaying a lack of ability to think clearly or a shortsighted overeagerness to accommodate his pagan audience. He was indicating his belief that the seat of human intelligence and conscience, as well as of emotion and reproductive capacity, was in a single location, and that it was to be found somewhere in the midsection rather than being distributed among the brain, the heart, and the liver. As it turns out, his view of human anatomy was mostly incorrect. But he was correct in assuming that his view accorded better with Hebrew Scripture. Moreover, the theological consequences of this "road not taken" may be worth another glance. The theological and psychological advantages of maintaining a "holistic" view of the human person have been reasserted in more recent times.[74] The correlate cosmological claim that God is fully present in the "lower parts" of the cosmos in preference to being more fully present "in heaven" is also receiving renewed interest.[75] Thus, Theophilus's apparently bizarre metaphor, once set into its fulller context, may constitute a profound and timely insight!

Chapter Two / FROM JOSEPH-JUSTE SCALIGER TO JOHANN GOTTFRIED EICHHORN: THE BEGINNINGS OF BIBLICAL CRITICISM

Jean-Loup Seban

The Protestant and Catholic Reformations of the sixteenth century aroused in Western Christendom an unprecedented and overwhelming, if not always exclusive, fascination with scripture. Johann Heinrich Alsted testified to this in his *Triumphus Biblicus* (1625), which contends that the Book of Nature is thoroughly contained in the Book of Scripture. Nonetheless, it was the Renaissance, essentially humanist and naturalist, that sowed the seeds from which the historical-critical method germinated in the seventeenth century and flourished in the late-eighteenth century. Giving the initial impetus to modern biblical scholarship, which spurred the long process of secularization of the Bible, was Lorenzo Valla's retrieval of Latin philology. The birth of philology in the fifteenth century brought forth an impressive array of proficient text critics, grammarians, translators, and biblical commentators in the course of the sixteenth and seventeenth centuries. Eventually the Bible had to forfeit its claim to quasi-divine status, as philologists treated it less as scripture than as one collection among others of historical narratives and ethical teachings.

Meanwhile in the world of science, two events of momentous proportions were heralding the watershed between medieval and modern times. One was the founding of the *Academia secretorum naturae* in 1560 in Naples by the nature philosopher Giambattista della Porta (1535–1615), and the other was the publication in 1616 of a discourse, *On the Natural Desire for Knowledge*, by the botanist Federico Cesi (1585–1630). Shortly thereafter he released the *Praescriptiones Lynceae* (1624), which became the manifesto of the empirically minded *Accademia dei Lincei*, in whose founding Galileo Galilei had taken part. Both events foreshadowed the collapse of the Thomist *entente cordiale*—the disruption of the medieval conciliation between the Book of Scripture and the Book of Nature—that the Endegeest meeting between René Descartes, the modernist, and Jan Amos Comenius, the biblical pedagogue, blatantly crystallized in 1642.

The scientific revolutions of the seventeenth century prompted an increasing number of biblical scholars to model their investigation of the Book of Scripture after the empirical method of nature philosophers. The popularization of philological and historical exegeses brought the *sensus literalis* to the fore.

The birth of modern biblical scholarship was set against an ideological background that reflected changing sociopolitical patterns. The ascent of commercial capitalism indirectly and variously affected the way scholars of all confessions appropriated the Bible, especially in the eighteenth century. On the rise since the fourteenth century, the bourgeoisie increasingly resented the growing discrepancy between its ascending economic status and the static sociopolitical role to which it had been confined in a feudal system that was artificially kept alive in most countries on ideological grounds, and in spite of the gradual social mutations due to the generalization of commercial capitalism. Post-Tridentine political theorists like Jean Bodin, Robert Bellarmine and Jean-Bénigne Bossuet reinvigorated feudalism in Catholic lands and even reinvented divine right monachism in order to legitimize statism, thereby promoting a monolithic system which ultimately turned out to be alienating to the bourgeoisie. On the other hand, some more advanced thinkers, such as Grotius, Spinoza, Pufendorf, and Locke, took the new middle-class mentality into account and proposed to reform the feudal system in Protestant lands where it had generally been kept unaltered by the successors of the sixteenth-century religious reformers. The eight Wars of Religion in France, and the later, infamous revocation of the Edict of Nantes; the pan-European Thirty-Years' War, and the Puritan interregnum in England, not to speak of the 1649 regicide, together conspired to create a general climate of lassitude toward religious dogmatism among members of the *Respublica litterarum* by the close of the seventeenth century. That feeling was further exacerbated in the eighteenth century by the countless misdeeds of religious enthusiasm, the arbitrariness of censorship, and the combined effect of the spiritual arrogance and cultural despotism of the consolidated religious orthodoxies. A few audacious scholars and determined men of letters, be they Roman Catholic, Anglican, Lutheran, Reformed, or Jewish, distanced themselves publicly from the official stand of their respective denominations, and even at times stigmatized, at the cost of their livelihood if not of their lives, what they deemed to be the cause of all evil in the world, be it dogmatism in some countries or scripturalism in others.

I

The sixteenth-century reformations prompted the decline of the four hermeneutical rules, which had been generally used by exegetes and preachers since Augustine. As early as 1512, the French humanist scholar Jacques Lefèvre d'Etaples, who inspired the Protestant Reformation, expressed a preference for the *sensus literalis*. Essentially literal, his epoch-making *Sancti Pauli Epistolae XVI ex Vulgata editione, adjecta intelligentia ex Greaco, cum commentariis* started a fashion that was widely followed, not only among Protestant and heterodox Reformers, but also, to a lesser extent among Catholic scholars. It should be noted that the emancipation of the *sensus literalis*, either grammatical or historical, for which the new philological instruments had been designed, was the concomitant of new theological axioms: scripture alone, scripture as self-interpreting, and the clarity of scripture (*sola Scriptura, Scriptura interpres sui* and *perspicuitas Scripturae*). It is furthermore not surprising that the *sensus literalis* found its most persuasive advocates among Reformed philologists such as Drusius (1550–1616), Isaac Casaubon (1559–1614), and Joseph-Juste Scaliger (1540–1609), the finest scholar of his day, to whom the French language owes the word *critique*. It is no less surprising, either, that the *sensus literalis* grew in importance in Roman Catholic biblical scholarship as a result of a general apologetic effort to answer Protestant claims. Of all seventeenth-century attempts at explaining and defending the Reformed doctrine of scripture, the *Isagoge seu introductio generalis ad Scripturam sacram Veteris et Novi Testamenti,* published in 1627 by André Rivet (1573–1651) against the backdrop of the Arminian and Amyraldian controversies, undoubtedly is the best informed and the clearest. One of Rivet's many criticisms was aimed at the Protestant scholastics who subjected scripture to their dogmatic prejudices. As for Socinianism, the first modern approach to dogmas, which often flourished on Calvinist soil, it also vastly preferred the *sensus literalis*. All the *Commentarii, Explicationes,* and *Paraphrases,* that either Faustus Socinus (1539–1609) or his followers in the *Ecclesia minor* produced, are based on a literal interpretation that they further rationalize.

Late Renaissance and early Baroque Catholic circles, where the Jesuits progressively took over the field of biblical scholarship, tended to neglect three of the hitherto popular four hermeneutical rules: the allegorical, tropological, and anagogical senses. An eminent Jesuit controversialist, Roberto Cardinal Bellarmino (1542–1621), who is remembered as Galileo's devoted interlocutor, argued that interpretation according to the literal sense could help settle controversial matters between opposing parties, in particular between the Church and the heretics. The growing popularity of the *sensus literalis* among Catholic preachers is traceable to the influence of a proficient biblical scholar from Flanders. A professor of scripture initially at Louvain and afterward at the *Collegio Romano,* Cornelius à Lapide (1567–1637) wrote hefty biblical commentaries. His much noted commentary on the Pentateuch of 1616 propounded in the *Prooemium* a convincing argument in favor of the *sensus literalis*. Lapide's argument was then developed and popularized in 1630 by another Jesuit, Giovanni Stefano Menochio (1575–1655), in *Brevis explicatio sensus literalis totius S. Scripturae,* which charted the course of biblical interpretation in post-Tridentine Catholicism. Roman Catholic literalism reached its apogee in the opening decades of the eighteenth century, when Dom Augustin Calmet

(1672–1757) of the Benedictine Academy of Moyenmoutier released his multivolume *Commentaire littéral sur tous les livres de l'Ancien et du Nouveau Testament* (1707–1716). In addition to the *Vulgata* and to a vernacular translation by Isaac Le Maître de Sacy, Dom Calmet's *opus magnum* offered an exhaustive commentary in French which popularized conservative scholarly opinions. Commonly read among the *philosophes*, it was Voltaire's favorite source of information on the Bible.

The Anglican tradition was no exception either. Though the flaws of mystical exegesis were not fully exposed before the Restoration, Anglican hermeneutics tended, on the one hand, to alleviate the four-level spiritual interpretation of medieval times, and on the other, to prevent literal exegesis from overpowering theology and society. *Of the Lawes of Ecclesiastical Politie,* Richard Hooker's masterpiece of 1593, had steered a middle course between the Tridentine clericalization of scripture, which assumed its insufficiency, and the Puritan exclusive scripturalism, which asserted its sufficiency. Likewise, latitudinarian divines of the likes of Bishop Edward Stillingfleet and Archbishop John Tillotson strove to achieve a satisfactory balance between the increasingly popular *sensus literalis* and the typological exegesis of the Eusebian tradition much valued in seventeenth-century England. A remarkable example is Ralph Cudworth (1617–1688), Regius Professor of Hebrew at the University of Cambridge, who is still remembered for his famous *True Intellectual System of the Universe* (1678), which failed to rally the English to the Cartesian cause. Like his associates More, Whichcote, and Smith, Cudworth was educated at Emmanuel College, a bastion of Puritanism, where he delivered two memorable sermons whose fusion of literal exegesis and historical inquiry is exemplary: *A Sermon Preached before the Honourable House of Commons* (1642) and *A Sermon Preached to the Honourable Society of Lincolnes-Inne* (1664). This notwithstanding, Cudworth frequently ventured beyond the confines of historical interpretation. A vocal opponent of Calvinist soteriology and Puritan predestinarianism, Cudworth, the neo-Platonist, was primarily concerned about securing a constructive relationship between Christian revelation and pagan culture. He therefore advocated, though not uncritically, the recourse to typological interpretation as a useful complement to historical exegesis. For, what ultimately mattered to Cudworth was to gain access to a higher truth, a metaphysical one. Much favored in seventeenth-century English literary circles, typology won the favor of clerical circles where it consolidated the preferential position of the *sensus literalis*. The grammatical or historical sense, and the typological sense, both, then constituted subsidiary senses of the prevailing *sensus literalis*.

It is no coincidence that the *sensus literalis* rose to prominence in Western Christendom at the time that the doctrine of literal inspiration was finalized in Reformed orthodoxy. In the *Institutes of the Christian Religion,* John Calvin had upheld a *revelatio interna*. His view was hardened by his successor Théodore de Bèze, the father of orthodoxy. As this doctrine was geared to justifying the

nonhuman origin of scripture, early-seventeenth-century Reformed theologians further elaborated on the external and internal proofs of the *revelatio interna*
on polemical grounds. They were responding to the Tridentine clericalization
of scripture. Entitled either *De Verbo Dei* or *De Scriptura sacra,* their often lengthy
treatises today belong to the classics of Reformed orthodoxy. As the matter of
the foundation of the authority of scripture became a major bone of contention
in post-Reformation Catholic-Protestant controversies, Reformed divines radicalized their teaching in order to strengthen their assailed position. Hence they
departed significantly from Calvin's and Bèze's moderate stand and developed
a closed system that was set inevitably on a collision course with the nascent
mechanistic worldview. What Reformed orthodoxy achieved amounted to a
reification. Scriptural inspiration became verbal inspiration. The divine character of canonical scriptures was solemnly proclaimed lest the Book of Scripture
would know either deception or fallacy. This new dogma eventually turned out
to be detrimental to Christian belief. For it failed, on the one hand, to offer
cognitive certainty as well as fiducial solace in untoward circumstances, and, on
the other, to wed the destiny of divine revelation to the fate of the Aristotelian
worldview. In retrospect, the doctrine of verbal inspiration merely provided
some temporary and utterly delusive comfort to those who suffered from an
unfathomed and unmastered *tremendum* in front of the disclosure of an infinite
universe at the heart of which the known world was no longer to be found.

Of the many divines who orchestrated this consequential shift of emphasis,
a systematician and a philologist deserve to be singled out for their exceptional
ascendancy over the Reformed tradition: Franciscus Gomarus (1565–1641),
professor at the University of Leiden and Jacobus Arminius's chief opponent,
and Johann Buxtorf (1564–1628), professor of Hebrew at the University of
Basel and immortal author of an *Epitome grammaticae hebraicae* (1605) and of a
no less influential *Thesaurus grammaticus linguae sanctae* (1609). Among other
teachings, Buxtorf taught that Hebrew was the language of God. The enthusiasm of many a seventeenth-century divine for historical and grammatical
exegesis was quite understandable in an age when critical collections of biblical
materials, such as Xantes Pagnini's *Veritas hebraica* (1623), Andrew Willett's
Hexapla in Genesis (1605), Salomon Glassius's *Philologia sacra* (1623) and Jacques
Bonfrère's *Pentateuchus Mosis commentarii illustratus* (1631), were made available
for scholarly endeavor. But the excessive reliance on the *sensus literalis* for the
establishment of truth, supernatural as much as natural, though no less explain-
able, is less understandable. For it mainly resulted from an apologetic desire to
preserve the authority of divine revelation, be it limited to the Book of Scripture
or extended to Tradition as well, in accordance with one's confessional allegiance.
Originating from that particular frame of mind of fifteenth-century nominalism, this desire for empirically ascertainable truth unfortunately prompted the
advocates of literalism to such an extreme as to challenge the newly emerging
natural philosophy on its own noetic grounds. It is incontrovertible that whereas

the primacy of the *sensus literalis* was apologetic in spirit, the emphasis on verbal inspiration was reactionary in essence. Both trends, however, were highly symptomatic of Modern Times in the making.

II

The year 1624 unmistakably augured the subversion of orthodox belief. In England, Herbert of Cherbury's *De Veritate* demonstrated the advantages of natural religion over revealed religion and thereby inspired those whose disaffection with Christian revelation caused the Deist controversy that convulsed the established Church. Meanwhile in France, a scholarly monograph on the obscure subject of punctuation, *Arcanum punctationis revelatum*, whose author, Louis Cappel (1585–1658), happened to be Moïse Amyraut's colleague at the Reformed Academy of Saumur, was sapping the very foundations of Reformed orthodoxy and, consequently, was posing a serious threat to the credibility of scripture. In fact, Cappel was merely restating Elijah Levita's conclusions, which he further consolidated by adducing historical, literary, and grammatical evidences. In *Masoret ha-Masoret,* published in Venice in 1538, Elijah Levita, a Jewish scholar of note, had contended that the vowel pointing was a Masoretic invention aimed at securing an accurate transmission of the Hebrew text. After giving this argument its final shape, Cappel dated the Masoretic pointing from the time when Hebrew dramatically fell into disuse among Jews, namely during the post-Talmudic period. Such an alarming thesis could not be left unchallenged. Hence, later in the century, the orthodox party mounted a vehement attack under the leadership of Buxtorf's son, Johann Buxtorf II (1559–1664), which concentrated on vindicating the antiquity of pointing. Based on a wealth of contrived evidences, Buxtorf's reply attributed the paternity of pointing to Ezra but failed to persuade the *critici sacri.* Biblical erudition had already gained enough of an autonomy to accept being silenced for dogmatic convenience without demur.

A few years later, Louis Cappel delivered the fatal blow that Reformed orthodoxy had vainly attempted to deter. Completed in 1634, Cappel's major work, *Critica sacra,* was eventually released in 1650 in spite of the unyielding opposition of his coreligionists. Ironically, it was the Catholics who facilitated this publication. Father Morin, an expert on the Samaritan Targum, shared Cappel's view and obtained the indispensable Royal Privilege, with the secret hope that it might weaken the imperious stand of the *Religion Prétendue Réformée,* even though its author was one of the *heretici.* Cappel's *Critica sacra* marked the turning point in the fortunes of Reformed orthodoxy, as it established both that the Masoretic text was not identical with the original Hebrew text—the *ipsissimus textus hebraïcus*—and that scripture had a literary history like any other book. It was self-evident to Cappel that God did not miraculously preserve the

Bible from human alterations. As expected, the orthodox rejoinder came in the classical form of *anathema*. The progressive strain of the mid-seventeenth century, which Cappel's scholarship embodied and which found a favorable reception among the theologians and orientalists of the Church of England, was officially condemned in 1675 by the *Formula consensus*. In line with the *Canon of Dort* of 1618, whose teachings it forcefully reiterated, the *Formula consensus* was a masterpiece of confessional reactionism, combining scientific ignorance with spiritual arrogance. This unfortunate document, which duly pleased England's Puritans, not to speak of their obscurantist New England heirs, as well as countless retrograde Dutch and Swiss Calvinists, bore the hallmarks of two luminaries of seventeenth-century Calvinism: François Turretini (1623–1687), a member of the Genevan *Vénérable compagnie des pasteurs,* and Gisbertus Voetius (1588–1676), a professor at the University of Utrecht, whose main claim to celebrity is to have opposed Copernicanism and to have barred the teaching of Cartesianism in the province of Holland for a time.

Like Stoicism, which made a temporary recovery in the closing decades of the sixteenth century, Platonism had been perceived from Augustine onward as essentially compatible with Christian belief, and had never aroused the ecclesiastical condemnation that Aristotelianism had incurred periodically. After enjoying a spell of revival in fifteenth-century Florence, Platonism surfaced again at the expense of classical Aristotelianism in the discussions on method and status in the *scientiae* among late-sixteenth- and early-seventeenth-century nature philosophers. The origin of what became yet another triumph of Platonism was the rise of mathematics, especially geometry, at the University of Padua. A subversive claim ensued which subtly brought into question the whole conceptual apparatus of the dominant worldview. The claim was that, owing to its superior if not absolute degree of certainty—*demonstratio potissima*—the mathematical method was the answer to the epistemological quest of an age eager to decipher the Book of Nature. Francesco Barozzi originally made the claim in 1560, in his *Questio de certitudine mathematicarum*. It was successfully fortified by Pietro Catena's *Oratio pro idea methodi* of 1563. The mathematization of Aristotelian physics, derived from a Platonic interpretation of the Stagirite, that Barozzi's conception implied the mathematization of Aristotelian physics, derived from a Platonic interpretation of the Stagirite; this met with expected vigorous opposition from a classical Aristotelian scholar of note, the Siennese philosopher Alessandro Piccolomini (1508–1578), author of an influential *Della filosofia naturale* (1565).

Piccolomini's counteroffensive failed to prevent mathematics from rising to epistemological prominence. In 1585, the Jesuits' *Ratio studiorum* endorsed mathematics as an auxiliary discipline in natural philosophy. A few years later, in 1589, a colleague of Galileo Galilei, Christophorus Clavius, senior mathematician at the *Collegio Romano,* released a commentary on *Euclid* which paved the way for the general endorsement of mathematics as a model science by nature philosophers. In applying mathematics to physics, nature philosophers attained a degree of certainty that neither the antique nor the medieval *scientia* ever imagined to be possible. Especially since fourteenth-century nominalism, there was a widespread assumption among academics that scientific explanations were *ex suppositione,* merely hypothetical. Thus nothing less than an epistemological revolution caused the gigantic struggle of worldviews, which in the end destroyed the credibility of Christian revelation. The new foundations of certainty, which gave birth to Descartes's and Spinoza's mechanical philosophy, were to have immeasurable consequences, as Johannes Kepler (1571–1630), the Lutheran astronomer, perspicaciously predicted in 1609, in a passage, since famous, of his *Astronomia nova:* "in theology the authorities, but in philosophy calculations shall have decisive importance." Predictably, *scientia divina* and *scientia naturalis* drifted farther and farther apart in the course of the seventeenth century, although the ambition to resurrect a fully integrated biblical-metaphysical-scientific system after the Thomist fashion was revived by some rationalist metaphysicians like Malebranche, Leibniz, and Wolff.

To most *novatores,* the nature of the challenge that the new natural philosophy represented to the established churches and to their interpretation of scripture was obvious beyond any doubt. Three of them deserve mention: Paolo Antonio Foscarini (1565–1616), Galileo Galilei (1564–1642), and Marin Mersenne (1588–1648). In January 1615, in the midst of the Copernican debate, a provincial of the Carmelite Order in Calabria tossed a bombshell that precipitated the Church's condemnation of Copernicanism in 1616. When Foscarini released his Copernican treatise entitled *Lettera sopra l'opinione de' Pittagorici e del Copernico,* Galileo was just a few months away from completing his notorious letter to Christina of Lorraine, which elaborately discussed the relation of science and religion. Foscarini's *Lettera* was an intrepid step, even though dictated by an apologetic concern. The purpose of the *Lettera* was to prove that, against all appearances, heliocentricism was contrary neither to scripture nor to doctrine. In support of his argument, Foscarini also ventured a heliocentric reading of scripture. However, Foscarini cautiously avoided taking a clear stand on the potentially dangerous issue of the relationship between natural knowledge and divine revelation, though he was preferentially leaning toward the hegemony of natural knowledge.

At the heart of Galileo's unpublished, yet widely copied, letter to Christina of Lorraine lay his desire to reverse the traditional attitude of exegetes and theologians. All his efforts concentrated, on the one hand, on drawing moral and natural truths asunder and, on the other hand, on depriving scripture of its illegitimate authority in scientific matters. At the same time he exalted the legitimate authority of the natural philosopher. It was Galileo's firm conviction that the conclusions of the exact sciences were binding whenever a scholar was interpreting a passage of scripture that referred to the natural world. Subversive though it appears, Galileo's hermeneutical rule was no novelty. As far back as the patristic era, Augustine had advised, both in *De Genesi ad litteram* and in his seventh letter to Marcellinus, always to interpret the word of God in the light of the truths of the natural sciences when the latter have been conclusively established. For an important matter was at stake: the unity of truth, its harmony and consistency. That unity, in Augustine's opinion, was by all means to be preserved from breaking apart. Restated in Benito Pereyra's *Commentariorum et disputationum in Genesim tomi quatuor,* printed in Rome between 1591 and 1595, Augustine's advice found renewed popularity among the *novatores* in search of authorities. History regards the Jesuit Benito Pereyra (1535–1610) as the age's most prominent Roman Catholic exegete. His monumental commentary on Genesis lays out a set of four hermeneutical principles that became familiar to Galileo at the time that he was writing his letter to Christina of Lorraine. It should be noted that Pereyra's fourth interpretative rule declares that the truth of scripture cannot be contrary to the true arguments and evidences of natural knowledge. It was a clever move on Galileo's part to enlist Pereyra, such a widely acknowledged authority on the Bible, in support of his own similar understanding of the relation of science and religion, but it failed to carry conviction and thereby to salvage Copernicanism.

Heliocentricism was to be Bellarmine's last victorious controversy. In January 1600, Roberto Cardinal Bellarmino, recently appointed to the Holy Office, had supported the condemnation for heresy of Giordano Bruno, an inspiring figure of late Renaissance metaphysics, who was subsequently burned at the stake on the Campo dei Fiori. In the wake of Foscarini's and Galileo's letters of 1616 the discord between the Tridentine *sacra doctrina* and the new science had grown to the point that the Holy Office could no longer deem innocuous a Copernican interpretation of scripture in the vein of Diego de Zuniga's *Commentaria in Job,* published in Toledo in 1584. When Galileo's much postponed treatise on the structure of the universe, *Dialogo . . . sopra i due massimi sistemi del mondo Tolemaico e Copernicano,* eventually appeared in Florence in 1632, no progressive cleric was in a position to calm the storm that it aroused or to impede the course of action taken by the Holy Office, which led to a trial.

Marin Mersenne, a French Minim Friar whose interests lay close to those of the *Collegio Romano,* provides a third enlightening insight on the biblical challenge of the mechanistic natural philosophy. An apologetic defender of orthodox Catholicism, especially against the then mounting threat of Pyrrhonian skepticism, yet an opponent of scholastic Aristotelianism, Mersenne attempted to reground knowledge in *La vérité des sciences contre les sceptiques ou Pyrrhoniens* (1625) and in *Harmonie universelle* (1636–37). As a *novator,* he strongly believed that mathematics and experience together provide the most effective means of understanding nature. In the early part of his career, Mersenne devoted much energy to the then much discussed issue of Adam's prelapsarian encyclopedic knowledge. The results of this investigation were collected in *Questiones celeberrimae in Genesim* (1623), which display a wide range of contemporary science. As an apology for Catholicism, his commentary on Genesis consisted in a literal interpretation from the vantage point of mechanical philosophy. The stand that Mersenne took in the preface was diametrically opposed to Alsted's view. It was a truly modern stand: the Book of Nature interprets and validates the Book of Scripture, since "the world is the book of God in which we ought continually to read." In England, the "Boyle Lectures," established in the closing decades of the seventeenth century in memory of the Oxonian physicist, spread a similar worldview. These public lectures, delivered at St. Paul's of London, were immortalized by two illustrious polymaths of the Church of England, both Newtonians and both foes of Deism, Richard Bentley (1662–1742) and Samuel Clarke (1675–1729).

The repercussions of Galileo's trial on the advancement of learning and the progress of biblical scholarship in the Society of Jesus were fatal. Caught in the midst of antagonistic duties to the Pope and to knowledge, the leading educational order of the age chose obedience over the pursuit of truth. It was not only a matter of survival in a time of crisis but also a matter of identity. Their founding father, Ignatius of Loyola, had emphasized the role of what he called "blind obedience" in a letter dating from 1553. In 1588, Bellarmine's *Tractatus de obedientia, quae caeca nominatur* had reminded some dissident Jesuits what *blind obedience* meant, namely, a pure, perfect, and simple obedience without discussion. This disciplinary principle inspired one of Claudio Aquaviva's letters of 1611, in which, as General of the Society, he enjoined the Jesuits to return to a solid and uniform doctrine, by which he meant the teaching of Thomas Aquinas in theology, and of Aristotle in natural philosophy. Galileo's trial rendered Aquaviva's injunction even more compelling. The fate of both Jesuit science and Jesuit exegesis was sealed in the wake of the trial. A biblical-Ptolemaic refutation of heliocentricism published in 1633 by the Jesuit Melchior Inchofer, under the title of *Tractatus syllepticus,* contributed to the diversion of Jesuit science from mainstream natural philosophy for ages. In spite of their continued commitment to astronomy, it was not until Pierre Teilhard de Chardin that the Jesuits caught up with the modern world. Jesuit exegesis, hitherto one of Christendom's most innovative, tragically fell behind. The Jansenists' Augustinian exegesis took front stage for a time. It was supplanted by Oratorian exegesis in the second half of the seventeenth century.

The Dutchman Cornelius Jansenius (1585–1638), bishop of Ypres, is mostly remembered for his controversial *Augustinus* (1640), which Jean-Ambroise Duvergier de Hauranne, abbot of Saint-Cyran, made into the charter of Jansenism. However, he once had been a professor of Holy Scripture at the University of Louvain. He left impressive commentaries on the Gospels (1639), the Pentateuch (1641), and the Old Testament sapiential literature (1644), whose historic effects can be traced throughout the history of Dutch and French Jansenism. In the preface to his commentary on Genesis, Jansenius enunciates a twofold hermeneutical principle: first, Moses must be read literally and any allegorical interpretation must be avoided, and second, as both Augustine and Pereyra had prescribed, one should listen to what the *philosophia naturalis* has to say, with the reservation however that the Book of Scripture prevails in the event of a conflict of opinion. Notwithstanding Jansenius's instructions, a type of spiritual interpretation, called figurism, regained popularity among the Jansenists as a result of persecution. Saint-Cyran excelled in drawing analogies between contemporary history and biblical history.

In spite of, if not because of, the ongoing discussions on method in the investigation of the Book of Nature, the Book of Scripture was much in the limelight of culture throughout the seventeenth century and well into the eighteenth century. Since Théodore de Bèze's tragedy, *Abraham sacrifiant* (1550), poets, dramatists, and composers regularly drew their inspiration from biblical narratives. Although Greek mythology and Greek tragedy remained a preferred source of fictional characters since the Italian Renaissance, biblical figures were far from being neglected, especially by writers and composers whose works pursued either an educational or an ethical goal. To correct a misconception, Protestant men of letters were not the only writers to cultivate the Christian Muse in seventeenth-century Europe. The Bible was as much a source of inspiration to Catholic as to Protestant *litterati.*

III

The latter half of the seventeenth century should have been a propitious time for the maturation of biblical criticism. Interest in the Bible was high and biblical commentaries proliferated. However, only one biblical critic, a reclusive and unfortunate French Oratorian priest, made a difference: Richard Simon. Johann Gottfried Herder, Johann David Michaelis, and Johann Salomo Semler hailed Simon (1632–1712) as the father of modern biblical criticism. Trained by the Oratorians and the Jesuits, Simon was a born scholar. He had a voracious appetite for learning and an inexpugnable craving for truth. He also was a contentious man. His deliberate controversy with the Jansenists and his inveiglement with Protestantism caused him as much prejudice as did his audacious scholarship. Simon succeeded in antagonizing both Catholics and Protestants. Despite repeated statements of loyalty to the Roman Catholic Church, like most contemporary *novatores,* Richard Simon encountered every obstacle the triumphant orthodoxy was capable of erecting in self-defense. He was received as a novice in the Oratory in Paris in 1662 and expelled from it in May 1678, as soon as Bishop Jean-Bénigne Bossuet had declared heretical his critical history of the OT. In July 1678, thirteen hundred copies of the *Histoire critique du Vieux Testament* were confiscated and burned. After a tumultuous career in Paris, Richard Simon ended his life in pious retirement in Dieppe, where he had been born.

The release in England of John Lightfoot's *Horae hebraicae et talmudicae* (1658–1674) provided all *critici sacri* an important tool. In addition to the Antwerp Polyglot, printed by Plantin between 1569 and 1572, which furnished an extended edition of the *Complutensis* of Alcala, they now also had two new polyglots at their disposal: the Paris Polyglot of 1645 by Guy-Michel Le Jay, and the London Polyglot edited by Brian Walton in 1657. As a result of foreign missions, non-Christian religions were increasingly drawing scholarly attention. In 1641, Isaac Vossius published in Amsterdam *De theologia gentili,* which was followed both in 1646 by the publication of Samuel Bochart's *Geographia sacra, seu Phaleg et Canaan,* in Caen, and in 1652–54 by the release in Rome of Athanasius Kircher's monumental study *Oedipus Aegyptiacus.* Vossius, Bochart, and Kircher discovered structural analogies between biblical figures and Egyptian, Syrian, Greek, and Roman mythologies. They shared the view that pagan myth was borrowed from the Bible. Pagan mythology was nothing but distorted Jewish tradition. In 1663, Herbert of Cherbury revealed the beauties of Greco-Roman religion in *De religione gentilium,* and several decades later, at the request of missionaries to China, Nicolas Malebranche drew Europe's attention to Asian religions in *Entretiens entre un philosophe chrétien et un philosophe chinois* (1707). Though still unsteady, the path was nonetheless cleared for the study of comparative religion.

The Oratorian phase was altogether prepared, accompanied, and discredited by the iconoclastic opinions of a handful of freethinkers and outcasts whose effects were devastating. At the height of the skeptical crisis of the late Renaissance, some *libertins érudits,* like François de la Mothe Le Vayer (1588–1672) and Giulio Cesare Vanini (1585–1619), had propagated corrosive opinions while claiming loyalty to the Church. They had implicitly challenged the divinity of scripture by arguing that Genesis proffered a fallacious image of man and of the world. The anonymous *Quatrains d'un déiste,* which widely circulated undercover, denounced many religious practices as contrary to nature and reason. La Mothe Le Vayer's *Dialogue sur le sujet de la Divinité,* one of a set of *Five Dialogues* published at Frankfurt in 1616, prefigured d'Holbach and Feuerbach. It contended the human origin of all religions. The influence of the *libertins érudits* had been limited, however, as the Church had been prompt in reducing them to silence. They were not able to do much harm to the establishment.

In revenge, Thomas Hobbes (1588–1679), Isaac La Peyrère (1596–1676), and Baruch Spinoza (1632–1677) much harmed the establishment; above all they shocked the learned world. Typical of seventeenth-century thought, the contentious Sage of Malmesbury envisioned Church and State as a united body, a remainder of medieval *corpus Christianum*; held theology and philosophy as the unitary foundation of all sociopolitical theory; and at times tackled theological and biblical themes. Though in line with Martin Bucer's *De regno Christi* (1550), and rooted in the Laudian brand of Anglican Erastianism, Hobbes's political philosophy bears many hallmarks of modernity. He was well acquainted with continental mechanical philosophy, and his justification of absolutism is solely based on anthropological considerations. He was often branded with atheism by his enemies, though the Bible plays a salient role in his theorizing on the State in both *De cive* (1642), and *Leviathan* (1651). Hobbes's recourse to the Bible was motivated by legal as well as typological interests. The Bible was above all the sourcebook of divine law, the criterion of the rules of life to which every Christian must conform, and additionally the record of the history of the ancient people of God commencing with Abraham. He was an absolute monarchist. OT patriarchs served as models for the sovereign of the commonwealth he envisioned. Hobbes much concerned himself with four current issues of a burning nature: the correct interpretation of scripture, the authorship of the Old and New Testaments, miracles that no longer occur, and the relevance of prophecy. His vantage point intentionally contraposed those of both Puritanism on his left and Romanism on his right. He was a liberal in doctrinal matters. His theories reflect the kind of rationalism and humanism that William Chillingworth embodied. Well informed about the latest developments in biblical scholarship, Hobbes denied Moses' authorship of the Pentateuch as well as Solomon's authorship of the Song of Songs and Ecclesiastes.

Isaac La Peyrère's denial of the biblical origin of mankind caused great alarm among Protestants, Catholics, and Jews alike. A jurist by profession, Isaac La Peyrère was born in Bordeaux to a prosperous Calvinist family, probably of Marrano origin. He was captivated by divine history and the election of nations. His philosemitic Messianism incurred the condemnation of the French Reformed Church in 1626. In 1640, he moved to Paris. There he met some of the leading minds of the age: Mersenne, Gassendi, Pascal, Grotius, and Hobbes, who formed or frequented the circle of his protector, the Prince de Condé. Two works brought him notoriety: *Du Rappel des Juifs* (1643), which deals with the fulfillment of Providential History and the conditions for recalling the Jews, and *Prae-adamitae* (1656), whose polygenetic theory of humanity's origin was anathematized. It is worth noting that in the nineteenth century the pre-Adamite theory was developed in America into a scientific explanation of the diversity of humankind by Samuel Morton and Joshua Nott and served to justify the superiority of the Caucasian race. By contrast with seventeenth-century historians, La Peyrère did not read Mosaic history as the basis of world history. The Bible is merely concerned with Jewish history. In order to facilitate the conversion of the Jews, La Peyrère proposed to harmonize Jewish and Christian Messianism and to create a Jewish Christian Church from which dogmas and ceremonies offensive to the Jews would be banned.

In the year 1670, upholders of orthodox belief and established religion, whether Christian or Jew, leafed through an anonymous Latin treatise with predictable repulsion. They promptly banned it as *liber pestilentissimus,* a most destructive book. The *Tractatus theologico-politicus* affranchised philosophy from revealed theology, assailed superstition and prejudice, censured religious intolerance, advocated freedom of thought, reduced miracle to *res naturalis,* emptied prophecy of any cognitive information, described the Bible as a mere guide for untutored minds, and demanded the separation of Church and State in an age that welded both on account of political absolutism.

A harbinger of modernity, Spinoza's hermeneutics was erected on a solid footing of philosophical dichotomies. First, he drew a sharp distinction between conservative and progressive theologians. The latter have the advantage over the former of trusting the *lumen naturalis.* Next, he contrasted *vana religio* with *religio catholica.* The former is the self-alienating historical religion based on cult, prayer, and alleged revelation, whereas the latter rests on reason and the Bible. Then, he contraposed *assentari,* which posits scripture as true and divine, with *credere,* which requires *a regula interpretationis,* a scientific method of interpretation. And finally, with amazing foresight, he distinguished truth from meaning.

Spinoza's radical departure from tradition parallels his antidogmatism and his historical positivism. By no means should the Bible be treated as the deposit of truth. Spinoza cautioned against any ontotheological appropriation of the biblical narrative and against metaphorical interpretation. Only the literal sense matters. Philology and history are the sole means of interpretation. *Lectio sola* is the sole reading Spinoza recommends. For it is not reconstruction that defines the task of the hermeneutist but deconstruction. For instance, Spinoza showed that the laws revealed to Moses by God were nothing more than Hebrew state legislation. Could there be a more subversive idea from the vantage point of a seventeenth-century political theorist? Following Abraham Ibn Ezra (d. 1195), a much praised Jewish scholar, Spinoza further concluded that the Pentateuch had been written ages after Moses. Spinoza attacked more than just religious orthodoxy.

It all reeked atheism to Samuel Clarke, the Anglican rationalist apologist. Even John Toland, an inveterate Deist whose *Christianity Not Mysterious* (1696) was geared at rationalizing, demythologizing, and moralizing Christian belief in a Socinian fashion, repudiated Spinoza by fear of disreputable association. In *Letters to Serena* (1704) he charged Spinozism with being "interely precarious and without any sort of ground, indigested and unphilosophical." In the year 1674, when Richard Simon discovered the *Tractatus theologico-politicus,* that Leibniz had introduced in France in 1672, Simon's *Histoire critique du Vieux Testament* was ready for publication. Nevertheless, he had the time to distance himself from Spinoza's attempt upon the divinity of scripture in the preface that he then wrote.

The Oratory graced the seventeenth-century world of learning with many talents. Besides Nicolas Malebranche (1638–1715), whose metaphysics combined Cartesianism with the Augustinian legacy, Bernard Lamy (1640–1715) signally enhanced the historical, philological, sociological, and anthropological understanding of the Bible and of ancient Israel with an authoritative *Introduction à la lecture de l'Ecriture Sainte* (1699).

41

Richard Simon's production as a critical biblicist may be divided into two periods: the OT period from 1670 to 1680, and the NT period, which culminates with the release of an *Histoire critique du Nouveau Testament* in 1689 and of an *Histoire critique des principaux commentateurs du Nouveau Testament* in 1693. His *opus magnum*, the seven hundred-page-strong *Histoire critique du Vieux Testament*, reissued in 1680 in Amsterdam, encompasses the entire field of OT scholarship. It deals with texts, versions, translations, and commentaries. Simon subjected them all to the sharpest scientific criticism. Casting aside the Tradition of the Fathers, which earned Bossuet's bitter reproach, Simon learned to historicize and to deconstruct a Hebrew text not only from the Jesuit philological tradition but also from the Rabbinic literalist tradition. Jewish philological analyses, like those of Kimhi, Jacob ben Hayyim, Abravanel, and Eliyahu Ashkenasi, helped him refine the tools of his trade. To love truth, to be unprejudiced and impartial, are, in Simon's opinion, the fundamental prerequisites to biblical criticism, which he believed to be the best means of ensuring the authority of scripture. For he viewed his scholarly commitment, whose purpose many questioned, as a service to the Church. In contrast with Hobbes, La Peyrère, and Spinoza, Simon did not directly deny Moses' authorship of the entire Pentateuch, though he established the presence of numerous corrections, interpolations, and additions. To account for these later alterations and at the same time to preserve the revelatory authority of the Pentateuch, Simon made a twofold hypothesis. He conjectured the existence of public writers in ancient Israel and postulated that they were inspired like the prophets. He then drew the obvious conclusion, that the public writers' contributions did not lessen the authority of the Pentateuch. Published in Rotterdam, the *Histoire critique du Nouveau Testament* comprises three volumes. The first is devoted to the NT text and discusses delicate issues of authorship. Released in 1690, the second volume deals with NT versions. The third volume, which dates from 1693, reviews medieval, Renaissance, and Reformation commentators. What is so unique about Simon's *critica criticorum* is that it was thoroughly devoid of any ulterior motive. Unlike Hobbes, La Peyrère and Spinoza, Simon's endeavor was solely motivated by scholarly passion. His biblical criticism was not aimed at grounding a political system, a theological-historical theory, or a metaphysics. He truly was a seventeenth-century Erasmus.

No one, not even his fiercest enemies, questioned Simon's status as a scholar among scholars. Everyone admired his voluminous learning. But there was little recognition and much reprobation in his own time for his positivist evaluation of biblical scholarship. Recognition came nonetheless, but in the second half of the eighteenth century from a physician, Jean Astruc, author of *Conjectures sur les mémoires originaux dont il paroit que Moyse s'est servi pour composer le livre de Genèse* (1753), and from the Lutheran scholars of Germany who perfected the historical-critical method that he had adumbrated. Simon had no following. He did not start a school, even though Etienne Fourmont could be cited as a disciple. Roman Catholic biblical criticism disappeared with Simon's death and did not reappear until the encyclical *Divino afflante spiritu* of 1943. There are many causes for Simon's lack of success. He was a hermitic scholar and a free spirit who tried to ignore the party line but lived in a country whose assaulted Tridentine Catholicism reacted tyrannically. His commitment to truth got him entangled in lethal controversies that left him without any supportive constituency. In a monumental *Perpétuité de la foy* (1669), Antoine Arnauld and Pierre Nicole had sustained the thesis that the eucharistic theology of Eastern Christianity was closer to Roman Catholicism than to Protestantism. Simon alienated the Jansenist party by stressing the weakness of their argument in *Fides Ecclesiae Orientalis* (1671). He should have got along well with Jean Le Clerc (1657–1736). They had much in common. Both were formidable scholars. Both were at odds with their tradition and disowned by their peers. Le Clerc was an Arminian and Simon a Molinist. Both were feared and isolated. Nevertheless, some futile matter of disagreement developed into a venomous and protracted polemic in the mid-1680s that only served Le Clerc's glory. Two other polemics, one with Pierre Jurieu about the fufillment of prophecies, and the other with an Oxonian don, Thomas Smith, on eucharistic theology, further ruined Simon's reputation among the Protestants.

Notwithstanding, it was Bishop Bossuet's thundering ire that shattered Simon's hopes. A man of reason and order, and a much celebrated sacred orator, Bishop Jean-Bénigne Bossuet (1627–1704) championed a strictly orthodox interpretation of Tridentine Catholicism, furnished theological justification for royal absolutism, defended the *Libertés* of the Gallican Church, and waged a merciless struggle against all forms of heresy, especially Protestantism. Was not Simon's fate predictable, even though silencing him only meant a Pyrrhic victory for the orthodox party? On the whole there were three ideological reasons for the eradication of unprejudiced biblical criticism. First of all, the *critici sacri* essentially proceeded to a negative critique. Theirs were works of deconstruction whose implications extended far beyond the narrow confines of their field. They drove a wedge between scripture and the word of God. They awakened suspicion about the reliability of scripture as a sourcebook of revealed knowledge. Second, the priority given to philology and history pushed into neglect the tradition of the Fathers, either mystical or doctrinal. It made the Church as sole authorized interpreter irrelevant. A third reason was to save the purpose and meaning of history. Along with the pre-Adamite theory and the emergence of Chinese and Mexican data, positivist biblical criticism challenged the current sacred history view that both Edward Stillingfleet's *Origines sacrae* (1680) and Bossuet's *Discours sur l'histoire universelle* (1681) epitomized. An alliance between the philological-historical method and the *philosophia naturalis,* of the kind that Spinoza and the English Deists concluded, rationalized the providential, naturalized the miraculous and demythologized the prophetic. Wittingly or not, the *critici sacri* contributed to the secularization of history that Giambattista Vico and David Hume later completed. Providential and prophetic history was put in jeopardy. World history was left adrift, without any interpretative key, and human society purposeless and meaningless.

IV

The Renaissance of biblical criticism happened not in Britain, whose established church abounded with scholars of stature, such as bishops Lowth and Hare, or in Catholic Spain, where it made an auspicious beginning, but in Germany, whose music, philosophy, and literature were captivating European culture. German *kritische Bibelwissenschaft* took front stage in the second half of the eighteenth century and remained unchallenged for two centuries. It all started modestly under the auspices of Philipp Jakob Spener (1635–1705), whose *Pia desideria* (1675) outlined a vast program of theological reform which focused on scripture and personal religious experience. In 1687 the *Collegium philobiblicum* was established in Leipzig. The founding of the divinity school of Halle by the Elector Friedrich III followed in 1694. Professor of biblical languages at Halle, August Hermann Francke (1663–1727), Spener's eminent disciple, created the *Collegium orientale theologicum* in 1702 and made Halle the mecca of Pietism. Carl Hildebrand von Canstein urged would-be preachers to study biblical languages. The creation in 1728 of the *Institutum Judaicum*, which involved the Michaelis family, further supported Halle's claim to the crown of biblical scholarship.

Pietism strove to invigorate Lutheranism stifled by scholasticism, to rekindle religious enthusiasm, and to restore the moral fiber of a country crippled by the ills of the Thirty-Years' War. Spener and Francke prescribed a drastic medicine: to turn away from doctrinal quibbling and to return *ad fontes*, to *Scriptura sola*. How to decipher the Bible thereafter became a priority among the Pietists as the doctrinal-catechetical framework of orthodoxy was relinquished. In 1693, Francke published a *Manuductio ad lectionem Scripturae Sanctae*, in which he elaborated on the notions of *scopus* and *affectus* that he had inherited from Johann Conrad Dannhauer's *Hermeneutica sacra* (1654). *Affectus* was a familiar concept in seventeenth-century thought, as Descartes's and Nicole's concern with the *passions de l'âme* illustrates. In addition, Francke drew a crucial distinction between *sensus literalis* and *sensus literae*. The latter is strictly philological, while the former allows for what Francke preconized, namely spiritual exegesis. Francke's *Praelectiones hermeneuticae* (1717) codified interpretative rules geared at providing theological, moral, and spiritual meaning. Another Halle scholar, Johann Jakob Rambach (1693–1735), followed suit and expatiated on the proper *ars hermeneutica* in *Institutiones hermeneuticae sacrae* (1724). The Pietists promoted philological investigation but did not confine their scholarship to the sole retrieval of the *sensus literae*. They expected more. Their hermeneutics paid special attention to *affectus*. The disclosure of the spiritual core that engages the human heart was the ultimate purpose of biblical scholarship.

Small wonder that the finest biblical scholar of the first half of the seventeenth century in Germany came from Pietist ranks. Perfecting philological rules that had been in part preconized by Johannes Coccejus and Gerhard van Mastricht, Johann Albrecht Bengel (1687–1752) published a Greek NT in 1734, to which he subjoined philological observations in 1743, the *Gnomon Novi Testamenti* that John Wesley read. Moreover, it is hardly surprising that the revival of mystical interpretation also originated from the Pietist bipolar exegetical tradition. It was achieved in a grand manner by one of Bengel's students. To ward off the *Aufklärung* that ebbed and flowed over Germany, Friedrich Christoph Oetinger (1702–1782) discussed biblical interpretation in *Inquisitio in sensum communem et rationem* and put together a *Biblisches und Emblematisches Wörterbuch* (1776). The originality of Oetinger's sacred philosophy, constructed around the concept of *Geistleiblichkeit*, stands in its Christosophic monism which incorporates Böhme's theosophy and Swedenborg's vision. The fact that Oetinger handed down Böhme's theosophy to Hegel and Schelling certainly accounts for his historical relevance. Nevertheless his symbolic hermeneutics is emblematic of the renaissance of the irrational in the late-eighteenth century. It derives entirely from the presupposition of a mystical affinity between the Book of Nature and the Book of Scripture. The relation of the *Logos* to the Bible, Oetinger contended, is analogous to that of the soul to the body. The *Verbum Dei* is incarnated in scripture as it is in nature. The hermeneutical task therefore consists in explicating the meaning of the biblical symbols and metaphors by which means the knowledge of God is mediated. The Romantic theologian and eclectic philosopher Friedrich Schleiermacher (1768–1834) was another epigone of the Pietist school. He left a hermeneutics, highly stimulating and seminal, that welded together the philological-historical approach of the humanist tradition, the christological interpretation of the Lutheran tradition, and the emphasis on the pious sensibility of the Pietist tradition.

Compared with Roman Catholic biblical studies, Lutheran biblical criticism rose to prominence relatively unhampered. The orthodox party no longer retained the means of imposing its doctrine of scripture *urbi et orbi*. However, the 1788 reactionary decree enacted by Johann Christian von Wöllner, Friedrich Wilhelm II's culture and justice minister, slowed the progress of the Enlightenment in the kingdom of Prussia for a decade. Born in the age of Pietism, biblical criticism matured in the age of Enlightenment. It largely owed its maturation to the emancipation of reason and the empirical propensity of the age. Nonetheless it was no easy coming of age. The road was paved with danger. The menace came not only from the apologists of the *testimony of the Holy Spirit*, but also, and more insidiously, from the radical *Aufklärung* or Enlightenment. While the orthodox, the fideist, the mystical, and the supernaturalist camped on one side of the road, the heterodox, the rationalist, the

Deist, and the naturalist stood on the other. Humanism and science commanded a scientific treatment of scripture as condition for the future of Christianity. Both countervailing forces, fanaticism and skepticism, struggled to impede the accommodation of Christianity to the modern world—the former by forcing a retreat of critical biblical scholarship into the safe haven of blind faith, and the latter by diluting into indifference the remainder of people's attachment to the Bible.

In sharp contrast with the French *Lumières*, the German *Aufklärung* did not forsake Christianity. Contrariwise, most *Aufklärer* embarked upon a quest for a reasonable Christianity. The English Enlightenment had set the tone. Besides, it was in full accord with the Philipist strain of Lutheranism. The Bible thus remained a cultural ferment as much in the secular as in the clerical *Aufklärung*. A collection of powerful thinkers presided over the most consequential cultural mutation in Germany since the Reformation. Leibniz, Thomasius, and Wolff were the progenitors of the *Aufklärung;* Mendelssohn and Lessing its blazing luminaries; and Kant its last and most critical interpreter. Gottfried Wilhelm von Leibniz (1646–1716), a quiet mystic, had propagated the refreshing vision of a friendly God, architect of the universe and guardian of the moral order. Christian Thomasius (1655–1728), a jurist, had denounced the absurdity of witchcraft, the inanity of superstition, and the barbarity of torture. Often hailed as *praeceptor Germaniae,* Christian Wolff (1679–1754) systematized and popularized Leibnizianism, establishing thereby the first academic philosophy in Germany since the demise of Aristotelianism. Just as Luther had molded German piety and German language, Wolff shaped German thought and German philosophical terminology. As a consequence, Protestant philosophy, theology, and biblical scholarship played a substantial part in Germany's cultural ascent to world leadership in the nineteenth century.

Seventeenth-century philosophers, whether rationalistic or empirical, perpetuated God's place at the heart of their worldview and preserved supernatural truth. For Descartes, God is at the origin of both knowledge and faith. There is in Cartesianism an epistemological parallelism between thought as product of consciousness and faith as volitional act prompted by grace, but no system of double truth. Descartes assumed the existence of what Leibniz later called preestablished harmony. A cautious thinker in a repressive age, Descartes advised reason to surrender to faith in case of conflict. In revenge, eighteenth-century *philosophes* deliberately shoved God to the periphery of the system, if they did not expel him peremptorily, and submitted revelation to the criticism of reason. They had little tolerance for propositions either transcending or opposing reason. At the height of the *Aufklärung*, in 1786, the *Berlinischen Monatschrift* published Kant's response to an issue raised by Moses Mendelssohn. The article is entitled *Was heisst: sich im Denken orientieren?* In a truly enlightened manner, the Königsberg philosopher, whose *Copernican Revolution* undertook reason's self-critical assessment, contended therein that "the final touchstone of truth is always reason." From Descartes to Kant, the relationship between natural and revealed truth essentially depended on the scope of the criterional power of reason. Though he was a teacher at the University of Halle, Wolff was by no means a Pietist. He was a rationalist—a Cartesian with a definite scholastic bent. Natural philosophy had no secret for him, nor did the Bible. In the wake of the irresistible seventeenth-century metaphysical dream, Wolff aimed to construct an encyclopedic synthesis on the Thomist model, a modern *summa,* a rational and universal worldview that reconciled *scire* with *credere,* knowledge with belief. Like Thomas Aquinas, Wolff unfolded a natural theology *but unlike the angelic doctor, he prioritized scrire* over *credere.* His natural theology was a rational theology. Like Descartes, Wolff differentiated revealed knowledge from natural truth, but unlike Kant, he did not reduce the former to the latter. As he put it, there is a twofold *connubium* of reason and faith. Wolff's semirationalism stands halfway between Descartes's strategic noninterference and Kant's resolute interference in *Religion Within the Limits of Reason Alone* (1793). In 1721, while delivering a rectorial address, Wolff had the audacity to compare Confucianism favorably to Christian ethics. His Pietist colleagues stood aghast at the suggestion that heathens were as capable of genuine morality as Christians. Consequently, Joachim Lange, Rambach's fanatic father-in-law, got him fired from Halle in 1723. As the tide of Pietism was receding, Wolff was reinstated by the king-philosopher Friedrich II in 1740. The *Aufklärung* was gathering pace.

Biblical proficiency was not uncommon among nature and moral philosophers of that time. Isaac Newton, for instance, spent considerable energy in his later years defending biblical chronology and interpreting the prophecies on the basis of modern science. His *Observations on Daniel and Revelation,* posthumously published in 1732, reclaim providential and prophetic history. Wolff was no less proficient in scripture, as his Latin treatises evidence; 310 biblical references and 71 quotations, mostly from the *Vulgata,* have been numbered. Most of them were used to buttress his rational demonstration of the existence of God in *Theologia naturalis methodo scientifica pertractata; Pars prior* (1736). All Christian theology, according to Wolff, starts with biblical exegesis and ends with practical theology. Divinely inspired, scripture is the *locus* whence revealed knowledge streams. Crucial therefore are the rules of biblical exegesis. Motivated by a sincere ecumenical concern, traceable to the Leibniz-Molanus dialogue of the 1680s, Wolff published an article about theological method, in 1707, entitled *Methodus demonstrandi veritatem religionis Christianae,* which purposed to lay the foundations for universally acceptable rules of biblical interpretation. Only a method, based on reason, experience, and observation, that is altogether logical and *wissenschaftliche,* can settle matters between the confessions once applied to the Bible. In order for the scriptural words, formulae and propositions to make sense, one should not only rely on the *sensus literalis,* Wolff argued, but also pay close attention to the historical context, the mores and customs.

The diffusion of Leibnizo-Wolffianism, the development of the natural sciences, and the emancipation of the historical and philological sciences together produced, amid a resilient orthodoxy and Pietism, a vast array of theologies and corresponding hermeneutics ranging from unyielding rationalism and pure historicism to unabashed supernaturalism. Wolffianism crystallized theologically into a new school, which historians dubbed *neology*. The neologists emphasized the biblical content of theology at the expense of the Platonism and Augustinianism of orthodoxy, and put the ethical content of scripture in the foreground. A Hamburg philologist who rode the high tide of rationalism was Hermann Samuel Reimarus (1694–1768). Born into a prosperous merchant family of the Hanseatic city, Reimarus undertook theological studies at Jena but turned to philosophy and philology when he realized that his faith in scripture was increasingly shadowed by a cloud of suspicion. He received his Master of Arts from Wittenberg University in 1716 and his Habilitation in 1719. A grand tour, during which he discovered the United Provinces and England, further widened his mental horizon. In 1723 Reimarus met Wolff. It was a philosophically decisive encounter. Wolff's rationalism and moralism, which ideally suited bourgeois intellectualism, greatly appealed to Reimarus, whose confidence in economic development, scientific progress, and the perfectibility of human nature epitomized the mentality of the eighteenth-century middle class. He was appointed professor of oriental languages at Hamburg's *Akademisches Gymnasium* in 1728, and, having reached the height of fame, was elected to the Academy of Sciences of Saint Petersburg in 1761. In his lifetime he was mainly known for three philosophical works: *Die vornehmsten Wahrheiten der natürlichen Religion* (1754), *Die Vernunftlehre* (1756), and *Allgemeine Betrachtungen über die Triebe und die Thiere* (1760).

For years Reimarus was secretly immersed in a major critique of the Bible, *Apologie oder Schutzschrift für die vernünftigen Verehrer Gottes,* which, as David Friedrich Strauss explained, prepared "to sweep away so unsparingly the edifice of the religious system of positive Christianity." The unabridged version of the *Apologie* was not published until recently, by Gerhard Alexander (1972). A selection of chapters from an early version had been published by Lessing in 1774 and 1777, under the title *Fragmente eines Ungenannten.* Lessing's discovery did not pass unnoticed. In the winter of 1777–78 a prominent Hamburg Lutheran minister started a polemic notorious for its virulence. Pastor Johann Melchior Goeze, who championed scriptural inspiration and infallibility, accused Lessing in a newspaper article of disturbing people's faith and refuted Lessing's *aufklärerische* dichotomy between Bible and religion.

Lessing responded in several short pieces that he, and not the Lutheran ministers, stood on Luther's side, furthering the advancement of Christianity. By impeding biblical scholarship and by obstructing its diffusion, Lessing concluded, Goeze and the clergy of his ilk act like little popes. In the preface to the *Apologie*, Reimarus formulates four preventions against orthodoxy which are reminiscent of Socinian rationalism, namely the discontinuity between catechetical and biblical teachings, the nonsensicality of the doctrine of the Trinity; the intolerability of eternal damnation, and the debasing example set by the Bible's many scandalous characters. If philology was Reimarus's forte, natural theology was his hobbyhorse. Religion is natural religion; theology is natural theology; and natural theology is rational theology. Rational theology deals with God, providence, freedom, and the immortality of the soul. For Reimarus the Deist, the *lumen naturalis* suffices in religious matters. Reason is the ground of knowledge *(ratio cognoscendi)*. History is not. However, for a revelation to be considered, it must occur by natural means and the information it conveys may transcend reason but never contradict reason. Revealed religion is conceivable only on the condition that it either expand or corroborate the noetic content of natural religion. Consequently, there is only room for a natural revelation. Supernatural revelation is excluded, and revelations that are allegedly historical, like the Bible's, are denied. Besides, there is no need for redemption, since there is no fall. Reimarus's hermeneutics is a corollary of his *Vernunftlehre*. Reimarus radicalized not only Wolffian rationalism, but also Wolffian hermeneutics. Like Hobbes and Spinoza, Reimarus disproved Moses' authorship of the Pentateuch and instead argued for Ezra as its redactor. He further maintained that NT mysteries and miracles, particularly the resurrection of Jesus, are frauds for which the apostles are responsible. What Jesus actually taught was a pure and exalted religion, rational and ethical. He was nevertheless misguided by the Jewish Messianic dream into assuming an ill-fated revolutionary role. For any allusion to Jesus in OT prophecies is equivocal at best. Expectedly, Reimarus strongly advised against allegorical interpretation. The retrieval of the *sensus literalis* by means of historical and philological criticism entirely fulfills the purpose of biblical scholarship. With Reimarus, whose unrestrained criticism presaged David Friedrich Strauss's demythologizing assault, the process of secularizing the Bible, which the Renaissance had initiated, was completed.

On the whole, biblical scholars shunned the extreme sentiments of either side. Fashionable though it was to be a naturalist in the late-eighteenth century, the neologist Karl Friedrich Bahrdt (1741–1791) failed to rally much support among biblical scholars. For understandable reasons, their readership, though basically receptive to novelty, remained conservative at heart. The secularization of the Bible loomed, sending a chilling message. Hence critical Lutheran biblical scholarship followed a *via media* between Reimarus's iconoclasm and the too credulous scripture principle. The privilege of ensuring the transition from Pietist exegesis to Enlightenment exegesis fell to a triumvirate of scholars: Johann David Michaelis, Johann August Ernesti, and Johann Salomo Semler. Possessing the necessary ingredients, they concocted the historical-critical method independently and for reasons embedded in their own history in the course of a couple of decades. Owing to a successful following among enlightened divines, their historical-critical method gained maturity with the neologists and their rationalist and supernaturalist successors, won recognition by the time of Heinrich Eberhard Gottlob Paulus (1751–1851), Martin Willhem Leberecht de Wette (1780–1849), and Wilhelm Gesenius (1786–1842); and became a hallmark of modern Christianity with Reuss, Wellhaussen, Renan, and Loisy.

Johann David Michaelis (1717–1791) was the son of Christian Benedict Michaelis, a theology professor at the University and the *Institutum Judaicum* of Halle. Raised in Pietist Halle, Johann David Michaelis received his early education at the *Weisenhaus,* where Sigmund Jakob Baumgarten (1706–1757), a famous Wolffian, taught him philosophy and theology. Wolffianism served well as an antidote for the ascendancy of his sanctimonious milieu but did not much erode his doctrinal orthodoxy. Under his father's influence, from whom he learned Hebrew privately, young Michaelis specialized in Midrashic Hebrew, Syriac, and Arabic at the University of Halle. He earned his doctorate in 1739, upholding a conservative estimation of the antiquity of vowel pointing. After a spell of teaching at Halle, he was appointed professor of philosophy and oriental languages at the University of Göttingen in 1750. Possessing a versatile mind, he edited the influential *Göttingische Anzeigen von Gelehrten Sachen* from 1753 to 1770. As a scholar who used historical criticism to buttress orthodox belief, he very much was in the public eye. The release in 1750 of an *Einleitung in die göttlichen Schriften des Neuen Bundes,* which addressed problems of language, textual origin, authenticity, and authorship, won him immediate academic acclaim. Regarding the origin of the Synoptic Gospels, he made the hypothesis of an apocryphal proto-Gospel. His 1760 *Compendium theologiae dogmaticae* struck a balance with the scripture principle of orthodoxy. He made a compromise statement: there are in scripture indications and traces of its divinity. His masterpiece, *Das Mosaïsche Recht* (1770–1775), offers a comprehensive study of Jewish law. The two-volume *Supplementa ad lexica hebraica* came out in 1786 as the crowning achievement of his scholarly career.

A Leipzig philologist, Johann August Ernesti (1707–1781), entertained the ambition of elevating philology to the highest theological status. The main feature of his seminal *Institutio interpretis Novi Testamenti* (1765) is a plea for grammatical exegesis. There is only one meaning to a text, Ernesti argued, the *sensus literalis.* By making philology the matrix of theology, Ernesti furthered the current process of dedogmatization of biblical history and biblical doctrines which crystallized in part in the emancipation of biblical theology from ecclesiastical dogmas.

Ernesti has been associated with the neologists, often reproachfully. Of this momentous triumvirate of biblical scholars, he certainly was the most enlightened, or at least the least bigoted. In any case, Johann Salomo Semler (1725–1791) is ranked today among the classic leaders of Protestant theology. A pupil of his, J. G. Eichhorn, paid him a well deserved biographical tribute in which he praised his mentor as "the preeminent reformer of our new theology."

Semler's autobiography of 1781–82 tells us that he was brought up in a milieu largely affected by Pietism. He was sent to the University of Halle and graduated with a degree in philosophy in 1750. Sigmund Jakob Baumgarten had taken a liking to him and became his mentor. After a year of teaching history and Latin poetry in Altorf, where he earned his doctorate, he was invited to take up a professorship at Halle. There he taught for some thirty-eight years and was elected rector three times. Semler did not have an easy life among his Pietist colleagues and often felt that he was struggling against the stream alone. He was a prolific writer. Although his writings address an amazing range of problems related to all aspects of Western history and culture, historical theology truly was his forte. His much awaited *Abhandlungen von freier Untersuchung des Canons,* which followed Muratori's trail, came out in four volumes between 1771 and 1775. They made history, not only because they established the historical origin of the NT canon on the basis of an unbiased historical and critical enquiry, but also because Semler demanded complete freedom of investigation for the biblical scholar. And that was no meager request. Much praised by the neologists, his 1774 Latin dogmatics, which appeared in 1777 in a German translation under the title *Versuch einer freieren theologischen Lehrart,* revolutionized the making of theology by ascribing a normative role to history. Taking issue with both orthodoxy and Pietism, he sundered theology from religion. Theology is a historical discipline. It is induced from the Bible scientifically. For Semler the Bible is undoubtedly a book that bears witness to God's revelation, but also, a human book written in human languages, a book whose making had a long and eventful history. Though refuting biblical inerrancy, Semler acknowledged a form of divine inspiration. The biblical writers received their knowledge from God. Reframing Calvin's *duplex cognitio Dei,* Semler distinguished in a Wolffian fashion between natural and special revelation. Whereas natural revelation is inherent to every human being, special revelation is restricted to scripture. The way Semler understood their relationship is emblematic of neology. Indeed, the purpose of the special knowledge additionally made available to man by God in scripture is either to ascertain or to augment natural revelation. Innovating further, Semler framed a new theory based on an old idea: the theory of accommodation. As scripture evidences, God has accommodated his message to the cognitive faculty and the moral capacity of the people of that time. Hence hermeneutics and the theory of accommodation are, in Semler's view, two sides of the same coin. It follows that the historical and cultural context, as well as people's modes of representation, provides essential information for the interpreter's judgment.

This unique triumvirate of farseeing and entrepreneurial scholars served as a catalyst for a tripartite biblical revolution: the completion of the historical-critical method, the birth of biblical theology, and the emancipation of hermeneutics.

Among the biblical scholars who brought the historical-critical method to successful completion, Griesbach and Eichhorn deserve to be singled out.

Semler's pupil Johann Jakob Griesbach (1745–1812), a NT scholar who first taught at Halle and later at Jena, is still vividly remembered on account of two achievements. Griesbach published in Halle and London simultanously, between 1775 and 1777, a *Novum Testamentum Graece*, a critical edition of the NT in two volumes that furnished a more accurate text than Erasmus's famous *Textus receptus* of 1633. There were some five hundred manuscripts at Griesbach's disposal among which the *Alexandrinus,* the *Vaticanus,* the *Codex Ephraemi Syri rescriptus* and the *Codex Bezae Cantabrigiensis* featured prominently. Beside textual criticism, Griesbach energetically concentrated on the Synoptic Gospels whose problem exerted some sort of fascination. For the benefit of his students, he published a Greek *Synopsis Evangeliorum Matthaei, Marci et Lucae* in 1776 at which occasion he made his famous hypothesis that Mark was composed of excerpts from both Matthew and Luke. He developed his theory in *Inquiritur in fontes, unde Evangelistae suas de resurrectione Domini narrationes hausserint* (1783). Matthew's priority over Mark as apostle and witness of the resurrection was further demonstrated on historical grounds in *Io. Iac. Griesbachii Theol.D. et prof. Primar. in academia Jenensi commentatio qua Marci Evangelium totum e Matthaei et Lucae commentariis decerptum esse monstratur* (1789–1790).

The greatness of Johann Gottfried Eichhorn (1752–1827), a formidable scholar who burned the midnight oil, stands out in his uncanny ability to synthesize the advancement of biblical scholarship over the ages. After completing his early education at the Heilbronn *Gymnasium,* Eichhorn matriculated at the University of Göttingen where he read theology with Johann David Michaelis and classical philology with Christian Gottlob Heyne. A successful promotion at the University of Jena in 1775 launched his academic career, which he furthered at the University of Göttingen. There he first released, mostly on his own, the *Repertorium für biblische und mogenländischen Litteratur* (1777–1786) and afterward edited the Leipzig *Allgemeine Bibliothek der biblischen Litteratur* (1787–1827). These periodicals bear witness to his vast command of the biblical field. His masterpiece, *Einleitung in das Alten Testament* (1780), which soon became a classic that is still read today, comprehensively reviews and appraises not only eighteenth-century OT historical-critical scholarship, but also the pre-Romantic and esthetic interpretations. Eichhorn considerably expanded the scope of the *Introductio ad libros canonicos Veteris Testamenti* that the Leipzig orthodox theologian Johann Benedikt Carpzov had published in 1721, and implemented Michaelis's historical-critical method with a desire to overcome neology in a manner that recalls Johann Gottfried Herder's hermeneutics. In the wake of Lowth's and Herder's study of Hebrew poetry, Eichhorn distinguished a variety of genres, which inspired Leberecht de Wette's 1823 commentary on the Psalms and, a century later, Hermann Gunkel's *Einleitung in die Psalmen* (1933). Heyne's influence is perceptible in Eichhorn's interpretation of OT myths. A myth, Eichhorn asserted, is a way of thinking and a mode of expression that is proper to the infancy of the human race. In 1783, Eichhorn published a German translation of Astruc's *Conjectures* and reactivated the Catholic Frenchman's documentary hypothesis. Henceforth, the Pentateuchal sources became a favorite issue among OT scholars. In his later years Eichhorn ventured in the NT field with equal success. Taking up Lessing's hypothesis, Eichhorn postulated a Hebrew or Aramaic common source for Matthew and Luke in *Ueber die drey ersten Evangelien* (1794). A comprehensive five-volume strong *Einleitung in das Neue Testament,* published in Leipzig, followed between 1804 and 1827.

Even so, Gotthelf Traugott Zachariä (1729–1777), another of Baumgarten's pupils, was the first to author a biblical theology, *Biblische Theologie oder Untersuchung des biblischen Grundes der vornehmsten theologischen Lehre* (1771–1775). However, the distinction between biblical and dogmatic theology was not clearly drawn until 1787. Eichhorn's pupil Johann Philipp Gabler (1753–1826) argued in a pioneering *Oratio de justo discrimine theologiae biblicae et dogmaticae* that dogmatic theology is didactical and philosophical, whereas biblical theology is *e genere historico,* or historical. For theology to have become a *genus historicum,* history had come a long way since Wolff. In regarding hermeneutics, it grew independent and expanded its sphere of influence to other domains over the ages. From Herder and Schleiermacher to Hans-Georg Gadamer, the science of scriptural interpretation irresistibly ascended the ladder of universality and, attaining a position held by mathematics in the seventeenth century and by physics in the eighteenth century, declared itself the science of understanding, the science of sciences.

Modernity demythologized belief, secularized history, and moralized society. There was no escape for the Book of Scripture. Wasn't it after all the sourcebook of an alleged divine revelation whose noetic and legal content was binding without appeal? Had the Bible not been an organ of truth and an instrument of power for ages? The day the clarion call *sapere aude* awoke reason from its dogmatic slumber the die was cast. Insidiously and sequentially, recovering from ages of oblivion and overcoming one obstacle after another, the Book of Nature gained an ascending, ever less challenged hegemony over every aspect of human life including the religious. Epistemology dominated the eighteenth century from its scientific height; it imposed a monism of method *urbi et orbi*. If Erasmian was the spirit of the age, Cartesian was its letter. The completion of the historical-critical method, its liberation from dogma, and its claim to self-sufficiency are clear symptoms of the momentous process of secularization to which culture and society, and ethics and politics were subjected and which accompanied the bourgeois ascent to ideological supremacy. The domestication of nature was insufficient. Scripture needed to be domesticated as well, lest the divine creation be left undomesticated.

Chapter Three / FACING JANUS: REVIEWING THE BIBLICAL THEOLOGY MOVEMENT

Steven J. Kraftchick

A lthough the more extreme advocates both of religious traditionalism and of modern rationalism wish it otherwise, neither tradition nor modernity can credibly dispense with the other. When biblical studies ignores this point, it becomes impoverished and endangers its future.[1]

In their fads, foibles, and follies, scholars are just as human as the members of any small town gossip association! It would be no great task to illustrate this from the lingo and novelties that pass current among us at this day.[2]

Secular intellectuals have largely stopped paying attention. They don't need to be told, by theologians, that Genesis is mythical, that nobody knows much about the historical Jesus, that it's morally imperative to side with the oppressed. . . .[3]

Introduction

It must be a mandate for New Testament scholarship within the context of the seminary to serve the well-being of the church. This mandate requires that the foremost task of the New Testament scholar is to beware of trivialization and to focus on the transparency of the biblical texts for the modern world.[4]

Any self-respecting redaction critic would spot the Bekerian hand here. With terms like "It must be the mandate," "beware of trivialization," and "the transparency of the biblical texts," this statement about the task of the biblical interpreter would be typical of J. Christiaan Beker. A pithy comment, deliberately ambiguous, but delivered in order to prompt a conversation about a difficult topic, characterizes Beker's work as a NT scholar. My hope with this essay, written in his honor, is to start such a conversation.[5]

Beker is surely aware that he is challenging a whole range of biblical scholarship by using terms like "trivialization." He also realizes that the biblical texts are often opaque for the modern world and that the task of making them transparent is anything but easy. But Beker's use of such terms is not accidental. His statement is a protest against the forms of biblical scholarship which he believes have hindered the elucidation of biblical texts for the present-day reader by focusing on the wrong aspects of those texts. Beker would not deny the legitimate and necessary function of critical historical inquiry, but he would question its worth detached from an end purpose. At stake for him is the responsibility of biblical interpreters to present analyses of biblical texts which translate not only into understanding but also into involvement.[6]

Modern biblical studies is, by the nature of its texts and the constituency of its audiences, a Janus-form discipline. Like the Roman god of beginnings it is constantly facing both inward and outward, forward and back. It must face backward because biblical texts are documents of a culture past, yet it must also face the present because in communities of belief those documents are understood as meaningful for modern life.[7] Given their nature as ancient documents, the interpreter must employ methods of historical analysis in an investigation of their content. Still, since that content is clearly religious in orientation and reference, the tools of historical analysis do not do justice to the claims made by those texts. Hence, the biblical scholar needs to give attention to how the texts' religious claims can be made evident and understandable.[8]

Biblical studies must face both inward and outward because it exists both in the academic setting and within the local church or synagogue. Since the communities of discourse to which it belongs do not conduct their conversations according to the same rules or ends, it must learn languages appropriate to each. Further, the ends of its labors for one constituency are not always seen as necessary or valuable for the other. Hence, the biblical scholar must also learn the art of translation between the languages appropriate to each.[9]

The trick has been not in recognizing this Janus identity but in acting in concord with it. To look both forward and backward at the same time is not easy and it is more likely that a biblical practitioner will take one of the views as her main task, hoping that her counterparts will take the other. Rarely, however, has this hope been realized. More often one or the other faces is attended while the other is neglected or, even more damaging, the two faces have been confused. The result of neglect is to make the appearance of the discipline bland. The result of confusion is to disfigure it. Eventually the neglect or confusion reaches a level that prompts a protest. Historically when protests have arisen they have used the term "biblical theology."[10]

When the protest takes this form, it highlights certain difficulties and problems that face a biblical critic, for example, the coherent relationship of the Bible's different documents, the question of the actual content of the Bible and whether the concept "theology" is accurate for describing it, and the relationship of that content to theological construction within the disciplines of systematic and dogmatic theology. In other words, questions about the plurality and nature of religious texts arise, and from these questions the authority of biblical texts in and for theological argumentation becomes a matter of interest.

The determination of which methods are appropriate for answering such questions also becomes a concern. Thus questions like: "In what ways are the methods of critical analysis to function?" "Are the proper methods for discovering the beliefs, desires, and understandings of the biblical writers being applied?" and "What is the place of the individual's religious commitments in the use and concern for interpreting the texts?" begin to occupy biblical scholars.

The serious debates over the identity, purpose, and methods of biblical interpretation which came to be called "The Biblical Theology Movement" are a form of this protest.[11] So too is Beker's mandate cited above. The Biblical Theology Movement argued that excessive attention to historical analysis, a lack of theological interpretation, and misunderstanding of the religious nature of biblical texts were derailing biblical studies from explicating the claims that were intrinsic to the texts it studied. As a result, biblical studies rendered itself inoperable except as an exercise in ancient history or philology. While these exercises had validity in their own right they did not exhaust the responsibility of the biblical scholar.[12]

Beker's warning to avoid the trivialization of biblical materials stands in line with the arguments of the Biblical Theology Movement.[13] Contained in his sentence are the coordinates between which biblical studies locates itself: communities of belief/the world in which those communities exist, analysis of the text/interpretation of the text. The interplay of those four points creates the parameters for biblical scholarship. Also contained in Beker's statement are the inherent difficulties of maintaining a balanced intersection among those points of reference. On Beker's read the discipline has become skewed because it has overindulged the analytical side and neglected the interpretive.

Given the difficulties contained in meeting the balance called for by Beker's mandate, I suggest that we look back to the Biblical Theology Movement for help. By looking at its attempts and at the reasons for those attempts, our own efforts to meet Beker's mandate can be aided. My suggestion is made for two reasons.

First there are, despite the shifts in the methods and understandings of critical analysis, sufficient similarities between the present state of our discipline and the state against which those scholars protested. Consider this recent assessment of the current state of biblical scholarship:

> Contemporary biblical scholarship considered from some angles seems to be in good shape. There are certainly more people with Ph.D. degrees in biblical studies than in any previous era. Regional, national, and international conventions proliferate and prosper. New journals are announced or appear every year. So many dissertations, monographs, books, and articles are being produced that

literally no one can even count much less be accountable for the yearly production. Measured quantitatively, the business . . . is booming.

Other perspectives, however, suggest that all is not well. As in other boom
industries, disquieting amounts of fraud and fakery appear. Overproduction itself
depreciates value. More than that, however, there are growing signs that the
energy and activity seem increasingly without direction. What is all this learning
about, to what is it directed, for whom is it any benefit?[14]

These two complaints: a hyperactive analysis with an underdeveloped sense
of purpose or direction and a tone deafness to the theological/religious claims
of the biblical texts reflect the critique of the Biblical Theology Movement.
Understanding how it attempted to resolve this imbalance, assessing its motivations for doing so, and viewing the critical response to it can be a benefit to
us in our own attempts.

Second, a review of this movement is also beneficial because the concerns
that prompted the protest are still operating. Those concerns were overshadowed and eventually not attended to because the critique of the Movement's
procedures and assumptions was so thorough. Proving that the solutions the
Movement offered were wrong did not make the reasons for the protest
disappear. The continued lack of attention to those concerns has contributed
to the "trivialization" against which Beker and Johnson are protesting. It would
be salutary to place those concerns back in the midst of our discussions.
Attention to the purpose of scholarly activity and to the circumstances in which,
and for which, that activity is performed ought to be an initial focus of the
biblical interpreter's responsibilities. One of the purposes of this essay is to do
that. We will neither solve the dilemmas posed with such attention nor resolve
its tensions, but a greater sense of the task can be gained and so perhaps a truer
reflection of the Janus form that this discipline assumes.

To highlight the concerns of the Movement I will present two of its representative voices: the NT scholar Paul Minear and the Old Testament scholar
H. H. Rowley.[15] Each presents an important aspect of the Movement, though
neither exhausts its various manifestations.[16] Others could have been chosen,
but Minear and Rowley serve our purposes since they express well the motivations of the Movement and its working assumptions.[17]

The Biblical Theology Movement

General Overview

The years after World War II saw an increased interest among biblical
scholars in the relationship of biblical materials to constructive theology. In
their review of the history of OT theology, Hayes and Prussner refer to these
years as a time when "the Bible and biblical theology came to occupy a place of

prominence and authority in theological studies which they had not enjoyed for years, probably not since the days of the Reformation period."[18] A confluence of the uncertainty after the war, renewed ecumenical exchange, and the founding of several new journals allowed the interest to grow.

At the center of this resurgence in biblical theology was the so-called Biblical Theology Movement. This movement attempted to transcend and provide an alternative to the Fundamentalist/Modernist debate with the hope of bridging the gap between them.[19] On the one hand—here agreeing with fundamentalist arguments—it affirmed the need for greater attention to the Bible's claims, language, and mindset for meeting and comprehending the conditions of the modern world. On the other, it maintained that the historical-critical methods of the modernists could not be eschewed. Whatever the consequences, historical analysis was necessary for public intelligibility and credibility.[20]

It also understood its task as providing a "reintroduction" to the Bible's theological dimension. Here, through the work of Emil Brunner and Karl Barth, the effect of neoorthodox understandings of the Bible was strong.[21] Scholars called for a "rediscovery of the Bible,"[22] and attempts to "reconcile the authority of the Bible with the authority of the knowledge gained through reason and experience,"[23] or for "a biblical religion, founded on and nourished by the Bible."[24] There was no claim that scholars should conform to a new set of insights or pay attention to more data, rather the call was for an increased attention to the theological implications of the biblical material. In that sense the Movement was like other forms of "biblical theology," an argument that something essential to biblical materials was being excised by current forms of investigation and analysis which needed to be recovered.

Besides its lack of theological sensibilities, previous historical-critical study was considered defective for two other reasons. First it had failed to recognize the distinctive "Hebrew mentality" that pervaded all the biblical material, both Old and New Testaments. Second, biblical interpreters had allowed the concerns and arguments of dogmatic theology to dominate the mode of theological interpretation of the Bible. The propositional nature of dogmatic theology overshadowed the nonpropositional nature of the biblical texts with the result that the distinctive nature and claims of the biblical material were misunderstood or lost.

Not all biblical scholars agreed with the Movement's assessment of the previous generation or with its proposals for solving the dispute with that generation. To many members of the biblical guild, the criticisms of biblical theology were simply a new form of old biblicism and its proposed breakthroughs weaker versions of critical scholarship from a previous age. The remarks of William Irwin are typical of this response:

> There can be no doubt that it is an expression, and in some degree a rightward move of the present which manifests itself variously all the way from a mild

conservatism to blatant reaction. Its cause, while frequently (and very dubiously) explained has never been satisfactorily analyzed. For it is all too glib to claim that its essence means personal confrontation with the biblical oracles or the effort to disclose the biblical relevance, religious or ethical, for the life of today—all this is very familiar; if one may use a pejorative of matters so serious, it is trite. Precisely this was the concern of the critical age, from which the theological movement would dissociate its genius. The scholars of that time were stirred by a vision of the vitalizing power of the Bible stripped of the accretions of the centuries and presented in its pristine freshness.[25]

To other scholars the problem was not that the biblical theologians misunderstood the past generation of scholarship, but a difficulty with the claim that biblical scholarship needed to appropriate ancient categories to make modern claims about the Bible's content and meaning. These scholars recognized the value in calling for theological interpretation but questioned whether the form proposed by biblical theologians was the only possible form of doing so. For example, in response to G. Ernest Wright's (a major voice in the movement) insistence that biblical theology could only be done in terms of biblical categories and that modern arguments ought to be filtered by those categories, H. J. Cadbury offered this caution:

> Now it is precisely in their frame of reference that the archaizers of Christianity are most insistent. They note correctly how unmodern the cosmology of the Bible is, and how inaccurate will be any understanding of the Bible which ignores its alien assumptions. But they insist that its assumptions should be adopted and they conscientiously try to do so for themselves and for their associates.
>
> This tendency shows itself in the movement to substitute biblical theology for theology. Now biblical theology is a legitimate and a necessary study. It should quite rightly be detached from that theology which is really a phase of general philosophy or metaphysics. The Bible can only be understood in the light of its own times and thought. Its whole attitude, for example, towards concepts like spirit, curse, blessings, or names, was more material, more automatic, than what our generation usually receives. The problem is: How far is it right and salutary to attempt to adopt as well as to understand this biblical outlook? Should it be normative for Christians today? Can it be superimposed in the thought of our time or made to replace that thought? Or are there some parts of it less applicable or valid than others?[26]

Cadbury goes on to argue that this form of archaizing has two perils: (1) a tendency to assume and thereby impose a false unity onto the Bible and (2) a form of verbalism, for example, investing particular terms found in the Bible with theological freight they cannot carry. Both these criticisms became crucial parts of the subsequent critique of the Movement offered by James Barr in *The Semantics of Biblical Language* and *The Scope and Authority of the Bible*.

Despite these responses, the Biblical Theology Movement maintained that a reorientation of biblical studies was necessary. This insistence occurred for at least three reasons. First, among some scholars there was a sense that social realities after the Second World War posed a genuine challenge to the claim that the Bible addresses meaningfully the human condition. The luxury of deferring an answer to that challenge while occupying oneself solely with questions of history was no longer one the discipline of biblical scholarship could afford. If before it could limit itself to historical research, it could no longer. Interpretation of that research that met the pressures of the world's situation was needed. From this perspective biblical interpreters ought to bring their scholarly efforts to bear on the genuine crises of confidence spawned by the war and its aftermath. To do anything less was to abdicate one of their prime responsibilities and to ignore an essential claim of the texts they interpreted. Here Paul Minear's comments are a prime example of the Movement's position.

Second, the Movement offered an internal criticism of previous historical scholarship. This was brought forth not because that scholarship lacked intellectual rigor, but because it lacked an integration of historical analysis with theological interpretation. That is, the form of history was inadequate. This occurred, it was argued, because there was a fundamental misunderstanding of the nature of the biblical texts and their view of history. According to the biblical theologians the biblical texts display an understanding of history as the medium of revelation. As a result, the biblical texts integrated reports of historical events (such as objective history of the acts of God) with interpretation of those events. Recognizing this conception of history—as the necessary and indivisible combination of event and interpretation—was a requirement of anyone who wished to understand the unique nature of the biblical materials. Moreover this recognition should regulate the sort of history one should do in order to rightfully interpret the biblical reports. To distinguish occurrence from interpretation, as history was typically done by their predecessors, was to lose sight of this and hence not actually be a history that did justice to the Bible.[27] Both Rowley and Wright raise this issue, and with Wright's *The God Who Acts,* it becomes a primary point of biblical theology.[28]

Third, following on the claim that the Bible presents a unique understanding of history, the Biblical Theology Movement insisted that the Bible be interpreted on its own terms and with its own categories: that is the biblical categories served as their own hermeneutic. Bringing categories from outside of the Bible would be illegitimate. Fundamentally this protest was two pronged. The first prong argued against the dominance exercised by dogmatic theology's categories in the investigation of the Bible. Even when biblical scholars eschewed this imposition, the influence of dogmatics was still too strong. The result was that dogmatic categories controlled the interpretations of the Bible and, conversely, that the Bible's own categories could play no critical role in constructive theology. The Bible was destined therefore to play an ancillary role at best, and more likely, to be used as a depository of proof texts at worst. The second prong of the argument considered the reliance of dogmatic theology on propositional expressions to make its arguments, but the Bible did not. According to biblical theologians the Bible displayed its own distinct mentality, a "Semitic" thinking that did not fit with the "Greek" propositional perspective. Thus, the propositional approach to biblical materials was both inappropriate and reductive. Either way, the categories and expressions that dogmatics used did not fit those of the Bible. As a result, the biblical materials were not properly understood. For the biblical theologians, maintaining this distinction between Hebrew and Greek thought was a necessary component for understanding the Bible. The interpreter must adapt to the Hebrew mentality and viewpoint if he or she desired to understand the texts. Though this distinction served as a general shorthand among biblical theologians, it became the cornerstone of Wright's *The God Who Acts,* and almost all of Wright's arguments are based on the necessity of this mental shift.

Generally, then, the Biblical Theology Movement, a protest against its predecessors' work, predicated two things. According to the biblical theologians its ancestors either lacked an overall purpose for their historical analyses or they misconstrued the Bible's claims as truth. To remedy this, the Movement argued for a greater degree of theological interpretation, which was based in the Bible's own categories, in order to understand and properly express its distinct claims about God and revelation. Anything less, though it might show great intellectual rigor and historical precision, would be only a prolegomenon to biblical interpretation. For a closer look at these general arguments we can consider the individual positions set forth by Paul Minear and H. H. Rowley.

Paul Minear

Essentially Minear is concerned with the claim and capacity of the biblical materials to address the human condition. His argument is that whether in antiquity or the present the biblical materials were/are able to interpret the world in a way that significantly challenges the world's own understandings and perspectives. Because of this he urges that the methods of the interpreter must be congruent with the Bible's claims. That means the scholar must move from the material of the biblical text to the appropriate methods and not from an assumed method to the materials of the text. Should one make the movement in reverse the biblical texts would then be forced into a framework that reduces their particular claims and vitiates their ability to address the modern world in any but a nontrivial way.[29]

Minear's desire for a biblical theology is based on three points. First, the social circumstances of the world require a biblical interpreter to take seriously the Bible's claims to present a message of hope. Second, not only do the present circumstances require a turn to a more theological orientation among biblical scholars, the imperative to do so arises from the message of the Bible itself. This suggests that the scientific-historical form of interpretation needs modification (or abandonment) because it is inadequate to fully comprehend and thoroughly express the main concerns of the biblical writers. Another viewpoint, one that allows the biblical expressions full voice, is required. Third, as a NT scholar, Minear focuses on the connection of biblical study to the life of the church. The church's vitality is directly proportional to the vigor of NT study. Since the Christian is a person transformed, that transformation impels "a renewed study of the NT." As a result, the "state of New Testament studies thus becomes an index of the state of Christian life and of the state of the Church. It is entirely pertinent, therefore, to raise certain questions concerning the vitality of current New Testament scholarship."[30]

Minear begins his questioning with a comment that the present scene among scholars was one of confusion and lack of focus. "No magnetic pole has been strong enough to force the alignment on theological grounds. . . . Schools have not coalesced about men or universities or denominations."[31] The confusion was the result not of a plurality of methods—for the most part Minear saw a consensus of method and observations—but of a lack of theological rigor. Minear argued that whatever divisions there were, they were due to technical issues rather than theological differences. In other words, debates centered around method and data rather than convictions about the interpretation of that data.

According to Minear, this was due to the lack of attention to the theological framework in which such study ought to take place and from which it derived a purpose. Minear argued that "biblical scholars do not take theology so seriously as to affect their vocational affiliations. The very absence of dissension is an important index of the vitality of 'NT Theology.' Only when theological issues are dormant can scholars lie down so peacefully together."[32] As a result, Minear called for specific attention to theological issues so that genuine agreement or disagreement might surface and not simply be eclipsed by technical wrangling masquerading as discussion.

This leads Minear to his second point. Even if technical activity were an endeavor to which a scholar might give credence and allegiance, it could no longer sustain itself given the social circumstances resulting from the Second World War. Minear describes the situation in almost apocalyptic terms:

The furies are loose and nothing is impervious to their attack. Old hopes and compacencies [sic] are shattered. The hollowness of old securities drives men furiously in search of new goals: a victory of arms, an American Century, a post-war world planned by the church and academic leaders to provide freedom and justice for all. But in many souls, disillusionment has bitten too deeply to allow easy substitutes to be effective. If new hopes are held, they are held gingerly, as illusions in disguise. A new program of self-help hardly suffices to drive out despair regarding all such programs. The crisis in external history becomes a crisis in internal history.[33]

And because of this new form of uncertainty "men have subjected theology and history to piercing scrutiny."[34] "Facing catastrophe with fear and trembling,"[35] a catastrophe of social and psychic orders, the world asks, "Is there after all a gospel adequate to this need?" Awaiting an answer from biblical scholars, men and women have "rejected as useless much that in a quieter day seemed essential" and "condemned as irrelevant most current study of the NT; all the while they detect in the early Christian witness a Word of judgment and salvation."[36] Minear, convinced that the NT can meet this scrutiny, calls for a form of investigation that brings to the fore this biblical word of judgment and salvation.

But the external crisis is not the primary one facing biblical scholarship; the real crisis comes from the emphasis of the NT itself. This is Minear's most important, in fact essential, reason for adjusting the goals and methods of biblical research. Viewing the significant scholars of past and present generations, Minear concludes that all "the aggressors in the theological wars" from Kierkegaard to Dodd to Bultmann took their "impetus from fresh contact with Christian faith in the New Testament."[37] Such contact challenges the mode of approach and the methods of analyzing the texts. "What is happening is this: the reappearance in sharpest focus of the inner contradiction between the testimonies of early Christians and the theological positions (presuppositions, methods, conclusions) of New Testament scholars. Instead of passively accepting judgment by its interpreters, the New Testament has turned the tables and is actively judging them."[38]

The primary means of scientific analysis had succeeded in producing hard effort and critical study, which, ironically, avoided interaction with the texts it purported to explicate. The results were, contrary to the expectations, a failure to understand the texts' primary concerns. Thus, the historicism that characterized modern NT scholarship "has assumed that the advancing application of scientific methods would enable us to determine and establish the character and validity of faith."[39] Because of the promises of such methods NT scholars have been reluctant to admit their limitation or "to push beyond them in dealing with the central witness of the apostles."[40] The inherent flaw here is that the biblical "witness itself resists the method and presents the historian with claims which the method itself cannot test."[41] The witness makes subjective claims, which the historian tries to understand objectively, the result is a failure to experience the actual arguments of that witness.

As historians, critics were correct in limiting their investigations, but Minear argues that an inversion had taken place. Minear granted that the biblical materials conflict with historical methods and that the historian "is perhaps justified in limiting his study more and more to such areas as may be cultivated by his tools." But he also argued that, "whether this is justified or not, it is what the typical American New Testament scholar has done. His methods have dictated the materials selected for study, rather than the reverse."[42] Historical critics were thus held captive by their methods and would necessarily elide crucial parts of the biblical messages. The external social conditions and internal biblical claims challenged this elision:

> As long as his sources present materials adapted to measurement by his methods, he may remain blissfully unconscious of his prison. He may happily busy himself with the problem of the date of Mark or the political conditions in Palestine. But the New Testament presents him with material of a different order. . . . His method, excellently adapted as it is to deal with events in human history, is not designed to describe and illuminate eschatological events.[43]

This meant that the biblical scholar's contentment with historical-critical inquiry was misplaced for it did not inquire into the Bible's own assessment of the world.

On Minear's reckoning, historical critics might be completely accurate in their findings, but fundamentally mistaken in their conclusions. Hence, he argues:

> His conclusions may be accurate but quite irrelevant to faith; he may contribute to knowledge but to parenthetical knowledge. He may be so concerned with what lies within the parenthesis of historical data that teacher and student alike forget what precedes and succeeds the parenthesis. In a period of spiritual poverty, when the radical character of the Gospel is submerged, the Church may be content with this procedure. But in a time of spiritual struggle, when the radical character of the Gospel reappears, the witnessing Church calls anew for confessional theologians and confessional historians.[44]

To break from this imprisonment Minear calls for "confessional theologians and confessional historians." By these terms he refers to scholars whose "faith transcends history [and] are rebellious against the limitations of those methods when applied to the ground of faith."[45] Minear recognizes that this call to confessional status requires a break with prevailing scholarly mores, particularly the claim to objectivity. The confessional historian

> finds himself in the predicament of being at once dependent upon historical events and independent of them. In faith he affirms the significance of an event which is historically both absurd and offensive. When he claims ultimate meaning for this particular happening, his colleagues with impeccable logic may charge him with obscurantist dogma. When he grants the absurdity of this revealed

meaning, thus declaring his independence of objective evidences, he becomes equally vulnerable to the charge of wild subjectivism.[46]

Thus, Minear realizes that confessional scholars will be resisted by secular historians, but he maintains that fidelity to the documents under consideration requires such a risk.

Here is a further reason Minear urged for a new biblical theology to emerge. As a resident in both the academic and ecclesial settings, the confessional scholar must meet two sets of concerns and understandings of meaning which differ quite markedly. Present-day biblical critics had met admirably the concerns of the academy, but had neglected those of the community of belief. However, to meet the needs of one (the academy) and neglect the needs of the other (the community of belief) was itself a violation of the biblical texts because those texts were written not simply to pass on information about the past but to use that information to instruct religious communities on how to live in their present. "Our Biblical theology has been the objective historical reconstruction of the strange ideas of a strange folk; their theology was a continuing response to God's redemptive activity in weaving the unique web of their destiny."[47] Thus, to argue that the interpreter's task is complete once the historical analysis is done is to disregard the intent of the biblical documents and to fail the expectations of the community for whom such documents contain contemporary meaning.

So Minear desires confessional historians and theologians who address both constituencies. He calls for teachers who "will not minimize the necessity for rigorous standards of historical accuracy, . . . will not short-cut the laborious procedures of research to gain comforting conclusions, or ground faith prematurely on the proximate results of their own study." But he also hopes that these same teachers will "let their existence as Christians determine their presuppositions: let the object of their study, such as the witness of early Christians, condition their methods; let their awareness of the tensions between man's history and God's Kingdom keep their minds alert to what belongs within the parenthesis of historical knowledge and what lies outside that parenthesis."[48]

There are important points to be made on Minear's behalf. First, he recognized the biblical texts as inherently texts of religious claims. So he argued that any interpretation claiming to be a full interpretation of such texts would need to take the insistence on the truth of those religious beliefs into account. One might be an ancient historian, but even then the history would be lacking if the religious component were not part of the narrative told. Hence, while any number of approaches might be valid, none would be sufficient if the religious dimension were not, at least, recognized and dealt with.

Second, Minear addressed an imbalance that is still felt in biblical studies, namely the fact that all interpretation need not be for consumption by the academy and that a natural place for theology to be done is in the local church or synagogue.[49] As that is the case, biblical scholars would find it necessary to consider not only the questions of other scholars but also those posed by the world in which they live.[50]

It will be clear that Minear's proposal did not fully consider the difficulties involved in placing historical rigor next to theological responsibility. Historical critics may be quick to point this out, but part of Minear's argument was that these historical-critical colleagues had also neglected these difficulties, in fact, overlooked them. We can see that Minear, as a confessional theologian did not fully construct a bridge from confession to academy, but he did recognize the need to do so, and he reminds us that his colleagues did not give enough (if any) attention to building a bridge from academy to confession. That Minear did not produce such bridges is not a surprise; neither did many of the other biblical theologians of the fifties. Nor is it a critique that eliminates the force of his observations. Rather it makes the need for attention to that task more clear. The necessity of constructing such bridges passes from generation to generation since former structures do not bear present weight well. We might decide to build different sorts of bridges but Minear's challenges to responsive and responsible scholarship remain matters to be undertaken.

H. H. Rowley

The Biblical Theology Movement also criticized the form of nineteenth-century scholarship that came to be known as "liberal" scholarship. Here Rowley's remarks serve as a prime example of the types of criticism the biblical theologians lodged against their predecessors, in terms of both substance and style. To a degree, Rowley's criticism is like that of Minear, but he goes farther than Minear in explicating the function of the ancient forms of witness. The heart of Rowley's argument is that since it was unaware of its presuppositions, liberal scholarship imported modern conceptions of history and fact into ancient narratives.[51] However, it also considered such conceptions to be shared by the ancient writers and, as a result, it misunderstood the characteristics of the ancient arguments and narratives. Based on those modern categories, the biblical materials were bound to appear inferior or in need of radical transformation. But Rowley disputes the use of modern categories of historical enquiry and formulates a case that biblical theology must recast its understanding of history in a manner more in line with the understandings found in the Bible. In this regard, Rowley is a convenient bridge figure between the critique of Minear and the program of Wright.[52]

Rowley acknowledges the debt that his generation owes to the scholarship of its ancestors. He also realizes that to expose its shortcomings "is as easy as it is profitless, and we who are in large measure the creatures of our age should not claim superiority to those who were the creatures of theirs and on whose labors we must build."[53] Nevertheless he argues that a true appreciation of that generation requires efforts which go beyond theirs. We will not show respect to those who precede us "if we stand merely where they stood and refuse to go forward to the new tasks which they have made possible."[54]

To make such moves forward means uncovering the limitations that we have inherited from that scholarship as well as appreciating its gains. Rowley catalogs two of these limitations. First "their view of the Bible was too atomistic."[55] This meant that liberal scholars focused too much on pre-text sources and matters of detail without attention to the overall import of a narrative. Second, the atomism occurred because the scholars were "under the influence of more preconceived ideas than they realized. In an age that was dominated by evolutionary theory, they shared that domination and applied that theory to their material."[56] Commitment to a scientific model of evolution required a particular kind of history. The result was that the evolutionary theory, when applied to the history of the biblical materials, resulted in an overemphasis on "the contrasts between prophet and priest, between Old Testament and New, between Jesus and Paul, and between the Synoptic and the Johannine writings. The unity of the Bible was gone, and it spoke competing voices."[57]

A corollary of scholarship based in a scientific model would be the required suspicion of the supernatural as a cause in the historical nexus. This required liberal scholarship to reinterpret, nonnatural occurrences in natural terms, or to eliminate them altogether, even if they were a prime subject of the biblical texts. Consequently, despite their intentions, these interpreters did not do justice to the materials they intended to analyze because, as Minear had pointed out, the philosophical prerequisites of the methods they had adopted dictated that the biblical material be read contrary to its own nature.

One of the compensatory moves for liberal scholarship was to focus on the genius of the interpreters: of Moses or the prophets, Jesus or Paul. The distinct nature of the Bible was to be found not in the events it reported but in the insightful interpretations that accompanied them. In other words, the authority of the biblical accounts was based in the genius of the interpreters, but liberal scholarship had argued that the events they supposedly interpreted did not occur. Rowley grants that attention to these ancient interpreters is crucial, they must be considered since "the bare fact of history would have achieved little without its interpretation, and it was through the great and inspired figures that this interpretation was given. Yet without the historical facts there could have been no interpretation of them. Both the objective fact and the prophetic interpreter must be equally remembered in any sound understanding of biblical religion."[58]

This failure to do history that was consonant with the texts under investigation is the heart of Rowley's critique. Distinguishing fact from interpretation, or focusing on imaginative interpreters of "non-events," to him meant misunderstanding the biblical form of history. To do this left one with "a body of ideas and principles divorced from the process out of which they were born."[59] It also implied that the truth of the Bible could be a set of distilled propositions, set free from the encumbering forms that the Bible used. Rowley disputed this and argued that the authority of the Bible is not found in "an abstract 'truth' of a revelation contained in its pages. It lies rather in the totality of the concrete fact and its significance. The interpreter of the Bible must therefore seek to apprehend the fact as historical fact, and must have a historical sense, relating the Bible first of all to its context of history and grasping the whole process through which the ideas were revealed."[60]

In other words, the problem with the preceding generation of scholarship was twofold, though the two aspects seemed to move in opposite directions. In the first case, those facts which history could uncover were dealt with in isolation. Minute pieces of ancient cultures were discovered but not integrated into a coherent narrative. In the second case, it had missed the distinctive forms of this history-telling which differentiated biblical religion from the religions of its neighbors.[61] Thus Rowley proposed that interpretation should be dictated by the nature of biblical religion. For him, the characteristic that defines biblical religion, that it shares with no other religion, is that "it is a religion that was born of history. It was not merely mediated through historical persons. It was mediated also through the events of history."[62]

As a result Rowley calls for a form of historical analysis that is as thorough as that of previous scholarship, but that is profoundly more theological. On his reckoning, only such a history could do justice to both the medium and content of revelation. He concludes:

> We need a more dynamic view of the Bible and its ideas. All is to be studied not only in and for itself, and in relationship to that which immediately preceded it and that which immediately followed it, but in relation to its lasting influence on the ages that followed. It is yet more to be studied to discern what is the veritable word of God which was mediated through it. For it is not enough to believe that God revealed some elements of his character in the events of history and that he revealed his will through the personality of the prophets. In so far as he revealed himself, the revelation is valid for all time; for his character is unchanging. It is therefore important to ask how far he revealed himself in each moment of the process and how far his word can be found in the word of prophet, lawgiver, and psalmist.[63]

Clearly in many regards Rowley's sentiments are correct. First, Rowley's form of protest centers on the nature of the historical enterprise and the commitments inherent in it. He recognizes that history writing is not value neutral, it implies commitments and worldviews. On his argument, the historical-critical paradigm of his scholarly ancestors gives away too much. Its commitments require that it transform the biblical narratives into something that they are not. In order to salvage the "truth" of the narratives from the nonhistorical form, nineteenth-century historical scholars had to extract some pure truth from this unfortunate form. Rowley, on the contrary, argues that the form is crucial for understanding the truth; the two are not separable.[64]

Rowley's recognition that no method is value neutral and his insistence that scholars reflect on the compatibility of method to material is still a pressing concern. In contemporary form the question of value commitment takes other shapes (social location of the interpreter, concerns for political or economic critique, revealing the concealed commitments of the dominant interpretive culture), but these shapes share Rowley's insight about the hidden commitments of any historical enterprise. Even so, for Rowley the question of how to claim truth value for narration remains unclear in his formulations. And if that is so, to "move beyond the preceding generation" requires that this generation take up the issues of making and justifying the truth claims of narrative. Recognizing the ideological commitments of an interpretive exercise is only an initial step; other interpretations must still be offered. Not surprisingly, this has become an essential part of theological debate, but it also should be part of the biblical scholar's concerns.

Second, Rowley underscores the need to take the narrative form of history seriously not just as a deposit of historical information, but as a form of history telling. Recently the narrative aspect has been exploited by biblical interpreters, but the question of how such narratives are understood as true remains a desideratum. Despite the proliferation of narrative approaches to biblical interpretation in recent years, few of those studies take up the relationship between narration and history.[65]

Some General Conclusions

First, the Biblical Theology Movement contested the propriety of the historical critic who claimed to have exhausted the meaning of the biblical texts when their historical conditions and value were explicated. The biblical theologians pitted themselves against this and argued that the meaning is to be found not there but in the theological claims of these texts. That is, the nature of the texts as intrinsically religious texts demands readings that give credence to this characteristic. "Lying at the center of this concern for a theologically oriented study was the conviction that the Scriptures were highly relevant for modern man."[66] Hence the biblical theologians argued for a different set of meanings which could also function as contemporary address.

The problem here is not, however, about which is the right meaning, despite the form of the protest. Rather it is a question of the audience that is addressed. That is, which side of Janus's face is being highlighted? The biblical theologians are protesting against a scholarship that only meets the needs of a section of academic discourse and neglects the fact that such texts also make religious claims for and about communities of belief. Here Jeffrey Stout's comments in

"What Is the Meaning of a Text?" are helpful.[67] Stout points out that in many cases where there is a dispute over the meaning of a text the debate is misplaced. The debate often is not over the text itself, but over the term "meaning." That is, "meaning" does not stand on its own but is always a matter of context. One must always ask "meaning for what?" Seen from that perspective the controversy between the biblical theologians and their predecessors was not so much over the meaning of the biblical texts but over the contexts in which they could be used and the methods appropriate to those contexts.

The second and third points of the biblical theologians' critique involve just this: According to the biblical theologians, historical criticism had claimed a hegemony over all venues of biblical interpretation. Not only did these theologians object to this, they argued that it was illegitimate to do so. They did so on two grounds. First, the needs of the community of belief did not fit with the needs of the positivism of secular history. Second, the nature of the texts required means other than historical analysis to appreciate their full potential and claims. Thus, the need for situating biblical studies in relationship to both the academy and to the church/synagogue, and the need for clarifying the means of analysis appropriate to each, form central parts of the biblical theologians' agenda.

This emphasis on the Bible's distinctive understanding of history had three other corollaries. First, revelation was by means of history. In the acts of God and their interpretation, the truth about God was mediated. God was known not by a set of facts, but by the narrative that recorded the divine actions in relationship to a chosen people.[68] Special place was accorded the biblical understanding of history which incorporated both event and interpretation.[69] How this was to be understood differed from theologian to theologian, but it formed a central tenet of the Movement.

Second, this narrative produced an underlying unity in the biblical text. History "as the vehicle for revelation provided an easy means to bridge the gap between the past and the present. Israel's history became the church's history, and subsequently our history."[70] As a result, attempts to show and maintain the unity of the testaments was a prime activity of these theologians.

The stress on revelation through history provided these theologians with a way to recover the historical events in an objective manner while maintaining that subjective interpretation was necessary for understanding them. Thus history was a record not only of human activity but also of divine interaction.

Finally, the biblical theologians insisted that the biblical texts ought to provide the categories for their interpretation. Neither the categories of dogmatic theology nor the rubrics of historical study were sufficient for uncovering and understanding the peculiar nature of the biblical material. The Bible's categories and its distinct manner of understanding history meant that there was a distinct biblical mentality. To understand the Bible, therefore, it was necessary to adopt its manner of conception.

The Critique of the Critique

Like most protest movements, the strength of the Biblical Theology Movement was its ability to point out the excesses and neglects of the previous forms of scholarship. But the strengths were also the weaknesses of the Movement. Despite the rhetoric of renewal and recovery, many of the distinctions it sought to draw between itself and its predecessors were distinctions in degree rather than in kind. Moreover, the distinctions it sought to draw between the Bible and its environment, Hebrew and Greek mentality, and the biblical understanding of history were quickly shown to be the result of imprecise research or muddled categories of thinking. Thus, much of the foundation of the Movement's solutions was eroded. Further, the solutions it offered often only covered over the difficulties, glossing the factors that prompted the protest in the first place.

One of the first to demonstrate the fragility of the Movement's distinctions was James Barr, whose well-known critique of the Biblical Theology Movement, *The Semantics of Biblical Language,* concentrates on the procedures of research and assessment of history.[71] In short order he demonstrated that: (1) there were not distinct categories of biblical thinking and, (2) that distinctions drawn between Hebrew and Greek thought, based on linguistic arguments, were not only untenable but based on an erroneous understanding of the semantics of language. Childs describes his book as striking "with such incisive and devastating criticism that the defenses appeared like a maginot line facing a new form of blitzkrieg."[72] The effect was devastating. As Childs notes, "Seldom has one book brought down so much superstructure with such effectiveness."[73] Sadly Wright, as the primary focus of Barr's attack, could only respond by noting that Barr was overly negative in tone.[74] On the grounds of linguistics, history, and analysis Barr had vitiated Wright's categories and proofs.

As devastating as Barr's criticisms were, to my mind the most important critical response came from Langdon Gilkey. In his article "Cosmology, Ontology, and the Travail of Biblical Language,"[75] Gilkey slowly, methodically, and inexorably destroyed the main tenet of a special understanding of history which the Movement had called the "biblical point of view." To do this Gilkey did not attempt to return to previous conceptions of history but demonstrated a fundamental confusion among the biblical theologians' main categories. The problem results from biblical theology's attempt to situate itself between fundamentalist and modernist procedures and stances. As Gilkey states it, contemporary theology "is half liberal and modern, on the one hand, and half biblical and orthodox on the other, i.e., its world view or cosmology is modern, while its theological language is biblical and orthodox."[76] The confusion results in using biblical terms but keeping modern content. This meant that the claim to use biblical categories was true only in form, not substance.

Gilkey showed that in repudiating liberal emphasis on the universal and immanent in revelation, the biblical theologians "have *not* repudiated the liberal insistence on the causal continuum of space-time experience. Thus contemporary theology does not expect, nor does it speak of wondrous divine events on the surface of natural and historical life."[77] But allowing for the necessary understanding of a causal nexus within history means that "a vast panoply of divine deeds and events recorded in Scripture are no longer as actually having happened."[78]

The tension exists because biblical language is univocal, for instance, "the words 'act' and 'speak' were used in the same sense of God as of men."[79] But contemporary theology, including biblical theology, uses such terms analogically. For contemporary theologians, unlike the biblical writers, the terms 'to act' or 'to speak' do not mean observable actions or audible speech when applied to God. The problem is twofold: first biblical theologians have not realized that the shift has taken place so they think that they are using the terms in the same way as the biblical writers and second, "unless one knows in some sense what the analogy means, how the analogy is being used, and what it points to, an analogy is empty and unintelligible; that is, it becomes equivocal language. That is the crux of the present difficulty."[80]

To show this, Gilkey proceeded to analyze the use of such terms as "mighty act" and "revelation" and found that on enquiry, none of the biblical theologians could give an account of exactly what God had done or revealed, at least not an account that squared with an understanding of the causal nexus of history. When pressed, it turned out that the biblical theologians argued that most of the acts recorded in scripture were simply interpretations by faith. Thus, when the actual doing of history was considered, the biblical theologians were forced to utilize the tactics of liberal theologians or be faced with the violation of their own commitments to a causal nexus for history. The one great exception to this inability which Gilkey found was the Exodus event, but even that unraveled under his questioning. Once more the "mighty act" turned out to be a natural phenomenon that became mighty only in the interpretation. Hence, the distinct category of "mighty act" turned out to be a null set. Gilkey's point was that despite their use of biblical terms, "when we [biblical theologians] analyze what we mean by these theological phrases, we can give no concrete or specifiable content so that our analogies at present are empty and meaningless. The result is that when we push the analysis further, we find that what we actually mean by them contradicts the intent of these theological phrases."[81] Since this formed the major cornerstone of the Movement, to show its fundamentally unstable nature was tantamount to destroying the major claims of biblical theology constructions. As Childs realizes, Gilkey's criticism, coming from one who could be categorized neither as a "classic liberal" nor as a fundamentalist and who understood the dynamics of the Movement, "was particularly painful because it raised the fundamental question whether the recourse of the biblical theologians to history had in fact succeeded in solving the old crux between the Conservatives and the Liberals."[82]

Gilkey's criticism also demonstrated that the problem of revelation and God's action within human history was a problem of systematic theology and philosophy of history. As such it could not be solved simply by insisting on biblical categories.[83] In fact, Gilkey argued that the rescue from the dilemma he had outlined depended on making an attempt to take cosmology and ontology more seriously, even if the Hebrew mentality did not do so. Second, it necessitated a greater attention to how God acts in "ordinary events," for example, how God is related to general experience. To ignore these endeavors was to pretend to let the biblical categories speak for themselves while covertly translating them into our own dialect. The results would be fatal, an interpretation would arise that neither convinced modern readers nor was true to the beliefs of the biblical authors. This, of course, was the exact opposite of the Biblical Theology Movement's purposes.

Conclusions

Given its short lifespan, one might argue that there is little reason to recall the voices of the Movement, especially since Brevard Childs already has provided a thorough and fair chronicle of its rise and decline in *Biblical Theology in Crisis*. Further, since the working suppositions which many of the biblical theologians held, such as the unique nature of biblical texts, the distinction of a Hebrew mentality from a Greek one, and the assertion of a special biblical history, were dismantled in quick order by the trenchant criticisms of James Barr and Langdon Gilkey, it might appear that there is little reason to return to them.

However, despite these observations, there may be some good reasons to remember this period in biblical studies. First, the Biblical Theology Movement is best considered as a protest against an overspecialization within the field of biblical studies and against the dominance of dogmatic theology in dictating how a biblical text ought to be classified. As we have seen above, there are enough voices among current biblical interpreters protesting against this overspecialization and trivialization of the biblical texts to show that the relationship of biblical materials to theological construction with which the biblical theologians were concerned is still an area of intense debate.

Second, the devastating criticisms of the assumptions and methods of the Movement hid from view the value of the motivations that prompted the biblical theologians to try such things. The attempts at integration, to give a focus to biblical analysis, to reconsider the nature of history and faith claims, and to relocate biblical studies within both academy and community of belief are still necessary and worthwhile discussions. Neglecting them is to our detriment.

These discussions may turn out to be heated sometimes, but they ought to be part of a biblical interpreter's responsibility. This is true because they give credence to the need to situate biblical studies within larger issues of theology and hermeneutics. But even if this were not so, at least the arguments would cause us to focus on substantive issues of the purposes of investigations and the ethics behind them.[84] More than that, they could very well be some of the first things biblical interpreters discuss rather than some of the last. If those discussions were part of initial work they would develop abilities to distinguish the goals of research and productivity. Some of the overload Johnson recognized would be alleviated because it would be deemed unhelpful or beside the point.

Third, even after pronouncing the Movement dead or at least moribund, Childs goes on to argue for the need to continue its efforts. He recognizes that there will be scholars who "will sigh in relief that this 'bout with the Bible' is now passed," but he also argues that "only a small group would suppose that the way was now clear for returning to the minutiae of the historicocritical scholarship without any continuing concern for the theological dimensions of the Bible or responsibility for the life of the church."[85] Childs's confidence about this has not necessarily been proven, but that only suggests the need to review the situation that prompted the biblical theologians to make these moves. As Childs recognized, it is not a matter of whether one will participate in biblical theology, only which kind.

At the start of this essay I suggested that the Biblical Theology Movement might be of help in accepting Beker's mandate. I want now, briefly, to examine some ways in which this could occur. The first way is a lesson learned from the failures of the Movement, the other ways are from its initial motivations as they were expressed by Minear and Rowley.

The critiques of Barr and Gilkey point to the excesses of the Movement. Barr's criticism deals primarily with procedure and exegesis while Gilkey's highlights flaws that can be attributed to the Movement's lack of attention to other instances of theology and an overall neglect of hermeneutics in general. The Biblical Theology Movement did more than resist the inroads of theology on exegesis, it argued that dogmatic theology itself was constructed incorrectly. The assertion that the systematic and dogmatic theology were ill-prepared to read the Bible resulted in a lack of attention to the concerns of those disciplines. As Gilkey pointed out, the mistake here was that ignoring the concerns did not cause them to disappear. In the case of the Biblical Theology Movement they reappeared under a different guise. Though biblical terms were used, contemporary content was implied. Dogmatic and systematic concerns are neither arbitrary nor capricious. They conceptualize significant interpretive issues that face all types of readers. Biblical readers are not exempt from the issues, and knowing how we are affected and indebted to the theological currents in which we exist helps guard against confusing contemporary concerns and interpretations (no matter how legitimate) with ancient ones.[86]

The Movement's inability to recognize this caused it to misread the texts it claimed to read better than its predecessors, because, like those predecessors, it tried to read its presumptions of truth and validity back into the texts. To some degree, this form of circular reading is unavoidable for any reader, but the circle need not be vicious. One of the ways that the Biblical Theology Movement could have avoided the self-deception that Gilkey notes is to have taken greater pains to interact with other theological disciplines. Even if it had decided not to do "theology" in a systematic or dogmatic manner and maintained its independence, the interaction would have had a salutary effect since it would have delineated modern theological positions from ancient ones. Even if one chose to privilege the ancient positions, as the Movement did, recognizing and restating those positions with integrity requires knowledge of present positions. If only to avoid confusing the two this would be true, but it is also necessary if biblical theology is to have any impact on those disciplines.

If that was a failing for the biblical theologians, the risk is no less the case today. As Johnson and Beker suggest, biblical interpretation done in isolation is context-free productivity at best and trivialization at worst. More positively, attention to the other theological disciplines lends a purpose for the study of biblical materials and this in turn helps one decide which avenues of enquiry should be followed and which texts are of more importance for present understanding of significant issues. To escape the historian's captivity, a realization that some pursuits are more valuable than others is essential. Otherwise all data have the same status. In a situation where no overriding purpose is recognized, the evaluation and necessity of the investigations becomes moot if not impossible. Determining the trivial from the valuable becomes an exercise of economics or institutional power.

A second lesson to be learned from the Movement's demise is the need for more attention to hermeneutics. By this term, I mean the conscious and public description of the reasons and process by which a text is to be appropriated from one context to another. Clearly this appropriation goes on, especially in synagogue/church contexts (but also by critics who eschew such affiliations), yet little attention is given to how these moves of appropriation are made. I do not suggest that this calls for yet another method or discussion of methods, rather we need to give direct attention to the actual moves that we do make.[87] As Stout points out, "A theology that hopes to converse on moral and other topics in a pluralistic setting like ours had better dispense with the quest for a method. There is no method for good argument and conversation—save being conversant—that is, being well versed in one's own tradition and on speaking terms with others." The suggestion of the Biblical Theology Movement was that the gap between the past and the present could be collapsed. In fact, that was not the case, as Cadbury had already suggested and Gilkey proved. That failure only highlights the need for recognition of the gap and continued efforts to deal with it.

Most present-day biblical scholars do, of course, recognize that gap but they are reticent to address its bridging.[88] Such scholars have followed Krister Stendahl's formulation of "meant and means" that allowed biblical scholars to leave interpretation to the systematicians.[89] Following this course implies that biblical theology becomes a historical discipline, but not a normative one. However, as Gerhard Ebeling remarks, "Even if we take these contrasts as a merely provisional characterization, yet it is clear that we cannot be content only to distinguish the two meanings of 'biblical theology.' Rather, the burning question arises: What is the connexion between them and where does the one pass over into the other? What is the relation between dogmatic and historical theology?"[90] Hence, even if the categories were as pure as Stendahl implied, the relationship between them would still need some attention.

Should we turn back to J. P. Gabler we would find that biblical theology was never expected to become a freestanding institution. In Gabler's project, biblical theology is a form of interface between the biblical texts and the present needs of dogmatic theology. In other words, though it is free of dogmatic constraint in its analysis of the texts, it nevertheless does answer to the dogmatic need for present-day exposition. In other words, the conversation with theology is a crucial part of the biblical interpreter's job. Sans this, there is not an actual location for biblical theology. Here Stendahl's form of détente dissolves. As Ben Ollenburger has already pointed out, there is no "means and meant" dichotomy.[91] The "means" is always present in determining the "meant," and the "meant" is suggestive for the categories of the "means." Ollenburger goes on to argue that the situation of the biblical theologian is, among other places, the church. That is, one of the impulses of the Biblical Theology Movement is on target: biblical scholarship does have a commitment to address the constituency made up of communities of belief. For, even if these are texts of antiquity, there are present-day communities who take them to be texts of the present as well. To claim the title *biblical* interpreter requires at least some form of recognition of this fact.

The need to present readings that justify the study of biblical texts is not restricted to those who would do theology or locate themselves in theological contexts. As Jon Levenson points out, forms of justification are also required of those who teach and study in nontheological settings. If one argues that these texts are simply one set of texts from antiquity (as a purely historical read is wont to do), then why should they be privileged over any other set of texts? That is, the need to think in systemic terms of justification is incumbent on anyone who wants to be known as a biblical interpreter rather than an ancient historian. In other words the Biblical Theology Movement's insistence that a purpose for investigation be considered is still worth taking seriously, whether one does theology or not. The protest against atomization made by the biblical theologians and mirrored in Johnson's remarks could be met, at least partially, if attention to this form of justification were given more thought, both in an outside of academic settings. Once more, the goals of the investigations needs attention if they are to have value and meaning to anyone but the practitioners.

When attempts are made, they are often in the form of methodological questions. But here the problem is, to use Jeffrey Stout's words, "preoccupation with method is like clearing your throat: it can only go on for so long before you lose your audience."[92] To join conversations in the academy or the community of belief, biblical theologians/interpreters will need to reflect on what they have to say that is worthwhile, and on how to say it in ways that are comprehensible. In other words, they will have to practice hermeneutics, not ignore or theorize about them. The best way to do this may be not to find a method but to submit our current practices of interpretation to critical scrutiny. Then we could see what seems to work and what does not, what is glossed over and what is privileged.

The Biblical Theology Movement did that with respect to the previous generation but not to its own work. It discovered the inherent commitments of allegiance to a method of interpretation and was blind to its own set of ideas and commitments in making exegetical and theological decisions. The result was the confused form of its own theology. Today this scrutiny seems equally crucial if only to escape the arrogance of assumption. But more than that, it ought to help us see how our own commitments to various approaches to a biblical text carry hidden freight. We have become adept at pointing to this among historical critical enterprises. It also ought to become a practice in viewing other forms of text explication and analysis.

Finally, the Movement opened the question of locating one's scholarship with regard to conversations outside of those held by other biblical scholars. This protest against a biblical scholars' enclave ought to be observed. Minear's recognition of a social context and public responsibility of the biblical theologian is as pressing today as it was when he wrote. The "crisis" of the world still exists, if not in the same form as he presented it, certainly to the same degree. Likewise, responsibility to a community of belief ought also to enter into the thinking of biblical interpreters, not to control their findings but to give them a purpose. If texts have meaning only in relation to a context, the same is true of the interpretations of those texts. Moreover, changing the context of interpretation requires different forms of discourse. Failure to attend to the different contexts in which the biblical texts are read and used is to cause the atrophy of one of Janus's faces. The faces of Janus require discussions of purpose and place before we start our investigations, not afterward. They require an honest appraisal of the past and a full recognition of the challenges of the present. To do otherwise risks the failure of trivializing the very texts we seek to value and by that process the de-facing of Janus itself.

PART TWO

THE PROBLEMS AND METHODS IN BIBLICAL THEOLOGY

Chapter Four / OLD TESTAMENT THEOLOGY: A DISCOURSE ON METHOD

Ben C. Ollenburger

The diversity that has characterized Old Testament theology from its beginning, and continues to characterize it, raises the question: What *is* OT theology?[1] Although the contemporary discussion of OT theology is especially concerned, perhaps even preoccupied, with questions of method, it has not yet settled that question. Indeed, the methodological discussion also raises a second question: What should we mean by *method?* In this essay I intend to pursue the second question, and in doing so I shall try to make the case that the first—What is OT theology?—may be answered, legitimately, in different and seemingly contrary ways.

A half dozen books published in English within the past decade devote themselves wholly or substantially to surveying the current methodological options in OT theology.[2] I will not conduct a similar survey in this essay, but will pay significant attention to J. P. Gabler (1753–1826), with whom such surveys typically begin. Gabler is a remote figure, and he wrote about biblical and not specifically OT theology. His remoteness, both historically and otherwise, is a benefit: it permits dispassionate discussion. That Gabler did not envision an OT theology separate from biblical theology is, in my view, relatively inconsequential for the questions of method that I want to pursue. On the other hand, the scope of his proposal makes Gabler unusually helpful for pursuing just those questions.

Discussion of Gabler will occupy this essay's first two sections. These will prepare for the third and fourth sections, dealing with complications that arose after Gabler and proposing the formal components of a method for OT theology. Finally, I will consider how and where theological considerations might figure in OT theology's method. My use of the term *method* may seem eccentric, but I hope it will become clear in the course of the essay.[3]

Johann Christiaan Beker, esteemed teacher and friend, will consider this essay an odd way to honor him, since he believes preoccupation with method to be a kind of voyeurism. The belief is not entirely mistaken, but watching biblical theologians from a distance is a way of acquiring the habit. I am still trying to acquire his.

I

Johann Philipp Gabler is credited with establishing the discipline of biblical theology, because he first provided a rationale for its independence from dogmatic theology. However, the point of its independence was, for Gabler, that biblical theology should provide for dogmatic theology a firm foundation in the truth.[4] Biblical theology could be independent, because Gabler had more or less securely in mind what its purpose was and how that purpose could be achieved. And because he defined that purpose in relation to dogmatic theology, and ultimately in relation to the practice of Christian faith—the aim of dogmatics—Gabler foresaw no tension between biblical theology's independence, on the one hand, and its foundational relation to dogmatic theology on the other. Dogmatics has the task, as Gabler believed, of articulating the Christian faith in relation to currents of thought that change with time, on behalf of Christian communities that are equally fluid. But those changing currents cannot be dogmatic theology's foundation, just because they are ever changing. Foundations have to be fixed, and Gabler assigned to biblical theology a constitutive responsibility for fixing them.

Naturally, this had a way of delimiting biblical theology's character. It had to provide dogmatic theology a set of timeless ideas whose truth would be both identified and guaranteed by their correspondence with universal truths of reason. The Bible is vastly different from a catalog of timeless ideas, so a certain amount of study—both historical and critical—would be necessary to identify them. First the ideas had to be identified and located as to time and place, then compared with each other, and finally evaluated as to their abiding validity. The matter of location was crucial for Gabler, because ideas are always clothed in manners of expression appropriate to their own time. Locating an idea historically is essential to removing clothes—ridding it of all particular and local manner of expression, so that the idea itself can be treated.[5] And the treatment consists, in the end, of assessing an idea's comportment with universal truths of reason.

Gabler's proposal for biblical theology, which I have just summarized, reflects a coherent method. That method has three principal components: (1) a rationale for the inquiry Gabler will conduct *as* biblical theology; (2) a clear conception of the material on which he will conduct that inquiry; and (3) a strategy for conducting it. Briefly examining these components may help us clarify what is at stake in methodological discussions about biblical theology and, by extension, about OT theology.

Gabler's rationale is straightforward: Biblical theology is an inquiry into scripture's diverse texts in order to derive from them those abidingly true ideas that dogmatic theology requires as its foundation. Implicit in this rationale is a particular definition of dogmatic theology. But Gabler's own order is the reverse: implicit in his definition of dogmatic theology is a specific rationale for biblical theology. Dogmatic theology has to elaborate the positive content of Christian religion in its own time, and that content has to be deduced from Christianity's sources.[6] It is a deduction that involves careful study of scripture, which cannot serve automatically as dogmatic theology's norm. Rather, scripture must be studied historically and critically, in order to determine what within it is truly revealed. The criterion of authentic or essential revelation is reason, but reason does not supply the content of that revelation; only scripture does. Dogmatic theology, which articulates the true, positive content of Christian religion, thus requires biblical theology and gives it its rationale.

Covered in Gabler's rationale for biblical theology is a definition of its aims: to compile an inventory of biblical ideas, and to identify by rational means those ideas within this inventory that are timelessly true.[7] These aims cohere with a particular conception of biblical theology's material.

Gabler's material is, obviously, the two Testaments of Christian scripture. However, that material acquires definition under the terms of a particular inquiry. Gabler defined scripture, under the particular inquiry of biblical theology—according to his definition of its rationale and its aims—as a corpus of mythical or poetic, and in all events primitive texts, reflecting in their diversity the location of their respective authors on different rungs of an ascending ladder of intellectual enlightenment. Scripture is thus the textual reflection of an evolution in rationality that proceeds by stages (a *stufenweise Entwicklung*),[8] and whose most significant leap occurs between the OT and the New.

The *material* of Gabler's inquiry, then, is a corpus of texts. But it is these texts as they are brought under the inquiry Gabler is prepared to conduct. He does not propose to inquire *whether* they express the variously useful religious ideas of individual authors. Neither does he propose to inquire whether they should count as scripture, and thus, under the properly critical investigation, as revelation. These assumptions, as we may regard them, are not *part* of the material on which Gabler will conduct his inquiry—he does not hold them open to inspection; rather, they are partially definitive of that material itself. This understanding of his material coheres with Gabler's definition of biblical theology's rationale and aims, and with his strategy for achieving those aims.

Gabler's strategy consists in a set of interpretive operations that put to work his judgments about biblical theology's rationale and aims, and about the material on which that inquiry (biblical theology) will be conducted. However, his strategy derives a part of its own justification from hermeneutical considerations of a general sort—judgments about how to interpret ancient ("primitive") literature, especially poetic or mythological literature. Drawing on precedents in classical and biblical studies, as he learned them from J. G. Eichhorn and C. G. Heyne, Gabler proposed a two-staged operation. The first stage involves the grammatical-historical interpretation of texts in order to determine their sense. The second stage involves an explanatory understanding the subject matter of the texts, which is to say their ideas, on the basis of a critical operation. This critical operation discriminates between historically particular forms of expression, such as those encountered in ancient creation myths, and the ideas clothed in those forms. Gabler referred to these stages as *Auslegung* and *Erklärung*—exegesis and explanation—respectively.[9]

These general hermeneutical considerations bear directly on Gabler's strategy for biblical theology. Under *that* particular inquiry, *Auslegung* corresponds to what Gabler called "true" biblical theology, while *Erklärung* corresponds, but only partially, to what he calls "pure" biblical theology. Pure biblical theology expands on *Erklärung*'s explanatory understanding of the texts to identify, by the criterion of reason, those "foundational ideas . . . that belong permanently to Christian faith."[10] The "undressed" biblical ideas passing reason's muster are open to restatement in dogmatic theology's contemporary idiom, and they provide dogmatic theology's foundation. This expansion beyond *Erklärung* is Gabler's appropriation of general hermeneutics to the strategy of a particular inquiry, biblical theology, according to its own rationale and aims.

II

Gabler was a rationalist. He preferred to call himself a "Christian rationalist," but he also acknowledged that "Labels decide nothing; mostly, they frighten the ignorant."[11] Whatever label Gabler merits, the details of his method have little contemporary appeal.[12] Each element of his method, as I have described it, would today elicit severe criticism. But it is because Gabler's method includes so many coherently and internally related elements, and because we know what criticisms to make of them, that it serves our heuristic purposes.

An obvious feature of Gabler's method is biblical theology's dependence on dogmatic theology. Biblical theology has its rationale in dogmatic theology, which also defines its aims.[13] In other words, not only does biblical theology exist, according to Gabler, just because dogmatic theology requires it, but the particular kind of inquiry biblical theology will be depends on a particular kind of dogmatic theology—in both cases, Gabler's rationalist kind. At the same time, Gabler insisted on biblical theology's independence from dogmatic theology: dogmatic theology does not determine what biblical theology will discover in its inquiry into the material, nor is that inquiry conducted *as* dogmatic theology. It is, rather, a free, *scientific* inquiry on which dogmatic theology waits and depends for its own foundations. But this claim seems precisely to contradict the one with which I began this paragraph. How can biblical theology depend on dogmatic theology while remaining independent of it?

Gabler could affirm both simultaneously because he distinguished between biblical theology's aims and its strategy. Like any other inquiry, biblical theology aims to achieve something, and apart from some definition of those aims it would be impossible to know what inquiry to conduct in the first place, let alone know how to assess its achievements. For Gabler, biblical theology is dependent on dogmatic theology, because the latter defines the aims of the former. But in the inquiry it conducts to achieve those aims, biblical theology is independent. Dogmatic theology cannot determine what ideas will be found clothed in Moses' primitive form of expression, or the temporal and local circumstances attending that form of expression, or the meanings of the Hebrew words Moses used.[14] It cannot determine when Moses wrote—or if he did—or how Moses' ideas compare with Isaiah's, or whether there is an identifiable coherence between their respective ideas that can participate in a larger, and more abstract, system of rationally validated biblical ideas suitable as dogmatic theology's foundation. Dogmatic theology can neither control that inquiry, much less conduct it, nor determine its results. It is an independent inquiry whose strategy is derived, in part, from general hermeneutical considerations defensible on grounds independent of dogmatic theology. That is to say, Gabler's interpretive procedures—the measures he applied to the texts in order to interpret them—were ones he shared, and for the same reasons, with what he considered to be the best historical and critical scholarship of his day, regardless of its interest in dogmatic or any other kind of theology.

In fact, biblical theology's emergence in the late-eighteenth and early-nineteenth centuries as an inquiry independent of dogmatic theology was a function of historical criticism.[15] Historical-critical study of the Bible represented a form of interpretation at odds with that of Protestant orthodoxy which could also, and legitimately, claim to embody a tradition of biblical interpretation. The biblical theologies that appeared in the late-seventeenth and early-eighteenth centuries intended to defend the legitimacy of this claim by pointing out the foundation of dogmatic topics, or *loci*, in probative biblical texts, or *dicta probantia*. This defense could only be successful, of course, if dogmatic theology itself represented the proper manner of interpreting the biblical texts. Historical criticism changed all this by insisting on a form of interpretation that did not begin in dogmatic theology and could achieve its aims without regard to it. As J. G. Eichhorn, Gabler's mentor and peer, put it: "I study . . . the texts of the Old Testament merely as a critical scholar; the dogmatician can make use of and assess my investigations as he sees fit."[16] Moreover, historical critics insisted that theirs was the *only* proper form of interpretation—applicable to ancient literature generally, whether profane or putatively sacred—which alone was capable of determining the one, historical sense of scripture.[17] In case biblical theology adopted a historical-critical strategy (for Gabler, this was not in question), its independence from dogmatic theology would be an inevitable consequence.

The challenge that confronted Gabler was not how to secure biblical criticism's independence from dogmatic interference, but how to secure dogmatic theology's foundations—in Gabler's view, these were necessarily biblical foundations—in view of its increasingly apparent asymmetry with historical-critical study of the Bible. His answer, of course, was "biblical theology." Since biblical theology had its rationale and aims given in dogmatic theology's need of it, biblical theology remained formally dependent on dogmatic theology. On one hand, this very relation of dependence required that dogmatic theology itself be modified: it had to become the kind of theology that *could* have its foundations in the historical-critical study of scripture. On the other hand, this required an adaptation of historical-critical biblical study to the precise need a revisionary dogmatic theology had of it. Gabler's answer was, again, "biblical theology," which would expand on historical-critical study by including a philosophical operation whose results—the identification of rationally validated ideas, free of local and temporal dress—were exactly what a new dogmatic theology required. Dogmatic theology itself could not determine what these results would be, but its very anticipation of them gave biblical theology its rationale and identified its aims—a rationale and a set of aims formulated in self-conscious recognition of what biblical theology was equipped to do.

Gabler did not intend biblical theology only to reform the traditional scholastic theology of Protestant orthodoxy with a more biblical dogmatics;[18] he also intended biblical theology to provide dogmatic theology a rationally defensible foundation in scripture. That scripture is theology's foundation was self-evident to Gabler, a Lutheran theologian. But any example of this foundation in a particular dogmatic theology must prove its intellectual mettle: it must be constructed of the best contemporary textual scholarship guided by the right hermeneutical theory, and to the results of that scholarship it must apply the critical canons of reason.[19] In this way, and proceeding independently, it will achieve the aims given in its relation to dogmatic theology, which provides its rationale.

III

As I have said, virtually every element of Gabler's method would today elicit severe criticism, though the specific criticisms offered would vary markedly. To explore those criticisms would require a historical account of developments in the various components of Gabler's method from his time to the present—developments in dogmatic (and systematic) theology, in philosophy, in exegesis, and in hermeneutics. For Gabler, biblical theology was a specific configuration of these components oriented to a particular inquiry. In section I, I described that configuration as constituting a rationale for biblical theology, including a definition of its aims; a conception of biblical theology's material congruent with its rationale and aims; and a strategy by which to conduct an inquiry on that material, congruent with, and partially definitive of, the rationale and aims of the inquiry itself. In section II, I described the articulation—as Gabler conceived it—between biblical theology's dependence on, and its independence from, dogmatic theology in relation to the questions that confronted Gabler and the resources he had for addressing them. The criticisms we would raise against Gabler's method reflect differences in the resources available to Gabler and us, respectively, but also differences in the actual questions we confront. A historical account would, precisely, *account* for these differences.

If we were to pursue such an account, we would find that biblical theology after Gabler, and even alongside Gabler, divided into two regions, with OT theology emerging as a relatively independent area of inquiry. G. L. Bauer wrote a separate OT theology while Gabler was still refining his own method.[20] We would also find that the methodological components of OT theology increasingly differed from Gabler's, and that the variety among those components has left us with the question raised at the beginning: What *is* OT theology? It will prove helpful, instead of answering that question, to suppose that naming some inquiry "OT theology" is to locate it historically, in the context of previous inquiries that suggest questions to be addressed and ways of (resources for) addressing them. Of course, a revisionist inquiry may propose that earlier questions were the wrong ones to ask, or that earlier ways of addressing them were misguided—or both. But especially a revisionist inquiry will locate itself historically, in order (put crudely) to show why its questions are more productive ones and why its resources provide better means of addressing them—as a way of justifying itself.[21]

The recent OT theology of Horst Dietrich Preuss is typical and instructive.[22] Preuss begins by saying what an OT theology must achieve: "a summary of the Old Testament's world of faith and witness" (1-2), which is to say, the theology "that the Old Testament contains and offers, but not that which has the Old Testament as its object . . . : the latter inquiry belongs rather to hermeneutics or to fundamental theology" (2). Further, OT theology is to be differentiated from the history of ancient Israelite religion. But this, Preuss recognizes, is not at all obvious; it constitutes one of the questions to be addressed by OT theology, and it is one of the questions OT theology inherits as its historical legacy. To show that this is the case, Preuss rehearses that history, beginning with Gabler (2) and continuing to the present (3-23). In this rehearsal, by means of which he situates his own inquiry, Preuss identifies seven orienting problems: (1) the relation of OT theology to the history of Israelite religion; (2) whether the OT's theology should be presented historically or systematically; (3) in case of the latter, whether a systematic arrangement should be derived from the OT itself or from outside it; (4) the evaluation of the OT's theology, and whether it should coincide with a historical or descriptive presentation, follow it, or be referred to dogmatic theology (8-9); (5) the relation between "history and kerygma"; (6) whether the OT has a theological "center," and in case it does have one, what it is; (7) the question of the OT theology's openness to "a biblical theology comprehending both Testaments of the Christian Bible" (16-17).

Preuss announces his own stance toward these problems (23-27), a stance justified, not on the basis of the inquiry itself, but on the basis of a critical discussion of that *kind* of inquiry's (OT theology's) prior history. In other words, Preuss identifies his inquiry as OT theology by situating it historically, and he justifies his stance toward that inquiry on the basis of a critical narrative of its history, beginning with Gabler. He does so, with one exception: he stipulates, in his book's second sentence, that OT theology is "a summary of the Old Testament's world of faith and witness." Preuss offers us no reason why we should believe this; he takes it to be self-evident. This self-evident quality of OT theology's aims is not peculiar to Preuss; to the contrary, indeed, it is typical. Ludwig Köhler stipulates, in the first sentence of his *Old Testament Theology,* that "One may give a book the title 'Old Testament theology' if it manages to bring together and to relate those ideas and thoughts and concepts of the Old Testament which are or can be important."[23] Edmond Jacob stipulates, in the first sentence of his *Theology of the Old Testament,* that "The theology of the Old Testament may be defined as the systematic account of the specific religious ideas which can be found throughout the Old Testament and which form its profound unity."[24] In his *Old Testament Theology in Outline,* in the first sentence under "Purpose and Scope," Walther Zimmerli stipulates that "Any 'Old Testament theology' has the task of presenting what the Old Testament says about God as a coherent whole."[25] Claus Westermann stipulates, in the second sentence of his *Elements of Old Testament Theology,* that "A theology of the Old Testament has the task of summarizing and viewing together what the Old Testament as a whole, in all its sections, says about God."[26] Werner Lemke stipulates that "Old Testament theology is an exegetical and theological discipline which seeks to describe in a coherent and comprehensive manner the Old Testament understanding of God in relationship to humanity and the world."[27]

This series of definitions is striking in at least three respects: (1) none of the authors cited mounts an argument in favor of his definition, but simply stipulates it at the outset;[28] (2) there is no material difference among the definitions, and any one could substitute for all the others; (3) in spite of complete agreement on the definition of OT theology's aims, the respective authors, not to mention a wide range of others, conduct markedly different inquiries. In other words, these stipulative definitions are uninformative. They take the place, I suggest, of a consideration of OT theology's rationale and aims, accepting as self-evident that OT theology can derive these from—and only from—considerations internal to biblical scholarship as a historical-critical, exegetical discipline. Thus, in Preuss's case, the historical narrative locating his OT theology *follows,* rather than precedes, the stipulative definition he offers of OT theology's aims: OT theology aims at "a summary of the Old Testament's world of faith and witness."

Between Gabler and Preuss there is a world of difference. G. L. Bauer, to whom I have already adverted, not only introduced OT theology as an independent area of inquiry, but also collapsed the two stages of Gabler's method into one, historical-critical strategy. In significant respects, OT theology in the nineteenth century represented a continuing effort to make good on Gabler's promise, as it came to be interpreted, of a consistently historical-biblical or OT (or NT) theology. In some quarters, there were specifically philosophical or theological reasons why OT or biblical theology *should* have a historical character. Among others, Wilhelm Vatke and J. C. K. von Hofmann proposed such reasons, but Vatke's Hegelianism and Hofmann's salvation-historical theology both came to be seen as impositions on the material itself.[29] Through the nineteenth century there was increasing pressure, not only to take into account the historical character of the OT, but also to give OT theology a thoroughly historical orientation.

While a form of this orientation had characterized OT theology from Gabler on, and had been given particular importance among conservatives from Steudel through Riehm,[30] critical historical investigation of the OT culminating in Wellhausen changed things dramatically. Wellhausen, drawing on the work of Wilhelm Vatke, Abraham Kuenen, Eduard Reuss, and K. H. Graf, reconstructed Israel's literary history on the premise that the prophets preceded the Law. Wellhausen's reconstruction was thorough and compelling, and very effective. If the Law is historically later than the prophets, contrary to the canonical order and to previous assumptions, then a historically oriented OT theology based on previous assumptions seems precisely to *lack* a basis. Naturally, this required changes in OT theology, which could no longer—at least not uncritically—trade on earlier historical reconstructions. But an even more significant effect was the change these developments brought about in the *character* of OT theology's historical orientation. They heightened OT theology's dependence, not just on a new set of historical reconstructions, but also (and what is more important) on the historical-critical strategies underlying those reconstructions. To put it another way: historical criticism seemed to provide the only means of justifying claims about the texts, their contexts, or their contents; to leave other kinds of claims without justification; thus to limit the range of justifiable claims OT theology could make.

James Barr summarizes the effect of this development, arguing that

the most important way in which historical reading has operated is not, as people suppose, its direct influence upon beliefs about what happened or who wrote this book or that and when. This . . . is less serious in the end than another factor: historical

89

reading has gained control of the *semantic* linkages within the text and its language. This is the deepest-lying shift of emphasis.[31]

In other words, and under this shift of emphasis, the OT does not refer to, say, a set of ideas or concepts that contemporary believers may, under appropriate conditions, hold in common with its ancient authors; rather, the OT's references are, in a peculiar way, intrasystematic. What the OT means, in any of its parts, is relative to historical criticism's ability to detect or to construct convincing semantic linkages within the OT itself; between the OT and the historical circumstances, political and cultic institutions, and rhetorical conventions within which it emerged; and between the OT and the Near Eastern environment of which it was a part.

By the end of the nineteenth century, this "control of the semantic linkages" seemed to make OT theology impossible, except as the history of Israelite (and Jewish) religion.[32] But this stalemate proved unsatisfactory to those for whom the OT's importance, or the importance of Israel's religion, was not exhausted by a reconstruction of its historical development. It was important to capture, *somehow,* the essence or the decisive features or the center of the OT, or of Israel's religion; OT theology should have this task. For some, like Herrmann Gunkel, this seemed unimportant in comparison with penetrating to the inner life of the OT's individual authors.[33] For Otto Eissfeldt, on the other hand, OT theology remained impossible within historical criticism's legitimate control of "the semantic linkages." He insisted that OT theology has to proceed, and to derive its structure, from faith—from the faith of the interpreter and the confession of the Church, and hence of a particular church. Historical-critical inquiry into Israelite-Jewish religion, Eissfeldt said, can and should play a critical role in relation to OT theology, helping to discipline its observations, but it cannot substitute for OT theology.[34] Walther Eichrodt argued, in response, that OT theology must remain a historical-critical discipline, "with the systematic task of a cross section through the developed whole [of Israelite religion], which should illumine the entire dynamic content of the religion according to its internal structure. . . . "[35] The role of faith is, for Eichrodt, incorporated within the subjective dimensions of historical inquiry itself, in the convictions and perspectives it brings to that inquiry.

Old Testament theology has continued for the most part within this post-nineteenth century trajectory. It has worked somewhere between the poles of Eissfeldt and Eichrodt without resolving them, trying to find ways of coping with the twin constraints seemingly imposed on OT theology: that it should somehow honor the semantic linkages over which historical criticism exercises a legitimate control, and that it has a theological assignment to honor as well—somehow. But in recent years a wider range of options has appeared, prompted by the availability of strategies that either expand on or diverge from historical-critical ones, and by broader attention to the kind of theological assignments

OT theology might be considered to have and to the ways in which it might legitimately honor them. More than that, all of the following have greatly expanded the range of questions OT theology can or must take into account: literary-critical and sociological studies; developments in hermeneutics from Gadamer to Ricoeur and Habermas, and beyond them; developments in contemporary theology affecting the ways in which scripture and theology are held to relate; attention to Judaism in light of OT theology's predominantly Christian character; and challenges to prevailing models of interpretation, and to its social interests and location, from liberation theology and feminism.[36] Today, virtually every inquiry in OT theology is revisionist. And any definition of OT theology as offering a summary of the OT, or of some dimension of it, begs a number of important questions.[37]

Two apparent consequences of these developments bear mentioning before moving to the next section. First, while the larger role Gabler assigned to biblical theology was *foundational* in character, OT theology has equipped itself to play a *critical* role. Neither dogmatic theology nor any other discipline, area of inquiry, or practice—religious, social, intellectual—has OT theology as its foundation. The OT itself may well be foundational, with respect to any or all of these, but the kind of inquiry OT theology can conduct is of a critical sort with respect to them. This is an unintended consequence of the distinction of biblical theology from dogmatic theology that Gabler introduced, and a function of the course OT theology has taken since Gabler. In short, it has become a *discipline,* in at least the restricted sense that it is prepared to address that range of questions congruent with a set of strategies (usually called "methods") deployed on material defined in a way congruent with them.[38] The strategies are not uniform, and recently they are not uniformly historical-critical ones; consequently, there is no uniform definition of the material and no uniform range of questions (compare, for example, Brevard Childs and Norman Gottwald).[39]

Second, if OT theology is to exercise a critical task, it can do so only in relation *to something;* understanding that task requires clarity about *what* OT theology stands in critical relation to, and *how* it can and should conduct itself in that relation. In other words, OT theology requires clarity about its method. Gabler remains a model of such clarity, even in spite of the long history between us and him.

IV

In the first section, I represented Gabler's method as comprising three formal components: a rationale for an inquiry conducted as OT (or, in his case, biblical) theology, which includes a definition of its aims; a conception of the material on which that inquiry will be conducted; and a strategy for conducting it. Essential to this configuration of formal components was Gabler's material definition of dogmatic theology, on whose behalf OT (biblical) theology was required. Dogmatic theology has changed since Gabler (it is, in North America, an endangered species), and it seldom any longer constitutes OT theology's rationale. Even so, a slightly modified version of Gabler's method, formally considered, can accommodate and account for OT theology's diversity, and it can help to make debates about OT theology more productive. I will propose such a method in outline form, followed by some explanatory comments.

A formal method for OT theology should reflect and permit reasoned judgments about the following components and their relation to one another:

(1) The *aims* of a particular inquiry;
(2) The *material* on which the inquiry is conducted;
(3) The *strategy* by which that material is brought under the aims of an inquiry and that inquiry carried out. A strategy will be determined in relation to:
    (a) certain *regulative ideas;*
    (b) certain *constitutive principles,* which may themselves derive from:
        (i) theories about the material;
        (ii) theories about (its) interpretation.

It may seem that this outline is general enough to include any version of, or proposal for, OT theology since Gabler. I believe (and intend) that to be the case. It is also general enough to accommodate virtually any inquiry in any field, so long as it interprets material. This level of generality at least accommodates disagreement about what OT theology *is;* moreover, it provides a framework for justifying, or assessing, claims about OT theology—claims such as Peter Dirksen's that two of the classics, Eichrodt's and von Rad's, are not OT theologies at all.[40] What Dirksen seems to mean is that Eichrodt and von Rad do not conform to his own definition of OT theology. Such disagreement is not surprising, even in light of the stipulative definitions that tend to occur on the initial pages of modern OT theologies. John L. McKenzie, in his unjustly neglected OT theology, makes this observation in his initial sentence: "Biblical theology . . . lacks generally accepted principles, methods, and structure. There is not even a generally accepted definition of its purpose and scope."[41] Since this is empirically the case, Dirksen's fundamental disagreement with Eichrodt and von Rad is no surprise. Truly surprising is Dirksen's claim that OT theology on his definition is both impossible and pointless, while inquiries like Eichrodt's and von Rad's—though failures at OT theology—are both possible and eminently worthwhile: to the benefit of OT scholars, they "will lead to a better knowledge of Israelite religion in its development;" to the benefit of Christian theologians, they "will bring to life many and manifold voices from Israel's past, voices from both writers and redactors, embedded in the OT, from the oldest layer of the text to the latest glosse [sic] or addition."[42]

This puts one in an interrogative mood. What sense is there in a definition of OT theology whose effect is to deny that the classic examples of it are examples in fact, while claiming that there can be no examples in fact and that, if examples were possible, they would be pointless? Why should we assign OT theology the impossible and irrelevant task, as Dirksen conceives it, of identifying "those theological ideas connected with the establishment of the Old Testament in its final form . . . ?" Why should we think that theologians would benefit from knowing—or knowing the debate about—the "religious impulses behind the growth of the [OT's] traditions?"[43] Answers to these questions may be at hand, but Dirksen does not hint at them. He begs the question of what OT theology is, how it should be conducted and to what end, who might benefit from it, and what that benefit might be.

Dirksen's brief article is instructive in its guiding assumption, that the aims of any inquiry presuming to count as OT theology are determined by strategies elected on other grounds. Since, as he assumes, OT theology accounts for the OT as a whole, its strategy must be of a redaction-critical sort, moving (as in his example) from reconstructed units within the book of Judges to their inclusion in a reconstructed " 'pan-Israelite' collection," then to that collection's inclusion in the Deuteronomistic history, on to the incorporation of that historical work in "the Old Testament as a whole," and finally to the interpretation of the original units within their new setting—an interpretation that needs to take into account the ideas of the canonizers, whoever they may have been, who put them in this new setting.[44] We do not know who these people were, or what ideas they had in mind, so OT theology turns out to be impossible; besides, Christian theology wouldn't be especially interested in these ideas, even if there were some way of finding them out.

The assumption that strategies devised to serve other interests must be those of OT theology, in such a way as to determine its aims, is pervasive. It is represented in the traditional notion that OT theology is the crowning achievement of historical-critical OT scholarship;[45] theologians, or people very much like them, should take note and consider the benefits, just because this *is* its crowning achievement. I do not want to contest the notion here, but I do want to insist that it requires justification. There may be reasons why inquiries conducted as OT theology should employ strategies other than (or in addition to) those of OT scholarship typically, or traditionally, and there may be reasons why such an inquiry should aim at something other than a summary of the entire OT, or of its statements about God, or of all those things that—in Ludwig Köhler's happy phrase—"are or can be important." Everything *can* be important; a method for OT theology should help frame arguments about what *is* important, so that an inquiry can aim at something. In his own words, one of which the English translator missed, Köhler spoke of those things that "are or can be *theologically* important."[46] With the adverb, Köhler introduces a pragmatic note into his definition of OT theology.

It is this pragmatic note that I want to stress and expand, upon suggesting that OT theology's methodological considerations need not confine themselves to what an inherited strategy makes possible (or impossible), or with what an inherited definition stipulates; they may include, and begin from, much more pragmatic questions. Terry Eagleton has made the point in relation to literary criticism: "It is not a matter of starting from certain theoretical or methodological problems: it is a matter of starting from what we want to do, and then seeing which methods and theories will best help us to achieve those ends."[47] In the outline I have proposed, this pragmatic consideration of ends to be achieved—of what we want to *do*, what aims we want to pursue—is included in OT theology's *strategy*, under the category of *regulative ideas*.

The term has a Kantian provenance.[48] For Kant, regulative ideas are transcendental rather than constitutive; they have a "regulative use, in directing the understanding to a certain aim. . . . "[49] In the same context, Kant speaks of "subjective principles which are derived, not from the quality of an object, but from the interest which reason takes in a certain possible perfection of an object," and he calls these "*maxims* of reason."[50] Kant requires that regulative ideas or principles be considered only maxims of reason—rational illusions generating useful hypotheses. We can adopt Kant's distinction between regulative and constitutive ideas, his view of regulative ideas directing the aims of understanding (or inquiry), and his association of regulative ideas with interested reason, without ascribing any inevitability to these ideas and without regarding them as transcendental in precisely Kant's sense—as the necessary conditions of inquiry, which can only be assumed and are not themselves open to debate. If we give the inquiry-directing regulative ideas, considered as maxims of reason, a pragmatic valence, we can implicate them dialectically in the inquiry itself.

For Gabler, the regulative ideas were embodied in the dogmatic theology he envisioned as the beneficiary of biblical theology's inquiry. What I am proposing as a method for OT theology permits this—it permits dogmatic theology to supply biblical theology's regulative ideas—but does not require it. It requires only that a case be made—that, in principle, a case *can* be made—of how dogmatic theology (or anything else) could, and why it should, guide the aims of OT theology's inquiry. But, in this instance, it also implicates dogmatic theology (or anything else) in the inquiry itself. That is to say, if dogmatic theology supplies the aims of OT theology's inquiry, that inquiry has dogmatic theology as its correlative object. Regulative ideas define the interests of an inquiry, but they do so in a serious way only if the inquiry bears critically on those ideas. Otherwise, OT theology is only an exercise, even if a very sophisticated exercise, in proof texting. As I said at the conclusion of section III, OT theology has prepared itself to exercise a critical task. Its regulative ideas define the aims of an inquiry, conducted as OT theology, by clarifying *what* OT theology stands in critical relation *to*. The range of possible candidates is limited only by the arguments that can be made in their favor.

Such arguments will include reference to the *constitutive principles* for conducting an inquiry. Regardless its aims, any inquiry requires a strategy—a (set of) procedure(s)—by which to conduct it. Regulative ideas, by joining interests with the aims of an inquiry, constrain the range of relevant strategies, but they cannot alone determine their precise character. If we should decide, with Gabler, that dogmatic theology provides our regulative ideas, and thus makes concrete our interests, we would not yet know how to proceed. For example, should we employ a version of historical criticism oriented to the reconstruction and understanding of tradition formation—on the order of Gerhard von Rad? Or should we employ a version of literary criticism oriented to the analysis of what the Bible does, the resources it uses, and what it achieves in constructing its stories and poems—on the order of Robert Alter?[51]

Different constitutive principles underwrite the interpretive strategies of von Rad and Alter. Further, their respective principles are independent of, and prior to, any direct concern for OT theology, whatever its possible aims. Theories of text and interpretation, of widely differing character and origin, relate von Rad's tradition-historical strategy and Alter's literary one to intellectual and interpretive domains broader than OT theology (von Rad) or biblical studies (Alter). It is entirely legitimate to argue, as von Rad seems to do, *from* a particular strategy, including the constitutive principles or theories of text and interpretation it comprises, *to* the aims of OT theology. Gabler makes a similar argument, on the basis of his conviction that historical criticism of his kind—and Heyne's and Eichhorn's—is the only acceptable means of determining a text's single sense. In each case, the argument is incomplete apart from a congruous definition. In Gabler's case, it is a definition of biblical theology's aims and the character of dogmatic theology. In von Rad's case, it is a definition he adumbrates at the outset: "The subject-matter which concerns the theologian is, of course, . . . simply Israel's own explicit assertions about Jahweh."[52] The "of course" is tendentious apart from the case von Rad actually makes in the course of his *Old Testament Theology* and in his substantial work that preceded it. It is a case that depends, first, on whether von Rad manages to show that the tradition-historical interpretation of OT texts, with its construal of *the material,* is itself defensible, compelling, and illuminating—and then on whether it is suggestive of something we may really want to *do* as OT theology, and of ends we consider worth trying to achieve.

That point, and the criteria for deciding it, need not be debated again here, since my purpose is only to suggest that reference to constitutive principles, perhaps including theories of text and interpretation, may figure in arguments about OT theology's regulative ideas—about the ideas themselves, and not just about which ones to have; and that correlatively or dialectically, the choice of regulative ideas elicits argument about constitutive principles. I have asked how we should choose between the representatively different strategies of von Rad and Alter, in case dogmatic theology provides OT theology's regulative ideas. If we conceive Christian theology along Wolfhart Pannenberg's lines, we may find von Rad more nearly compatible; if we conceive it as Hans Frei does, we are more likely to find in Alter the lineaments of a strategy for OT theology.[53] Sharper oppositions could be found than exist between either Alter and von Rad or Pannenberg and Frei, but even in these cases the differences are more than negligible. An OT theology determined to relate itself critically to Christian theology would have thereby made an important (and corrigible) decision, but it would then have crossed only the threshold of its methodological considerations. In these considerations, it may even need to argue a preference for Pannenberg or for Frei, or for an alternative to both; that is, it may need to conduct an explicitly theological argument.

V

Biblical scholars are often reluctant to conduct an explicitly theological argument, sometimes for good reasons: as James Barr contends, "they do not dispose of material that will enable them to judge and decide the question."[54] Judgments, if they are bound to be incompetent, are best avoided. But it is not only, and not even especially, a matter of the material's inaccessibility—biblical scholars master all sorts of material (theology is not harder than Akkadian)—as it is a concern to maintain the freedom, and the priority, of historical-critical interpretation. Jesper Høgenhaven, for example, insists that the "proper meaning" of the biblical texts is attainable only on a "historical reading," which is itself, he believes, a concomitant of their canonical status.[55] The notion of a singularly "proper meaning" is slippery, and it is currently under vigorous and justified assault. But what Høgenhaven glimpses, and Barr explicitly points out, is the inability of historical studies themselves to decide fundamental questions that divide theologians, or (what may amount to the same thing) to secure theology's—any theology's—foundations.[56] Two generations ago, when historical criticism's grip on the "semantic linkages" was still an inhibiting legacy, this issue could be evaded by means of a nearly eschatological reservation. Johannes Lindblom's counsel, in 1934, is representative: OT theology exhausts its responsibility when it has "given the dogmatic theologian and the philosopher of religion reliable material which they can then use for their particular ends."[57] It is hard to imagine what would constitute pertinently reliable materials apart from the consideration of particular ends, since, in the nature of the case, *particular* ends vary widely—not only between dogmatic theologians and philosophers of religion, but among both parties as well. Karl Rahner's remarks on this reservation are apt:

When you simply leave the work of bridging the gap between exegesis and dogmatic theology conveniently to us, and we poor dogmatic theologians want to take up this work . . . then you are the first to shout—admit it—that we dogmatic theologians understand nothing about exegesis, and that it would be far better if we left it alone rather than dabbling in it in a clumsy sort of way! Who then is to do this job that must be done?[58]

Rahner's question persists, but so does OT theology's reluctance. As I would argue, this reluctance is a material issue within OT theology, whose method should include a place for debating it. John J. Collins's recent proposal exemplifies both the issue and the method. Collins agrees that OT theology should be of a critical sort; he means by this that historical criticism should remain OT theology's "context."[59] The distinguishing feature of this context is its "demand for evidence and reasoned calculation of probability"; biblical theology will apply this demand to "the critical evaluation of biblical speech about God," in order to "clarify the meaning and truth-claims of what was thought and believed from a critical perspective" (8). More to the point: historical criticism's "primary contribution to biblical theology . . . lies in its clarification of the various genres in the biblical text," and thus of "the truth claims that can be made for a biblical passage . . . " (9).[60] Collins applies this point to the biblical narratives, whose genre is "story." This fact about the narratives, presumably satisfying evidential demands and having a calculated probability (Collins mentions only a shift in interpretive sensibilities [10]), means that they cannot be "judged only as historiography"; "they do not provide the bedrock of certainty that theologians have often sought." And, according to Collins, this shift from history to story also "abandons the last claim of biblical theology to certain knowledge of objective reality" (11).[61] Historical criticism, says Collins, recognizes that the biblical narratives, as "story," are the work of human imagination, and that they are fiction; they are poetic expressions of reality and can "be read as proposals that open up new ways of viewing life" (12). Biblical theology, then, in all its genres, is the expression of an "experiential, symbolic theology" (12). Evidently, Collins here means by "biblical theology" the Bible's own experiential expressions.

Collins's proposal for critical biblical theology makes only negative use of his remarks about genre: since the genre of the Bible's narratives is story, they cannot be treated as history. That they are experientially expressive poetic fictions seem not to figure in critical biblical theology, which attends, not to the workings of the Bible's narrative/poetic fictions, but to their *assertions:* "biblical assertions about God" (13). Moreover, the attention biblical theology gives these assertions is guided by "a view of biblical religion as a functional system where myth and cult are supporting devices to regulate the conduct that is at the heart of the religion" (13). Collins does not argue for this functionalist approach, except to note that historical criticism "lends itself most readily to it" (13), and that "assertions about God . . . are most easily explained as rhetorical devices to motivate behavior" (14). This is so because historical criticism, and thus a critical biblical theology, is unable to establish the truth of assertions about God, or whether they are "well founded" (14). It can establish, presumably—Collins hedges here—the social function of these assertions.[62]

Finally, Collins gives reasons why critical biblical theology, in his sense, is not only critical but *theological.* A functionalist (the characterization is mine) "account of biblical God-language is in itself a theological exercise, since it clarifies our use of theological language. It also has some warrant in the Hebrew Bible, where *miṣwôt* are the end of history . . . and ethical performance is more important than belief " (14).[63] This kind of biblical theology is "reductionistic," Collins admits, if it claims to be exhaustive. It avoids reductionism by also recognizing the biblical texts "as proposals about metaphysical truth, as attempts to explain the workings of reality" (14). However, there are such diverse proposals in the Bible, and diverse "philosophical systems" in contemporary culture. "It is not within the competence of biblical theologians as such to adjudicate the relative adequacy of metaphysical systems." Whether a critical biblical theology is possible "depends on the model of theology we are willing to accept." It *is* possible, Collins says, if we understand theology "as an open-ended and critical inquiry into the meaning and function of God-language" (14). Exactly.

Collins's proposal is illuminating—in the first place, because it exhibits all of the formal components of Gabler's method, and all of the material ones as well. It depends on a particular model of theology (though philosophical, not dogmatic) to articulate biblical theology's aims. These aims are mutually congruent with a particular conception of the material (for Collins, fictional works of imagination serving functional ends) and a particular strategy supported by constitutive principles—theories of text and interpretation. For both Gabler and Collins biblical theology's inquiry-directing regulative ideas are represented as "theology," defined in a way congruent with, and (particularly for Collins) on argument from, the theories supporting biblical theology's strategy. For Collins, a particular "model of theology" is the condition of a critical biblical theology's possibility (14); this is a stringently *regulative* idea. It includes a congenial (13) theory of religion as a functional system, and coheres with certain constitutive principles—historical-critical ones—to define biblical theology's aims.

Collins's proposal is also illuminating because each of its components is open to debate, and is in fact the subject of debate. Collins takes particular, contested positions on the genres of Hebrew narrative; the relations among history, historiography, fiction, poetry, truth value, and truth claim; "the value for theology" of biblical narratives; the explanatory power of a functionalist sociology, and its compatibility with other theorists he cites, like Ricoeur and Sternberg (are *they* compatible?); the capacity of historical criticism to offer functionalist explanations that enjoy *any* probability (as opposed to a rhetorically suggestive possibility); the nature of theological language and of theology itself; and the relations among truth, metaphysics, theological propositions, and biblical narratives. That the positions Collins takes on these matters are contestable is no criticism; they are contestable in the nature of the case, and it is greatly to Collins's merit that he recognizes, at least implicitly, that *any* biblical (or OT) theology will take or entail positions on them. Nor is Collins necessarily to be faulted for not actually making a case for certain positions he takes, such as on the need of a philosophical system as a "yardstick by which to assess metaphysical truth" (14). Even if he treats certain controverted positions—including the one I just named—as if they were self-evident, he thereby exposes them, and thus his proposal as a whole, to productive argument. In his concrete instantiation of a method, Collins elicits argument across the widest possible range of issues and interests.

But what of Karl Rahner's question? Collins's reluctance to enlist in the effort Rahner calls for is grounded in his commitment to historical criticism as constitutive in (or of) biblical theology's strategy. But the reasons he gives for this commitment are pragmatic: historical criticism serves "as a forum for dialogue between people of different views" (8), and "it still commands the allegiance of the great majority of biblical scholars, including most of those who work in biblical theology, and with good reason, since it provides a broad framework for scholarly dialogue" (15). In other words, because the majority of scholars practice it, it provides for scholarly dialogue; and because it provides for scholarly dialogue, the majority of scholars practice it. Circularity aside, dogmatic—or, in Collins's terms, confessional—theology does not provide that forum or broad framework for scholarly dialogue; biblical scholars have different views, different confessions, and even different faiths.[64] Besides, "historical criticism is not compatible with a confessional theology that is committed to specific doctrines on the basis of faith" (14).

Collins's emphasis on dialogue—on a particular dialogical community, as we may say—is salutary. Even so, the particular community to which he points is exceedingly small, and the range of its interests, limited by the set of strategies comprising it, is narrow. The dialogical community and its interests can be expanded, even if those interests are concrete and particular, and even if the strategy remains largely the same. In her feminist prospectus on biblical theology, Phyllis Trible proposes no replacement of historical criticism, but she does propose putting it to use—and, where necessary, modifying or going beyond it—in the particular interests of a feminist biblical theology whose dialogical community extends far beyond the academy or one of its parts.[65] Moreover, the concrete expression of those interests is, in a general sense, confessional: feminism "opposes the paradigm of domination and subordination in all forms, most particularly male over female. . . . " It is also confessional in a specifically theological sense: "Theologically, the rule of male over female constitutes sin" (281).

Trible does not claim to derive this confessional claim directly from the exegesis of a text, nor does she insist that the exegesis of any text must yield results confirming it: "The approach [exegesis] does not guarantee the outcome" (289). In other words (in mine), Trible distinguishes clearly between regulative ideas and constitutive principles. Trible's *regulative ideas,* which include the conviction that exegesis provides material for reflection, and her *constitutive principles,* including literary analysis and a feminist hermeneutics, shape the aims of her proposed inquiry conducted as biblical theology: "it would focus upon the phenomenon of gender and sex in the articulation of faith" (292). The aims are not limited to a demonstration of that phenomenon in the Bible; they extend as well to "models and meanings for authority," and specifically "the authority of the Bible" (294).

Collins asks what aims, and what regulative ideas, are appropriate to historical criticism. Trible asks what use to make of historical criticism, if the aims of an inquiry are guided by certain regulative ideas. Trible's conception of biblical (or OT) theology is not less critical than is Collins's. The questions that concern her are more particular and more concrete than are his; but they are also more "existential" than are Collins's, and inclusive of a broader community's interests. The elements composing her instantiation of a method are just as open to debate as are Collins's, and the most crucial ones are not resolvable on the constitutive principles proposed. Historical criticism no more confirms a functionalist theory of religion than literary analysis does a theory of gender and sex (280); to expect otherwise would be to assign OT or biblical theology a foundational role in relation to them. Which does not mean that these theories must be held uncritically, just because they function as regulative ideas, or that arguments in favor of or against them have no place within the method. To the contrary. It only means that those arguments will not be strictly historical-critical or literary-analytical ones. When Collins proposes to put a functionalist theory of religion to historical-critical use, he assumes the truth of that theory; the same is true, *mutatis mutandis,* of Trible.[66]

These considerations apply as well to dogmatic theology. Robert Morgan speaks of the "critical function of historical knowledge" in suggesting that "a theological criticism which uses historical research as its instrument presupposes the legitimacy of the theological perspective which it seeks to correct."[67] Including dogmatic theology within OT theology's regulative ideas need not impinge on the freedom and integrity with which historical criticism, or any strategy including it, is pursued. If "dogmas" arose in the course of a community's—or of many communities'—attention to these texts, there seems to be no necessary reason why OT theology should insulate itself against the detailed results of that attention.[68] And if, as Nicholas Lash says, the principal form that this "attention" takes in Christian communities consists "in the life, activity and organization of the Christian community," such that "Christian practice consists (by analogy with the practical interpretation of dramatic, legal and musical texts) in the performance or enactment of the biblical text: in its 'active reinterpretation' "[69]—if this is so, then OT theology can assume a concrete and particular role, a critical role, in relation to that performance. It can do so by including the communal norms (call them "dogmas") of this "performance" among its regulative ideas.[70]

Old Testament theologians have a long-standing concern to avoid the imposition of alien schemes or categories on the biblical texts. I want to honor that concern, which cannot be turned one-sidedly against dogmatic theology, as if it should be uniquely disqualified from OT theology's methodological considerations. Biblical interpretation of any adequate kind is at root philological—what George Steiner calls "the philological enactment of our experience of meaningful forms."[71] That experience embraces obligations and opportunities, Steiner says, as well as hope, trust, and fundamentally the extension of courtesy. Philology's first step is a lexical courtesy—*cortesia*, as he says—extended as extravagant attention to words (155-56). The second stage of philological reception is "an exact sensitivity to syntax" (157). The third level is semantic. "It denotes the executive passage of means into meaning. But this passage is incommensurable . . . ," because "the words, the syntax, the formal arrangement, the relevant material or notational code" enter immediately into a context that is unbounded. "There is a sense, perfectly concrete, in which an exhaustive, a tautological analysis and understanding of any semantic or semiotic act would be an analysis and understanding of the sum total of being itself." This is so, Steiner says, because "all semantic-aesthetic phenomena, all acts of meaning out of verbal, material or acoustic form, are themselves of the informing context of our lives in the manifold of being." In consequence of its unboundedness, context is always dialectical, and "the history of context in respect of meaning is the context of human history. The interactive proceedings between them are in perpetual, finally incommensurable motion" (162-63).

One form of response to this perpetual motion is Judaism's unending commentary, whose own dilemma receives a rabbinic answer in "moral action and enlightened conduct": exposition finally has a point (41). It is what Steiner calls "answerability," which is "interpretative response under pressure of enactment" (8). Steiner rightly distinguishes these two—answerability compelling action and answerability constituting it, as in the staging of a play—but he does not set them against each other. We may go further in relating them, along with Lash, by seeing the life of a community as performance, and as the most fitting interpretation of these texts—texts that are canonical even on Steiner's definition of a canon as "the guarded catalogue of that speech, music and art which houses inside us, which is irrevocably familiar to our homecomings" (184).[72] Philology is unending, ever incomplete, even (especially?) when its material is irrevocably familiar. Performance is also unending and partial in its own way, but it nevertheless claims to be, confesses itself to be, an interpretation under pressure of enactment.

If dogmatic theology, or another kind, puts itself in the service of this performance, and does so by redescribing it in ways that are also performative, even interpretive, and even under pressure of enactment—for performance can also be rhetorical and discursive—then it need not be, and cannot be, defined as "hermeneutic punctuation, as the promulgation of semantic arrest" (44). If it does impose alien categories on the texts, then it does so in the hope of a homecoming to what is irrevocably familiar but also perennially new. Old Testament theology trades on this hope. By including it in its regulative ideas, OT theology implicates dogmatic theology (or another kind) in the inquiry it conducts. It places itself in critical relation to dogmatic theology by putting those ideas to work and thus to test, not in opposition to dogmatic theology, but in accordance with what it claims to be and to do.[73] I do not know whether Collins expects that biblical theology will implicate a functionalist theory of religion, or Trible a theory of gender and sex—whether their inquiries will have a critical relation to these components of their respective strategies. These theories may not have anything to gain or to lose from the practice of philological courtesy on texts irrevocably familiar, and perennially new, to particular but broad and diverse communities; dogmatic theology does.[74]

Perhaps Karl Rahner would not have conceded that these remarks suggest an answer to his question. However, one could imagine a current exigency consisting in dogmatic theology's relation to scripture, not only as its basis, its object, or its methodological problem, but as that guarded catalogue of literature irrevocably familiar to a community's homecomings. It is surely part (just *part*) of dogmatic theology's task to describe (thickly) a community's continuous and iterative performance, and to describe it with reference to the criteria of its adequacy and truth. In the exercise of this task, dogmatic theology makes use of doctrines. Suppose we define a doctrine, using Peter Ochs's terms, as "a context-specific propositional formulation of the transformational tendency symbolized by the scriptural text," and as "a representative instance of a community's method of interpretation."[75] And suppose OT theology should exercise a special concern for the "retextualization" of such propositional formulations and doctrines by the extension of a well-formed philological courtesy, on behalf of a community's homecomings—so that they might be homecomings to what is newly familiar, and whose transformational tendencies might be newly discovered, resymbolized, and reformed on behalf of better, more adequate, more truthful, and in all events, richer performance.

Under this supposition especially, OT theology could play a critical role, since the OT is but tenuously the location of the Christian community's homecomings. The point is not to domesticate the OT to a community's doctrines or its dogmas by the unflinching application of its method of interpretation; it is, rather, to expose transformational tendencies not yet represented or inadequately represented or positively denied in a community's performance or in its doctrines, and perhaps impatient of its method of interpretation. Nor is the point only a formal one, correct in itself, by which the use of critical instruments presupposes the legitimacy of the perspective it wants to correct. Materially, a community's doctrines, contextualized in a history of performative interpretation and reflection on it, equip someone at home in them with immensely powerful descriptive resources. There is no point refusing these resources, unless enfeeblement counts as a virtue. Which is not to say that these resources are unerring just because they are powerful. *Not* saying so is the critical space in which biblical theology initially gained its purpose. It continues to be an exceedingly wide space, accommodating the sharply focused proposals of Collins and Trible, but also the vast canvas on which Hans Urs von Balthasar paints *The Glory of the Lord*.[76]

VI

Beginning with Gabler and concluding with these extended comments, I have given disproportionate attention to the *possible* (as opposed to necessary) relation between OT and dogmatic theology. That attention reflects certain interests and choices of my own, including an interest in the church's use of scripture. To some, like Heikki Räisänen, this is unnatural. "If one is free to choose," he says, "it seems natural to take a broader view."[77] The view Räisänen then goes on to take seems to me narrow and abstract by comparison, but one *is* free to choose. It is not, finally, a matter of placing limits on the kinds of inquiry OT theology can conduct, or on the interests and purposes those inquiries can serve. Nor is it a matter of ending debates about the kinds of inquiry, and about their guiding interests and purposes, by appealing to someone's sense of what is natural. It is a matter, as I have here conceived it, of opening the widest possible range of questions to the widest possible arguments.

What I have proposed as OT theology's method is intended to serve such wide-ranging argument. A method, as I am proposing, is not just a strategy for conducting an inquiry, nor is it just a theory governing that strategy, or both. It is also a discursive framework for justifying a particular strategy in relation to specific aims, regardless the direction in which the justification proceeds. It may proceed from any point within the framework: from a conception of the material, from certain constitutive principles, from a set of pragmatic aims, or from a set of regulative ideas; regardless of where it starts, it is incomplete until it considers the other points as well, none of which follows necessarily. That this discursive framework should be OT theology's method does not require every inquiry to satisfy its requirements in order to count as an example of OT theology. It suggests only that any actual instance of, or any proposal in OT theology, implies or depends on judgments of the kind I have mentioned. The categories under which I have placed those judgments may prove inadequate. That will not matter, so long as the judgments themselves receive the kind of attention they deserve, and if the biblical texts receive the richly diverse attention they permit with an appeal that amounts to a demand.

Chapter Five / NEW TESTAMENT THEOLOGY

Robert Morgan

The phrase New Testament Theology (NTT), closely related to biblical theology, refers to modern biblical study's analysis and presentation of the theological ideas of the NT. It is used in a narrower and broader sense, and this distinction needs to be noted before exploring a different and more serious ambiguity caused by a weaker and a stronger use of the word *theology* in this phrase.

The narrower sense of NTT, or "the theology of the NT," or "Biblical Theology of the NT," refers to the few dozen textbooks bearing these names. They survey and summarize the theological ideas of the NT, as understood by a modern biblical scholar. But that original reference has led also to a broader use of the phrase to classify the many thousand scholarly productions detailing one or other of the individual items included in the textbook surveys. Thus the theology of a particular writer, or even a writer's use of some particular theological word, is also generally classified as biblical or NTT.

This use of the word *theology* in discussing the linguistic background and history of theological ideas without reference to their truth or reality raises the more serious division of opinion about NTT: whether, or in what sense it is really *theology*. That is not so much a dispute about what gets included in the discipline called NTT, as about what counts as theology, and about ways of doing theology. The notion of doing "theology as scriptural interpretation"[1] has been popular in Reformation and neo-Reformation Germany, but less so in the English-speaking world, and especially less so since the so-called Biblical Theology Movement of the 1940s and 1950s fell into justified disrepute.[2]

Most biblical scholars see their task as describing and, in part, explaining some first-century patterns of Christian belief, but they disagree about how if at all this relates to the task of expressing a contemporary Christian form of belief. Prior to the Enlightenment biblical statements could be taken as true and as contemporary theology. Now it is necessary to distinguish between a biblical author's theology and our own, and neither the claims of the Bible, nor those of modern theology to tell the truth about God, are uncontested.

The Enlightenment's effective criticism of the older equation of the biblical text with revelation, and the subsequent loss of confidence in Western Europe and America in discourse about God, account for both the emergence of modern NTT and its methodological difficulties. A presentation of the theological ideas of the NT is no longer automatically theology in the strong sense of making a contemporary truth claim. But the communication and appropriation of these ideas is as essential to Christian faith and theology as ever. How they are presented therefore remains a legitimate religious interest and it is scarcely surprising that this evolved into a modern theological discipline.

Our account of this discipline, NTT, will show how other good scholarly interests have sometimes overshadowed religious interests within academic study of these texts. One reason for this is that theology's proper use of all available rational methods has sometimes drawn it in directions suggested by the methods themselves and away from its original aims. Since all truth is welcome to theology, and ultimately germane to it, this is not a cause for regret. Theological advances have been made by the disinterested pursuit of truth. But other legitimate interests must also be served, and Christians need to be taught how to read their foundational texts. NTT explains what is written in a way that relates the texts to the modern readers' own belief systems. Calling this religiously-oriented interpretation "NTT" implies not merely that it speaks of God, but that it claims to tell the truth, and not only the historical truth of what the texts are saying, but a religious truth valid today.

That is a bold claim which will make some biblical scholars invert Luther and "thank God that they are (not) theologians" (WA 40, 1; 207, 17-18). The weaker, nontheological sense of NTT is more in accord with the limitations of their professional expertise. The stronger sense can be left to dogmaticians. But these are rarely biblical specialists, and it shows. NTT requires dual citizenship, in biblical scholarship and in theology. But it brings risks beyond the inevitable limitations in the knowledge of those who span several disciplines. Theologians who interpret the NT are open to attack from two sides in particular: from other scholars who suspect them of fixing their history and exegesis to suit their theology, and from believers suspicious of methods developed under European rationalism and laden with asumptions hostile to traditional supernaturalism.

Fortunately for the integrity of the discipline, most NT theologians are trained in historical criticism and understand that theology also makes claims to truth in the public arena. It therefore cannot retreat into a ghetto where a private language and beliefs are authorized by an infallible scripture. It must relate the knowledge of God it claims is mediated by scripture to whatever rational inquiry has to say about these texts. Christian theology may start with the shared convictions of the religious group, but as it articulates, defends, and where necessary, criticizes and modifies some of the group's beliefs it is subject to the intellectual norms of the day. Even if its claims can be fully appreciated only from within, by living the life, they still have to be generally intelligible, and must avoid saying anything that is patently false.

This condition for the truth of theological claims demands biblical criticism as well as biblical theology. It has destroyed precritical identifications of the Bible with the revelation of God, rendered much theology based on this implausible, and stimulated new accounts of the saving revelation of God in Jesus Christ.

Some dispense with the notion of revelation altogether, since precritical ideas of revelation have been destroyed. But most Christian theology has retained the notion even while revising it, because most Christians still affirm a decisive revelation of God in Jesus, varying from the naive and ungrounded (but not necessarily untrue) assertion that God is loving like the historical Jesus was loving, to a more serious account of what religious people mean by God and how some of them claim to be confronted by God in the risen Lord Jesus Christ through word and sacrament. If a NTT, therefore, is not merely a historical presentation of early Christian ideas, but also in some sense a contemporary presentation of Christianity, it will contain a theory of revelation involving an understanding of God and Godtalk, history, human existence and faith, and Jesus' life, death, and resurrection. Where that is no longer implied, the discipline tends to lose its properly theological character. *Theology* in NTT then becomes a classificatory label for the ideas being analyzed, no longer the attempt to articulate a truth from and about God.

The analysis which follows aims to clarify and defend this theological view of NTT, and to suggest how it can be developed. It will show how different theories of revelation account for some of the differences between NTTs, and how all these genuine NTTs differ from other legitimate aims in biblical scholarship which eschew modern theological interests. It can therefore join forces with Wrede[3] in attacking the misleading use of the phrase NTT to describe the nontheological task of classifying or arranging and presenting historically the theological ideas of the NT. But it joins forces with Bultmann[4] against Wrede in defending a theological conception of the discipline: NTT properly so-called.

All NT study involves the interpretation of texts. The value of the word *interpretation* in a discussion of NTT is that it directs our attention to the interpreters and the kinds of writing about the NT they are attempting, not simply to the text itself, as the word *exegesis* does. *Theological interpretation* describes a kind of interpretative activity, not the kind of text being interpreted, and not the method being used. It uses ordinary linguistic, literary, historical, and other methods to present the material, but is guided by a theological aim to communicate the theological messages in the text on the assumption that they have something (Christian) to say to the present.[5] It teaches Christians how to read their scriptures and invites others to look at the Bible this way. It is a kind of practical or applied hermeneutics.

What makes a presentation of NT ideas, or theological interpretation of the NT, function theologically by reflecting a contemporary understanding of Christianity is the *user's* setting it within a (usually implicit) theory of revelation. Without that it is ancient history, perhaps contributing to the theological enterprise, but not itself theology, and so not properly NTT. This theory of revelation is generally unstated, and it is not always possible to detect whether a NT scholar is working with a theory of revelation or not. Neither is it necessary to know. The term *user* covers both writers and readers of NTT. A nontheologian's descriptions of the NT material can function as theology for readers whose views of revelation allow them to see a contemporary religious truth in what is being presented, even if the modern biblical scholar intended no such thing. That provides some justification for calling any presentation of its theological ideas NTT. But so long as we are considering modern authors rather than readers it is better to reserve the phrase for attempts to write theology by interpreting the NT theologically.

But that is to anticipate. The following so-called defense of NTT will rest on some necessarily brief allusions to the history of the discipline. It is written to salute Christiaan Beker, a NT theologian whose scholarship serves both historical and religious truth, and in hope of winning some agreement from him through its debt to another NT theologian we both revere, the now aged eagle of Tübingen, Ernst Käsemann.

I

Before the more serious question about theology in the strong sense is addressed through a sketch of the discipline's history, the minor distinction between textbook overviews[6] and the discipline itself deserves some brief comment.

The great nineteenth-century German handbooks of NTT surveyed the field and presented their authors' own conclusions, sometimes summarizing the state of the most reputable scholarship in justification of those conclusions. Both specialization and increasing scholarly diversity make such ambitions unrealistic today. Knowledge is advanced by monographs and articles which deal with a small part of the field and provide room for scholarly interaction with alternative arguments and conclusions. Surveys of research are now limited to particular topics in series such as *Aufstieg und Niedergang der Römischen Welt* or *Erträge der Forschung*. But that does not mean that overviews are superfluous— only that their functions have in part changed. The greater the scholarly diversity, the more need there is for the mapwork that overviews or textbooks can provide.[7] They can propose and illustrate how a wider field should be viewed.

The wider field called NTT is naturally described in terms of the discipline's data—"the theological ideas contained in the NT." But they can be analyzed and presented in several different ways, depending on what purpose is being served. Historical presentations have been favored, because that is the obvious way to organize data from the past, and it allows the different pieces to illuminate one another in being related and made to produce a larger picture. But the larger historical picture, interesting and valuable as it is, has not usually been the final goal and main purpose of NTT. Like other theology it has often been geared toward contemporary religious faith and practice, suggesting how these texts may be understood in relation to Christian faith. This theological aim is best handled through a textbook overview of the discipline. Free of the obligation to argue each point in detail as in NTT can provide a view of the material geared to the particular question that concerns modern theology: how it should be read today in order that its religious potential may be realized.

If that now sounds remote from the aims of much biblical scholarship, even some NTT (if not biblical theology), it shows how far the scene has changed in recent years. Some of the best NTT over the past twenty years has been written by systematic theologians. That is not to reproach biblical scholars who wish to move "beyond NTT,"[8] but a line of defense for those who still wish to fulfill its traditional aims. There is room for a plurality of interpretative aims and standpoints. Many seek to do justice to the authors' own views of their subject matter and some of these think that despite cultural changes its essential message is true. A sympathetic understanding of an ancient text may or may not lead to agreement with it, but a mind closed to that possibility is as likely to distort as one which fails to take seriously the historical distance.

The history of the discipline offers support for a theological definition of its aims. It was scarcely necessary to say so in the nineteenth century, but NTT has usually aimed to speak of the God that Christians worship, not simply to present ancient religious ideas. That involved interpreters relating their historical perception of these texts positively to their modern understanding of Christian faith as based on biblical revelation. This view of NTT is confirmed by the opinions of those who prefer to direct NT scholarship along other, more exclusively historical paths. William Wrede proposed that NTT should be renamed "the history of early Christian religion and theology" (n. 3 p. 116), since this is what it had, by 1897 (in his circle), become. Wrede's historical acumen makes his program attractive, but Heikki Räisänen is right to deny, and Wrede wrong to suggest, that this admirable proposal is the only option for intellectually serious NT interpreters.

This ecclesial theological task of interpreting the NT in ways that communicate its religious message rather than simply mining it in the service of other interests, sometimes upsets its own conservative constituency by insisting on truth even in the teeth of tradition. But that is theological education, and quite different from giving historical stones for theological bread.

The story of theological bread going hard in biblical studies is doubly interesting. It involves the secularization of scholarship, which can be welcomed by all lovers of rationality and truth, including theologians. But it also involves competing conceptions of Christianity. The struggle to preserve NTT as a properly theological discipline has sometimes reflected a theological argument about which versions of Christianity are authentic: the argument between traditional Christianity, Catholic and Protestant, and the newer version born of the Enlightenment and more or less influential in the West to the present day. Our survey will show NTT to be a conservative enterprise, conserving the biblical tradition by interpreting it, radical in the sense of attending to the roots of the Christian symbol system, but not uprooting it by replacing the Jesus Christ of NT faith with the speculative reconstructions of Jesus rightly and interestingly essayed by historians and apologists alike.

For reasons of space it is necessary to concentrate on textbooks and methodological discussions, where the writers' theological aims are clearest. These have the further advantage of raising a problem that is central for a NTT that as theology seeks to guide the Christian church: the problem of the theological unity of the NT in the face of its historical diversity. For how can a collection of conflicting witnesses define Christianity?

Overviews also raise the important questions of what should be included in a NTT—above all whether a section on the "historical Jesus" is appropriate, but also whether noncanonical documents like 1 Clement and hypothetical documents such as Q should be discussed. There are, then, advantages in concentrating on textbooks, overviews, and methodological discussions. But it must be remembered that they are secondary and derivative. They depend on an understanding of the discipline itself as that is reflected in the vast body of work covered by the broader use of the phrase.

Outside the German universities where lecturing obligations encouraged the production of ponderous *Lehrbücher* the broader use is more common. English and Welsh teachers like Hoskyns and Dodd, Moule and Barrett, or Americans like Keck and Martyn, Brown and Fitzmyer, have all written plenty of NTT without writing *a* NTT. What makes much of their work *theology* is not simply its subject matter but their and their readers' understandings of the subject matter, and consequent engagement with it.

This does not mean that only believers can write NTT, though in practice most who try to express Christian belief through interpretations of NT writings are at least sympathetic to it. The confessional task of theology involves advocacy, but its equally important critical task is best safeguarded by the widest possible range of viewpoints being represented. There are three things that are necessary for writing Christian theology, including NTT: a serious interest in the claims of these texts; a mind open to the possibility that their talk of God may disclose a truth about the world and human existence which would by definition be decisive; and the historical and literary knowledge essential for any intellectually responsible interpretation of the NT data.

II

The broader use of the phrase NTT, which refers to the discipline itself, is more common today. But the narrower usage referring to textbooks is more original, and takes us to the beginnings of the modern discipline.

G. L. Bauer's[9] choice of title for his great textbook, *Biblische Theologie des Neuen Testaments* (4 vols., 1800–2), indicates the origins of NTT in the older biblical theology. Bauer's division of biblical theology into divisions, OT and NT, was the first and natural consequence of treating the subject historically. This had been proposed in 1787 in the inaugural lecture of his colleague in Altdorf, J. P. Gabler, "On the proper distinction between biblical and dogmatic theology and the correct delimitation of their boundaries"[10] which is rightly seen as the birth hour of modern NTT even though the phrase does not occur. Its proper distinction was later celebrated for giving biblical studies a historical discipline, a relative independence from dogmatics. On the contrary, his aim was to secure the authority of at least parts of the Bible for Christian theology by sifting out as merely contingent those parts which he thought could not possibly be relevant to contemporary Christianity. The historical analysis was to be undertaken for a Christian theological purpose, not for the sake of historical reconstruction itself. That is why it was still "biblical *theology*" not biblical history, even though it must use historical methods.

The most influential aspect of Gabler's proposal was its *two stage* character, which has become the usual way for biblical scholars to understand the relationship of their historical description to theological appropriation.[11] They have not usually explained how to change gear from stage one to stage two, and this model is largely responsible for the common feeling that a theological education based on biblical criticism fails to prepare candidates for Christian ministry. But the alternative model, which conflates the two stages, is also open to theological objection. It preserves the theological meaning of the text at the cost of weakening its capacity to challenge the assumptions of its interpreters.[12] The solution is to distinguish the two tasks, and to recognize that the second involves the first, but to deny that the first must be completed (which it never is) before the second can begin. They overlap, but are guided in part by different aims or interests. Interpreters can start with whatever contemporary interests take them to a text and proceed through an interplay between these and whatever historical, literary, sociological, religious, and other insights emerge from the text itself.

Gabler's methodological proposals were taken up with some change of emphasis by G. L. Bauer, whose aim was also still theological: to separate truth from error and show Christianity to be a rational and divine religion. What was no longer credible (such as the mythical material) was modernized, because Bauer's presentation of the content of the NT in the historical form appropriate to such a descriptive task was intended to validate his own modern understanding of Christianity.

Expressing Christianity through a presentation of the biblical material presupposed a view of revelation as timeless truths. Contingent matters like Paul's instructions on women's veils are set aside. Following Semler, the Word of God or revelation is no longer identified with scripture. But biblical theology of the NT was still *theology*, as it had been when in the older biblical theology biblical statements were taken directly as contemporary Christian truths. It was still the attempt to *express* Christianity as the truth from God, even though the criterion of truth was now human reason rather than the Bible itself. Bauer was not merely describing ancient religion. So long as the content of the Bible coincided at least in part with the moral dictates of eighteenth-century reason it was possible for him to call it revelation and construct biblical theology out of it.

Gabler and Bauer on the other hand, and the older biblical theology of Protestant Orthodoxy[13] and Pietism[14] on the other, provide us with the beginnings of a typology for classifying NTTs, and a criterion for evaluating them. As attempts to mediate what the NT says in a way that illuminates contemporary Christianity, they naturally hinge on how their modern authors understand the revelation of God in Jesus.

Some twentieth-century analysts like Barth doubt whether *revelation* is an appropriate category for describing what the theological rationalists Gabler and Bauer find in the Bible. They learn nothing new from it. For the older orthodoxy the locus of revelation was the texts; the rationalists placed more emphasis on the moral and rational judgment of the interpreters. But this twentieth-century antithesis between revelation and reason is overdrawn. The moral sensibilities of these "neologians" had already been informed by their Christianity and the biblical traditions, and in any case, our moral and intellectual response has to find a place in any credible theory of revelation. The real problem with their notions of revelation, and so with their NTT, despite its exegetical merit, becomes visible when they eliminate not only women's veils but also any of the Bible's religious dimensions which fail to correspond to their own beliefs and expectations. Their theory of revelation allows the texts insufficient power to challenge contemporary assumptions. Whereas the earlier biblicist theory was too hard to accommodate new knowledge, and being brittle, broke on its incompatibility with perceived truth, this rationalist (and later liberal) alternative is too soft to allow scripture to confront its Christian readers with the authority of the God they worship. Is there a third way which both avoids the irrationality and absolutism of biblicism, while also allowing scripture to mediate the revelation (Word) of God?

111

The answer is a theory of revelation which combines the Enlightenment's respect for the modern reader with Orthodoxy's respect for the text. But before that was found, the nineteenth century saw a more radical turn from the text which almost destroyed the NTT. This was made possible by an erosion of the belief in biblical inspiration and the biblicist view of revelation associated with that. These had sustained the older biblical theology and even (residually) the Enlightenment's rationalism. But their decay coincided with the new interest in the history *behind* the texts, which eighteenth-century criticism had learned to distinguish from the texts themselves. This new interest in history could be combined with a new belief in a revelation behind the texts wherever history was interpreted metaphysically by German idealists or was thought to include *salvation facts (Heilstatsachen)* by some conservative theologians, but any such move to the history behind the texts throws the phrase NTT into question. The phrase refers to twenty-seven texts, not to the history for which they are some of the sources. On the other hand, the NT itself bears witness to a patch of history that it considers decisive for God's involvement with the world, and this historical reference has to be included in any Christian account of revelation, or theory of how and where God is now known. Sifting the NT for historical knowledge of Jesus is a necessity for modern theology, and cannot now be excluded from NTT. The only question for NTT is how this legitimate interest can be appropriately included in a presentation of the NT data.

Since NTT aims to interpret these documents, it should satisfy its historical interest in Jesus in a way that works with the grain of the NT itself: not by using modern historical reconstructions to attack the biblical portraits, as the Enlightenment critics and their successors have done, but by confronting each portrait with those fragments of historical truth that seem well-established, and so challenging each evangelist's interpretation by reference to the person they claim to be interpreting.[15]

This piecemeal integration of modern historical knowledge into NTT's discussions of the witness of the four evangelists incorporates the historically contingent truth about Jesus within its representation of the larger truth about him (Christology). The older orthodoxy found revelation in the text, and had no sense of the *historical Jesus* as distinct from that, and so no place for this in their biblical theology. Their neoorthodox successors mistakenly claimed no theological interest in the question. The Enlightenment radicals and liberal Protestants located revelation in the historical Jesus and so had no need of the theological witness of the text and no use for the discipline that communicated that. Some nineteenth-century theologians solved this problem of the necessary reference to the historical figure as reconstructed by modern scholarship by including their reconstructions of Jesus in their NTTs. They could even make these central (no mere appendix) because their historical portraits of Jesus owed so much to their own Christianity. That compromise held firm only so long as radical gospel criticism was held at bay. This explains why that criticism was so bitterly resisted.

But the future lay with the radicals, and the most important figure is F. C. Baur (1792–1860). On occasion he theologically interpreted the central *texts* (Paul's Epistles, Matthew whom he thought closest to Jesus, and the Fourth Gospel which he thought the climax of NT thought), reflecting the Enlightenment view of Jesus and anticipating Bultmann on Paul.[16] But what made all his historical research contribute to a NTT was a theory of revelation based on the metaphysical interpretation of history that Baur had learned from Schelling and (after 1834) from Hegel. His *Lectures on NTT* (1864) were not published until after his death, but from 1831 on, all his bitterly contested historical criticism of the NT contributed to a reconstruction of the history that was the vehicle for an idealist Christian theology. He was plainly writing Christian theology, not the theologically empty history preferred by what was shortly to be called positivism. His conviction that the divine Spirit was moving dialectically through the historical process enabled him to speak of God through his research and motivated him to start work at four A.M. in the Tübingen winter without heating in order to get the history right.

Given this coincidence of history and theology it was natural for the theologian Baur to absolutize historical research and judge previous NTTs by the adequacy of their historical scholarship. Half-baked history was bound to result in half-baked theology. His own synthesis proved vulnerable to further research which showed that Christian history was more variegated than his dialectical model had allowed, and that Paul did not mean by *Spirit* what Plato had.[17] The dissolution of the synthesis discredited attempts to base a theological interpretation of the NT on the historical development of its ideas or doctrines, and the fading of idealism devalued Baur's interpretations even before they were historically undermined by Droysen's recognition that the Hellenistic age differed from Hellenism. Baur's successors continued his historical research, but abandoned his Hegelian vision of the theological meaning of the whole process. Something of his vision survived in the relatively nontheological history that remained when its philosophico-theological key was jettisoned, but NTT was bound to decline as historical research flourished without the metaphysics that had given it theological meaning.

Baur's last pupil, Otto Pfleiderer, continued to maintain an idealist synthesis of history, philosophy, and theology, but others admitted a gulf between their philosophical theologies and their biblical research, and failed to bridge it in an overarching NTT. Their understandings of Christianity drew on biblical resources (Jesus and Paul in particular), but instead of interpreting afresh the theologies of the biblical witnesses they concentrated on reconstructing the religion and morality of Jesus and the religious experience of Paul. The theological ideas of the Gospels and Espistles were explained and sometimes explained away as imports from the surrounding world, rather than interpreted as appropriate expressions of the gospel which NTT could retrieve for contemporary Christian faith and modern theology.

One of the best books between Baur and Bultmann is Bossuet's *Kyrios Christos* (1913, 2nd ed. 1921, Eng. trans. 1970). It shows how the liberals' history of religion could lead to theology, but scarcely to NTT. This fascinating history of the Christ-cult contains enough evaluation to show where Bossuet himself stands. His finally negative evaluations of the whole development are compatible with giving a description of the theologies contained in the NT, but not with unfolding a modern theology in accord with the NT. New Testament Theology can include an element of theological criticism *(Sachkritik)* of particular NT formulations.[18] But that is based on an understanding of the gospel which depends on these witnesses themselves. It presupposes a sense of what they intend, and is therefore incompatible with Bossuet's wholesale theological criticism of the NT witness. The break with NTT occurs where modern reconstructions of Jesus are made into the norm against which the NT witnesses are themselves measured. The truth about Jesus is indeed for Christians the norm against which all witnesses are to be measured, including the Gospels, but for them that elusive truth includes also a theological evaluation informed by scripture and absent from most historical reconstructions.

Historical research on Jesus is thus an ingredient in modern Christian theological interpretation of the NT. But to *replace* the theological witness of the texts with a reconstruction of what lies behind them, and then to build one's results into a new liberal theology, leads to a radically different version of Christianity from that of the NT writers themselves. It may be called Christian, because it contains elements of traditional Christianity, but this is not the place to comment on the truth or value of Christian humanism; this comment is used only to point out that decisions about which scholarly tasks to undertake may affect one's version of Christianity, and vice versa. New Testament Theology generates versions of Christianity in tune with the NT witnesses; giving priority to historical research on Jesus leads to more liberal versions which claim the authority of the historians' reconstructions of Jesus rather than that of the NT witnesses. Believers must prefer the truth as they see it, but only one side can claim much continuity with earlier versions of Christianity. Whether that matters again depends on one's view of revelation. Some forms of Christianity are undercut by claims which deny to earlier centuries a genuine saving knowledge of God in Christ.

Baur and Bultmann interpreted NT texts theologically as well as reconstructing history, and so wrote NTT. Whether their respective interpretations are orthodox or not, they are theological, so it is not a category mistake to attach that label.[19] Harnack, J. Weiss, and Bossuet also wrote Christian theology by interpreting Christian tradition, but, like Baur on other occasions, chose forms of historical theology (for example, historical Jesus research, history of ideas, German history and culture) better suited to their liberal standpoints than

NTT. It would be odd to call these reconstructions orthodox or heretical, and that shows how much more they are history than theology. Whether finding a theological interpretation orthodox is considered relevant to its truth depends on one's theory of revelation, how and where God is known.

Historical research leads theology in a liberal direction when it destroys old syntheses and makes the disturbing history of Jesus the focus of theology. But history can also be a conservative force. A hermeneutical form of theology like NTT is more likely to preserve a more traditional form of Christianity because it accepts the tradition and attempts to interpret classical Christian documents in ways that respect the intentions of its authors. But the tradition is so variegated that within this traditional shape, radical new developments can be proposed. Thus despite their modernizing philosophical theologies the NT theologies of Baur and Bultmann remain closer to traditional Christianity than Harnack's *Essence of Christianity,* which makes the historical Jesus central.

The representative liberal Protestant NTT is H. J. Holzmann's *Lehrbuch der neutestamentlichen Theologie* (1896–97, 2nd ed. 1911), the long-awaited monument of the acknowledged leader of the then-blooming liberal NT scholarship. The extent to which the historical form of the discipline had effectively buried its theological motivations is startlingly evident in the way Wrede *(Über Aufgabe und Methode der sogennanten neutestsamentlichen Theologie)* could attack what he considered its ecclesial residue as simply a failure to carry out the task of NTT (so called) consistently. Modern admiration for Wrede's 1897 call for the dissolution of NTT into "the history of early Christian religion and theology" reflects a biblical scholarship now partly alienated from its religious matrix. His argument that this transformation had already, in effect, happened in current biblical study, and that he was simply demanding consistency, is even stronger today. It signals the end of NTT and so demands an answer from any advocate of the discipline.

It is important to distinguish two elements in Wrede's brilliant essay: his excellent arguments concerned with the historical description of early Christian thought, and the logically independent thesis that this is what NTT essentially is or should be. Bultmann largely accepted the former when a generation later he grouped the smaller NT writings together and included the Apostolic Fathers in his presentation, as historical perspective demands. But Bultmann did not accept Wrede's view of the purely descriptive aims of the discipline any more than Baur would have done. He limited his own theological interpretation to the two NT witnesses who could be fitted into his existentialist bed, but these presentations of Paul and John are NTT in the proper sense of theological interpretation, even though the book as a whole is cast mostly in the form of a historical reconstruction.[20]

Bultmann's new synthesis followed Barth's appeal for a theological interpretation of the biblical witness. It partially fulfilled that hermeneutical program while combining it with some of the best of liberal scholarship. But that was later. In 1897 history dictated the aims as well as the methods of biblical research.

Bultmann's subsequent convictions about the theological and hermeneutical character of NTT were not anticipated by his liberal teachers and predecessors. Holzmann almost conceded Wrede's case by the weakness of his brief response. Wrede had criticized him for restricting himself to the canonical writings. Holzmann's defense[21] was more pragmatic than principled. He rightly pointed to the use of these writings in the church, but gave no account of how Christians' historically responsible reading of scripture relates to their belief in a revelation of God in Jesus Christ. He no doubt agreed with Wrede that the relationship of the NT to contemporary Christianity is a matter for dogmatics, not NTT. They were right to see here a theological question, not one that biblical scholars have to answer unless they are also theologians. But it is precisely to this question that NTT originally owed and still owes its very existence. The older liberals' answer involved a retreat from the NTT because it associated the Christian claim to revelation with the history rather than with the NT texts themselves. Some of their successors have seen the difficulties in both theories and abandoned the notion of a revelation of God in Jesus, mediated through scripture and Christian witness. The alternative is to base one's NTT on a theory of revelation that does justice to the history (and metaphysics), the text (and context), and to the reader's response to that witness.

Holzmann could have replied to Wrede that the aim of NTT is to present the biblical material in a historically responsible way that is intended to inform, communicate, and correct contemporary faith and theology. Holzmann could have supported his statement by reference to the history of the discipline. Even his use of categories drawn from subsequent dogmatics, much criticized by Wrede, could have been defended as assisting in the understanding and appropriation of the biblical witnesses by modern theologians whose own understanding of Christianity is often expressed in those terms. That would not be a good defense if (as Wrede thought) these categories actually distort the biblical witness. But Christian theological categories are not wildly appropriate to the NT, and may well assist analysis of this material. The main justification of their use in NTT, however, is not descriptive and analytic, but hermeneutical: they can serve as a bridge between those ancient authors and the Christian faith, and theology of at least some modern readers, and so help them to read the NT in a Christian way.

When liberal theologians such as Gunkel, Wrede, and Bossuet preferred categories associated with religion to those of classical dogmatics which no longer expressed their own modern Christianity, they too were building hermeneutical bridges. Paul Wernle wrote about *The Beginnings of Our Religion* (1902–04), J. Weiss about the religion of Paul, and Harnack the religion of Jesus, all forging links between their own faith and their scriptures, only using modern concepts rather than those of classical dogmatics. Their retreat from NTT did not, in most cases, stem from religious indifference or theological weakness, nor can their preference for modern categories be faulted. Bultmann later used modern categories to great effect. The liberals' withdrawal from what seemed to them an outdated way of doing theology followed their detaching Christian belief in revelation from the biblical text and ideas. Associating it instead with the history behind them involved a new view of Christianity, born in the Enlightenment and bred by Romanticism. It inherited theistic belief and was genuinely committed to the historical Jesus. It also admired the religious genius of Paul. But it associates the NT witness to Jesus less closely with the contemporary question of God than traditional Christianity has always done.

The temptation to substitute history for theology, historical reconstruction for theological reflection on the NT texts, is strongest in relation to Paul, because in these Epistles far more than in the Gospels, historical projections about the author are both possible and essential to plausible interpretations of the documents themselves. The tasks of historical investigation and theological reflection are bound to overlap. But if the phrase NTT is taken to imply a theological reading or indication that the texts speak of the God who is not described but worshiped, then (at least until another theological theory about history like that of German idealism captures the Christian imagination) the primary focus must be on the existing texts. These, not their sources or authors, are what Christians confront when they listen to the witness of scripture. It is here that they find witness to God that confronts or challenges their preconceptions and expectations.

The historian provides scaffolding, as in some literary interpretation. This assists any understanding of an ancient text, including the kind of understanding that relates the text to contemporary faith by combining historical and evangelical methods with the interpreter's own religious discourse. New Testament Theology's focus on the text rather than the history behind the text does not, as in literary formalism, deny the historical particularities of textual interpretation. But Paul's Epistles will best be treated separately, contrary to much current practice, because they are separate texts, though a substantial introduction can set them broadly in context and summarize what is presupposed by them all. Second Corinthians can be treated as unity, but if interpreters are convinced by a theory that denies its integrity they should reflect that in their presentation. The author arguably takes priority over his editors in the interpretation of his Epistles. Canonical shape does not demand priority over what one judges historical reality. It is the texts themselves that count, not the idea of the canon, or even the form given to the texts by an editor.

It is possible to criticize the liberals' primary focus on the history behind the text as ultimately destructive of NTT while welcoming their use of categories drawn from the scientific study of religion. These provide many Christians with a better conceptuality for theological appropriation (and so for NTT) today than those of dogmatics, because they provide the most helpful terms for reflecting on one's own faith. They can be used as well to interpret the texts as history, and are more likely to persuade others when applied to existing texts than when applied to the highly speculative reconstructions of early Christian history.[22]

Like all NTT, using these new conceptualities to interpret the texts runs the risk of modernizing. That underlines the necessity of Wrede's historical critique. Distortion must be identified and corrected for theological as well as historical reasons. The Church wants to hear what the texts are actually saying and wants to subject itself to this biblical witness. Its descriptions of the material ought therefore to be at least as persuasive as those that are not theologically motivated. Modernizing distortion is an ever-present risk in NTT, just as archaicizing is the danger in a theologically uninterested historical study of the NT. Neither discipline is to be judged by its failures.

There is thus good reason to accept Wrede's historical criticisms of his contemporaries' NTTs, but no reason to accept his unargued dismissal of the theological discipline itself. The popular notion of a victorious historical scholarship gradually overcoming theological prejudices contains some truth. Historical research has progressed and has discredited some NTT. But that sets the stage for an updated NTT that takes due account of the improved state of historical knowledge as well as the changing philosophical and religious climate. Changes in human knowledge and sensibility make particular theologies and NTTs outmoded, but do not discredit theology or NTT as such. Räisänen concedes the legitimacy of such an ecclesial NTT (p. xviii), while preferring to direct university research along Wrede's secular path.

The best explanation or excuse for Wrede's extraordinary unwillingness to take seriously the theological character of NTT, such as its function as a bridge between biblical scholarship and modern Christianity, was the use of this bridge by conservative scholars who clung to a residually biblicist view of revelation and could be suspected of blunting the edge of criticism to make it compatible with their own beliefs. But instead of simply criticizing their bad history and incredible theology, he dismissed their enterprise in principle. B. Weiss and W. Beyschlag, for example, were right to see Christian belief in revelation as the presupposition of biblical theology, even if their views of revelation were unsatisfactory. They saw that theology presupposes the faith of the religious community and is a function of its life, unfolding its beliefs and relating these to the rest of current knowledge. But instead of exploring the crucial point of how revelation is to be understood, Wrede brushes their claims aside as scarcely worthy of serious consideration.

His brief remarks (ET p. 183 n. 4) do, however, lift the veil on his own feeble thoughts on the subject of revelation. They show that he saw no third alternative beyond the old biblicism that identified the Bible and revelation on grounds of inspiration, and the old rationalism (still current among philosophers of religion) that looks at a claim to revelation and makes a judgment about it. Both theories contain some truth—an adequate Christian doctrine of revelation takes both the Bible and human reason seriously. But both views are untenable, one because it is irrational, the other because it undercuts the claim of revelation to transcend reason and morality. These can falsify claims to revelation, because what is untrue in reason and morality cannot be true in faith. But they cannot establish or authenticate such claims.

The revival of NTT in the present century followed from a new account of revelation. Bultmann's kerygmatic theology, rooted in Schleiermacher and Herrmann as well as in Luther and Kierkegaard, presupposed the faith of a religious community as it communicates and unfolds this in terms which respect contemporary knowledge. Wrede, by contrast, assumed that NTT was scholarship, not confessional theology, and he did not consider whether it might not possibly be both. In circles that distinguished sharply between *wissenschaftliche* and *kirchliche* theology[23] it was important to insist that biblical scholarship was "scientific," genuine history, just like any other area occupied by that most prestigious discipline in late-nineteenth-century German university research.

There were and still are good reasons why theologians should do their ancient history in ways that can be acknowledged by other historians. The interface between religious faith and contemporary awareness of truth depends on theology abiding by the rules of the secular methods it uses. Preserving its own integrity requires knowing when to stop using them, and not forcing them to perform tasks they are not designed for—such as establishing miracles or speaking of God. Historical research in Wrede's day was generally as positivistic as the philosophical climate, and that set stricter limits to its contributions to theology than had been acceptable a generation or two earlier. This brought a day of small things for liberal NTT. It had married the spirit of German idealism and found itself a widow when this philosophy that embraced religion was replaced with one that opposed it. Instead of looking for theological and philosophical support for a new theological interpretation of the NT that would synthesize the results of historical and exegetical study in a new theological framework, most biblical specialists now concentrated their intellectual energies on the historical tasks and left the question of religious appropriation to personal statements and popular lectures. Religion seemed optional, more a matter of taste than truth. The contrast between that and the two great pillars of NTT is striking. Baur and Bultmann made themselves philosophical theologians because they wished to interpret NT theologically, for example, as speaking a truth that invited a religious response. Their theological convictions about the NT demanded philosophical sophistication as well as rigorous historical scholarship to express them.

Not that their syntheses were wholly satisfactory, even in their own day when they could claim more philosophical support than a later generation would concede to them. Baur's system reduced NTT to the first chapters of the history of dogma and required the whole of history to make sense of speaking of God.

Bultmann avoided Baur's need for too much history, but settled for too little. His redefinition of history *(Geschichte)* in terms of the historicality or historicity *(Geschichtlichkeit)* of human existence does not correspond to what most people call history. But both these giants correctly identified the aim of NTT to provide a modern theological interpretation of the texts, one that expresses Christian faith for its own day, in the historically and exegetically responsible mode that modern assumptions about truth require.

As anticipated by Kähler, Bultmann found that Barth's retrieval of Luther's emphasis upon the Word of God preached, dovetailed with his own history of traditions research. This disclosed older traditions being actualized in proclamation and resulting on occasion in the "event" of revelation and its faith response. That found expression in theological statements which were therefore to be interpreted not as doctrines but as accounts of believing self-understanding. Paul's Epistles contain several anthropological and soteriological concepts, and so lend themselves to theological interpretation in terms of their understanding of human existence and the transformation of this by faith's obedient response to the Christian proclamation. The Fourth Evangelist also said enough about the word and faith (and little enough about the historical Jesus) to be fitted illuminatingly into the pattern of Bultmann's existentialist theology. The other NT writers fared less well theologically and were pushed to the periphery of Bultmann's NTT as materials for its historical framework.

Bultmann's presentation of the NT materials does not, in principle, abandon the traditional aim of showing how it is relevant for Christian faith and theology today. But his synthesis in fact finds a theological use for only two of the NT witnesses. That is a bit thin and was unlikely to satisfy other Christians whose faith depended more on the Synoptic Gospels.

There were two reactions among his own pupils, both remaining within their teacher's history of traditions framework: a new attention to the theologies of the synoptic evangelists, and the so-called new quest of the historical Jesus. The former led to a mountain of redaction-critical scholarship with ever-decreasing contemporary theological significance. Much of it has advanced the historical aspect of the NTT without attempting to show how the Gospels inform contemporary Christianity.

The "new quest" was theologically suggestive, but made more contributions to systematics than to NTT, despite the leadership of such distinguished NT theologians as Käsemann, Bornkamm, and Conzelmann. For all its theological importance (which Kähler, Barth, and Bultmann had underestimated, in justifiable reaction to the quest's earlier distortions of traditional Christian belief) and Bornkamm's attractive program of seeking the history in the kerygma of the gospels and the kerygma in the history,[24] even this more subtle historical Jesus research did not fit into a discipline aiming to present the Gospels' theological witness. It now looks like a failed attempt to mix two essentially different operations: the quest of the historical Jesus and NTT (cf. n. 15).

The theological interpretation of the Gospels in NTT must have an eye to all available historical knowledge of Jesus. Only so can it claim to be respecting and testing the evangelists' claims to be speaking of the historical figure. It can also benefit from redaction critical suggestions about the evangelists' aims and methods. But its task is, in principle, different from that of modern historical research. The final aim of NTT, like all living contemporary theology, is to speak of God. Its particular task is to do this in and through its responsible presentation of the NT.

Barth's prefaces to his *Romans* were explicit about this and so recalled Christian theological exposition of the NT to its primary task, which had apparently been buried under the massive weight of a flourishing historical research. That research is both valuable and necessary, but without the theological significance it had had for Baur, it had threatened to replace theological reflection on the NT. As a critical scholar, Bultmann achieved what Barth did not: a synthesis of historical exegetical research and theological interpretation. But like Baur's a century earlier, Bultmann's was also vulnerable to philosophical obsolescence. Existentialism is not quite dead, but is recognized as inadequate to the demands of today. Like systematic theologies, NTTs are built for their own generation, not for eternity. Also like Baur's synthesis of philosophy, theology, and history, Bultmann's synthesis was subject to historical corrections that would erode and partially discredit it, though coming at the end of the golden century of historical criticism (1831–1930), rather than at the beginning, its historical judgments have fared better than Baur's. This synthesis was also less brittle than Baur's, because it did not depend so directly on such risky judgments as chronology. Nevertheless, it now belongs to the history of NTT as a monument from which to learn rather than an answer to the theological questions of the 1990s.

The history of NTT since Bultmann raises the question of how much has yet been learned from the master. The generation of Bultmann's main German pupils continued to live in the shadow of his theological synthesis even as they questioned some of its historical foundations. Käsemann challenged aspects of Bultmann's Pauline interpretation and provided a new synthesis of historical reconstruction and theological interpretation.[25] But by criticizing John, he reduced his main standing ground in NTT from Bultmann's two witnesses (Paul and John) to one (reinforced by the historical Jesus)[26] and even his Lutheran interpretation of Paul had been challenged by subsequent historical research.[27] The series of lesser NTTs which have appeared since Bultmann's classic have done as little to advance the discipline methodologically as Bultmann's immediate predecessors and contemporaries.[28]

Our comments on the history of NTT from Gabler and G. L. Bauer through F. C. Baur, to Bultmann and beyond, have insisted that its generally unspoken aim has been to present the theological ideas of the NT in a way that indicates something of their relevance for contemporary Christianity. The discipline has naturally used historical methods to describe and arrange the theological statements of these writings, and that has involved distinguishing between the witnesses and abandoning any attempt to draw a unitary doctrinal system from them. But its theological aim to guide contemporary Christianity by communicating the NT message requires us to distinguish it from histories of early Christian thought, helpful as such frameworks have been in clarifying the differences and interrelationships between these witnesses.[29]

Some hint of this contemporary theological dimension of the discipline is contained in the anarthrous phrase "theology of the NT." Bultmann and some others who use it know that there is more than one theology in the NT and clearly reject the old idea of a unitary doctrinal system (vol. 2, p. 237). The phrase is usually taken as shorthand for "the theological ideas of the NT," but as in the phrase NTT the anarthrous singular also suggests that any new presentation, which is inevitably an interpretation of the NT witnesses, expresses the modern author's own single theology. Bultmann's *Theology of the New Testament* is a modern theological interpretation of the NT witnesses but as such it also communicates the one theology that emerges from one man's engagement with these writings at a particular time. [30]

Baur's understanding of the revelation of God as Spirit in the historical process allowed him to see his historical reconstruction of the thought as contributing to the Christian truth about God in history. Insofar as they abandoned this untenable and dangerous theory of revelation, the later liberals took the theology out of NTT, or (in Wrede's case) inserted a "so-called." Conversely, it was the neoreformation theory of revelation that allowed Bultmann to remove Wrede's *sogenannte,* and write theology through his biblical interpretation. Neither the biblicists' reliance on an inspired text, nor the historicists' reliance on what lay behind the text provided a credible theory of revelation. Kerygmatic theology drew fresh attention to one of Luther's ways of speaking of God when it located the revelation event in the proclaimed Word that could change the self-understanding of its hearer.

In both cases, as in the earlier cases of biblicism and rationalism and in later liberalism, the theory of revelation (or lack of it) provided the key to the modern NTT. That is because a NTT aims to speak of God by interpreting the NT, and because religious and theological talk of God is based on tradition or a claim of revelation. Reason has a critical but rarely a foundational role. It is religious communities that preserve traditions and make a claim to revelation. The Christian claim refers to history, to written texts, and to contemporary oral proclamation and appropriation or reception—all of which invite the use of reason and imagination. But different theologies emphasize different elements in this mix, and all those reviewed so far can be criticized for underemphasizing one or another element that is essential for adequately expressing the Christian claim that the decisive saving revelation of God has found, and still finds, expression in Jesus of Nazareth, crucified and risen, remembered and proclaimed in the community of his followers.

Bultmann's sermon-centered theory of revelation, happening on occasion at about eleven o'clock on Sunday mornings, had the merit of directing attention both to the individual believer and to the contemporary life of the religious community in which God is acknowledged, as well as to the biblical text itself. A theory of revelation today must surely relate it to (1) contemporary faith and life as well as to (2) the foundational event which provides the focus of trust, obedience, and worship, and to (3) the documents which direct the former by bearing witness to the latter. But this rather punctiliar theory of revelation and faith does less than justice to the historical and narrative dimensions of the foundation event, the biblical witness, and human experience.

These deficiencies can be corrected, and Bultmann's positive emphasis upon the hearer of the Word preached can be developed by revising his NTT in terms of the newer literary interest within biblical scholarship. His interpretations of Paul and John stretch historical scholarship beyond its normal limits,[31] and are more easily defended within a literary frame of reference. Bultmann offers plausible modern readings of some NT texts, true to what he considers the fundamental intentions of the authors, rather than accurate historical reconstructions of the author's thought. This shift to a literary paradigm is actually suggested by Bultmann's own emphasis upon "interpretation" over "reconstruction." The literary model could be developed by parallels between this emphasis upon the contemporary hearer of the Word and recent interest in the reader (and reader response) in some literary theory.

There is nothing inherently theological about literary study of religious literature, such as the Bible. In fact it is quite likely to be less theological than historical study, because it is usually less interested in the original authors and their subject matter. But these new approaches offer new possibilities for NTT because some literary theories about reading are similar to some Christian belief in how the revelation of God in Jesus Christ is mediated through the biblical literature.

NTT does not *ground* belief in God in Jesus Christ when it provides doctrinal or historical information—essential as such traditions are for actualizing the revelation of God in Jesus Christ today. Scripture interpreted by NTT functions, rather, by confirming and reinforcing, or challenging and correcting, the reader's already existing sense of God and relationship to God. NTT cannot make even this happen, but it can introduce and present the biblical material in ways that make it more likely to happen, and that remove false stumbling blocks.

Belief in the truth of God's revelation in Jesus is not compelled by NTT. People become Christians for various reasons, few of them directly connected with Bible study. The truth of Christianity is presupposed within the community in which NTT is usually written,[32] and is understood in various ways. Individual NTTs reflect this diversity among believers. But unlike historical Jesus research which has often been the launching pad for a modern Christian theology at odds with all the NT witnesses, NTT aims to represent these accurately, even when signaling some theological criticisms. Even Bultmann's demythologizing, an unusually critical *(Sachcritik)* example of NTT, assumes the essential truth of the NT witness and Christianity. Its main weakness (in the judgment of more traditional theologians) lies in its narrowing the witness of the NT writers by an interpretation that eliminated (contrary to Bultmann's stated intentions) essential dimensions of the theology contained in the mythical language. Like all NTT, it hinged on a judgment about what in the NT is essential to Christianity, and what is not. Most theologians find more than the existential aspect essential.

Most NTT is less programmatic, less selective, and less explicit than Bultmann's demythologizing. Because it presents the material through literary and historical judgments that are open to the critical scrutiny of all biblical scholars, NTT finds a home within a pluralistic biblical scholarship. But its success as NTT lies in articulating its author's own theology through its representation of one or more biblical witnesses, not only in representing these convincingly.

One attraction of the literary frame of reference is that it is hospitable to a greater variety of plausible readings of the biblical text than historical study, and so maximizes the possibilities for NTT. The corresponding problem is that the plurality of readings seems to undercut the capacity of scripture to act as a critical norm for Christian faith, excluding versions of Christianity that conflict with the general thrust of these diverse writings.

But this objection can be countered by a consideration of the "soft" way in which scripture has usually functioned as a critical norm. Measuring a serious theology or religious practice against the witness of scripture has rarely provided hard and clear-cut answers. It is itself an intepretative activity, part of an ongoing conversation within the church about what Christianity essentially is, and how the scriptures are to be understood. The challenge to show one's continuity with the NT often reveals the theologian's true colors but does not of itself settle the question of truth.

The revival of NTT associated with Barth and Bultmann was made possible by their appreciation of their own (Reformation) theological tradition and their willingness to introduce this, or the question of God which it posed for them, into their biblical study. Barth's exegetical practice has seemed wayward to historical critics. Bultmann's narrowed the scope of both history and theological interpretation by demanding they coincide. A literary frame of reference and appropriate theory of literature could do better justice to the intentions of them both. It would accept the plurality of interpretations that is a fact of theological life today but without surrendering to a textual indeterminacy that renders any Christian theological use of the Bible as a source of information and a critical norm impossible.

Literary approaches to NTT have their dangers but so too do historical approaches. As a product of modern rationalism, historical criticism has been subversive of theology except when it has been harnessed to a theology or religious

124

philosophy. That is reason enough for theologians to be aware of and to enforce its limits—to use it as a necessary tool, not allowing it to set the whole agenda for biblical studies. Historical study's surprising attraction today for conservative Christians untouched by the nineteenth-century alliance with idealism lies in its seemingly providing the one correct answer to what a passage of scripture means. We should not dispute the success of historical exegesis in discrediting untenable interpretations of individual passages and books, but not even a much stronger exegetical consensus than exists could establish the meaning of scripture as a whole. That would in any case be necessary only if scripture functioned as a norm by means of a single correct interpretation that excluded distortions. In fact, it functions more by helping generate countless new *positive* understandings of the gospel. Critical judgments are then made by theologians and other competent believers in light of their whole experientially tested appropriation of the tradition. One who has learned from NTT to understand the scriptures in a Christian way will be able to make critical judgments about false developments in Christianity; but the role of scripture in this process, and so of its interpretation by NTT, is mainly the positive role of generating understandings. The critical function of refuting false accounts is a more complex operation.

A negative doctrinal criterion, designed to exclude rival interpretations, is found toward the end of the NT timespan at 1 John 4:2 and more clearly in the *homoousion* at the Council of Nicea. It is more a function of creeds and confessions than of scripture, even though the problematic word "canon" suggests that this is how scripture is intended to function doctrinally.[33] Luther and his successors have, on occasion, drawn from scripture (such as from parts of Paul's Epistles) a negative criterion for clarifying the gospel in opposition to a prevalent misunderstanding, but this tactic is productive only within the larger context provided by a much broader Christian use of scripture. If absolutized it leads to Marconism.[34] This tendency was aggravated by NTT, so long as Lutheran interpretations of Paul were plausible, because Paul's key position for the historical study of Christianity, together with his theological profundity, gives him undue weight in a historically oriented NTT.[35] Non-Lutherans have to structure their NTTs in a way that subordinates Paul's theology to the gospel he and the other NT witnesses proclaim. That means, in practice, subordinating the Epistles to the Gospels, as Schlatter did,[36] while avoiding Schlatter's critical blindspots. A more literary orientation facilitates this.

Writing NTT through a biblical scholarship more oriented to literary approaches need not be set in harsh opposition to the historical paradigm that reigned supreme throughout most of the nineteenth and twentieth centuries. Some criticism of a positivistic historical scholarship is necessary, but historiographical theory today is well aware of the literary character of historical (even modern historical) narrative.[37] Theologically committed biblical historians and literary critics alike need to consider which theoretical frameworks are most fruitful for Christian theology. An orthodox Christian will want her NTT to remain bound to a literary theory which takes seriously the historical and metaphysical reference of the texts as well as their impact on the reader or hearer.

These brief suggestions point in a different direction from that taken by Bultmann's pupils. These scholars adhered strictly to the still dominant historical framework of NT scholarship and sometimes occupied positions closer to his liberal Protestant predecessors.[38] Without disputing the importance of the controls on NTT exercised by historical exegesis, the alternative hinted at here would build on elements in both Barth's and Bultmann's biblical interpretation which can be more readily defended within a literary frame of reference. Bultmann's stature as a NT scholar has led most other historians to concentrate on his critical judgments. But his theological interpretation is misjudged if historical criteria alone are applied. More is involved, and his greatest contributions consisted of the illumination brought to some of the NT texts by his integrating his linguistic and historical scholarship with a theologically suggestive philosophical conceptuality.

Bultmann's philosophical categories are not so fashionable today, almost seventy years after his conversations with the early Heidegger. We may agree with him and with Luther that talk of God involves talking of our own human existence, but we are unlikely to speak of human existence in such a one-sided individualistic way as Kierkegaard or some later existentialists did. Religious talk of God speaks also of society and the cosmos and NTT needs to draw these wider perspectives into its interpretations. The best way of doing so is by reflecting on the character of religious texts, and that requires a theory of religion.

Just as NT and other Christian theologians have to be selective among theories of history and literature, so too among theories of religion. Marx and Freud can contribute to theology and NTT through their contributions to our understanding of the human, but their theories of religion are demonstrably false. Kierkegaard's theory of religion is attractive and profound, but one-sided. Contemporary anthropologists of religion such as Clifford Geertz offer theories of religion that fit the empirical data better and leave open the possibility of belief in God, and so the possibility of theology, including Christian theology—even one that proceeds by interpreting some important Christian texts in a specifically Christian way.

That needs to involve reconstructing Paul's or the evangelists' religion. With the help of history, the social sciences, and a theory of religion, efforts in that direction are possible. But a NTT need not be so ambitious. Its aim is to make intelligible what these texts have to say about the revelation of God in Jesus Christ. A modern theory of religion that both fits what they say and makes sense to the contemporary student will provide the necessary language for interpreting the NT theologically.

A NTT in the literary paradigm, for example, an attempt to *interpret* this *literature* theologically, will respect the integrity of each of the NT texts by treating each writing separately, contrary to Wrede's broad-brush historicism. But without imposing a unitary doctrinal system it must presuppose and articulate an essential unity to these texts.[39] Granted their literary and historical diversity, their function as Christian scripture demands some view of their unity. But this unity resides in the one Lord the witnesses proclaim, the one faith they share and aim to evoke, the one baptism they all presumably shared as initiatory ritual into the (in principle) one *ecclesia* scattered around the Mediterranean world, and the one God and Father of the Lord Jesus Messiah. It does not reside in one theology or doctrinal system. The Christian religion constantly generates a variety of theologies, and while it is important to explore what these texts reveal of their author's theologies, it is a mistake to look for the unity of the NT at that level. Even partially conflicting theologies are compatible with a unity of faith.

Accounts of this unity are determined by the interpreter's perspective and reflect a view of the identity of Christianity itself. It is not possible to demonstrate historically that every writer shares that common faith, but it is necessary to show that every writing can plausibly be read on this assumption. Christians rarely derive the form and content of their faith directly from scripture, but they can use scripture to support and challenge their faith only on the general assumption that it agrees with itself and with them about who God is, and who Jesus is (in whom God was, is, and shall be revealed) and where salvation is to be found. That is the central content of scripture for Christians, given definitive shape subsequently in the Christian dogma of Trinity and Incarnation, and spelled out in a succession of theological articulations (Christologies, soteriologies, ecclesiologies, and so on).

The God of Israel is the one God of all, and the Man from Nazareth in whom his followers see God's decisive loving intervention on their own and the world's behalf, and the Spirit through whom both God and Jesus are defined in relation to believers, are the subject of NTT that has found some partial expression in the symbolic language of these texts. It is this symbolic language, speaking of the salvation event and process, the community, its memory and its hope, and the norms of behavior that were seen to follow from it, that NTT presents in such a way as to inform and nourish contemporary Christianity.

The biblical expression of these ideas and ideals varies with the author, time, and place, but those who relate them to their transcendent referent will seek to identify a unity that does not impose on them a false uniformity. It is not the date of the parousia, for example, much less an opinion about its cosmic manifestations, but the ground of their hope that unites the NT witnesses and should unite all Christians. Not their christological formulations, but the structure of the revelation of God in Jesus that they acknowledge; neither the details of their marriage discipline nor the patriarchal assumptions of the day, but the identifiably Christian ideal in marriage; not the organizational form of their ministries, but the tasks to be fulfilled.

The unity of the NT that NTT must postulate came into conflict with the historical methods and results of the discipline when precritical orthodoxy found this unity in a web of doctrinal statements drawn from scripture and identified with divine revelation. When revelation is located instead in the life of the community that listens to scripture, the Spirit is not bound so tightly to the letter. It leads disciples into the truth of God as they propose and test new doctrinal formulations and make new moral decisions. The unity that the Spirit brings is found in the fellowship that the NT message creates, not in these inspired texts as such. It is compatible with differences among the witnesses and honest disagreement about the meaning of these texts within a common set of Christian assumption to which all parties subscribe. Within that fellowship, differences can be faced and either resolved or lived with. The unity of the NT, acknowledged and shared by orthodox Christians, consists in their witness to the one God of Israel whose love for the world is being revealed through the Spirit to Jews and Gentiles in the proclamation of Jesus Messiah. If (on the limited evidence available) James and Jude saw that less clearly than Paul and the evangelists, they do not contradict it, and are simply less central traditions for subsequent Christian witness.

There is no difficulty in believing that all twenty-seven books were written by Christians expressing a common faith in God revealed in Jesus, but expressing it in different situations with different intellectual and conceptual resources. It is possible to be critical of particular formulations, even whole books (cf. Luther on James) without threatening a unity that lies in the gospel that they all, more or less, adequately express. Indeed such theological criticism *(Sachkritik)* will be necessary to allow the modern interpreters' *Sachexegese* (exegesis oriented to the theological content of a text) to reflect their own understanding of the gospel. That goes beyond the normal bounds of historical interpretation (cf. n. 31) and opens the door to subjectivism, as Barth saw in opposing Bultmann (n. 18). But the only way he could close it was by reverting to a more biblicist view of revelation. There is no final escape from the dangers of subjectivism in Christian faith, but these can be minimized by insisting that the whole scriptural witness be considered, even if it cannot all be accepted as equally true to the gospel, and by trusting to the consensus of the whole community to provide controls against individual theologians' distortions. Theology, like all interpretation, involves risk.[40] Experiments have to be made and interpretations of the gospel tested in the experience of the wider constituency.

Both theological interpretation and theological criticism of a NT text or document are done in the light of the interpreter's own understanding of the gospel, but using modern historical and exegetical methods to determine the meaning of the texts. The unity of faith, if not theology, among the various NT authors and even more theological interpreters has made NTT possible within the historical paradigm of NT scholarship. The situation was always more difficult, perhaps impossible, in OT theology and in biblical theology as a whole.[41] A Christian theological interpretation of the OT is bound to be selective and critical in a different way than a historical presentation of Israelite religion, and the question of how this reading of the OT is related to NTT is by no means easily answered.

But since a theological NTT is defensible only as part of a biblical theology[42] (or theological interpretation of Christian scripture which contains Old and New Testaments, with or without Apocrypha) the attempt must be made, in any defense of NTT. Release from the historical framework of most biblical theology opens new possibilities here too.

A Christian theological interpretation of the whole scripture needs to recognize (as biblicisms do not) that scriptural traditions are not all equally important for Christians. The NT is more central than the OT, because it stands historically and theologically closer to the Christian foundational revelation event of God in Jesus Christ, indispensable though the faith of Israel was and still is for this finding understanding and expression. The religious value of those OT documents for Judaism is not the concern of NTT, however important it is in other contexts that Christians appreciate this. What for Judaism is the decisive revelation of God (Torah) is relativized and relegated to religious tradition for Christians by the coming of the Messiah. It is no disrespect to Judaism to recognize that Leviticus does not have the same weight for Christians.

The faith of Israel, reflected in the OT, is presupposed by all the NT writers. This needs to be made explicit in a NTT, which should therefore include far more OT content than is customary. One might even imagine a NTT which contained more OT than specifically NT content, in order to underline the importance of what is taken for granted in the NT and Christianity. A Christian biblical theology or theological interpretation of the whole Bible could well be in effect a NTT adequately filled out with OT content. It would draw its shape from Christianity, not from the scriptures themselves. These provide its materials.

This hermeneutical guideline called biblical theology does not, however, exhaust the significance of the OT for Christian faith and theology any more than NTT exhausts the uses of the NT for systematic theology and devotion. The Hebrew canon and the Septuagint are both such rich resources that Christians will want also to hear them in their own terms, and will depend on biblical scholars to assist this, even if our theological evaluation of what these scholars offer is determined by norms external to these writings. In other words, "secular" literary and historical studies of the OT are needed as well as Christian theological interpretations which use these methods and relate their results to Christian faith.

But such pointers to the shape of a biblical theology and insistence on the insufficiency of NTT on its own, take us beyond the theme of this essay. They are included only to underline our contention that the theological character of NTT implies its orientation to Christian scripture. A NTT that did not speak of the OT would be inadequate both to the NT authors' witness to the revelation of God in Jesus Christ and to most modern interpreters' understanding of this. We are forced back upon the misleading phrase *biblical theology,* despite its biblicistic associations. These are less of a problem in North America, where prestigious chairs in biblical theology have absorbed the sea change wrought by historical criticism, than in Europe where many critical biblical scholars are still embarrassed by the conservative resonances of the phrase.

Embarrassed conservatism ends these reflections on an autobiographical note. Mailing them across the Atlantic, their European author is conscious of inhabiting a world closer to Goldsmith's "Deserted Village" than to Newark airport. Even some Oxford colleagues find the form of Christianity it presupposes strangely attached to the doctrinal tradition, and insufficiently oriented to the liberating praxis of the gospel. And the remarks of Wayne Meeks in *The First Urban Christians* about "an antidote to the abstractions of the history of ideas and to the subjective individualism of existentialist hermeneutics" (p. 2) are well taken. I hope this argument is open to these necessary variations and that NTT at the end of the century will be as interested in ethics as in doctrine, and will make as much use of social as of literary theory. But orthodox Christianity is more closely tied to the symbolic language of the NT in doctrine than in ethics and spirituality, and ideas or beliefs are inescapable in theology. The point is to try and get them right.

The account of NTT given here has admitted to a kind of conservatism, and runs the risk of reinforcing the status quo. That risk is unlikely to be serious so long as the religious status quo stands in such visible need of theological criticism from a NT perspective. But this account does presuppose and reinforce the view that to be appropriately called Christianity, any contemporary restatement should be able to claim a strong continuity with the NT and subsequent versions considered broadly true to it. The tendency of NTT to reinforce that *normal* Christianity is at odds with the conceit that theologians spend their time on the boundary, exploring new possibilities and reflecting on new experience. That enshrines a truth and biblical scholarship, especially historical Jesus research, and has been a motor of theological innovation, some of it healthy. But NTT is a matter of theological education, and this involves conserving the tradition by weeding out error and passing it on in a form that allows its truth to be recognized. Individuals may work on the frontiers, but the discipline has to be defined from the center. Frontier work in theology deserves support even (especially) when it is farthest from what is specifically Christian, but the best support for it is a strong center. It is all God's world and theologians should be the last to underestimate the freedom of the Spirit. But what Christians believe about how and where God is most certainly known underlines the case for a theologically educated clergy that can interpret scripture. An academy persuaded by the success of the natural sciences to reward originality over learning, and research over study, is inimical to the cultivation of a tradition. Theology, including NTT, dances to a different drummer.

Chapter Six / HISTORICAL-CRITICAL METHOD, THEOLOGY, AND CONTEMPORARY EXEGESIS

J. J. M. Roberts

Introduction

In recent years, one has seen a veritable explosion in the writing and publishing of biblical commentaries. All sorts of new commentary series have begun appearing, and some classical old series have resumed publication after a hiatus of many years. At the same time there is a great deal of discussion and no little uncertainty about what a biblical commentary should be, about the proper task of exegesis.[1] The discussion is due, in part, to the dissatisfaction preachers and church teachers have felt with the older commentaries. The complaint is often heard that the older commentaries are interested only in the dry and boring, if not deadly, details of textual minutiae and hypothetical historical reconstruction; and that they offer no theological direction for the preacher's reflection on the text. The reason for this, many critics say, is that professional biblical scholarship has been dominated too long by the historical-critical methodology introduced at the time of the Enlightenment.

Historical-critical methodology was always the bogeyman of fundamentalist biblical scholarship, but now it has become the bogeyman for much wider circles of theological scholarship in this so-called postcritical age. It is not uncommon today, even in scholarly circles, to blame historical-critical scholarship for making the Bible inaccessible to the average person. As the Yale theologian George Lindbeck formulates it, "It is now the scholarly rather than the hierarchical clerical elite which holds the Bible captive and makes it inaccessible to ordinary folk."[2] Though Lindbeck does not make the historical-critical method solely responsible, he does imply that it has contributed to the contemporary Christian community's loss of biblical literacy, to the loss "of a generally intelligible and distinctively Christian language within which disagreements can be expressed and issues debated."[3] Biblical scholars have also joined the chorus of critics. Brevard Childs has been a persistent and long-time critic of the theological inadequacies in the historical-critical approach to the Bible,[4] but even if one disagrees with his critique of traditional historical-critical scholarship,[5] his comments have been restrained and measured compared to the charges leveled against the method by other biblical scholars. Note the comments of James A. Sanders:

> Hans Frei has put it very well: the biblical story has become eclipsed by the work of the very professionals in seminaries and departments of religion who seem to know most about the Bible. In the rhetoric of today, the experts have lost perspective on the very object of their expertise. A colleague calls biblical criticism bankrupt. For some, it has reduced the Bible to grist for the historian's mill, the province of the professor's study. Something like the very opposite of what Albright and George Ernest Wright intended has taken place: often the Bible has been reduced to the status of a tell which only the trained expert with hard-earned tools can dig.[6]

Or compare the following comments of Walter Wink, the colleague to whom Sanders referred, from a book whose first chapter bears the sensational title, "The Bankruptcy of the Biblical Critical Paradigm":

> Historical biblical criticism is bankrupt. . . . The historical critical method has reduced the Bible to a dead letter. Our obeisance to technique has left the Bible sterile and ourselves empty. . . . It was based on an inadequate method, married to a false objectivism, subjected to uncontrolled technologism, separated from a vital community, and has outlived its usefulness as presently practiced.[7]

Finally nontheological and theological critics alike attack the method for being overly concerned with historical questions, with the search for external referential meaning, for not being satisfied with the internal, narrative meaning of the text.[8]

Given this widespread climate of opinion, and the fact that I have just finished one major commentary and am working on two more, my interest in these new trends is deeply existential. At the same time, I am concerned about the integrity and continuity of the scholarly enterprise. Though I feel no compulsion to offer a blanket defense of the historical-critical method as theoretically conceived, much less as it has been practiced by the many different scholars in the field, I am deeply suspicious of the current tendency to denigrate previous OT scholarship. The disparagement of the historical-critical method as a dead end that, if not responsible for all the current problems in the field of biblical exegesis, must be transcended if one hopes to achieve theologically relevant and compelling exegetical results for the contemporary community of faith, seems to me to lead to a far narrower dead end of its own.

The important article of George Lindbeck previously cited may serve as a useful framework for a discussion of these issues.[9] In it he argues that it was a particular way of reading the Bible that created and sustained the communal faith and identity of the early Church. Lindbeck defines this classic herme-neutic as reading the Bible "as a canonically and narrationally unified and internally glossed (that is, self-referential and self-interpreting) whole centered on Jesus Christ, and telling the story of the dealings of the Triune God with his people and his world in ways which are typologically . . . applicable to the present."[10] This hermeneutic began to break down at the time of the Enlight-enment, according to Lindbeck, and its loss is largely responsible for the present biblical illiteracy and the lack of a central core of commonly acknowledged beliefs in Christendom today. In his view, the creation and sustaining of such communally held beliefs is dependent on a central core of privileged and familiar texts which project imaginatively and practically habitable worlds. That means that these privileged and familiar texts must supply followable directions for coherent patterns of life in new situations. According to Lindbeck, to again make the Bible followable in our day, one must regain this classic hermeneutic of the past.

How is a biblical scholar to respond to these claims of Lindbeck? In a very general way, I think one can agree with him. At least in broad terms, I would claim that to read the Bible as a unified whole means telling the story of the Triune God's dealing with his people and his world in ways that are typologically applicable to the present. I would certainly claim that scripture provides the interpretive framework for all reality for me, and for the Christian community to which I belong. On the other hand, Lindbeck's formulation harbors numer-ous problems when one tries to apply it in detail to the reading of the biblical text. What do canonical unity, narrational unity, and self-referentiality actually imply for the exegesis of particular prophetic texts?

Canonical Unity

First of all, what precisely is meant by "canonically unified whole"? Does this mean that one reads any particular book in the light of all the other canonical books? If that is so, the question as to which canon is meant rises immediately. Lindbeck speaks of the Hebrew scriptures and the Hebrew Bible in a way that suggests that he follows Childs in basically identifying the OT canon with the canon of the Masoretic Text.[11] That, however, was definitely not the OT canon of most Christian churches until the time of the Reformation. Their OT canons, whether they used the LXX, the Vulgate, or other translations, typically con-tained additional books and followed a different physical arrangement of the material. Any "canonical" reading of the biblical text that wants to claim the support of early Christian interpretation must be broad enough, therefore, to accommodate this diversity in both content and arrangement of the canon.[12]

Second, how can one protect a canonical reading of the text, say of Isaiah, from the charge that one is simply reading all sorts of later Christian meanings into the text? How can one make sure that one is reading Isaiah and not simply using it as a pretext for hearing only Paul or some other NT writer? If one reads Isaiah as part of the ongoing story of God's dealing with his people, one can be open to the larger canonical context while respecting the historical fact that this represents an earlier chapter in the story. Openness to the canonical context of the fuller story need not result in collapsing the distinctive message of Isaiah into a carbon copy of later New Testament texts, but it does require a willingness to take historical development seriously in order to avoid this danger.

The necessity to take historical development seriously should make one cautious about playing off a canonical meaning of a text against a historical one, as though the canonical meaning were certain and the historical one were only putative and reconstructed. Lindbeck is guilty of this when he asserts that in the classic hermeneutic "the use and therefore meaning of the text . . . was the one it had in the canon-forming situation, not in some putative historically reconstructed original one."[13] In addition to the lack of clarity as to what is meant by this expression, his formulation overlooks the fact that any "canon-forming situation" is itself the construct of a historical reconstruction.[14] The formation of the canon was a long process; it was not completed at one time, and the reasons for the particular canonical shape of individual books, and often even of individual pericopes within a book, are usually obscure and hardly to be attributed to a particular moment in the course of that process. "Canon-forming situation," then, is not a very helpful concept to clarify the appropriate approach to exegesis.

Third, to read a biblical book as scripture in the light of the larger canon need not imply any contrast to a reading motivated by philological or historical purposes. It is simply not true to say, as Lindbeck does, that "to read Homer's *Odyssey* for philological or historical purposes . . . is to turn it into something other than an epic poem."[15] Any decent historian who expected to extract useful historical information from Homer's *Odyssey* would have to be constantly aware of the text's genre. He or she would have to read the text as an epic poem before one could expect it to yield any useful historical information. Moreover, even canonical readings cannot dispense with philological and historical concerns. If one is going to read the Bible with any understanding at all, one must learn the scripts, the morphology, the syntax, the vocabulary, and the literary conventions of the languages and periods in which it was written. And for an ancient text like the Bible, that inevitably involves historical as well as philological research. The historical-critical method is not responsible for the difficulty of interpreting the biblical text. Any ancient text from a different culture composed in a foreign language would present similar difficulties, and neither Lindbeck's classical hermeneutics, nor any other kind, can sweep these difficulties away and magically clarify the meaning of the Bible to the general public.

Narrational Unity

Lindbeck's characterization of the Bible as a "narrationally unified whole" also needs further specification. If he means by that phrase that all parts of the Bible contribute generally to the one story of God's dealing with his people, it is a useful concept. However, one must be careful to avoid overstressing narrative as the fundamental theological category for revelation. If the older scholarship overstressed history as the mode for revelation, recent scholarship seems tempted to simply substitute narrative or story for history, forgetful of the fact that narrative is subject to many of the same objections that were raised against history.

In the first place, much of the Bible does not qualify as narrative in any meaningful sense. The legal collections, the wisdom books, most of the pro-phetic books, many of the Psalms, and the epistolary material of the NT are simply not narrative literature. To try to interpret these materials in detail with interpretive categories derived from narrative literature is sure to result in gross misrepresentation.[16]

One can illustrate this issue with specific regard to a prophetic book. A typical prophetic book consists of a mixed collection of oracles given by the prophet at different times and occasions during his prophetic ministry, and this collec-tion is usually expanded by the commentary and additions of the prophet's disciples, editors, and later scribes. Some of the oracles in a prophetic book may have a brief notice informing the reader what the historical occasion behind that particular oracle was, and such a notice may take the form of a more extended narrative. Yet even in the case of Jeremiah, which has relatively extensive narrative material, the majority of the oracles are without a narrative framework. Moreover, despite the enormous effort that has gone into the attempt to uncover the principles behind the present literary arrangement of the oracles in the various prophetic books, there is very little agreement on this matter with respect to most books. If one were to look for a contemporary analogy to the literary form of the prophetic book, the closest parallels would be a book of sermons or a collection of meditations with extensive marginal notations. Given this literary form and the fact that the principles of literary arrangement are uncertain and at least open to the possibility of being largely haphazard, meaningful reading of such a work will concentrate on individual oracles rather than on putative literary links between contiguous oracles. If one wants to put a particular oracle in a larger context within the book, one will read it over against other oracles on the same subject, or, when this can be known, against other oracles given by the prophet in the same historical context. Literary placement in the collection may count for less than similarity of message or of historical background. Thus a critical, if not *the* critical issue in the interpretation of a prophetic book will be the correct delimitation of the extent of a particular oracle. This way of reading the material is dictated by the genre, and no concept of canonical or narrational unity can override this elementary observation of the character of the material to be read.

One could, however, take Lindbeck's claim for canonical and narrational unity as a claim that the reading of a particular passage in a prophetic book should be controlled by the literary arrangement of oracles in the book. Brevard Childs clearly makes such a claim when he argues that the placement of Isaiah 40–66 in the same scroll with the oracles of Isaiah of Jerusalem has dehistoricized the oracles of Second Isaiah so that they should be read canonically as though they were from the eighth century BCE.[17] In my opinion, this is sheer nonsense, and it certainly cannot claim the support of the history of interpretation. It is true that Isaiah 40–66 was attributed to Isaiah of Jerusalem because these chapters were included in the same book as the oracles of the eighth-century prophet, but in terms of the actual interpretation of individual passages the ancient Christian interpreters paid very little attention to the literary shape of the book. Classical interpretation of a prophetic book actually interpreted discrete passages, not the prophetic book as a whole. Prophetic books were read, not as coherent, unified wholes, but as collections of discrete prophecies, each of which could stand on its own as a word of God. In general, there was very little interpretation of any biblical book, even the genuinely narrative ones, in terms of the structure of that book as a whole.[18] Interpretation concentrated not on books, but on relatively short pericopes. It tended to be quite atomistic, unified only by the belief that all of scripture was the word of God. Therefore any passage in the Bible could be invoked to help explain whatever difficult passage one was reading at the moment.

There are exceptions to my general portrayal of the literary character of prophetic books. In the case of Habakkuk, for example, I would argue that one was dealing with a work that reflected a self-conscious compositional unity. It may be composed of discrete oracles given on different occasions, but these oracles have been put together in such a way as to create a narrativelike structure in which the theological point depends on the text's sequential development of the argument. Even in the case of Habakkuk, however, one cannot elevate the final form of the text to the final arbiter of theological meaning, because after the creation of this compositional unity, late marginal glosses were added to the text which confuse the message.[19] In Hab 2:5-20 the nations who have been oppressed by the Babylonians sing a taunt song over the Babylonian king in which they describe his terrible oppression of other peoples. In 2:12 they address the Babylonian king as one who builds his city with bloodshed and establishes his town with iniquity. Following this address, in 2:13b one finds the statement:

> So that the peoples exhaust themselves only for the fire,
> And the nations grow weary for nothing. (author's translation)

In the context of this saying and in the context of the larger pericope's function within the book as a compositional unity, the meaning of Hab 2:13*b* can only be that Babylon's oppression of the other nations has prevented these nations from enjoying the fruits of their own labors. It is an indictment of the selfish cruelty of the Babylonians. This verse, however, is partially quoted in the later oracle in Jer 51:58, and there it is applied to the doom of the Babylonians. A still later reader of Habakkuk, influenced by this Jeremiah passage, wanted to impose this interpretation on Hab 2:13*b,* and to do so he bracketed it with two glosses. He introduced it with the comment in 2:13*a:* "Are not these things from Yahweh of Hosts?" and he ended it in 2:14 with a partial quotation of Isa 11:9: "For the earth will be filled so that it knows the glory of Yahweh as the waters cover the sea" (author's translation). Both comments miss the passage and are clearly recognizable as secondary glosses. One can interpret what the glosses mean, but one cannot interpret the whole context in the light of these glosses, because the glossator did not interpret, much less understand, the whole text. Why, then, should we accept any canonical or narrative theory that would allow the latest pre-Jamnia glosses to control our reading of whole pericopes?

Self-Referential and Self-Interpreting

Lindbeck's principle of scripture's self-referential and self-interpreting character is also problematic. It was formulated as a corrective to the tendency in historical-critical scholarship to be so concerned about the historical background of the text that the actual narrative meaning of the text was lost. A good example of the problem is presented by Speiser's treatment of the three stories in Genesis where the patriarch denies that the matriarch is his wife and claims instead that she is his sister. Speiser argued that the motif arose from a later misunderstanding of an early social custom, known from sixteenth-century BCE Nuzi, where a man could give higher status to his wife if he also adopted her as his sister.[20] However one judges the accuracy of Speiser's historical argument, which has been seriously challenged by other scholars,[21] it does not have any clear bearing on the present form of any of the stories in Genesis. Whatever the background of those stories, the exegete must ask what they mean in their present shape, and Speiser largely ignores that question. Thus Lindbeck's principle is the reaffirmation of the importance of a narrative *qua* narrative. What does a story mean as a story? The introduction of historical information actually extraneous to the story is no contribution to the interpretation of the story as such, and far too much of that has been done. When interpreting literature composed of a people's myths, legends, sagas, or dramatic treatment of quasi-historical heroes of the past, one must allow the literary work to create its own world of reality. Particularly in books like Genesis or Job, the question of historicity should not be allowed to crowd out the more important question of meaning.

On the other hand, when a work like Samuel or Kings refers to known historical events, sometimes just in passing, it hardly makes sense to restrict interpretation to the internal referential world of the book itself. If a book refers to external events, a more profound knowledge of those events than what is actually narrated in the book itself may be necessary for a proper understanding of the work.

In modern fictionalized narratives set in the contemporary world, an author often depends on his or her audience's knowledge not only of contemporary culture, but of recent history as well, in order for the work to make sense. If one were to interpret such a work to a foreign audience five hundred years later, when such knowledge could not be presupposed, one would have to supply much of that missing "historical background" for that later audience to understand the work. The same is true for the interpretation of many biblical narratives.

Moreover, biblical books like Kings and Chronicles claim to be more than historical romances: they make theological claims based on their construal of Israel's history. When a modern work offers a theological critique of contemporary society based on historical events, say the internment of Japanese-Americans in World War II or the killing of civil rights activists in the South, an interpretation of the meaning of that work, if it is to go beyond saying what the work claims, to an evaluation of how one should react to those claims, must ask how accurately the work has portrayed those historical details. One need not get every historical detail right in order to sustain a particular interpretation, but a gross misrepresentation of historical facts would certainly render any interpretation dependent on that misrepresentation suspect. That is one reason why biblical scholars in general have a higher respect for the theology of Kings than that of Chronicles. It is rooted in a less tendentious treatment of historical detail. The point, however, is that the interpretation of biblical books that refer to external events requires the interpreter to raise historical questions. An interpretation of the Bible that limits itself to a referential system totally restricted to the biblical narrative itself does not take seriously the actual character of the biblical literature.[22]

If the referential system of even narrative literature cannot be restricted to the "imaginative" world created by the narrative itself, how much less is that the case with nonnarrative literature? Prophetic oracles in particular make all sorts of passing allusions to historical events without providing any narrative framework for an adequate understanding of those historical events. Even when one reads the prophets in the context of the whole Bible, one still finds no clue to the significance of many of these allusions. References to Calno, Hamath, Carchemish, and Arpad (Isa 10:9) would remain unclear were it not for the Assyrian inscriptions and the historical reconstruction they make possible.

Were it not for the Greek historians, the full significance of Second Isaiah's references to Cyrus would not be known, and this is not a modern discovery. The exegetes of the ancient Church, those model practitioners of the classic hermeneutic, also quoted Herodotus and other secular Greek sources in their interpretation of the biblical material.

Moreover, the understanding of a detail in the text may sometimes require the reconstruction of the historical event that lay behind that text from scattered hints in the biblical text itself. This controversial point may be illustrated from an equally controversial detail in Isa 7:3:

> And the LORD said to Isaiah, "Go forth to meet Ahaz, you and Shear-jashub your son, at the end of the conduit of the upper pool on the highway to the Fuller's Field. (author's translation)

An attentive reader will ask why God told Isaiah to take his son Shear-jashub with him when he went to meet Ahaz. The text in Isaiah 7 raises the question, but it provides no answer to it. We know from Hos 1:3-9, however, that prophets sometimes gave symbolic names to their children as a kind of living embodiment of their prophetic message. Isaiah (8:18) refers to the children God had given him as "signs and portents in Israel," and that suggests that he too gave symbolic names to his children. There were certainly two and probably three— Shear-jashub, Immanuel (often identified as the king's son for insufficient reasons), and Maher-shalal-hash-baz. Now all of the symbolic names that Hosea gave to his children are explained in the passage that refers to their naming. The same is true of the name of Isaiah's third child, Maher-shalal-hash-baz. The name means "Hasten booty, hurry plunder!" and Isa 8:3-4 explains the prophetic judgment implicit in the symbolic name:

> The LORD said to me, "Call his name Maher-shalal-hash-baz; for before the child knows how to cry 'My father' or 'My mother,' the wealth of Damascus and the spoil of Samaria will be carried away before the king of Assyria." (author's translation)

If this was the normal pattern in the giving of symbolic names, why does Isaiah 7 not explain the significance of the name Shear-jashub? The name means "A remnant will return," but a remnant of whom shall return from where? Does it convey a positive meaning or a negative meaning? For whom is it positive or negative? If one limits oneself to the present text of Isaiah 7, these questions cannot be answered.

There is another passage in Isa 10:20-23, however, where the phrase Shear-jashub occurs twice. The present shape and context of this passage requires that one read it as an oracle from the period of the Assyrian crisis. There is impressive evidence, however, that verses 16-23 dated originally to the period of the Syro-Ephraimitic war and were intended at the time as a threat against Israel, the northern kingdom.[23] In other words, these verses were originally composed around the same time as the events described in Isaiah 7 took place, and they explain the meaning of the name Shear-jashub: "A remnant will return, the remnant of Jacob, to the mighty God. For though your people Israel were like the sand of the sea, only a remnant of them will return. Destruction is decreed, overflowing with righteousness" (Isa 10:21-23).

In the context of the Syro-Ephraimitic war, this can only mean that the Israelite army threatening Jerusalem will be destroyed, and only a remnant of the hostile northern kingdom will survive. Thus the name Shear-jashub originally conveyed a message similar to that of the name Maher-shalal-hash-baz. It pronounced judgment on the north, but hope for Judah. In my opinion, it is only by such a historical reconstruction of the original meaning of Shear-jashub's name that one can answer the long disputed question of whether Isaiah had a positive concept of the remnant. In the original historical context this ambiguous concept was positive for Judah but negative for Israel, and that suggests that Isaiah may have preserved a similar ambiguity in his later reuse of this concept when applied to Judean society alone. Judah's judgment was certain, but Isa 1:26 nonetheless implies the survival of a positively evaluated remnant. If this discussion has any merit, theological significance cannot be limited to the final form of the text as Lindbeck and Childs seem to demand: one's perception of earlier forms of the text affect the way one reads the final form.

Conclusion

Thus, three of the main principles of Lindbeck's definition of the classical hermeneutic are ambiguous, problematic, or subject to significant abuse. His critique of the way in which the historical-critical method has been applied has its valid points. Whether it is legitimate to criticize exegetes of the church for not carrying their task far enough, for stopping before addressing the theological concerns that the text raises, is not as self-evident as Lindbeck and other critics imply. There may, in fact, be some good reasons for the hesitancy of scholars to press on in this area. As Barr has persuasively argued, this hesitancy may arise out of the nature of the theological enterprise itself, from the fact that theological exegesis is an interaction that takes place between the factuality of the text and the prior theological expectations that people have due to the particularities of their own religious or nonreligious backgrounds.[24] Unless the commentator is addressing a very particular religious community whose theological presuppositions he or she knows well, the contemporary theological reflections of the commentator are apt to appear scattered and unfocused, and a commentary addressed to such a particular community is apt to strike other readers as tendentious or peculiar.

On the other hand, particularly if Barr's analysis is correct, Lindbeck and other critics of the historical-critical method do not have enough respect for the continuing contribution of this approach to the task of interpretation. One cannot dismiss this approach *in toto* as now outdated without losing the ability to achieve a critical understanding of ancient documents, and the preservation of this ability is a goal that has profound theological, not just historical, ramifications.

PART THREE

PROPOSALS FOR BIBLICAL THEOLOGY

Chapter Seven / STANDING ON GOD'S PROMISES: COVENANT AND CONTINUITY IN BIBLICAL THEOLOGY

Bernhard W. Anderson

Introduction

The Christian community shares with the Jewish community a common Bible, in Christian terms called the Old Testament; but it rereads these scriptures with a *discrimen*, a discriminating judgment, that perceives dimensions of continuity and discontinuity. This has been emphasized by my friend and former colleague at Princeton Theological Seminary, Chris Beker, to whom this essay is presented with great appreciation. In a penetrating study of the function of the word of Hab 2:4 in the Epistle to the Romans, he traces both continuity and discontinuity with the testimony of the Hebrew scriptures. He concludes that Paul's interpretation of this passage, as well as of Gen 15:6, "may be a promising start for a consideration of Romans as a model for a Biblical Theology."[1]

I would like to pick up on Beker's "preliminary observations" by exploring the theme of the promises to the people of God, set forth in the ancestral history (Genesis 12–50) and related OT passages. The dialectic of continuity and discontinuity operates in the Christian perception that these promises have been endorsed by God's revelation in Jesus Christ.

Heirs of the Promise

In various ways writers of the New Testament express their conviction that the life, death, and resurrection of Jesus Christ is the climax, and in a sense, the fulfillment of God's purpose, traceable to the time of creation and worked out particularly in the life of Israel, the people of God. Today Christian worshipers share this conviction when, in the Communion Service, they join in praising and thanking God "for the goodness and love which you have made known to us in creation, in the calling of Israel to be your people, in your word spoken through the prophets, and above all in the Word made flesh, Jesus your Son." Creation, the call of Israel, the prophets, Jesus Christ—that is the sequence of the great story that unfolds in the perspective of Christian faith.

Above all it was the apostle Paul who stated this view in terms of the promises made to the ancestors. To the church at Rome he wrote that Christ "became a servant to the circumcised" (the Jewish people) in order to demonstrate "God's truthfulness" (or "faithfulness"), and this was done "in order to confirm the promises given to the patriarchs, and in order that the Gentiles might glorify God for his mercy" (Rom 15:8-9 author's translation). So, the welcome to the Gentiles did not mean laying aside or abrogating the promises made to Israel. God is faithful, and does not go back on a word of promise. "The word of our God will stand forever," as a great prophetic poet exclaimed (Isa 40:8). Rather, this welcome means that the Gentiles, along with faithful Jews, are also heirs of the promises to the people of God. To the church at Corinth Paul said that all God's promises of salvation have been affirmed by Jesus Christ. "For in him every one of God's promises is a 'Yes.' For this reason it is through him that we say the 'Amen,' to the glory of God" (2 Cor 1:20).

One wonders why early Christian interpreters, who took seriously the OT witness to God as creator of heaven and earth, spent so much time in the exegesis of the OT. Why didn't they just proclaim a monotheistic creed: God is the source and ground of all existence? Why didn't they, like the wisdom writers of Israel, point to the order of creation and urge people to find peace, security, and well-being by attuning their lives to that cosmic order? The answer, I think, is to be found in something that they considered more exciting, namely, that Christ threw the doors open so that all persons may be invited into the community known as the "people of God" or as Paul says explicitly in Galatians "the Israel of God" (Gal 6:16).

In the Epistle to the Romans, Paul develops the theme that membership in God's people, whether Jew or Gentile, "depends on faith." The reason that it depends on faith, he says, is "in order that the promise may rest on grace and be guaranteed to all [Abraham's] descendants, not only to the adherents of the law but also to those who share the faith of Abraham" (Rom 4:16). The upshot is that all those who share the faith of Abraham are "children of Abraham." "For," says Paul, "he is the father of all of us, as it is written, 'I have made you the father of many nations' " (Rom 4:16-17). If this is so, it may be added, Christians should not regard the Scriptures of Israel as the literature of another people (Jewish Scripture) or as a Hebrew Bible which may be studied objectively (as in academia). Rather, as Paul says elsewhere, "these things were written down for *our* instruction, upon whom the end of the ages has come" (1 Cor 10:11 author's translation). These are Christian scriptures too.

The Promises of Grace to the Ancestors

When Paul declares that "Abraham is the father of us all," that is, all who share Abraham's faith, he alludes specifically to Genesis 17 where at the time

146

of God's making an everlasting covenant, the patriarch was given a new name signifying a new relationship: no longer Abram (meaning "exalted Father") but Abraham, which is construed to mean "father of a multitude" (Gen 17:5). So, let us turn to the ancestral history (Genesis 12–50) to see what the promise—or, better, "the promises," for God's promise has several facets—entails. After studying this part of the OT, especially Gen 12:1-3 and chapter 17, we shall discover, I believe, that in Christian discernment there are both elements of continuity and discontinuity.

The ancestral history that unfolds in Genesis 12–50 is not just a historical preface to the Exodus—the story of people who drifted into Egypt, became slaves of the mightiest emperor of the day, and eventually experienced liberation from Pharaoh's yoke of bondage. It is also, and fundamentally, a theological preface to the story of the people of God and especially the crucial experiences of Exodus and Sinai. Viewed theologically, the ancestral history is the beginning of the history of the promise. For the theme of God's promise is the thread that binds together the various episodes and movements of this story/history. Indeed, the dynamic of the story is the promise that is ever on the way toward its fulfillment, despite setbacks and times of testing.[2]

The theological meaning of the ancestral history does not have to be deduced from the movement of the narrative; it is clearly spelled out in a sequence of divine addresses that punctuate the unfolding story. One of these addresses is found at the very beginning, at the point of transition from the primeval history to the ancestral history. Here the theme of the promise is introduced programmatically (Gen 12:1-3). In the translation of the Jewish Publication Society, this bridge passage is translated:

> The LORD said to Abram, "Go forth from your native land and from your father's house to the land that I will show you.
>> I will make of you a great nation,
>> And I will bless you;
>> I will make your name great,
>> And you shall be a blessing.
>> I will bless those who bless you
>> And curse him that curses you;
>> And all the families of the earth
>> Shall bless themselves by you."
>
> (Gen 12:1-3 TANAKH)

In this passage, which the TANAKH arranges in poetic form, the promise includes two elements: that Abraham's descendants will become "a great nation"—elsewhere a numerous posterity[3]—and that their relationship with God will benefit all the families of the earth.

147

It is striking that the promise of land is not explicitly mentioned in this poetic formulation. Silence on this matter has been taken to mean that the composer of the old epic tradition ("the Yahwist") played down this aspect of the received tradition. The theme of promise of the land, writes Hans Walter Wolff, "is reduced by the Yahwist almost to a footnote," that is, the subordinate sentence in 12:1 (RSV), "Go . . . to the land that I will show you"); rather, the Yahwist prefers to emphasize the promise of descendants. Indeed, "the result of Yahweh's blessing (in 12:2a) is not land, but a beneficial, abundant vitality, a power for life."[4]

However, the argument is not convincing. At the outset (12:1) Abram is summoned to go to the land that Yahweh will show him; and a few verses later, when Abraham is at Shechem, Yahweh appears to him in a vision and says: "To your descendants I will give this land" (12:7). Indeed, it is important to realize and emphasize that the promise of land is an essential element of God's promise. Later in the book of Genesis, whenever the promise is repeated and summarized, land is always included, often along with the two other elements of increase in posterity and relationship with God that will benefit other peoples. For instance, in the Jacob story, when Jacob is in flight from Esau's wrath and is in danger of losing the land, God appears to him in a dream at Bethel and renews the promise:

> "I am [Yahweh], the God of Abraham your father and the God of Isaac; the land on which you lie I will give to you and to your offspring; and your offspring shall be like the dust of the earth, and you shall spread abroad to the west and to the east and to the north and to the south; and all the families of the earth shall be blessed in you and in your offspring." (Gen 28:13-14)

The promise of land runs through the whole Pentateuch and reaches its most forceful elaboration in the sermons of Moses to the Israelites in the book of Deuteronomy, just as they were on the verge of crossing the Jordan River and entering into the promised land.

Divine Promises and Covenant

Notice that in the ancestral history, priority is given to God's promises. Promises were given *before* God made a covenant with the people; indeed, God's covenant was given for the purpose of solemnizing and guaranteeing the validity of the promises.

That is the way it is in the old epic tradition found in Genesis 15. The storyteller says that Abram has doubts about two of the divine promises: how can he know that he will have a great posterity when he has no son (Gen 15:1-6)? Nevertheless, he put his trust in God's word of promise and—as we read in a famous biblical statement—this trust was accredited to him as righteousness, that is, right relation with God (Gen 15:6).[5] In the second part of the story (15:7-21), Abraham questions God about how he can know that he will possess the land when the Canaanites are still in it. God's covenant, sealed by a strange blood rite and a solemn divine oath, is made to certify the promise: "On that day the LORD made a covenant with Abram" (15:18).

The covenant of promise does not free one from obligations; indeed, in the parallel chapter 17, God summons Abraham to "walk before me and be blameless." The covenant recognizes Abraham's integrity and responsibility. The emphasis falls, however, upon the giving of promises, not laws. No wonder that Paul, in his proclamation of God's grace in Jesus Christ, went back before the Mosaic covenant of obligation to the Abrahamic covenant of promise. Abraham was held up as the great representative of the faith which is a trusting response to God's word of promise.

The seventeenth chapter of Genesis is one of the most important theological treatises in the OT. This chapter sets forth the divine promises that are guaranteed to the people in the Abrahamic covenant of grace. Again, the divine promises are threefold, though they are nuanced differently than in old epic tradition (Genesis 12).

First, Abraham and Sarah will have a numerous posterity (Gen 17:6): Abraham will be "the father of a multitude of nations" (v. 4)—recall the pun on the name of the patriarch (Gen 17:5). Similarly, it is said that Sarah will be a "mother of nations; kings of peoples will come from her" (v. 16). This assurance of the fruitfulness of the people of God was picked up later by a prophetic poet during the period of the exile, when it seemed that Israel was barren and had no future:

> Look to the rock from which you were hewn,
>   and to the quarry from which you were dug.
> Look to Abraham your father
>   and to Sarah who bore you;
> for he was but one when I called him,
>   but I blessed him and made him many.
>   (Isa 51:1-2)

Second, this covenant assures God's special relationship to, and presence with, the people of Abraham and Sarah; for *El Shaddai* ("God Almighty") promises to "be God to you and to your offspring after you" (Gen 17:7). This promise points forward to the priestly passage in Exod 6:2-9 where El Shaddai discloses the personal name of God to be used in prayer and worship: "I am [Yahweh] . . . and . . . I will take you as my people, and I will be your God. You shall know that I am [Yahweh]" (Exod 6:7).

In this view the people of God are a worshiping community that is allowed to invoke God by the personal name that signifies identity and relationship. To worship God is to call "on the name of [Yahweh]" in times of distress, as in the psalms of lament (Ps 116:4); or to "call on the name of [Yahweh]" in times of deliverance from trouble, as in psalms of thanksgiving (Ps 116:12-13).

③   Third, the Abrahamic covenant is connected essentially with the land. The language is that of a formal, legal grant: "I will give to you, and to your offspring after you, the land where you are now an alien, all the land of Canaan, for a perpetual holding" (Gen 17:8).

✓   The "everlasting covenant" *(berît ʿolām)* assures the claim upon the land as an "everlasting possession" or "possession in perpetuity" *(ʾaḥuzzat ʿolām)*. As in the royal grants widely practiced in the ancient world,[6] in this legal arrangement, the donor—usually in recognition of past loyalty—binds himself unilaterally by oath to give property permanently. So in this case the grant of the land is based on Yahweh's oath, is given in recognition of Abraham's past loyalty, and is unilateral, for no specific obligations are imposed.

The real estate dimension of the covenant with the ancestors is highlighted in the storytelling Psalm 105, where it is said that

→
> [Yahweh our God] . . . is mindful of his covenant forever,
> of the word that he commanded, for a thousand generations,
> the covenant that he made with Abraham,
> his sworn promise to Isaac,
> which he confirmed to Jacob as a statute,
> to Israel as an everlasting covenant,
> saying, "To you I will give the land of Canaan
> as your portion for an inheritance."

(Ps 105:8-11)

The Problem of the Promise of Land

The real estate aspect of the theme of the promise is fundamental and at the same time problematic. This hit me with full force when I took part in a seminar sponsored by the Native Ministries Consortium of Vancouver, British Columbia, in the summer of 1992. This was my first experience of teaching the Bible to native peoples from the United States, Canada, and elsewhere. Walking in their moccasins, so to speak, and trying to see through their eyes gave me a new appreciation of the difficulty and challenge of interpreting the Bible in the modern world.

What proved to be most troubling was the theme of the promise to the ancestors of Israel, especially the promise of the land of Canaan (Gen 12:1, 7). In Gen 15:18-21, an archaic covenant rite guarantees the possession of the land whose boundaries are given:

On that day [Yahweh] made a covenant with Abram, saying, "To your descendants I give this land, from the river of Egypt to the great river, the river Euphrates, the land of the Kenites, the Kenizzites, the Kadmonites, the Hittites, the Perizzites, the Rephaim, the Amorites, the Canaanites, the Girgashites, and the Jebusites." (Gen 15:18-21)

Here it is clear that God's gift of the land is at the expense of the native peoples who are listed in pedantic detail. Similarly in the story of the burning bush, Moses is assured that God will deliver the Israelites from bondage in Egypt and bring them "to a good and broad land, a land flowing with milk and honey." This promise will be realized, however, by dispossessing the indigenous peoples: "the Canaanites, the Hittites, the Amorites, the Perizzites, the Hivites, and the Jebusites" (Exod 3:8).

I must confess that before the conference I had concentrated on the promise to Israel and had not thought too much about its consequences for the native peoples. Those ancient peoples flourished for a while in a small corner of the ancient world and then disappeared from the historical scene, though some of them—for example, the Hittites—have been rediscovered by modern archaeologists. However, in the presence of Native Americans who lost their land to invaders, I became uncomfortable about the land dimension of the promise to the ancestors and took a new interest in those forgotten peoples.

The problem of the native peoples is exacerbated in the book of Deuteronomy, which picks up the theme of the promised land and brings it to a sermonic climax. In his valedictory address to the Israelites, as they are on the verge of crossing the Jordan and ascending the West Bank, Moses announces that the land is God's gift and declares that they are to take it by force from the native inhabitants, "nations larger and mightier than you" (Deut 9:1). In strong language, the invaders are told to "make no covenant with them and show them no mercy" (Deut 7:2); rather, they must "break down their altars, smash their pillars, burn their sacred poles with fire, and hew down the idols of their gods" (Deut 12:3).

To be sure, some powerful reasons for this negative attitude are given. The Mosaic sermon warns that the Israelites may be "ensnared" by aspects of native culture (Deut 7:25); further, they are told that God is dispossessing the native peoples not because of the Israelites' "righteousness" but because of "the wickedness of these nations" (Deut 9:4). Nevertheless, it is easy to see how native peoples of North America, Australia, the Hawaiian Islands, and elsewhere, who feel the hurt of loss of their land and destruction of their cultures, would be turned off by the theme of the promised land. Moses' exhortation could be used as a justification for taking land and destroying native culture, as has happened again and again since Columbus's arrival in the New World.

While reflecting on this difficult problem, I found much help in an essay by Wendell Berry, "The Gift of Good Land"—the title essay of a collection of essays dealing with ecological and agricultural subjects.[7] Berry is an essayist, novelist, and poet—not a professional biblical scholar; and for that reason his essay is peculiarly refreshing and challenging. He proposes to turn to the book of Deuteronomy as a way of developing a biblical basis for ecological responsibility. "The giving of the Promised Land to the Israelites," he writes, "is more serviceable than the story of the giving of the Garden of Eden, because the Promised Land is a divine gift to a fallen people."[8]

In speaking of a "fallen people," Berry is using traditional language. What he means, I believe, is that any people—not just ancient Israel—receives God's gifts in a historical situation where self-interest and human pride tarnish them. The theme of God's gift of land to a people, he says, "sounds like the sort of rationalization that invariably accompanies nationalistic aggression and theft," and he draws attention to "the similarities to the westward movement of the American frontier." Early American pioneers, as we know, believed that they were marching into the promised land. Berry observes that, whereas the movement into the American frontier produced an ethic of greed and violence, the Israelite conquest of Canaan from the very first was informed by an ethic of responsibility based on the view that the land is God's undeserved gift. To quote the essay once again:

> The difficulty but also the wonder of the story of the Promised Land is that, there, the primordial and still continuing dark story of human rapaciousness began to be accompanied by a vein of light which, however improbably and uncertainly, still accompanies us.[9]

The "vein of light" which pierces the "dark story" of human aggression and violence surely shines in the story of God's promises to the people of Israel, including the promise of land. That light of the Torah is seen, for instance, in the book of Deuteronomy, whose basic teaching is that the land is God's gift. Deuteronomy teaches that, since the land is God's gift, the people should live on it with a humble sense of gratitude, that they will dwell on it long if they heed God's imperatives for justice, and that they should exercise "good husbandry," thereby displaying a reverent concern for God's good earth. Surely, it is important for the Christian community, which is heir of the promises to the ancestors, to heed this teaching. Nevertheless, there are difficulties with the promise of the land which Christians must face seriously, especially when the matter is considered in the light of God's revelation in Jesus Christ. Let me offer the following proposals to Christians, who are sensitive to the experience of native peoples, as they reflect on the theme of the Promised Land.

First, the story of the promise to Israel's ancestors pertains to a people of the past—ancient Israel. The story is, as we say, "historically conditioned." It was not intended to provide a divine mandate for other people in other times and historical situations to engage in territorial expansion at the expense of native populations. It is important for us to say that this story belongs to *the past*, when the people of Israel were struggling to find a place in the sun and to understand their God-given vocation. In this respect, I believe, historical criticism can perform a great service to the church.

Second, the story is about an ancient people who—like every people and nation from time immemorial—has been inescapably involved in what Berry calls a "dark history" of struggle for power and for land. Hence, the formulation

152

of God's promise to ancient Israel has an ideological coloration. Just as the promises of grace to David provided the justification for the Davidic throne (see Psalm 78, especially the conclusion in vv. 56-72), so also the promise of land to Abraham and his descendants provided a theological rationale for the conquest of Canaan. This sociological dimension of the story is another evidence that the Word (revelation) of God comes to us in human words, words that are colored by their historical and social setting.

Third, in the perspective of the faith of Israel, God works through the sufferings, dislocations and tragedy of human history to achieve a purpose that ultimately will benefit all peoples and nations. Indeed, Israel—represented by Abraham and Sarah—is summoned to a special task that, in some sense, will yield blessing to "all the families of the earth," the third of the divine promises to Abraham (Gen 12:3). A prophetic poet, writing in the time of the Exile, perceived that this was the deepest meaning of Israel's whole history:

> And now the LORD says . . .
>> "It is too light a thing that you should be my servant
>> to raise up the tribes of Jacob
>> and to restore the survivors of Israel;
> I will give you as a light to the nations,
>> that my salvation may reach to the end of the earth."
>
> (Isa 49:5-6)

Perhaps native peoples, who have been overrun by invaders, may one day say in retrospect that some good came of it after all. In Vancouver I discovered, however, that the hurt is still too great for native peoples to say in the words of Joseph: "Even though you intended to do harm to me, God intended it for good" (Gen 50:20). As a black student observed, such positive statements are more easily made by the oppressor than by the oppressed.

Christian Reinterpretation of God's Promises

Let me bring this discussion to a conclusion by returning to the base from which we started: the announcement that, since people of faith are children of Abraham and Sarah, "we" are heirs of the promises. As we have seen, NT interpreters—especially Paul—are emphatic on this matter. Paul declares that all of God's promises are affirmed or endorsed by Jesus Christ. People of faith are children of Abraham and therefore "heirs of the promises."

Here again it must be said that Christian rereading of the Scriptures of Israel perceives both continuity and discontinuity. Yes, there is continuity between the old and the new; but there is also discontinuity. The promises are nuanced differently. Since the doors are thrown open so that Gentiles may enter the community of faith, the result will be that "the Israel of God" will have great increase in numbers. Furthermore, the relationship with God through Jesus Christ, which is the basis of this community, will benefit all the families of the earth.

What about the promise of the land of Canaan? Notice how Paul treats this matter:

> For the promise that he would inherit *the world (kosmos)* did not come to Abraham or to his descendants through the law but through the righteousness of faith. (Rom 4:13 italics mine)

This is a stunning reinterpretation of the theme of the promised land. Of course, in Hebrew, as students of the language well know, the word *'eres* can mean either "land" in the sense of a bounded territory or country, or it can signify "earth" or "world," as in Ps 24:1: "The earth is the LORD's and all that is in it." The choice of the larger meaning of the Hebrew word introduces a universal dimension that is discontinuous with the Hebrew scriptures.

To be sure, Paul could have found support in Jewish circles for this reinterpretation. Early rabbis, influenced by the universality of the third promise to Abraham ("all the families of the earth"), said that Abraham was the heir of the whole world, indeed, of "heaven and earth."[10]

In this larger sense, which transcends the limitations of ethnic territory and national ideology, Paul declares that the promises to Israel's ancestors have been endorsed by God's revelation in Jesus Christ. Living in the promise provides an opportunity for the Christian community to proclaim the gospel to the ends of the earth.

As Rosemary Ruether rightly points out, however, there is danger in this reinterpretation of "land" as "cosmos," namely that the concrete relation to the land, presupposed in the Abrahamic covenant, will be lost. She observes that as Christianity developed, "the concrete eco-justice perspective" of the OT faded, "to be replaced by a cosmological and spiritualized understanding of the work of Jesus as Messiah." She continues:

> Even though Christianity claimed to be the people of the "new covenant," the covenantal concepts of relationship to the land would be discarded. Christianity replaced the Jewish ethnic view of peoplehood with a universalist imperial view of God's "new people."[11]

In conclusion, it should be repeated that Christian rereading of the history of the promise perceives elements of both discontinuity and continuity. The discontinuity shows that the promise, in Christian understanding, transcends the OT limitations of the Promised Land. The continuity, which needs to be perceived more clearly today, indicates that, as in the book of Deuteronomy, the covenant binds people to the good land and calls them to assume responsibility for the environment, so that we and our children after us may live long on the earth which the Lord God has given us.

Chapter Eight / CREATION AND COVENANT

Patrick D. Miller

The God of the Old Testament is both *qōnēh/'ōsēh (samayim wā)'āres*, "Creator/Maker of (heaven and) earth,"[1] and *sōmēr habberît*, "keeper of the covenant."[2] Both rubrics incorporate vast numbers of texts and theological themes. Together, creation and covenant bid fair to represent the whole of the theological subject matter of the OT. The question, however, of what the creation of the world has to do with the covenant with Israel, or God's creative activity with God's covenant-making, or how these two are parts of a whole, interactive and conjoined in some fundamental fashion, is a much debated matter. The aim of this essay is to explore particular ways in which these two dimensions of the activity of the God of Israel have been understood, and to suggest how their integration is theologically significant or contributes to the integration of other features of the OT, or of theology in general, features that are often dealt with separately or seen to be in serious and unhelpful tension.

I

Throughout the history of the interpretation of scripture, there have been various ways in which the many realia and relationships to which covenant points have been seen to provide a large framework for speaking about the theology that is found there and more particularly the theology of the OT. Such moves hardly ever involve a claim that covenant encompasses everything but that it is the dominant theme or theological structure for the whole.

That is surely evidenced in its simplest form in the choice of the term or rubric "testament" *(diathēkē)*. While the English translation suggests the meaning of "will" or provision for an estate—and Pauline usage of *diathēkē* has some of that connotation (for example, Gal 3:15-18)—the appropriation of the Septuagint's use of *diathēkē* for Hebrew *berît*, "covenant," clearly represents a claim that in the two parts of the canon we encounter God's covenant with humanity, and more specifically with Israel and the Church. The use of the term suggests that the primary way of understanding the canon, and especially the interrelationship of its parts, is as the testimony to God's commitment to redeem and create a people; God's binding of self to a community in a formal way. That the notion is strongly present in both Testaments and that the OT speaks of and anticipates a new covenant are sufficient grounds to claim that this rubric may be a way of identifying the primary unity in the canon. What is immediately clear, however, is that there is a tension between the *unity* found in the two covenants, whether understood typologically or in terms of the history of promise and salvation, and the *contrast* proclaimed in various ways in the New Testament between the old covenant that was clearly God's doing but inoperative under the Law, and the new covenant that is fulfilled in Christ. For a long time, such an understanding has been the source of theological wrestling and debate, particularly for the way in which it seems to set aside the "old" covenant and its scripture. That debate, however, is not the point here. It is simply to recognize in this nomenclature an early indication that the structure of covenant, involving God's commitment and human response—in whatever variety, tension, or conflict its various manifestations may suggest—is the fundamental theological subject matter of the canon.

The emphasis upon this sequence of old and new covenants in Calvin's theology, as well as that of Bullinger, is well-known. The development of that emphasis into the federal theology of the late-sixteenth and early-seventeenth centuries,[3] however, was the impetus for "the first serious attempt to escape entirely from the influence of tradition and historic confessions of faith and to theologize in a purely biblical manner," an attempt found in the work of Johannes Cocceius.[4] Biblical theology has its primary precursor in his *Summa doctrina de foedere et testamento Dei* (1648), in which he set forth a theology around a succession of covenants, "a notion of distinctive temporal stages operative in the history portrayed in scripture."[5] Cocceius divided history into two covenants: a covenant of works, or of nature prior to the human fall, when humanity was able, by nature, to obey God's commandments; and a covenant of grace in the time after humanity fell into sin, the dividing point being the Proto-Evangelion in Gen 3:15, promising the defeat of Satan and, by inference, the coming of the Messiah. The latter period itself may be divided into three economies or dispensations, the antelegal dispensation of the patriarchs with law a matter of conscience, the legal period in which grace was mediated through the Law, and the postlegal period in which the Law is fulfilled in Christ and divine grace is available to all. The whole of history from creation to consummation is held together by this sequence of covenants. Within this system, the point of discontinuity is not between the Testaments but between the two covenants, that is, in the Fall. Such a way of seeing the theological break is foreign to most developments before and after, but is worth noting because while there is clearly no explicit reference to covenant, or emphasis upon works in the first three chapters of Genesis, the early chapters of Genesis do assume a working relationship between God and human beings that is breached in Genesis 3, and the rest of the story flows out of what happens between Genesis 3 and 11. Here, of course, is the basis for a "history of salvation," the history that grows out of the Fall.

This covenant theology had a greater impact upon confessional and systematic theology, for example, the Westminster Confession of Faith and Catechisms, than it did upon biblical theology, although the later development of a history of salvation approach to the wholeness of scripture is directly indebted to Cocceius. For much of the time between the seventeenth and twentieth centuries, however, biblical theology focused more on the religion of Israel and the uncovering of a unity in the ideas of scripture, rather than in the historical-theological unity found in the succession of covenants claimed by federal theology. In the modern period, however, the centrality of covenant came back into the picture in the work of Walther Eichrodt, who claimed to see in the covenant between God and Israel, the unifying center of the OT.[6] Covenant is for Eichrodt "a convenient symbol for an assurance much wider in scope and controlling the formation of the national faith at its deepest level, without which Israel would not be Israel."[7] Eichrodt acknowledges that there is much in the OT that does not have to do directly with the covenant. But he argues that everything is seen in the light of, and in relation to, that understanding of the particular relation between God and Israel, the redemptive activity of God to claim a people that would live as God's people ("I will be your God and you will be my people"). When he comes to speak about God and the world, however, there is very little explicit reference to the covenant and, as is frequently noted, little implicit sense of the impact of the covenantal relationship between God and Israel on the relation of God to creation. Eichrodt devotes less than one page to that question, and there his only point is that the creative work of God is imbued with moral purpose in the light of the covenant.

Eichrodt's insistence on the significance of the covenant for OT theology was echoed in America in the less systematic work of G. Ernest Wright, whose *God Who Acts* may be the most widely read piece of biblical theology to arise on the American scene. While arguing the priority of election over covenant, he saw in the interrelation of those two realities—God's gracious election of Israel as God's own people, and the covenantal relationship that set before them a way of living under God, both of which reflect history as the primary sphere in which God is revealed—"the chief clues to the theological understanding of the whole Bible."[8] The focus on history and the playing down of nature as the sphere of interest of the pagan religions, however, meant a consequent inattention to creation except for the creation and role of humankind. In similar fashion, the large sphere of wisdom had little place because "it does not fit into the type of faith exhibited in the historical and prophetic literatures. In it there is no explicit reference to or development of the doctrine of history, election or covenant."[9]

It is not surprising, therefore, that counter voices have been heard in the years following the impact of these two seminal voices. They are of two sorts: one is the move to play down the role of covenant in the history of Israel's religion, claiming that, as a framework for the fundamental relationship between Israel and Yahweh, it is essentially a Deuteronomistic construction. The fundamental work representing this perspective is Lothar Perlitt's *Bundestheologie im Alten Testament*,[10] but there are a number of other similar studies.[11] While historical judgment about the origin of the covenant in Israel does not necessarily settle the question of its theological significance, the result of this trend has been some lessening of emphasis upon covenant, generally, though there are notable exceptions.

The other direction that has developed in the more recent period has been a renewed focus upon creation and its centrality in the OT and its theology. Implicitly addressing Wright's perplexity over what to do with wisdom, Zimmerli made a persuasive case for seeing it fundamentally as a part of a theology of creation and quite unconnected to covenant.[12] That is reflected in the explicit taking up of creation matters in Proverbs and Job and also in the widespread interest in world order that is characteristic of wisdom. Wright's rejection of wisdom was to be expected in a theology that focused upon history, election, and covenant. A turn toward creation opened up room for serious theological dealing with the wisdom literature and its theology.

That turn was fully made in H. H. Schmid's seminal essay, "Creation, Righteousness, and Salvation: 'Creation Theology' as the Broad Horizon of Biblical Theology."[13] In sharp contrast to von Rad's influential essay in which he argued for the historical and theological subordination of creation faith to the *Heilsgeschichte*,[14] Schmid claimed that creation theology is the foundation of biblical theology. Particularly in the light of his earlier work on righteousness as world order, Schmid drew in many aspects of the OT to make the following sweeping claim:

> All factors considered, the doctrine of creation, namely the belief that God has created and is sustaining the order of the world in all its complexities, is not a peripheral theme of biblical theology but is plainly the fundamental theme. What Israel experienced in her history and what the early Christian community experienced in relation to Jesus is understood and interpreted in terms of this one basic theme.[15]

II

While Schmid represents a powerful attempt to reverse the covenant dominance by seeking to make creation the all-encompassing rubric for biblical or

OT theology, other more recent works reflect an effort to think about the relation of covenant and creation in the biblical texts. Although only a few examples can be cited—and they are quite varied in approach—they suggest fruitful directions for biblical theology.

One way of dealing with both of these themes in some sort of unity is precisely to see them as two major theological themes that stand in either a dialectical or compatible relation to each other. That is, they exist together, either in tension with each other, or as variant forms of a single ideal. In the work of Walter Brueggemann, both covenant and creation as ways of understanding God's relation to Israel and the world, play a significant part in a complex dialectical approach to OT theology. Both of them are part of what he calls a "contractual theology" that shares much in common with other ancient Near Eastern theologies and is "the foundational construct for Israel's faith."[16] "This theology of coherence and rationality . . . is an assertion of *creation theology*, the sense that the world is ordered and governed" (italics mine).[17] Such contractual theology, reflected in the Mosaic covenant where Israelite religion is couched "in a political metaphor with sanctions and a rule of law" and in the "much more frontal and full-blown covenant theology" of the Deuteronomists as well as in the sense of "orderliness and coherence in life" of wisdom theology, serves to legitimate the existing structures and order of life.[18] It is, therefore, subject to, and in need of, radical critique because it is open to exploitation. That critique comes from within Yahwism and the OT by "the embrace of pain as a posture of both Yahweh and Israel"[19] found in the lament prayers of Moses, Jeremiah, Job, and in the Psalms as well as in the stories of the Flood and of Sodom and Gomorrah and in Hosea 11.

In this programmatic way, creation and covenant are joined together as foundational for Israelite faith and OT theology, but as such are also problematic. This is especially the case with creation theology, for in other works Brueggemann has suggested that the Mosaic covenantal trajectory exercises a liberating and critical function against the more triumphant and dominating royal theology, which is itself rooted in covenantal structure, but also much more controlled by the "imperial propaganda and ideology" of creation theology. There is, thus, an ambiguity in the way that both these dimensions of Israelite faith function, but the covenantal stream is more ambiguous and capable of either legitimating or subverting than is the creation stream.

Jon Levenson has proposed to see in covenant and creation "variant idioms for one ideal—the exclusive enthronement of YHWH and the radical and uncompromising commitment of the House of Israel to carrying out his commands."[20] The variants are found in the expression of God's creative activity presented in the combat myth and in the covenantal structure as it is represented in the suzerainty treaty analogies.[21] This ideal, in Levenson's opinion, is the only thing that "monotheism" can mean with reference to Israel. The great threat to monotheism so understood is defection, which "in the mythic [for

159

example, creation] idiom takes the form of a challenge to YHWH's supremacy among the gods" and in the covenantal idiom "takes the form of Israel's worship of other gods. . . . "[22]

Like Brueggemann, therefore, creation and covenant come together in a quite foundational way in Levenson's theology. For him, they function, in effect, as the vehicle for "monotheistic" faith. He too, sees a problem in the theological outcome of these variant idioms. It is not, however, in the legitimating character of the ideal but in its precariousness, the fragility of God's control over the forces of chaos, as well as of God's reign over Israel. Covenant and creation are not ambiguous, nor at odds, but they are always under threat of undoing.

Another possibility for understanding the relation of creation and covenant is found in the history of religion sphere, particularly in the work of Frank Cross. Indeed, Levenson's approach is a Jewish theology that makes sense to many Christian theologians, not only because of its general theological acumen and sensitive handling of biblical texts, but also because it works out of categories familiar from the work of his teacher, Cross, as well as that of other scholars in interpreting Israelite religion out of its Near Eastern context.

Within the history of religion perspective as set forth by Cross, the conjoining of creation and covenant is found in the characterization of the deity.[23] That is, Yahweh emerges as the God of Israel out of two pre-Yahwistic mythological and religious streams. One is the worship of the clan or tutelary deity, the god of the ancestor, who was the patron of the clan, joined in kinship or covenant to the clan and its leader, and existing in the special relationship that such a structure carried with it. The other stream is the worship of the high god El, who, among other aspects of his role as head of the Canaanite pantheon, was the transcendent creator god, the primordial father of gods and human beings and creator of heaven and earth.[24] The god of the ancestors, however, was in all likelihood this high god Amorite Ilu = Canaanite El. Furthermore, El was not only the creator deity but also a social god who existed in covenantal or kinship relations with kings and others. In a Hurrian text at Ugarit, El actually bears the epithet *brt* = "covenant" in the form *il brt*, "El of the covenant."[25] Furthermore, Cross has argued for a long time that the name of Yahweh, the covenant-making God of Israel, means "he creates" and that the name together with the epithet "Sebaoth" ("Hosts") comes originally from a cultic name of El, "He who creates the hosts."[26] What this means, then, is that the creative activity of God and the covenantal relationship with the human community are conjoined in the very nature and origin of the deity. Yahweh who chooses Israel and is bound in covenant to the community, is also the creator of the heavens and the earth, as well as of the community itself.[27]

Cross goes on to develop in some complexity, though not always in direct reference to creation and covenant, the relation of these themes in the history of Israel's religion. Indeed, the claim of his major work, to describe the interplay of Canaanite myth and Hebrew epic in that history, is in effect a working out of the relation of creation faith and covenant faith, broadly understood. The following summary quotation is a good indication of what he is about:

> In the cult of the league . . . themes of mythological origin can be detected, standing in tension with themes of historical memory or enhancing redemptive events by assimilating them to primordial events. These mythic features are to be found especially in archaic psalmody, which underwent less shaping in transmission than the prose. It is this more or less subdued mythological element of the old time that breaks out afresh in the cultus and ideology of the monarchy. This movement is counterbalanced by the great prophets who, while influenced by the royal cult and its liturgical style, recall the more austere themes of the covenant forms of the league, its legal language, and its relatively minor use of mythological material. As late prophecy and remnants of the royal ideology flow together to create the early apocalyptic movement, we may say that the old mythological themes rise to a new crescendo, though even in the apocalyptic the expression of Israel's faith is still firmly controlled by a historical framework. The primordial events of creation and the eschatological events of the new creation are typologically related but are held apart by the events of human history so that, unlike the movement of myth, the primordial event and the eschatological event never merge in a cultic "Now."[28]

Another example of a contemporary effort to work out the relationship between creation and covenant is found in the recent work of Rolf Rendtorff, especially in two essays that are somewhat programmatic and part of the prolegomena to his OT theology currently in progress.[29] Explicitly and self-consciously Rendtorff sets his approach as "close to that of Brevard Childs."[30] That is, his way of describing the theological interplay of creation and covenant follows a line of direction from the programmatic attempt of Childs to focus scholarly attention on the final or canonical form of the text.[31] Not accidentally, therefore, Rendtorff begins with the first two books of the Bible, which is how he thinks an OT theology ought to begin.[32] The dynamic interplay of creation and covenant is seen in the beginning of the biblical story where creation is the "given" (in the double sense of that term) and covenant the means by which the given remains a gift and a possibility for human existence. In developing this, Rendtorff places a weight upon the Noachic covenant that is rather unusual in contemporary biblical theology, as he himself recognizes.[33] His own summary best represents his position:

> The Primeval History in Genesis 1–11 and the Sinai story in Exodus 19–34 show a parallel structure. In both cases the first gift of God (creation [Genesis 1–11]/covenant [Exodus 19–34]) is endangered by human sin and threatened to be destroyed because of God's wrath. In both cases God changes his mind because of (the intervention of) one man (Noah/Moses). In both cases God promises not

to bring destruction again (on humanity/on Israel), and in order to confirm that he (re)establishes his covenant *(běrît)*. Now neither humanity nor Israel lives in the original situation of creation or covenant, but in a restored one, which is spoiled by human sin but whose continuous existence, nevertheless, is guaranteed by the *běrît* God himself has established.

The use of the word *běrît* in other texts between these two key stories shows a network of references and interrelations whereby human involvement in the covenant as a response to God's gift is emphasized in different ways: circumcision is the first "sign of covenant" as a response to God's promise to Abraham (Genesis 17). Obedience to the commandments is Israel's response to God's guidance and gift of the covenant (Exod 19:4-6; 24:3-8), and the sabbath as a "sign" of the "everlasting covenant" (31:12-17) links Israel's religious life to the first covenant by which God restored the creation once and for all (Genesis 9).[34]

Creation here is not the broad horizon of OT theology. In this analysis, covenant plays the larger role. Creation, however, is perceived as the divine gift and the presupposition of human existence. The nature of human existence as it is lived out, however, always threatens the gift and the presupposition. God's covenant promise with Noah is the means by which the gift is restored and continues as gift and presupposition. Furthermore, covenant itself is both gift and preserver of the gift. In the Sinai story, it is God's gift for the establishment and maintenance of Israel as a community under God's rule (though Rendtorff does not particularly lift up how the Sinaitic covenant addresses the problem of human existence identified in Genesis 1–11). But it is also the means by which God overcomes the problem of Israel's sin (Exodus 32) and reestablishes the relationship and the gift of covenant (Exod 34:10, 27-28).

What is seen of the necessary and significant connection between covenant and creation at the beginning of the OT is found in other parts also. Implicitly, Rendtorff claims, the conviction of wisdom that creation and its orders may be trusted, does not arise out of the creation itself, for creation is always threatened and endangered by what goes on continuously in it that is not good. It is only by God's covenant with Noah, God's self-obligation to keep the creation going despite the evil in it, that one can trust the creation and its orders.[35]

In the prophets, the Noah covenant as the guarantee of creation appears again. For Deutero-Isaiah, it is both a guarantee of creation and a model and prototype for God's dealing with Israel after the catastrophe of the Exile (Isa 54:7-10). The Babylonian exile is comparable to the Flood, but as on that occasion, so now also a restoration happens through God's covenant, the "covenant of peace" (*běrît šalôm*—v. 10).[36] In Ezek 34:25-31, we hear again of that covenant of peace after the Exile, only here nature is drawn in also. The wild animals who have taken over the empty land will give it up again to its inhabitants. Rain will come at the right time and the earth will yield its increase.

162

Seed time and harvest will again take place, as God had promised in the Noah covenant.[37]

Creation and covenant, therefore, are inextricably bound together according to Rendtorff, and it is only through that binding that either human existence or Israel's existence can be maintained. One notes along the way of Rendtorff's argument how crucial is the methodological direction set by Childs. The Genesis and Exodus texts are interpreted as they present themselves without reference to prior stages or their literary complexity. Rendtorff acknowledges this diachronic disinterest in passing, but clearly does not see it as a problem.[38] The canonical/end-form reading of the text that Childs has pressed so vigorously has opened up for Rendtorff a new way of thinking about creation and covenant.

III

While there are other theologians who are pressing the question of how God's creative work and God's covenanting activity are related,[39] those discussed above offer major and generally programmatic proposals. In various ways, one can see in them indications of some of the consequences for OT theology, and indeed for theology and ethics more generally, of the answer(s) to that question. To illustrate its significance, let me identify two different long-standing tensions in OT theology for which the interrelation of covenant and creation may be crucial, either by way of helping resolve them or by providing analogous structures for doing so.

Nature and History. The dichotomy between nature and history has been a continuing problem in biblical theology. Illustrative in the modern period is again G. Ernest Wright. While his emphasis upon the God who acts, included God's acting in the creation of the world, its real focus was an acting in history. The centering of that activity, and thus of OT theology, in election and covenant without a serious attempt to see them in close relation to creation, led to a focus upon history as not only the realm of the divine activity but also the primary concern of human response. The sphere of wisdom, where nature comes into play in significant ways, remained outside his purview. Nature was a concern of the ancient Near Eastern "background" against which (Wright's terms) Israel's focus on election and covenant was set.

The dichotomy finally will not work because nature is historical and history takes place within nature. What that means theologically and morally for the human community, however, cannot be fully or properly determined by a theology that focuses exclusively on covenant. It is worth noting that Wright's student, colleague, and longtime friend, Frank Cross, for whom creation and covenant-making are central in the origin and nature of Israel's God and its religion, has made one of his rare forays into theology precisely at this point,

163

examining the redemption of nature as a biblical theme in "an attempt to recover the wholeness and unity of human and natural history that stamp the language of the Hebrew Bible."[40] In Second Isaiah, Cross sees new epic and new myth fully joined. The prophet describes the history of salvation in a new epic, a new Exodus and Conquest, a new universal covenant, a renewed heaven and earth, a new creation, and a new redemption embracing Israel, humankind, and the rest of nature. What Cross worked out as an understanding of the history of Israel's religion has now an explicit theological implication: "in the biblical epic of redemption, we find a wholeness and unity in the grand process that we call in our language human and natural history."[41]

Against this vision of a "grand process" and a "wholeness and unity," Brueggemann sees a more scarred terrain and a more tenuous whole. There is, within his theology, a suspicion of creation faith leading to a focus more upon the sociohistorical and less upon the natural order. While covenant in one of its forms and manifestations (Davidic) is drawn into the royal theology and its legitimation of human structures of control, covenant in another form (Mosaic) remains also the fundamental critique of creation theology. Brueggemann, therefore, is more willing to risk a covenant-focused theology but seeks to hold them in dialectic relationship because he sees such a dialectic in the OT. A theology focused upon historical actuality can become ossified, but that is more likely with one that is rooted in the natural order. He has been critical of process theology precisely at this point.[42] It is rooted heavily in creation and nature without the subversive and liberating force of the Mosaic covenant, the context in which human hurt may sound its voice against the natural order of things. In support of that tilting of the creation-covenant / nature-history axis, some have pointed to von Rad's strong insistence on the subordinate character of creation faith in the OT in his 1935 essay[43] as a joining with Karl Barth's resistance to natural theology at the crucial point in German theology when National Socialism wished to understand even the nation as an order of creation.[44] They saw precisely the structure-legitimating danger of a creation theology without the critique or control of God's historical activity and covenant-making.[45]

But the shift away from, or the subordination of creation may leave us ill-equipped for another natural catastrophe, the ecological disaster in the modern world. If National Socialism, with its perverted appropriation of natural and creation theology destroyed human life and society in an unprecedented fashion, we are slowly finding out that Marxism in its communist form has so corrupted the natural world in its pursuit of a classless society, for example in Russia and the former East Germany, that it may become unlivable as a context for God's covenant with human beings and no longer the matrix of divine blessing as the Priestly writer saw it (Gen 1:26-31). Indeed, according to the biblical story, the Exodus and covenant with Israel grew out of the threat to the actualization of the creation blessing by Pharaoh's oppressive treatment of the

Hebrews (Exodus 1).[46] The trajectory of God's liberating and covenant-making activity arising out of the Exodus has to be so understood that it does not become the vehicle for letting nature be overwhelmed by history with all the devastating effects that move threatens. The covenant of peace, as it is adumbrated in the prophets is precisely a binding relationship that includes not only God and humankind, but the natural order as well (such as Ezek 34:25-31). If, in the 1930s, the covenant in its largest sense—and certainly in its form in the First or Great Commandment—was set against the threat and actuality of tyranny and mass destruction that sought to attach itself to a structure-legitimating order of creation and a natural theology, at the turn of the millennium, it may be equally crucial to set creation against a narrowly limited covenantal theology that lacks the moral and theological tools to handle the threat and actuality of the destruction of the natural world in which history continues to transpire but may yet expire.

Here, it would seem the effort of Rendtorff to focus theological attention on the little-attended Noachic covenant is a pointer in the right direction. We have concerned ourselves more with the interplay of Mosaic and royal covenants (for example, Brueggemann, Cross, Levenson,[47] and Anderson) when it may be that the theological enterprise needs to discern the relationship between Mosaic and Noachic covenants. Rather than legitimating a particular political order or dynamic, or a particular theological establishment, by rooting it in creation, the Noachic covenant legitimates *God's* structures of creation for humankind, precisely those that belong to the natural world's capacity to sustain the matrix of history. The covenantal benefit, however, includes nature itself and not just humankind.[48] That is, we tend to make a distinction between nature incorporating the material world and the creatures inhabiting it, leaving history to refer to the realm of human life and activity. The Noachic covenant views matters differently. The natural environment is secured in covenant with human and natural creatures. The covenant with Noah restores and secures the creation for the benefit of the creatures, animal and human. Human treatment of the natural world, therefore, is a matter not only of the attitude toward the creation, but also how humankind receives the promise, which it shares with the animal world.

Furthermore, the Noachic covenant involves a recognition of human corruption and sin, before the divine destruction of the creation but also after its restoration. In Jeremiah, the daring assertion is made by the Lord that the sins of the people "have turned away . . . the rain in its season, the autumn rain and the spring rain" (Jer 5:23-24). The Noachic covenant is a guarantee of the created order on God's part but not a license for violence and corruption on the part of the human creature. For such corruption can threaten the creation and its order. Rendtorff has called attention to the phrase in Gen 8:22, "*As long as the earth endures,* seedtime and harvest, cold and heat, summer and winter, day and night, shall not cease," and suggested that we can so disturb the earth

165

in lasting fashion that the alternation of day and night, summer and winter, is broken by the permanent night and the permanent winter, what we call "nuclear winter," and the alternation of cold and heat is broken by the "warming" of the planet, so that the fundamental conditions for God's promise in the Noachic covenant, "so long as the earth remains," are altered.[49] In a quite different way than that of which Jeremiah speaks, it may be possible once more that "your iniquities" will turn away "the rain in its season." In the face of such a potentiality, taking place before our eyes, theology and ethics need to rethink how the obligation of the Mosaic covenant and the promise of the Noachic covenant may provide the resources for shaping human action in a different sort of way, or at least for understanding how we have doomed ourselves.

Levenson's work is important precisely at this point. He insists that it is out of God's ongoing activity against chaotic forces that covenant comes. God's vigilance in keeping chaos in confinement[50] is "simply a variant of God's covenantal pledge in Genesis 9 never to flood the world again."[51] If creation is done and finished, then the covenantal structure of relationship binding God and humankind is a separate matter unrelated to the ongoing of creation. But if the creation is an ongoing work of God against chaotic forces, and if it involves the human and other aspects of creation, then covenant may be the structure for binding human and divine in the struggle against evil and for creation. The prophets, at least, saw the negative side of this possibility.

Israel and the Nations. A further tension in OT theology potentially affected by, or examined in the light of an understanding of creation vis-à-vis covenant is the question of the relation of Israel and the nations of Israel and the world. One of the most obvious ways in which these two horizons take one into that question is in the recognition that the creation traditions of the OT go broadly and deeply into the religious traditions of the nations of Israel's time and the connections between the God of Israel and the gods of the nations, while the covenant tradition, in its Mosaic form at least, identifies Yahweh particularly with Israel and marks Israel off from the nations: "Now therefore, if you obey my voice and keep my covenant, you shall be my treasured possession out of all the peoples" (Exod 19:5).

But the contrast between the universal/creation and the particular/covenant that is suggested there does not fully reflect the complexity of the way(s) creation and covenant meet in the OT, and especially with regard to Israel and the nations. Here again, the Noachic covenant needs to be taken into account.

The nations are a part of the created order, the outcome of the blessing of God in the completion of creation.[52] The restoration of the creation after the Flood involves also the restoration of humanity as a part of that creation and of the renewal of the blessing (Gen 8:17; 9:1, 7) through the lineage of Noah (Gen 9:19). So also the establishment of covenant with Noah is an establishment of covenant with all of humankind. The text makes this point repeatedly and thus with much emphasis. The universal covenant with humankind as a way of perpetuating and maintaining the creation incorporates the nations of which Israel is a single part.

The nations, therefore, are susceptible to the same divine *blessing, mercy,* and *redemption* as is Israel. Three texts particularly suggest that:

1. Genesis 17 is the Priestly account of the covenant with Abraham, the same tradition that sets forth in full the Noachic covenant in Genesis 9. It also marks the separation of Isaac and Israel from Ishmael and the Ishmaelites, clearly indicating that God's covenant is with Abraham and his descendants through Isaac, not Ishmael. But in Gen 17:20, the creation blessing of God (Gen 1:28; 9:1, 7), which is echoed in partial form previously in words to Abraham and Sarah (vv. 2, 3, and 16), is set forth in its most complete form *with reference to Ishmael:*

> I will bless him and make him fruitful and exceedingly numerous; he shall be the father of twelve princes, and I will make him a great nation.

The obvious point is well made by J. G. Janzen: "It is as though every rhetorical means is used to balance the covenant in Isaac with the general creation blessing in Ishmael."[53] Precisely the creation blessing, renewed in the everlasting covenant with Noah, sets one of the nations, Ishmael, on a plane with the seed of Abraham, with whom God has entered into everlasting covenant.

2. In Jonah the total focus is upon the nations and Israel's attitude toward them. The anger of the prophet is because he knows that the Lord of Israel is "a gracious God and merciful, slow to anger, and abounding in steadfast love, and ready to relent from punishing" (Jonah 4:2). Here the prophet quotes one of the oldest liturgical and confessional formulae in Israel's faith and one that in its literary—and probably historical—context was intimately associated with the character and activity of God as the one who makes covenant with Israel.[54] Jonah, the prophet of the covenant people, knows that the covenant God is merciful and gracious—*toward even the hostile nations.* The covenant with Moses and Israel does not exclude the nations from the covenantal mercy and steadfast love that is at the heart of Israel's own experience as the people of the Lord.

3. It is also the case that the other nations, including those with whom Israel has been at deep enmity, are the beneficiaries of the same kind of redemptive activity as delivered Israel from Egyptian slavery in the Exodus. Amos makes that very explicit:

> Did I not bring Israel up from the land of Egypt,
> and the Philistines from Caphtor
> and the Arameans from Kir?
>
> (Amos 9:7)

So also in one of the Isaianic oracles concerning the nations, the Egyptians are promised that "when they cry to the LORD because of oppressors, he will send them a savior, and will defend and deliver them" (Isa 19:20).

The covenant with Noah, therefore, has incorporated the whole creation, including the nations, in the blessing, the compassion, and the redemption of God arising out of the promise to maintain the creation. Mosaic covenant does not stand against that or mark out a special place for Israel. That raises the question, quite naturally, of what that covenant does mean for Israel if the Noachic covenant is the larger framework that both establishes a natural order as the matrix of human and historical existence, and creates the conditions for God's compassionate and redemptive activity to become available for "every living creature." It surely means that Israel, too, shall continue to benefit from the blessing, compassion, and redemption in covenantal relation with the Lord.[55] But there is a particular role that Israel is to play that is not necessarily a part of the universal covenant with the nations. That role is not given a uniform definition in the biblical literature. But it does seem to have to do with the nations, both implicitly and explicitly. Amos speaks of a special relation the Lord has with Israel: "You only have I known of all the families of the earth" (Amos 3:2). He seems to have in mind the election of Israel "to keep the way of the Lord by doing righteousness and justice," an election that is set in the context of the promise to bring blessing to Abraham that he and his seed after him may be the means of blessing for the nations (Gen 18:17-19).[56] To the extent that the servant in Deutero-Isaiah is to be understood as Israel, the way of justice is further indicated as an explicit task vis-à-vis the nations (Isa 42:1-4). But if for Amos, the covenantal relation means a way of righteousness and justice in the world, in Exod 19:3-6, that special covenantal role for Israel is to be the people who minister as a priesthood in the world, standing before the world in behalf of God and before God in behalf of the world. Later, Deutero-Isaiah will speak of this task also, but in different language: "I will give you as a light to the nations, that my salvation may reach to the ends of the earth" (Isa 49:6). Presumably, yet other definitions of that covenantal particularity may be identified. But it rests in an obedience that is in some sense quite purposeful and, whether Noachic, Abrahamic, or Mosaic, has to do with the manifestation of the divine promises for the nations as well as for Israel.

The horizon of creation and the horizon of covenant thus meet in various and often complex ways. That interaction is theologically complex but an accounting of it in biblical theology has been, and remains, a matter of no small urgency. It has to do not only with getting our theology straight, but with how to live in this world and with one another.

Chapter Nine / A SHATTERED TRANSCENDENCE? EXILE AND RESTORATION

Walter Brueggemann

The Exile—as event, experience, memory, and paradigm—looms large over the literature and faith of the Old Testament. Together with the restoration, the Exile emerged as the decisive shaping reference point for the self-understanding of Judaism.[1] Moreover, the power of exile and restoration as an imaginative construct exercised enormous impact on subsequent Christian understandings of faith and life as they were recast in terms of crucifixion and resurrection.

I

We may take as foundational for our theological reflection three propositions that are beyond dispute:

1. The Exile was indeed *a real historical experience* that can be located and understood in terms of public history.[2] It is clear that a considerable number of persons were deported by the Babylonians, though different accounts yield different results. In any case, much of the leadership of the community was deported. It is conventional to conclude that the sociopolitical situation of the exiles was not terribly difficult, though Smith has made a strong case for the notion that, in fact, the deported Jews in exile faced enormous hardship.[3]

2. While the actual number of persons exiled must have been relatively modest, the Exile as a theological datum became a governing paradigm for all successive Jewish faith.[4] That is, the experience, articulation, and memory of the Exile came to exercise influence upon the faith, imagination, and self-perception of Judaism quite disproportionate to its factual actuality. As a result, the Exile became definitional for all Jews, many of whom were never deported. Part of the reason that a modest historical fact became a dominant paradigm for self-understanding, no doubt can be understood in terms of the exercise of

social imagination and social power by the Jews who were in exile, who insisted upon and imposed their experience on Judaism as normative for all Jewishness. The community of the deported established ideological, interpretive hegemony in Judaism, insisting that its experience counted the most. Such a sociopolitical explanation, however, does not fully account for this interpretive turn in Judaism.

In addition to the interpretive authority of the exilic community in the political process, the intrinsic power and significance of the Exile must be acknowledged. Since the Mosaic articulation of covenantal faith, built as it is around stipulation and blessing and curse—an articulation appropriated in the prophetic tradition—Israel has been subject to the moral seriousness of its own covenantal-ethical enterprise. Thus the Exile required, power politics notwithstanding, construal in Israel in terms of those covenantal categories. As a result, the Exile is an event not only of historical displacement, but of profound moral, theological fracture.

That moral, theological fracture generated two primary responses. On the one hand, the paradigm of exile/restoration is concerned with the *moral failure* of Israel, so that exile is punishment and judgment from God. This is a dominant stream of "*golah* theology," voiced especially in the tradition of Deuteronomy. On the other hand, however, it is clear that the crisis of exile cannot be contained in the categories of covenantal sanctions. Thus there was also the posing of urgent questions concerning *the fidelity of God* that are more profound than a simple moral calculus of blessing and curse. These questions are voiced, for example, in the prophets, in the priestly tradition, and perhaps in Job. Thus the immediate questions of *moral symmetry* and the more subtle question of theological fidelity created a large arena for Israel's venturesome theological reflection.[5]

3. The experience and paradigmatic power of the Exile evoked in Israel a surge of theological reflection and *a remarkable production of fresh theological literature*.[6] The Exile decisively shattered the old, settled categories of Israel's faith. It did not, however, lead either to abandonment or despair.[7] Israel was driven to reflect on the moral, theological significance of exile. The characteristic tension between acknowledgment of shattering on the one hand, and the refusal of despair and abandonment on the other hand, required, permitted, and authorized in Israel daring theological energy which began to probe faith in wholly new categories which are daring and venturesome. Indeed, it is not an overstatement to say that exile became the matrix in which the canonical shape of OT faith is formed and evoked.[8] In that context, the old traditions are radically revamped and recharacterized,[9] and the theological process strikes out in quite fresh and inventive ways.

These three factors, historical experience, paradigmatic power, and inventive literary imagination, are crucial for recognizing the context of the Exile as decisive for shaping OT faith. These three factors, however, in and of themselves, do not constitute a theological probe. They are the context for such a probe. Our intention here is to push beyond historical-literary issues to theology proper.

II

The literary-historical-cultural aspects of the Exile have posed the general, overarching question of *continuity and discontinuity.* This rubric permits us to consider a number of subpoints in relation to the general problematic. The dominant Wellhausen paradigm for OT history and interpretation revolves around the question of continuity and discontinuity.[10] Wellhausen's powerful model insisted upon a significant discontinuity between the earlier faith of Israel and the later development of Judaism. It is not clear to what extent Wellhausen's model was designed to critique and even depreciate later Judaism, which he found inferior to earlier prophetic faith, nor is it clear to what extent that depreciation was either motivated by or served (unwittingly) a kind of anti-Semitism. In any case, very much critical Christian scholarship has regarded the emergent faith of the Jewish postexilic community as inferior, so that a clear line has been drawn from the earlier prophetic faith to the New Testament.[11]

Distinct from Wellhausen's powerful paradigm, none has thought more carefully and perceptively about the question of continuity and discontinuity than has Peter Ackroyd. In a series of four articles, Ackroyd has carefully and judiciously reflected on the crises of history and culture, and the powerful drive for continuity in the midst of the cultural, historical break.[12] Ackroyd has considered the ways in which cult objects (temple vessels), theological constructs, and reutilization of textual formulations have served the concern for continuity.[13] It does not surprise us that in the end Ackroyd concludes that continuity is the overriding reality for Judaism:

> The restoration and the destruction are all of a piece; discontinuity is resolved in the discovery of a continuity within it.[14]

There are two very different reasons why Ackroyd comes down on the side of continuity. First, there was in and through the Exile, a surviving continuity of vibrant Judaism as a community. As a historical fact, the Jews did indeed have continuity, and they claimed that continuity for themselves. Second, Ackroyd poses questions of social history; he is concerned with the community over time and through time. Moreover, Ackroyd is interested in institutional sociology, and therefore is attentive to the gestures, textual and otherwise, which sustain continuity. A historical critic could hardly entertain the notion of deep discontinuity, so that there is an inevitable bias toward continuity in our common work of criticism.

I do not at all suggest that Ackroyd has misconstrued the data, for his historical methods serve well to understand the community that lives in and through an ongoing tradition. I suggest, however, that Ackroyd's analysis has not, in fact, penetrated beyond cultural, institutional, community-generated continuities to the more difficult theological question, namely, what happened to God in the process of the Exile? Or to put the question more critically, what does the text say happened to God?

In putting the question in this way, a methodological acknowledgment is required. To do biblical theology, I suggest, requires us to leave off the kind of critical observation that stands outside the text, and to enter into the dynamic that operates inside the text and its claims. Or to put it differently, biblical theology, unlike historical criticism, requires us to approach the text more "realistically," as though this were indeed a word about God and about God's life, very often a word from God about God's life.[15] Such an approach may appear critically to be naive, but it is the only way we have to penetrate the difficulty of God's own life in the Exile.[16]

When we ask a theological question of the text, as distinct from a literary, historical, or sociological question, the issue of continuity and discontinuity takes on a different configuration. Whereas concerning literary, historical, and sociological questions, one can point to evident continuities that override discontinuities (as Ackroyd has done so well), a theological focus on the rendering of God's own person as a character in Israel's large drama of faith is not so unambiguously on the side of continuity. The texts attest that the Exile constituted a significant crisis in God's own life. As a character rendered in Israel's "covenantal discourse," as a character central to the plot of Israel's self-presentation, God is deeply impinged upon by the crisis of the Exile.[17] The theme of continuity asks whether the character of Yahweh continues to be the same character in, through, and beyond the Exile. The theme of discontinuity asks whether (and to what extent) the character of God is decisively changed by the crisis of exile, for example, if God ceases to be in some crucial way who this God was heretofore.

The evidence is not clear and consistent. The articulation of the text, nonetheless, makes clear that the displacement and suffering of exile breaks something of God's own self, both permitting and requiring Yahweh to be presented in a different way. It is clear that such a substantive theological argument depends upon a) the texts being taken as "realistic" speech about God, and b) the metaphor of personhood as the governing image, so that a rendering of the person of God in this drama is what is available to Israel (and derivatively, available to us). Clearly, there are in the Exile literary continuities through reused speech formulae, historical continuities through genealogy, and sociological continuities through cultic acts and gestures. These continuities, however, all appear to be organized to cope with the peculiar reality of discontinuity with which God struggles.

In putting the theological question in this way, I note two implications that more directly relate to Professor Beker's own work and writing. First the continuity/discontinuity of Israel's God in exile is a theological counterpart to the christological problematic in the NT concerning the relation of the "Jesus of history" to "the risen Christ."[18] The NT Church struggles to assert continuity in the person of Jesus through the events of Good Friday and Easter, but also must assert that in those events there is a decisive, transformative discontinuity in the person of Jesus. So it is as well concerning the God of Israel in the Exile.

Second, Beker's own poignant and remarkable discussion of suffering and hope is a reflection on the power of hope in the midst of suffering.[19] Beker's mode of expression asserts that hope confronts and overrides suffering. An alternative model might be that hope arises precisely in and through suffering. In either case, the life of the God of Israel in the midst of exile, a life of suffering in solidarity, and of powerful resolve against displacement, is a life which struggles for continuity in the brokenness. I mention this connection to Beker's work in order to suggest that the question I pose is an intensely practical issue, for Israel sees through this crisis of God how real suffering is, how seriously suffering is taken, and how suffering impinges even upon the life of God, both to shatter something old in God's own life, and to evoke something utterly new in God's life.[20] cf his note!

I have selected three texts from different exilic sources which explore different dimensions of the way in which God is voiced.[21] To be sure, one can understand the different voices in these texts critically, such as, to explain their different theological claims by referring to the literary, historical sources. But if one is theologically "realistic," the diverse voicings evidence the struggle in God's life over the way God will be God in the face of such a crisis.

III

The critical problems concerning the history and unity of the first text, Deut 4:23-31, are considerable.[22] They are made more complex by the dominant judgment of two redactions by the Deuteronomistic tradition.[23] Specifically vv. 29-31 are widely judged to be a secondary redaction.[24] Thus the text may be composite. In any case, the entire passage as it stands reflects a concern about the Exile. Verse 26 speaks of "utterly perish from the land," and v. 27 of "scatter." The phrase "from there" (v. 29) no doubt refers to exile, so that the text as we have it advances from a warning about exile (vv. 23-28) to a situation in exile and an anticipation after exile (vv. 29-31). And if vv. 29-31 are indeed an intrusion, as critical study has concluded, then they are an intrusion reflective of God's new exilic situation.

In this sustained and extended speech, Moses traces a remarkable move in the character of Yahweh. Put concisely, Moses voices Yahweh *before* exile and *after* exile around the geographical/temporal reference to "from there" (v. 29). Prior to "from there," Israel is not yet "there," not yet in exile, nor is Yahweh yet addressed "from there." Prior to exile, Mosaic Israel is defined by the demands, sanctions, and warnings of Sinai. The burden of the speech of Moses is that attentiveness to the Torah is the condition for remaining in the land (vv. 25-26). The theological dimension of this preexilic warning is that Yahweh is "a devouring fire, a jealous God" (v. 24), a God who will brook no rival and tolerate no disobedience. The entire warning and urgency of Moses grows out of the character of Yahweh, a God who is uncompromising about demand. Thus the ominous warning of Moses is appropriate to preexilic Israel and grows from the jealousy of Yahweh.

Were the character of Yahweh sustained into exile in continuity, we would expect Israel, in exile and beyond exile, to continue to deal with a jealous, uncompromising God. The God who is available "from there," however, is not the devouring God from preexile. In the middle of the text, in the middle of Israel's experience, and we may believe, in the middle of God's life with Israel, there is a new "there"—exile. When Moses continues his testimony about the God with whom Israel has to deal, everything is changed. Of course one may say that this change reflects layers in the redactional process, and therefore different theological perspectives. Or the change may only reflect the pastoral emergency of the Exile when the producers of theological literature said something different to meet new needs. If, however, we are to do theology, what emerges in the text is a real break in God's way with Israel, such as a real break in God's way of being God. Now there is no more talk of devouring fire and jealous God. Now Moses speaks of a "merciful God" (v. 31). The *'el qannā'* (v. 24) has become the *'el rahum* (v. 31); the one who scattered in anger is the one who will not forget covenant.

There is, of course, continuity in this God to whom Moses bears witness. If one follows the rhetorical pattern of the text, however, there is also a discernible discontinuity in the move from *'el qannā'* to *'el rahum.* This God who keeps the same name has ceased to be, so far as the text is concerned, a jealous, devouring God and has now become a God of compassion. Of course one may conclude simply that one need not say everything about God in every sentence, and that the God of Israel has all along been *'el qannā'* and *'el rahum.* That, however, is not the way the text works. I submit, rather, that in this one text, the voice of Moses expresses a profound break in the character of God, and that break makes visible the emergence of a God of compassion whom Yahweh has not been before in this text, an emergence evoked by the Exile.

Thus we may provisionally suggest that as hope arises in the midst of suffering, hope that did not heretofore exist, so the mercy of God is evoked, formed, and articulated just here. The formal reality of discontinuity permits a substantive assertion of compassion. And if one follows Trible's notion of compassion as "womb-like mother love,"[25] then the Exile becomes the place where the character of God turns in a quite fresh direction.

IV

Perhaps the most remarkable text for our theme is Isa 54:7-10. Having just utilized the metaphor of a wife (Israel) deserted by her husband (Yahweh; vv. 4-6), the poem asserts the restoration of the relationship when the husband takes a fresh initiative to restore the relation. Within this metaphor, the husband makes two quite distinct assertions, each reiterated in a parallelism. First, "I forsook you" ('azabtik), "I hid my face" (histarti).[26] Second, "I will gather you" ('qabbesēk), "I will have compassion" (rihamtik).[27] The contrast of the husband's two moves are: abandon/gather; hide/have compassion.

Three interpretive questions may be posed about these assertions: Was the abandonment a real abandonment? Was the absence a real absence? Did God in truth abandon covenant partner Israel? The wording of the poem is candid and unambiguous. The abandonment is real and complete, without qualification.

Such an assertion is difficult when there is a felt need to claim that God's resolve is unbreakable, for example, when continuity is stressed in every circumstance.[28] Thus John Calvin seeks to find a way around the clear statement of the text in the interest of continuity:

> When he says that he *forsook* his people, it is a sort of admission of the fact. . . . What the prophet says in this passage must therefore refer to our feelings and to outward appearance, because we seem to be rejected by God when we do not perceive his presence and protection. And it is necessary that we should thus feel God's wrath, even as a wife divorced by her husband deplores her condition, that we may know that we are justly chastised. But we must also perceive his mercy; and because it is infinite and eternal, we shall find that all afflictions in comparison are light and momentary.[29]

Such a reading, however, clearly goes against the wording of the text itself. Serious theology is placed in jeopardy when texts are, in this way, explained away. Calvin's comment is an example of the way in which a concern for theological continuity (transcendence) wants to outflank and override the text.

In the face of postwar tragedy in Europe, Kornelis Miskotte voices a much more sober reading of the text, directed against an interpretative posture like that of Calvin:

> The very first thing that is said here makes it clear that this situation actually cannot be understood on the two-dimensional level of experience and its interpretation

175

[so Calvin]. It is a real abandonment. And those who did not recognize and understand it as an actual abandonment by God are now compelled to hear it proclaimed as God's own word. It was an actual abandonment by God. Without this proclamation of the (partially recognized and partially unrecognized) abandonment by God, the prophetic word is not in the full sense the word of God. He scattered the people, he hid his face from them. The fact is that we have actually lived under the condition of this act; but it is only the Word that reveals to us that it is an act of God.[30]

Miskotte's reading poses much more difficult theological questions than does the reading of Calvin, but it surely is more faithful to the text. The poem asserts a profound discontinuity without qualifications, as Israel's condition vis-à-vis God. All transcendental guarantees about God are shattered; God's goodness in Israel is decisively broken. It is instructive that it is Miskotte's European experience of discontinuity that both permitted and required a radical rereading of the text.

The break in abandonment and anger is "for a brief moment" (*rega;* vv. 7-8). We may ask, as Israel must have asked, how long is a *rega* ? The word suggests that while the abandonment by God was total and without qualification, it was only for an instant. Or we may reverse the proposition: the abandonment was only for an instant, but long enough for it to be massive, total, and decisive. The other uses of *rega* do not illuminate us very much because they are the same appeal to brevity, but to decisiveness.[31] That is "a moment" is long enough for a total inversion or transformation. I suggest that in this word as it is used here, we are at the crux of the issue of discontinuity and continuity for Israel in exile. The time span of the break interests us because we wonder if it was so brief that the carryover of God's commitment still prevails.

In considering "for a moment," perhaps an analogy will aid us. The moment of God's abandonment is like the effect the breaking of an electrical circuit has on a digital clock. The breaking of the circuit may be only for an instant. To my unscientific observation, it appears that sometimes the circuit breaks briefly when the power goes off, but not so long as to disrupt the time reporting of the clock. The clock continues to function through the brief break in power. At other times, or with other clocks, the seemingly same disruption of current does break the functioning of the clock, and it must be reset. In both cases the break is "for a moment," but in one case continuity persists, and in the other it does not. Thus the "instant" of circuit breaking is a delicate one, and one does not know when a clock (or one clock rather than another) will be disconnected and cease to function accurately.

In like manner, this poem, I suggest, intends us to focus our theological attention on the instant of the breaking of God's loyal love. We are left by the poem to ponder whether the "breaking of the circuit" of God's faithfulness precludes the continued function of the covenantal commitment of God. It is for Israel a close call; whether or not the current leaps the break for Yahweh determines continuity or discontinuity for Israel. This poem deliberately lodges the entire issue of continuity and discontinuity on the freight of one word, a word so delicate we cannot decide precisely. Thus the hard verb "abandon" is set next to the adverb "for a moment," and there the matter rests. The verb in the end is more decisive than the adverb. The husband did indeed abandon the wife in wrath; but it was only for an instant, "a twinkling of an eye."[32] It was enough of a circuit break to cut the connection, briefly, but decisively.

This double statement of the acknowledgment of real abandonment by God is followed with a counter theme introduced by an adversative conjunction:

> but with great compassion I will gather you . . .
> but with everlasting love I will have compassion on you,
> says the LORD, your Redeemer. (vv. 7-8)

Miskotte comments on the "reverse" of the rejection:

> This at the same time reveals that this word is a saving word—by reason of the fact that the event [for example, the Exile] is now past and is no longer the ultimate truth about our condition. . . . Therefore the church must be all the more aware of the reverse side of this truth, namely, that grace, which is the annulment of judgment, confirms and corroborates the judgment as God's judgment. In the multidimensional realm of his freedom, God does not arbitrarily pass from one to the other, from yes to no, from rejection to acceptance. He resists the resistance. He breaks the rebellion by breaking his own heart.[33]

Abandonment, wrath, and *hiddenness* are countered by *steadfast love, compassion,* and *redeemer.*

Because of the adverb ʿolām, we may inquire about the relation of the negative and affirmative triads. When ʿolām is rendered "everlasting," we might conclude that God's hesed was at all times operative, for example, before, during, and after the abandonment. On that reading, the abandonment by the husband does not cut deeply, and an underlying continuity is affirmed in spite of the hiddenness of God's face (so Calvin). An alternative reading, however, does not regard the qualifying ʿolām as mercy before and during, but only after the abandonment. Thus the relation of rejection and embrace is not an ongoing parallelism whereby hesed denies ultimate seriousness to abandonment, but the two are sequential. Hesed arises out of, after, and in response to the rejections, so that hesed stands on the other side of the discontinuity, and not in powerful opposition to the discontinuity. Thus the "everlastingness" of ʿolām is into the future, but not through the past of Israel's exile.

Thus we may answer our three interpretive questions: 1. The abandonment is real and not only "seems" so; 2. The abandonment is *for an instant,* but long

177

enough to matter decisively; and 3. The promised *hesed* is *after and in response to* the abandonment, and not in its midst as an antidote. The upshot of this reading is that there is discontinuity in God's own resolve for Israel, a discontinuity that evokes, permits, and requires a new response by the compassionate God who is redeemer.

This reading of discontinuity is sustained by the following lines in vv. 9-10. "This[the Exile] is like the days of Noah" (RSV).[34] God swears "from wrath" *(miqṣop)* and from "rebuking" *(migʿār)*, as Yahweh "swore that waters would not again pass over the earth" (cf. Gen 8:21-22, 9:11). In the analogue of the Flood, it is clear that the promise in Genesis is a promise that it will not happen "again"; it is a promise *after* the Flood which precludes its replication.[35] There was a real flood, a real release of chaos, a real abandonment of the earth which left creation bereft of God's protective care. Thus in the flood story, the promise and assurance do not persist through the Flood, but come in sequence after the discontinuity of the Flood.[36] The analogue supports our reading vv. 7-8 as a statement of deep discontinuity, with the same "again" implied; that is, the exile of abandonment will not happen again, as it manifestly has happened this time.

The sequencing of abandonment and compassion in v. 10 is not a denial of recently experienced discontinuity, but an assurance against future discontinuity. Mountains and hills are juxtaposed to God's *hesed* and *berît sālom*.[37] Now in light of the promise, God's compassionate resolve is more reliable than the ordering of creation. That assurance is given and received post-Flood, post-Exile, postabandonment. Thus out of the massive discontinuity of chaos (flood, exile), God arrives at a new, overriding resolve for fidelity and compassion which wells up out of the discontinuity. The husband who has abandoned now embraces. The God who has been wrathful acts in compassion. The relation that has been breached is now solidified. Out of discontinuity comes a profound decree of continuity, after the discontinuity. The text exhibits no interest in and makes no comment on how it is that the newness arises out of, from, and in the midst of the break. The movement of this sequence is not unlike the sequence we have found in Deut 4:23-31; in Isa 54:7-10, it is from wrath to compassion; in Deut 4:23-31, it is from jealousy to compassion. The situation of exile features a profound recharacterization of God.

V

The cosmic reference of Isa 54:10 which contrasts "mountains and hills" with "steadfast love and covenant of peace" leads us to our third text, Jer 31:35-37. These verses immediately follow the new covenant passage (vv. 31-34). The announcement of "new covenant" appears to accent the discontinuity between the new covenant and the old covenant which it is not like (v. 32). Indeed, the

178

dominant tendency of the Jeremiah tradition is to accent the discontinuity of exile. Oddly, vv. 35-37, immediately following, are a stunning statement of continuity. These verses counter the main tendency of Jeremiah and make a high claim of continuity. Whereas Isa 54:10 acknowledges that the structures of creation may indeed "depart" *(mos)* and "be removed" *(mot)* in this text it is assumed that the "fixed order" of creation will not "depart" *(mos)*.[38] In Isa 54:10, God's *hesed* to Israel is more reliable than creation; in this text, God's guarantee of Israel "all the days" is as assured as the fixed order of creation which is utterly assured. Thus the argument on the same subject, to make the same claim, is stated very differently. Whereas Isa 54:10 moves beyond the experience of discontinuity to make its claim,[39] our verses appeal to the experience of continuity to make a similarly large claim.

This assertion of utter continuity is not one we expect in Jeremiah. It is as though the tradition cannot finally settle the matter of continuity and discontinuity. Each time it makes an assertion, it must follow with a counter assertion. As a result, even in the Jeremiah tradition, preoccupied as it is with discontinuity, there is added this counter voice that insists that God's guarantee of Israel is not and cannot be disrupted.[40] The ostensive protasis-apodosis structure of the passage, twice voiced, appears to be governed by a conditional "if"; the rhetoric, in fact, denies any conditionality (against the grain of Jeremiah), and assumes an unconditional relation between God and Israel. In this text, even the Exile allows no disruption in Israel's life with God because of God's steadfast love and fidelity. Unlike Isa 54:7-8, Israel's partner does not abandon and does not act in wrath.

VI

We may take these three texts, Deut 4:21-23, Isa 54:7-10, and Jer 31:35-37, as representative of the theological reflection evoked by the Exile. These three disclosures together suggest that the issue of continuity and discontinuity was for Israel an urgent issue, one that admitted of no simple or settled solution. Four observations arise from this analysis:

1. While the historical, sociopolitical dimension of the Exile is hardly in doubt, the Exile cannot be treated simply as a historical problem concerning the continuity of the community. The Exile is *a deep problem for the character of Yahweh,* as well as the community of Israel. Thus exile constitutes a profound theological problem and must be treated theologically as a crisis for God. The texts we have considered are all decrees in the mouth of God, for example, disclosures of a moment in God's own life which cannot be explained simply as a historical or sociological issue.

2. The theological crisis that these texts enunciate and with which they struggle is that *the transcendence of God is placed in deep jeopardy* by the Exile. From this it follows that even God's abiding commitment to Israel is at risk, impinged

179

upon by the reality of the Exile. It is our common theological propensity, as indicated by Calvin, to exempt God from such jeopardy, to imagine that at bottom, Israel's God is not subject to the terms of the historical process. Such transcendentalism, of course, offers assurance, but must necessarily refuse to take either the text or Israel's experience of exile with real seriousness. These texts entertain the thought that God is radically vulnerable to the realities of Israel's life.

In making this affirmation, Israel breaks with magisterial "common theology" that reduces God to a part of a fixed, predictable retribution system.[41] Such a "common theology" cannot countenance the Exile as a crisis for God, and cannot entertain the stunning affirmation concerning God's own life which emerges in the midst of such jeopardized transcendence.

3. The texts assert the jeopardy of transcendence but cannot finally adjudicate the extent or depth of that jeopardy. That is, the texts refuse to come down cleanly either for continuity or discontinuity. In each case the text tends to counter the tradition in which it is embedded. Deuteronomy 4, which ends in compassion "from there," counters the familiar "theology of command" featured in Deuteronomy. Isaiah 54 is embedded in the vibrant affirmation of exilic Israel, but pauses over God's radical abandonment in the Exile (cf. 40:2). The affirmation of continuity in Jer 31:35-37 lives in tension with the Jeremianic inclination to discontinuity. In this way, the texts keep the question of the jeopardy of God's life with Israel delicately open. Every tilted statement is promptly corrected by a counterstatement, thus permitting no statement to be a final one. Israel's way of doing theology, or more fundamentally, God's act of self-disclosure, bespeaks a profound and ambiguous lack of closure that resists every systematic closure.

4. The texts *move toward God's compassion.* This is true more directly of Deuteronomy 4 and Isaiah 54 than of Jeremiah 31, but see Jer 30:18, 31:20, 33:26. Indeed, God's compassion seems to be the primary and powerful theological emergent of the Exile. The exile evokes new measures and fresh depths of compassion in the character of God. Taken pastorally, the articulation of God's compassion is a humanly needed assurance. Taken theologically, the Exile evokes in God a new resolve for fidelity, a resolve that was not operative prior to the hurt and dread of the Exile.[42] That resolve on God's part is, to be sure, seeded in old texts (cf. Exod 34:6-7); the Exile, however, provides a rich array of texts voicing this newly central and newly appreciated theological datum. The Exile permits God to become toward Israel whom God was not.[43] The fresh characterization of God seems to arise, inexplicably, but freely in, through, and out of exile. The tone of God's speech toward Israel is dramatically transformed through this terrible jeopardy, a jeopardy that God shares with Israel.

VII

The Exile is the moment in the history of Israel and in the life of God when an irreversibly new theological datum is introduced in the horizon of faith. In conclusion, I suggest three dimensions of our interpretive work which are impinged upon by this theological reality emerging in exile:

1. The paradigm of "exile and restoration," which has as its theological counterpart God's abandonment and God's new compassion, provides crucial and decisive categories for understanding the crucifixion and resurrection of Jesus and the NT "*dialectic of reconciliation.*"[44] While trinitarian theology has opened a variety of ways of getting from Friday to Sunday,[45] the typology of exile suggests

  a. that the abandonment of God is real and decisive, albeit brief, and

  b. that the God who is evidenced in Easter is decisively different from the God who abandons and is abandoned on Friday.

The theological reality of the Exile warns against any protective transcendentalism in the midst of the failure of God's life with Israel and Israel's life with God.[46] Thus NT theology might take more seriously this paradigm which comes to govern the imagination of Judaism, as a way of reflecting upon the abandonment of Jesus and the rule of the risen Christ.

2. The new theological datum of exile impinges upon the crisis of modernity and postmodernity in theology. There is in the Exile a decisive disclosure of God that should warn us against certain theological temptations. Three aspects of our crisis occur to me in this connection.

  a. Much theological work has been a search for universals, an attempt to articulate "truth" that lies outside the concrete experience and testimony of the confessing community.[47] Against every such universal, the claims of the biblical God come down to particular moments of embrace and abandonment, to particular verses of texts, and to particular moments (*rega*) of crisis. More than anywhere else in the OT, in the Exile Israel faces "the scandal of particularity" in all its pathos. Such an exilic voicing of God stands powerfully against any would-be universals.

  b. Much of theology, particularly as voiced in conventional confessional traditions, has sought to voice God in transcendental categories which leave God freed from, and untouched by, the vagaries of historical discontinuity. The disclosure of God in these exilic texts refuses such a posture and allows no certitudes about God out beyond the jeopardy of discontinuity.

  c. The moral propensity of modernity is ragingly enacted in the brutality expressed in technological categories, most dramatically (but not exclusively) in the Holocaust. It may indeed be that the Exile is no adequate paradigm for the technological brutality quintessentially expressed in the Holocaust;[48] nonetheless we are the generation that has witnessed massive hurt generated through technological strategies that bespeak the power of death and the absence of God. The technological production of massive pain makes all our conventional theology open to questions, and drives us to the more elemental categories of God's presence and absence, God's abandonment and reemergence.[49] In the exilic texts, human failure evokes God's absence and abandon-

181

ment; *mutatis mutandis,* our shameless linkage of brutality and technology may evoke a moral calculus that requires God's absence. It may, however, be that same shameless linkage of brutality and absence that evokes God's reemergence in a fresh posture. In, with, and under the brutality and pain, God emerges anew as the generator of human possibility.[50] The new theological data of exile has much to teach us about our current theological situation, much that we should already have learned but did not.

3. The importance of the new theological data of the Exile not only offers decisive material for the shaping of NT theology and crucial illumination of a substantive kind for our current theological task. Its major offer to us is the suggestion of new ways of doing theology in poetic, narrative forms that eschew conventional modes of discourse, that offer God as a speaker in the poetry, a character in the narrative plot, a God who moves in and through terrible disjunctions to newness. Thus the rhetoric of these texts shapes God's own life with Israel

a. "From there" (Deut 4:29),

b. "but . . . but," (Isa 54:7-8), and

c. "if . . . then, if . . . then" (Jer 31:35-37).

Such a way of theology is concrete, particular, and inherently subversive of every settlement, spilling over from daring rhetoric into public reality, where exiles must live and trust.

It is a delight to join in congratulations to Chris Beker and in expressing gratitude for his work. His own study, marked by pain, candor, and hope, is a model for doing exilic theology which mediates new possibility. Our common work in OT, NT, and systematic theology now is gathered around new questions, new modes of discourse, and new public possibilities. If we are able to get beyond ourselves, we may discern clues in our own "break point," that God's old transcendence is at risk, and that God may make new compassion-shaped resolves. Both God's risk and God's new compassion-shaped resolve refuse and resist domestication, either through our certitude or through our despair.

Chapter Ten / WISDOM LITERATURE AND EXPERIENCE OF THE DIVINE

Kathleen M. O'Connor

Introduction

Aspects of Wisdom literature that in the past caused it to be ignored by biblical theologians are the very features of the literature that are provoking its rediscovery today. Wisdom's preference for daily concerns of human existence, for example, its attention to creation, its depictions of God as mysterious and elusive—perspectives that once kept wisdom on the edges of historically oriented biblical theology—now seem to provide essential theological resources for a postcolonial, postmodern world.

Criticisms of Old Testament theologies based primarily on historical and prophetic books are emerging from many communities around the globe today. Interpreters with new perspectives, working self-consciously within previously unrecognized social contexts, object to theologies that portray divine human relationships in categories of domination and subordination, that portray God in exclusively male language, and that emphasize Israel's election and sense of difference from the nations.[1] Some find these theological perceptions to be so inadequate for contemporary contexts that they advocate abandoning the Bible altogether as a basis for Christian theologies.

This essay proposes that the Wisdom literature (Proverbs, Job, Ecclesiastes, and the Deuterocanonical or Apocryphal books of Ben Sirach and Wisdom of Solomon) contains alternative theological visions that can modify and expand traditional OT theologies to meet some of these challenges. This is not to suggest, of course, that the Wisdom literature escapes cultural assumptions of the ancient Near East so as to be directly relevant to contemporary concerns. It is to claim, instead, that emphases and orientations of this literature reflect different experiences of life and of God from the prophetic and historical books. It is Wisdom's expression of these different experiences that enable it to provide alternative theological witnesses for contemporary appropriation.

After beginning with a brief methodological discussion, this essay describes broad theological currents of Wisdom literature that expand and challenge historically oriented biblical theologies. The essay then turns to an investigation of personified Wisdom in the book of Proverbs to show that personified Wisdom is a symbolic expression of Israel's experience of God that emerges from the nation's own theological process of mythmaking. The essay arises from feminist debate and its search for alternative understandings of God and of human relationships that include and liberate.

Methodological Considerations

To be commensurate with the literature from which it arises, biblical theology must not only retrieve language, symbols, and fruitful analogies to serve the contemporary community in its search for God. It must also uncover experiences of God expressed in the text and the rhetorical purposes hidden in the text, and present them to modern readers in contemporary terms. These requirements arise from the nature and function of literature.

Sean McEvenue observes that literature functions to create vicarious experience for its readers.[2] Presenting more than ideas and information, literature re-creates life. Its appeal extends beyond so-called rational capacities of readers to address, as well, affective and imaginative capabilities. In this way it invites readers to experience for themselves realities encoded in the text. In Paul Ricoeur's terms, literature creates symbolic words that readers enter, worlds "thick with meaning," where more is experienced than can be articulated or comprehended and where language communicates something of the original experience.[3]

The interplay of all the elements that compose a piece of literature, its language, structure, and voice, contribute to its recreation of experience in an artistic unity.[4] Biblical theology, therefore, must concern itself with the whole of a literary piece in order to recover something of that original experience,[5] because it is the experience expressed by a text that gives it power to change people, to alter and inflame imagination, and thus, to affect behavior. But if literature is artistic creation, it, nonetheless, does not exist in an aesthetic realm apart from history. Literature, and biblical literature in particular, has social functions: it is designed to persuade, to provoke, and to influence its "implied readers" toward behavior in concrete social and historical situations,[6] even though those situations are not always recoverable.

This means that historical-critical analysis is required for interpreting biblical literature and, thus, for biblical theology. Because biblical texts are ancient documents, reading them is a cross-cultural act. Historical-critical tools enable readers to make the imaginative leap across cultures required to enter the world created by any ancient text.[7] Biblical theology, however, cannot limit itself to historical inquiry, nor to abstract summaries or paraphrases of texts. Its task includes consideration of both the whole of a text in order to grasp the experiences it articulates, and the responses it hopes to motivate. It must not only attend to what texts explicate but also to what they imply, and perhaps what they omit, as it seeks to uncover that "surplus of meaning" that dwells in a text and to understand its rhetorical and ideological purposes.[8]

This essay explores contributions of Wisdom literature to biblical theology by articulating some ways wisdom communicates Israel's experience of God. It looks not for themes and doctrines, but for expectancies, assumptions, and perspectives; what I call "broad theological currents," implicit in the text that reveal something of the experience of God that the texts communicate.

Some Theological Currents of the Wisdom Literature

Revelation in Ordinary Life. According to the Wisdom literature, experience of God occurs in daily existence, in the quotidian struggles, doubts, and joys of life. It is these that reveal God,[9] not primarily the heroic, miraculous, or broadly political as in the historical and prophetic books. Wisdom's elevation of ordinary life is not expressed in an explicit or thematic way; it is implied and understood throughout the literature.

The sayings in the book of Proverbs, for example, address daily concerns, decisions, and the interactions of mundane human existence, such as relationships in the community and how to live a full human life. Proverbs' introductory chapters (1–9) do not contradict this direction but sharpen it into a choice to be made in the marketplaces of human life (Prov 1:20, 8:1) between life and death, between wisdom and folly.

Similarly, the book of Job explores, from many perspectives, problems of human suffering and the possibility of finding God in the midst of that suffering. And though it seems likely that Job symbolizes exiled and restored Israel, the book creates the world of one individual concerned with domestic and local matters. The book of Ecclesiastes, likewise, ignores historical narratives to investigate the value of human work and the limits of human knowledge, and it advises readers to live daily life with gusto.

Even the Greek books of Ben Sirach and Wisdom of Solomon give primary attention to daily concerns. Ben Sirach's instructions recapitulate and develop the instructions of Proverbs, and Wisdom of Solomon provides guidance for living in righteousness and gaining wisdom. When these two books do turn to historical reflections, it is to bring historical traditions under the aegis of Wisdom.

Wisdom's assumption that the locus of divine revelation is daily existence does not deny the significance of the historical and political, for daily life is historical life, but it broadens theological horizons to include within the sacred the lives of ordinary people, intimate human relationships, domestic life, and the routine labor that "maintains the fabric of the world" (Sir 38:34).[10]

Openness to Humanity. The historical and prophetic books focus Israel's attention inward, on Israel's election and particularity, and thereby create Israel's identity over against other peoples, an identity based on what Paul Beauchamp calls "un principe de difference."[11] The Wisdom literature, by contrast, implicitly turns from a sense of Israel's difference to reach outward. Its spirit is ecumenical, moving beyond a sense of nationalism toward a recognition of its common citizenship in the world.

Personified Wisdom, for example, addresses a broad audience, not the chosen, not Israel, but the "simple," all who have not yet become wise (Prov 1:22, 1:32, 8:5, 9:4). Job is a great wise man from the East, an Edomite, not an Israelite, and both his human predicament and its resolution resonate across cultures and faiths. Similarly Qoheleth ignores specific questions of Israel's faith to investigate the meaning of any human life. The absence of typical categories of Israelite religious thought in the wisdom books, and the inclusion of characters and audiences other than Israelite, imply a change in social condition for the Israelite community. But more important for this study, they suggest a theological shift in which Israel comes to express its experience of God as the God of all peoples.

By contrast, the works of Ben Sirach and Wisdom of Solomon assume that Israel received unique revelation. Nonetheless, these two books create a conversation between Greek wisdom and Jewish wisdom.[12] Neither book abandons a sense of Israel's chosen status, but both borrow from Hellenist culture, accept its questions, and attempt to dialogue with its wisdom.[13] The Wisdom books, therefore, lead outward in the direction of dialogue and respect for the cultures and beliefs of others. They are characterized by an "openness that permits a real recognition of the other and a positive evaluation of otherness,"[14] and they provide a beginning for a biblical theology that challenges tribalism and triumphalism.

The Ungraspable Deity. The primary concern of the Wisdom books is not God but the struggles of human life. These books come around to God almost reluctantly, but when they do speak of God, they do not contradict the historical and prophetic books. Rather they express their experiences of God in different terms. Generally they avoid depictions of God in judicial, royal, or political language. They do not imagine God as an intervening deity, a *deus ex machina* who steps in to fix history's chaos. They prefer, instead, to speak of God in the role of Creator. But even this characterization withholds as much as it reveals.

When the passages about personified Wisdom (Prov 8:22-31, Ben Sirach 24, Wisdom of Solomon 7–9) refer to God's work of creation, for example, their purpose is to establish Wisdom's antiquity and authority rather then to explore God's creative deeds.[15] The sayings in Proverbs also assume God's creative role without exploring it (Prov 14:3, 16:4, 16:11, 17:5, 20:12, 22:2, 29:13), and

Ecclesiastes declares outright that creation is impenetrable to human probing (1:2-11). Only when God speaks from the storm in the book of Job (38:1–42:6) does the Creator's activity receive expansion; yet even here God remains beyond Job's grasp. God's creative actions reveal the breadth of divine care of the cosmos and its inhabitants, including Job, but they also obscure solutions to Job's dilemma, neither addressing his suffering nor answering his questions. And although God remains free of restriction and is respectful of human freedom,[16] the book of Job expresses an experience of a deity who remains veiled by the vastness of creation.

Even as it insists on God's transcendence and incomprehensibility, however, the Wisdom literature also portrays God in immanent and intimate terms when it speaks of personified Wisdom. It is the thesis of this essay that Israel came to articulate its experience of ancient Near Eastern Wisdom as an encounter with God, not some foreign deity, but its own God, symbolized by the figure of personified Wisdom. In this interpretation, Wisdom is not merely a literary device, nor a personification of order in creation, nor an hypostasis of an aspect of God; she is Wise-God, Israel God. She is the personification of God's own wisdom, a mytho-poetic expression of divinity that both complements and challenges depictions of God found elsewhere in the Hebrew Bible.

Wisdom as Experience of God

With few exceptions, biblical scholarship has not identified Wisdom with God.[17] It is true that the majority of interpreters have placed Wisdom in the transcendent mythological sphere, but they have preferred to view her either as a hypostasis of a quality of God or as a goddess borrowed from a neighboring religion and demoted to serve as a subordinate to Yahweh, rather than a symbol of God in her own right.[18]

By contrast, recent sociological interpretations perceive Wisdom as a product of social impulses within Israel that drew upon the lives of historical women for their imagery. Joseph Blenkinsopp, for one, claims that Wisdom and her opposite, Stranger Woman, were created during the Persian period to discourage exogamous marriage among returned exiles.[19] Claudia Camp,[20] whose theory has gained wide acceptance, claims that social forces propelled the transformation of female imagery into the exalted figure of Wisdom. These forces included renewed emphasis on the home in the postexilic period, the consequent elevation of the status of women, and the need for a mediator between God and the people to replace the defunct monarchy.

However, neither mythological nor sociological interpretations of Wisdom are fully adequate. Mythological readings generally view Wisdom as an anomaly in Israelite faith, an adopted alien goddess whose power was controlled by subordinating her to YHWH, even though there is no consensus regarding the identity of this original goddess. Sociological interpretations are no more successful because, in order to join Wisdom to the lives of real women, they have had to suppress goddess imagery and mythological features of the texts. There is, however, a third position that both accounts for the text's mythological nature and understands Wisdom as the product of creative theological thinking within Israel.

In studying the influence of Wisdom on early Christology, Elisabeth Schüssler Fiorenza[21] speculates that Israelite personification of Wisdom resulted from a mode of theological thinking that she calls "reflective mythology," a theological process by which a community "appropriates a living myth," adapts and develops it for its own purposes to create a new myth.[22] According to this proposal, personified Wisdom gained prominence in Israel as a genuinely transformed myth to meet the crisis of the goddess that confronted Israel in the Hellenist period.

Richard J. Clifford believes that personified Wisdom appeared in Israel as early as the seventh century BCE, as part of a polemic against Canaanite religion.[23] Martin Hengel also proposes that Wisdom appeared to meet the crisis caused by neighboring Wisdom goddesses, but he proposes dating Proverbs 1–9 in the early Hellenistic period.[24] Given the international character of Israelite wisdom literature, it is not unreasonable to imagine that such a process of "reflective mythology" began in Israel in the Persian period or perhaps even earlier as a theological response to threats created by competition from neighboring Wisdom goddesses, but there is insufficient data to decide the matter of dating with any firmness.

Besides both allowing for creative theological thinking within Israel and giving due attention to the texts, the hypothesis that Wisdom arose through Israel's theological reflection on neighboring myths to become a new myth also accounts for another aspect of the biblical passages. It helps to explain why earlier poems about her, notably the poems in Proverbs, are more subtle in identifying her with God, whereas later texts in Sirach and Wisdom of Solomon do so more directly.[25] Wisdom emerged in Israel through a long process of struggle and reflection, as the community slowly came to understand its experience of Wisdom as an experience of its own God. Wisdom, therefore, was not incorporated into Israel's religion as an alien deity but developed as an indigenous product of Israel's struggle to understand God in light of international Wisdom.

Feminists have resisted interpretations of Wisdom as divine because some believe that recognizing Wisdom's divinity also requires accepting her as subordinate to a male God.[26] Feminist suspicion is completely appropriate. Both Wisdom Woman and Stranger Woman are male creations that project onto women all that is good and bad in human nature. As stereotypes they harm women by failing to represent them as human beings, and they also misrepresent men by portraying them as helpless victims of preying females. Despite these difficulties, however, personified Wisdom transcends her patriarchal origins precisely because she is not representative of historical women, nor is she ultimately subordinated to YHWH; she is a symbol of God. Whereas Strange Woman dies a literary death, never reappearing in the texts after Proverbs 9, Wisdom takes on a life of her own, developing in biblical tradition, becoming increasingly identified with God, and standing as God in the world (Sirach 24, Wisdom of Solomon 7–9). What follows is an exegetical investigation of passages that personify Wisdom in the book of Proverbs (1:20-31, 3:13-18, 8:1-21, 8:22-31, 9:1-6, 31:10-31). Lack of space prevents a related investigation of Wisdom's portrayal in the Greek books of Ben Sirach and Wisdom of Solomon.

Wisdom in Proverbs

Ultimately poetic portrayals of Wisdom imply that she is God, not merely an aspect or quality of God, but a symbol and an expression of God; she is Wise-God. As symbol, Wisdom provokes readers' imaginations by means of suggestion, association, and relationships. She is a separate being that partakes of the reality that she symbolizes, so that ultimately she is indistinguishable from the Creator. She is what Ricoeur would call a "category mistake,"[27] that combines female and deity to say something new about God and that seeks to evoke devotion to Israel's God in the face of international Wisdom.

Proverbs identifies Wisdom with God subtly, indirectly, by allusion and suggestion. To do so, it uses stratagems of characterization. It makes claims for her that elsewhere are made only for God; it grants her roles usually ascribed to God; it describes demands she makes upon her followers that only God makes.

The dramatic poem that introduces Wisdom (Prov 1:20-33) presents her as a prophet and, at the same time, draws an analogy between her and God. Like a prophet, Wisdom calls in the public places of the town (vv. 20-21), in squares and marketplaces of human life. She accosts the "simple" by "crying," "shouting," and "raising her voice" (vv. 20-21). But when this prophetlike figure gains their attention, she departs from her prophetic role to make a promise fitting only for God (v. 23).

Most translations obscure intimations of divinity in Wisdom's promise by translating the two cola of Prov 1:23 in closely synonymous terms, "I will pour out my thoughts to you ('abi 'ah lākem ruhi); I will make my words known to you."[28] Translated this way, the verse simply states in two parallel ways Wisdom's intention to announce a message to her audience in the mode of a prophet. However, another translation of the verse is possible. "I will pour out my spirit to you, I will make my words known to you" (1:23, my translation). Instead of conveying a meaning identical to the first cola, the second cola "heightens"[29] or "focuses" the previous cola.[30] In the first cola Wisdom pours out her spirit, that is, she gives herself *(ruhi)* to her followers; in the second cola, she specifies an aspect of that self-gift, the communication of her words.[31] What Wisdom promises her audience is what God promises, the gift of herself.

Support for this interpretation comes from the unusual phrasing of the first cola in which the verb *nb'* ("to pour out") takes *ruah* as its object. It is true that *nb'* usually relates to "pouring out" from the mouth,[32] but elsewhere in the Hebrew Bible when verbs of "pouring out" make *ruah* the object, God is the subject, the one who pours our *ruah.*[33] This suggests that in Prov 1:23 Wisdom pours out her spirit to her followers in the same way God pours out the divine spirit to prophets.[34] Her promise, therefore, appears as disclosure or revelation akin to divine revelation.[35]

It is herself, her *ruah,* that Wisdom reveals to the simple. The poem's warnings against rejecting Wisdom (vv. 24-32) heighten intimations of her divinity. Those who refuse to listen to her meet the same resistance as those who refuse to listen to God in the book of Jeremiah. She will not listen to their cries (vv. 26-28), just as God refuses to listen to the people (Jer 14:11-12, 15:6, 16:11-19). Furthermore, the poem insists that to repudiate Wisdom is equivalent to rejecting God—the consequence of either is death (vv. 31-32).

Proverbs' first poem about Wisdom has clear rhetorical purposes, namely, to persuade the audience of the life and death stakes involved in relationship with her. To live, the simple must obey her. Like God, Wisdom demands absolute allegiance from her followers and grants life to all who do. The poem assumes that relationship with Wisdom is equivalent to relationship with God; to heed either is to condemn oneself to death (vv. 31-32), but to accept is to gain life and peace (v. 33).

The next poem that features Wisdom (3:13, 18) also identifies her with God, this time by celebrating the benefits she brings to her followers. True happiness, the poem announces (3:13, 18), results from exclusive dedication to Wisdom. In an astonishing assertion the poem claims that "all that you desire cannot compare with her" *(wekol-hapāsekā l'ō yiswu bah,* 3:15). Wisdom not only transcends the value of wealth, but like God, she exceeds all human desire. The poem continues to identify her with God by giving her control of life and making her the dispenser of wealth. "Length of days are in her right hand, in her left are riches and honor" (3:16); she is a tree of life to those who "lay hold of her" (3:18 author's translation).

The daring nature of these theological claims is underscored by the Septuagint's modification of them. Instead of setting Wisdom above "all that you desire" (3:15), the personal fulfillment of human longings, the Greek translation suggests a reduction in her importance. She is more valuable than "everything of value" *(pan de timion).* Moreover, it explicitly states that Wisdom is not God; she is only like God *(ōs epi kurion,* 3:18).

The rhetorical purposes of 3:13-18 are similar to those of 1:20-33. Both attempt to motivate the audience to pursue Wisdom with absolute devotion. To incite such commitment, 3:13-18 equates the benefits of Wisdom with gifts that in the Hebrew Bible are God's alone to give.

Wisdom's next poem (4:5-9) does not characterize her as a divine being, but neither does it deny her that status. Since the poems about Wisdom represent a connected literary tradition, they must be read together. Such a reading tactic insists that claims made about Wisdom in one poem carry over into those that follow. Wisdom is the same character in Prov 4:4-9 as the one who appears in earlier poems in the book, and so she must hold the same status here as there. This poem seeks to evoke single-minded devotion to her (4:6-8) by highlighting the dignity, indeed, the nobility that accrues to her followers as she bestows crowns upon their heads (4:9).

Proverbs 8–9 contain a cluster of loosely united poems about Wisdom (8:1-21, 22-31, 32-36; 9:1-6). Of these, the first two focus on Wisdom herself, the second two on her relationship with her followers.

A tactic the opening poem (8:1-21) uses to describe Wisdom's value to humans is to repeat or reinterpret other biblical passages. For example, vv. 1-9 repeats Wisdom's invitation to the simple of Prov 1:20-23;[36] Proverbs 8, however, abandons the genre of prophetic address in which the invitation was originally expressed (1:20-33) in favor of the ancient Near Eastern speech form of aretology in which a goddess praises herself.[37] Hence, Prov 8:1-21 and the poems that follow (8:22-31, 32-36) by their very genre cast Wisdom as a divine being.

Proverbs 8:1-21 also reappropriates the estimate of Wisdom's value from Prov 3:15, "All that you desire cannot compare to her (8:11)." Prov 3:11 meets the same fate in the Septuagint as did 3:15 *(pan de timion ouk azion autēs estin)*. Wisdom's value is subtly diminished.

Finally in more complex ways Prov 8:14-16 reinterprets 1 Kgs 3:3-15. In the narrative passage from 1 Kings, Solomon prays for a discerning mind that he might govern wisely (1 Kgs 3:9) and discern justice (3:11). In response to his prayer, God gives Solomon the gift of wisdom, a "wise and discerning mind" *(lēb hākām wenābon,* 1 Kgs 3:12; Heb 3:11). All that this gift involves for Solomon is an intensification of his ability to know what is just and to govern wisely.

Proverbs 8:14-16 also speaks of the gift of Wisdom to rulers, but the wisdom offered here is more than the gift of wise judgment, however divinely given. She is a personal agent who not only makes kings wise, it is she who enables kings to rule at all *(bî melākim yimlōku,* 15a and *bî sārim yāsru,* 16a). In the Hebrew Bible, to enable kings to rule is a prerogative of God (1 Kgs 3:7). God chooses kings (1 Chr 28:4), regrets making kings (1 Sam 15:35), and brings kings to nothing (Isa 40:23).

When Wisdom promises to bestow riches and honor upon her disciples (Prov 3:13, 21), she takes to herself yet another of God's activities in 1 Kings 3. In that passage God is so pleased with Solomon for requesting only wisdom and not riches that God grants him everything—wisdom and riches and honor *(nātati lāk gam-ʾōser gam-kābod,* 1 Kgs 3:13). In the Proverbs poem Wisdom offers the same things to her followers. She gives them herself and promises them riches and honor as well (ʿōser-wekābod, 8:18, and see 8:21).

When she makes these promises, she is assuming divine powers. Proverbs 8:1-21 portrays Wisdom as if she were God, the one who fulfills all human desires, who performs God's deeds and gives the gifts God bestows. Moreover, she herself possesses "counsel, sound wisdom, insight and strength" (8:14), qualities of the ideal king (Isa 11:2), and of God (Job 12:14).[38]

The next poem, Prov 8:22-31, has long claimed central attention in the discussion of Wisdom in Proverbs. It is this poem that creates the chief problem for the thesis of my investigation because it distinguishes the characteristics of Wisdom and God and appears to subordinate her to God. But instead of emphasizing Wisdom's inferiority and subordination, the poem functions rhetorically to identify her with God, to make unmistakable her divinity, and to identify her so thoroughly with the Creator that she herself takes God's place in the world.

Although Prov 8:22-31 continues the aretology of vv. 1-21, it shifts attention from Wisdom's authority and benefits to her mythical origins and relationships. Several translation difficulties bear upon the poem's interpretation but solutions to them elude consensus. One such term is qānāni (8:22), from qānāh, which may mean "create," "beget," or "acquire."[39] That many translations render the word, "The Lord created me," is probably due, in part, to the influence of the LXX which reads kurios ektisen me ("The Lord made me"), and perhaps also due to theological presuppositions of interpreters regarding the subordinate status of Wisdom.[40] However, the LXX version of Proverbs consistently demotes Wisdom from her exalted role in the Hebrew text, replacing intimations of divinity with precise subordinating terms and correcting the MT in ways that diminish the status of Wisdom.

If qānāni is translated "acquired me," then the verse implies that Wisdom once existed independently of God. Since poetry employs language to gain connotation as much as denotation, however, all the nuances of qānāni serve together to create an atmosphere of mystery and uncertainty regarding both Wisdom's beginnings and her relationship to the Creator. Regardless of the translation the interpreter chooses, the main assertion of the verse is that Wisdom and God shared a unique relationship before (rēʾ sit) creation began. The poem reinterprets Israel's creation myths (Genesis 1–3, Psalm 104) not to provide instruction about creation, but to identify Wisdom with the Creator.

The literary structure of the poem has received detailed attention in articles by J.-N. Aletti and Gale A. Yee[41] who agree that the poem divides into three stanzas (vv. 22-26, 27-29, 30-31). Yee, in particular, draws attention to the chiastic structure of vv. 30-31 that highlights their climactic role in the poem. Neither of these analyses, however, advert to the unity between the first two stanzas created by the surprisingly long list of temporal clauses (8:23-29). Each verse from 22 to 29 contains two temporal clauses except for v. 26 which contains only one. These clauses create a lopsided structure, a long prodosis, that builds a tension not resolved until vv. 30-31.

On the surface, the temporal clauses describe the work of creation in luxuriant detail but their underlying purposes are theological. Their attention falls not upon creation but upon Wisdom's presence before and during the entire process of creation. She was there at the beginning (vv. 22-23) before anything was created (vv. 24-26), and she was there (šām ʾāni, v. 27) when it all occurred (vv. 27-29). These verses celebrate her transcendent status as one who exists forever (mē ʿolām, v. 23a) and who does not depend upon the earth for existence. In insisting upon Wisdom's presence at creation, the temporal clauses establish her antiquity and her authority; she is older than anything humans know, older than the earth itself, and a privileged witness of creation. But the most important function of these verses is to declare that God and Wisdom have been mysteriously joined to one another from the beginning.

The apodosis (vv. 30-31) resolves the tension and clinches Wisdom's connections with the Creator. "Then," that is, during all these acts of creation, "I was beside him like an ʾamon" (v. 30a). This line asserts unequivocally, albeit ambiguously, Wisdom's status as companion to the Creator. Like the first line of the poem in its use of qānāni, v. 30a uses an untranslatable word to name that relationship. Lang proposes five defensible translations of (ʾamon).[42] The first two, "infant" and "darling child," subordinate wisdom to God; the last three, "confidant," "artisan," and "master worker," present her as God's associate, companion, or cocreator, the one at his side participating in creation.

For the second time this poem employs a puzzling polyvalent term to speak of the relationship between Wisdom and the Creator, and again the word's nuances converge to establish a perplexing intimacy between the two, an intimacy of relationship and of labor. The remainder of v. 30 reinforces that intimacy. She was "daily his delight (sa ʿasuvim) rejoicing (mesaheaet) before him always" (v. 30b).[43] His delight is focused on her "all the time" (bekol ʿēt), daily or continuously.

The second conclusion that the apodosis provides forms a chiasm with v. 30b and expresses in the language of myth Wisdom's present role. Wisdom rejoices (mesaheaet) in the inhabited world and delights (wesa ʿasu ay) in the children of humans" (v. 31). In her joy, she brings together God, the earth, and humans. What this verse highlights is not God's delight but Wisdom's. It is her involvement with the earth and its inhabitants that forms the climax toward which the poem has been driving. Throughout the poem, Wisdom reports events and tells them from her point of view; it is her location, activities, and relationships that receive attention. The poem is not interested in God but in Wisdom and her relationship to God, to creation, and to humans; it subordinates God to Wisdom by using God to point to her.

These verses hint at the unthinkable. They imply that Wisdom is God's child, or God's darling, perhaps even God's consort,[44] or that she is cocreator, architect, or artisan with God. They heighten her status even further by showing

193

that she is God's delight, and ultimately they subordinate God to her. By contrast to the MT, the LXX version reduces the theological shock of the passage by making God, not Wisdom, the central character in the poem's climax: *euphraineto tēn oikoumenēn suntelesas kai eneuphraineto en nuiois anthrōpōn* ("For he delighted when he completed the world, and delighted among the children of humans," 8:31). Wisdom drops from view as God alone receives explicit and exclusive credit for creation, and God, not Wisdom, rejoices in humanity. The LXX reduces Wisdom's role because in the last verse of the Hebrew poem she takes the place of God.

The Hebrew poem does not subordinate Wisdom to God; it identifies her with God. She does God's work. She creates the earth, she lives in intimacy with humans and with all creation. She is God present to the world, a symbolic representation of God's being, a manifestation of the deity in the guise of Wisdom. Proverbs 8:22-31 functions to make this identification clear. Wisdom is not a separate deity from Israel's God but, from the beginning, one with, and an expression of, that divinity. To persuade the "implied reader" of this is the rhetorical purpose of 8:22-31.

After the previous poems have established Wisdom's authority and divinity, the next poem (8:32-36) presents the demands she makes to "the children of humans," and it continues to identify her with God. To obtain her favors is to obtain "favors from the Lord" (v. 35). She exhorts her "children" to listen to her instruction (vv. 32-33), the content of which is again herself (vv. 35-36). Humans must respond to her revelation actively by listening, watching, and waiting for her (v. 34); they must commit themselves to her completely. Just as the prophet Amos urged the people to "seek God and live" (Amos 5:4, 6), Wisdom promises that "whoever finds me finds life," whereas those who hate her choose death (vv. 35-36). This poem, like Prov 1:20-31, urges commitment to Wisdom by depicting her as God who demands absolute loyalty from humans and rewards them with life.

The final poem about Wisdom in this collection portrays her as a hostess at a banquet (Prov 9:1-6). The meal takes place in the house that she herself built. Only one architectural feature, the house's seven pillars, describes the house (9:1). Although some commentators think that seven pillars merely indicate that the house is the home of a rich woman,[45] others find mythological traces in the metaphor.[46] In support of the latter view, the Hebrew Bible elsewhere uses architectural features to describe the cosmos. The earth, for instance, has foundations (Prov 8:29; Ps 104:5) and a cornerstone (Job 38:6). It has pillars supporting it from below (1 Sam 2:8), and pillars or a firmament above (Job 26:11; Gen 1:6-8, Gen 6:11).[47] Wisdom's house has seven pillars, therefore, to present her house as the world she created.[48] The poem presents Wisdom as the Creator who prepares a banquet for all who accept her invitation to the table of life.

The house motif also appears in the closing poem of Proverbs (31:10-31). Thomas P. McCreesh has shown that the poem is a summary of the entire book of

194

Proverbs and that the woman it praises is Wisdom herself.[49] In his view a loose narrative thread joins this poem to previous poems about Wisdom. In chapter 9, for example, Wisdom invites her followers to come to her house and eat at her table; in Prov 31:10-31 "the time of courtship, of learning is over."[50] She lives with her followers in her household, gives them the blessings which she has promised, cares for them in intimacy and companionship, provides them with all good things of life, and gains them honor as they rise in praise of her (31:28).

Taken together the poems about Wisdom in Proverbs present an enigmatic character. Although occasionally they distinguish her from the deity, most often they identify her with God. They grant her divine powers and prerogatives, provide her with transcendent origins, portray her as worthy of absolute loyalty, imply that she herself is Creator, and declare explicitly that she gives and withholds life and wealth.

The poems about Wisdom must be read together as a literary and theological stream that serves the same rhetorical purposes. They attempt to alter the imaginations of readers by persuading them that their God is Wise-God and that they do not need to abandon Israel's God to live with Wisdom for she and God are one. She is God among humans. Through a variety of allusions, images, and metaphors, they assert that to live with Wisdom is to live with God. It is she who frames the book of Proverbs, giving an explicit theological character to the sayings of chapters 10–30.

Conclusion

Personified Wisdom is the product of a long process of mythopoetic thinking in which Israel draws upon a pool of goddess myths from the ancient Near East, reflects upon them, and transforms them into a new myth in Israel. This new myth served ideological purposes that remain obscured by time, but it seems likely that personified Wisdom gained a place in Israel's faith to meet the challenge created by international Wisdom goddesses.

Israel's theological reflection on its experience of international Wisdom lead to the insight that to live in Wisdom is to experience God, not a new God, but Israel's own God. This insight is consistent with the insistence of the Wisdom literature on the inability of humans to define or confine the deity who remains always beyond the reach of language. In contemporary rereadings of the text, Wisdom offers biblical theology a symbol of God who breaks the boundaries of gender and nationality, who relates to humans in intimacy and mutuality, and who joins them to the earth and to one another at her banquet of life.

Chapter Eleven / PAUL AND THE CANON OF THE NEW TESTAMENT

Hendrikus Boers

Chris Beker rendered an important service to New Testament, specifically Pauline, scholarship by raising the issue of the center of Paul's thought in *Paul the Apostle.*[1] The coherent center of Paul's thought "is not a theoretical proposition that is subsequently applied to sociological contingencies. . . . Rather, Paul's coherent center must be viewed as a symbolic structure in which a primordial experience (Paul's call) is brought into language in a particular way."[2] Much of the discussion which followed the publication of Beker's book on Paul has concerned the nature of this symbolic structure.

The issue I am called upon to address in this article expands the scope of what Beker has suggested to the entire NT. Something similar to his suggested "symbolic structure" rather than a "theoretical proposition" or conceptual unit also holds the promise of providing coherence in our understanding of the canon of the NT, without reducing it to a single theoretical proposition or conception, whether it is "Jesus' own understanding of his relationship with God, with his disciples and with the kingdom" as argued by James D. G. Dunn,[3] or an existential self-understanding, as proposed by Herbert Braun.[4] Braun avoids interpreting the self-understanding as an unchanging idea by maintaining that the "believing self-understanding in the New Testament is an occurrence and event which takes place again and again."[5]

The problem with every attempt to formulate a unity or constancy in the NT in terms of a single factor is that it does not allow for the real differences and even contradictions that are also present. Even Braun's understanding of the constant factor as an "occurrence and event which takes place again and again" could not prevent the criticism of Ernst Käsemann that what he proposes does not apply to the entire NT, but only to Jesus, Paul, and John.[6] It is not my intention here to enter into a discussion of those issues. What I will propose is not intended to answer criticism such as Käsemann's, but moves completely outside the framework of the earlier understanding of the issue, similar to Beker's argument in favor of a structure rather than a single "theoretical proposition" or conception. In that way the question whether or not the point of view of a NT author can be accommodated diminishes in importance. In my proposal, the particular views of the NT authors are no longer what count but rather the relations established between them by their presence in the canon.

What is at issue can be clarified by recalling an insight by the philosopher Gottfried Martin on meaning in philosophy, specifically metaphysics. According to Martin, if we consider the multiplicity of metaphysical systems from the point of view of their answers, we are confronted by confusion in philosophy, but if we consider them from the point of view of the questions to which they are proposed answers, we encounter the richness of philosophy.[7] Important for our purposes is Martin's understanding that contradictory propositions in philosophy can both be true, and can be proven as such. The task of philosophy is to find and clarify the contradictions, to prove contradictory propositions, and to investigate the meaning of the contradictions and the grounds for their occurrence.[8]

A similarly positive approach to contradictions also characterizes the interpretation of myth by the anthropologist Claude Lévi-Strauss. According to him, what is distinctive of mythical in contrast to positive (philosophical) thought is that mythical thought accepts contradiction, and provides a way of dealing with it.[9] He maintains that the logic of myth, which accepts and tries to cope with contradictions without trying to resolve them, is as rigorous as positive (philosophical) logic, and that in the final analysis there may be little difference between the two forms of logic, because the real difference between them concerns less the operations of the mind than the subject matter to which they are applied.[10] He expresses the hope that we may "discover some day that the same logic is operative in mythic thought and in scientific [philosophical] thought, and that the human being always thought equally well."[11] It is thus important to note that in Martin's observations we encounter an acceptance in philosophical thought of the contradictions which Lévi-Strauss considers characteristic of mythical thought.

Actually we encounter such acceptance already in the late Plato concerning the question whether reality is fundamentally unchanging (as in Parmenides and in Plato's own theory of ideas) or in constant flux (as in Heraclitus). In the Sophist Parmenides in the guise of the Eleatic stranger insists that the young Socrates accept as true the view of the "friends of ideas" that reality is unchanging, as well as the contradictory view of those who claim that all of reality is constantly changing. "For the philosopher it will be necessary . . . to call real and the whole *(to pan)* whatever is unchanging [as well as] what is subject to change."[12] In *Le Mythe de Sisyphe* Albert Camus elevates the acceptance of this kind of contradiction to the fundamental principle of his thought. He refers to it as the posture of the absurd which occurs when a person seeking happiness and reason encounters the irrational. "The absurd is born from this confrontation between the human call, and the unreasonable silence of the world."[13] It arises from the "divide between the spirit which desires and the world which deceives: my nostalgia for unity, this broken universe, and the contradiction which binds them."[14] To destroy either term of this opposition is to destroy it all.[15] The absurd person does not "proceed to . . . a leveling out" which, for the sake of clarity, abandons one of the terms of the contradiction; the absurd "does not abandon reason completely and [in desperation] admit the irrational,"[16] because "[the] absurd has meaning only to the degree that one does not agree to it."[17]

I propose a structure grounded in such contradiction as the basis for an understanding of Paul and of coherence in the canon of the NT. Needless to say, it is an extreme radicalization of Beker's suggestion of a symbolic structure. And yet, unless one proceeds with such a radical solution, it would be impossible to come to an understanding of either Paul, in particular, or the NT canon as a whole which does not eliminate crucial features. Anything less would inevitably be, to use Camus's term,[18] a leveling out of the range of meaning which comes to expression in the NT.

I begin with Paul because, in his thinking, not a single view comes to expression, but at least two that are fundamentally opposed. They occur in tandem in Rom 4:4-5, "For the person who works the reward is not considered as a kindness, but as what is due, but for the person who does not work, but trusts in him who justifies the ungodly, his [or her] trust is reckoned as justice" (author's translation). Paul's praise of good works in Romans 2, representing the first view, is unsurpassed, but here in Romans 4 his intention is to argue in favor of the second, that justification is by faith without works. In 4:7-8 he presents Abraham not only as not having had good works on which he could rely when he was justified, but as a sinner, basing his reasoning on scripture, Ps 31:1-2 (the LXX). It is important to note, however, that Paul's reasoning in Romans 4 does not pose justification by faith against justification for good works as such, but against justification through works of the Law as the sign of being a Jew.

The issue in Romans 4 is whether one can be justified only and exclusively by being circumcised and thus subject to the Law, that is, by being a Jew, or whether a Gentile could be justified as well. Justification through works of the Law in Rom 3:21–4:25 does not refer to the doing of good works, but to circumcision and the Law as the exclusive functions of justification. The theme of Romans 4 is given in 3:29-30, "Or is God of the Jews only? not also of the Gentiles? Indeed, also of the Gentiles, since it is one God who justifies the circumcised out of faith, and the uncircumcised through faith" (author's translation), and is reinforced by 4:9-12, "This blessing, then [which David pronounces on the sinner in Ps 31:1-2], is it on the circumcised [only], or is it also on the uncircumcised? For it is said, Faith was reckoned as justice for Abraham. How was it reckoned? While circumcised or uncircumcised? Not circumcised, but uncircumcised. And he received the sign of circumcision, a seal of the justification of faith while uncircumcised, so that he would be the father of all who believe while uncircumcised, that it would be reckoned to them, and the father of the circumcised for those who are not only circumcised, but also follow in the footsteps of the faith of the uncircumcised Abraham" (author's translation). The point Paul makes with his reference to Abraham having been circumcised after he had already been justified by his faith is the same as the one he made earlier in Gal 3:17 that the Law which came four hundred and thirty years later could not invalidate a testament that had been ratified by God so as to destroy the promise. Paul's point is that Abraham had been justified as a Gentile, which, from a Jewish point of view, as Paul understands it, is equivalent to being a sinner.

But even though the limitation of salvation to the Jews, not justification for good works, is what Paul negates when he posits justification by faith against justification through works of the Law in Rom 3:21–4:25, justification by faith and justification for good works are nevertheless also contraries in his thinking. Justification by faith means to be justified by God as a kindness (Rom 4:5, cf. 4:16), without the benefit of good works; justification for good works, that is, to be rewarded for good works, is not a kindness, but in accordance with what is one's due (Rom 4:4). What is involved in these statements can be clarified by means of a logical square. Whereas the opposition between justification through works of the Law and justification by faith can be placed on a logical square, revealing the logical relationships between them, it is not possible to place the opposition between justification for good works and justification by faith on a single square.

Paul brings the opposition between justification through works of the Law and justification by faith to expression most clearly in Gal 2:21*b*, "if justification were to be through the Law, then Christ died in vain" (author's translation), and 2:16*b*, "in order to be justified through the faith of Christ, and not from works of the Law" (author's translation). The following logical square clarifies what is involved. The lines above "justification by faith" and "justification through works of the Law" at the bottom corners of the square signify negation.

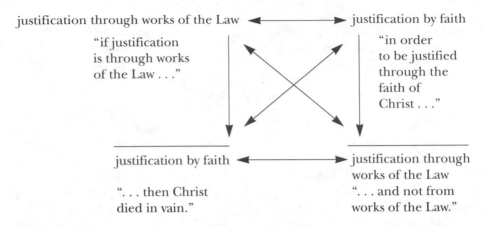

justification through works of the Law ⟷ justification by faith

"if justification is through works of the Law . . ."

"in order to be justified through the faith of Christ . . ."

justification by faith ⟷ justification through works of the Law

". . . then Christ died in vain."

". . . and not from works of the Law."

The square makes it clear that justification through works of the Law and justification by faith are actually not logical contradictories, but contraries. The logical contradiction of justification through works of the Law is its negation, as the diagonal line from the top left to the bottom right reveals: if justification through works of the Law is the case its negation is not the case. Inversely, if negation of justification through works of the Law is the case, justification through works of the Law is not. The same applies to justification by faith and its contradiction, the negation of justification by faith. In Paul's thought, justification through works of the Law and justification by faith are contraries, illustrated by the upper horizontal line on the square. Only one of them can be the case, not both of them. If justification through works of the Law is the case, it implies that justification by faith is denied, as Paul states in Gal 2:21*b,* and the left vertical line of implication shows. Similarly, if justification by faith is the case, justification through works of the Law is negated, as Paul states in Gal 2:16*b,* and as the vertical line of implication on the right shows.

It is important to note that the lines of implication point down only, which means that the negation of justification by faith does not imply justification through works of the Law. Similarly the negation of justification through works of the Law does not imply justification by faith. Logically neither justification through works of the Law nor justification by faith have to be the case. Both subcontraries—on the bottom corners of the square—can be the case. What is crucial for our understanding of Paul is that both the contraries on the upper horizontal line, justification through works of the Law and justification by faith, cannot be the case. The relationships on the square are so tight that what is said in terms of one relationship can be said in terms of another as well. For example, what is said with regard by the relationship of contrariety is said in a different way by the relationships of implication. That justification through works of the Law and justification by

200

faith cannot both be the case is equivalent to saying that justification through works of the Law implies the negation of justification by faith, and that justification by faith implies the negation of justification through works of the Law.

The relationships between the various expressions may appear so obvious as to make their clarification on a logical square fruitless. But note what happens when one tries to clarify the relationship between justification by faith and justification for good works on a logical square. Since in Paul's thought, justification by faith and justification for good works can both be the case, they appear not to be logical contraries. Are they then subcontraries, both of which can be the case logically? But that would mean that the negation of justification for good works implies justification by faith; similarly, the negation of justification by faith would imply justification for good works. Furthermore, since both contraries cannot be the case logically, it would mean that if justification by faith is negated, justification for good works cannot be negated. The same would apply for the negation of justification for good works. In both cases the lines of implication would make this clear. All of this is of course nonsense. But what then is the logical relationship between justification by faith and justification for good works? That question brings us to the center of what is involved in Paul's thought, and in the canon of the NT.

Paul himself reveals the difficulty of making sense of this relationship when he tries to discredit an understanding of opponents who draw what appears to be the logical conclusion from his proclamation of justification by faith without works of the Law in Rom 3:8, "As some blaspheme and contend that I say, Let us do evil so that good may come about," and of imagined readers in Rom 6:1, "Shall we remain in sin so that [God's] kindness may become abundant?" and 6:15, "Shall we sin since we are not under the Law, but depend on [God's] kindness?" (all verses author's translation). The opposed reasoning is fundamentally the same in all three cases: being justified by faith (through God's kindness) implies that one should do evil (which includes the negation of doing good). The logic is that justification by faith through God's kindness is contrary to the doing of good works (and the negation of doing evil), as on the logical square above, but with "doing good works" replacing, or taken as the equivalent of "justification through works of the Law."

That Paul repeats the argument, first as an accusation by opponents, and then in the reasoning of imagined readers, is an indication of how much it must have bothered him. In the case of the opponents he provides no argument, but merely pronounces a curse on them. With regard to the twice repeated argument of imagined readers in Rom 6:1, 15 his reasoning is that being in Christ implies being freed from sin, which makes it inappropriate to continue living in it. In Paul's reasoning, being in Christ and continuing in sin are contraries. He does not prove his point though. Notwithstanding the length of his reasoning, he merely asserts the opposed view that being in Christ implies that one should refrain from sin, contrary to the understanding that justification through God's kindness implies that one should sin in order that God's kindness may abound, or because one is not under the Law. The problem is that he cannot take justification by faith and sinning as logical contraries because justification for him is justification of the sinner, that is, someone who sins, as he argues, for example, in connection with Abraham in Rom 4:5-9 by proving from scripture that Abraham was a sinner when he was justified. According to Paul the sinner is justified unconditionally by faith.

Paul may have been drawn into this line of argument because, as a Jew, by accepting the justification of Gentiles he had to assume that it was as sinners that they were justified. And so he equates justification by faith with justification of sinners. By proving in Rom 2:1–3:20 that the Jews too are sinners, he is able to maintain that they too could be justified only by faith. The condemnation of the Jews in Rom 3:9-20 functions to equate them with Gentiles, and so dependent on faith for their justification. Even though his reasoning in Romans 2 concerns good works in general, Paul was unable to distinguish consistently between justification for good works, which he affirms, and justification through works of the Law as the sign of being a Jew, which he rejects. This lack of differentiation makes it understandable why he ends up interpreting a Gentile who fulfills the just requirements of the Law as cryptically a Jew, obviously understood in a positive sense (Rom 2:25-29). Inversely, it also makes clear why he found it necessary to prove from scripture that Abraham had been a sinner when he was justified (Rom 4:6-9), giving support to his argument that at that stage Abraham had not yet become a Jew through circumcision (v. 10).

Paul's intention may actually not have been to teach specifically that justification by faith was the justification of sinners, at least not in the unqualified sense in which it has become understood. Even though what he wrote in Galatians, Romans, and Philippians gives reason for such an understanding, it may nevertheless not have been what he intended, but the result of his failure to differentiate between justification of a Gentile and justification of a sinner. In Phil 3:4b-6 he claims among his other virtues as a Jew that he was unblemished with regard to righteousness through the Law (v. 6b), which must mean that he was justified as a Jew who fulfilled the Law, not as a sinner, as a Gentile. But even as a Jew he was justified as if he had been a Gentile, "through Christ I considered [all of that] a loss" (v. 7b, cf. vv. 8-9 author's translation), probably in the sense of Rom 4:12, according to which, in addition to the uncircumcised, Abraham became the father "of the circumcised for those who are not only circumcised, but also follow in the footsteps of the faith of the uncircumcised Abraham." However, it could be only in a Jewish sense that he claims to have been unblemished with regard to righteousness through the Law; he did come to understand his persecution of the Church as evil. In 1 Cor 15:9 he says that he was unworthy of being an apostle because he persecuted "the church of God." In the development of his thinking, justification of the Gentiles was probably primary, from which followed self-evidently that it was the justification of sinners, and from there the tendency to consider justification by faith as equivalent to justification of a sinner.

I argue above that in his reasoning, Paul was unable, as have been his interpreters until only recently,[19] to distinguish between justification through "works of the Law" as a technical expression for being a Jew and justification for good works. In Romans 2 he argues that the true meaning of justification through works of the Law is not achieved through the mere fact of circumcision and reliance on the Law, but by fulfilling its just requirements, but then, in Rom 3:9–4:25 he moves to a negation of justification through works of the Law without clarifying the transition from the one meaning to the other, probably also not in his own mind. The transition occurs inconspicuously in Rom 3:19-20.

In v. 19, Paul pronounces a final condemnation on those who are under the Law, based on the quotations from scripture in vv. 10-18, "We know that what the Law says it says to those who are under the Law. So that every mouth will be shut and the entire world will be subject to God's judgment," and then, in v. 20, he states, "because through works of the Law no-one will be justified before him, for through the Law is the recognition of sin" (author's translation). Here all the ambiguity in Paul's understanding of works of the Law is revealed. On the one hand, he maintains that it is not possible to be justified through works of the Law, "for through the Law is the recognition of sin," as he had just demonstrated from scripture in vv. 10-19. The sole purpose of the Law is to condemn, contrary to what he argued in chapter 2. But then, yet a third conception of the Law emerges, the Law as the sign of Jewish privilege. Romans 3:20*b* marks the transition from the one meaning to the other. That no one will be justified before God through works of the Law, on the one hand, refers to the condemnation of the Jews by scripture (vv. 10-19), summarized in the statement that the Law brings the recognition of sin (v. 20*b*), and, on the other hand, is the basis for the argument which follows in 3:21–4:25 according to which works of the Law signify a false reliance on Jewish privilege as the exclusive and self-evident means of justification. Rather than differentiate between the different meanings of works of the Law, Paul allows them to flow into each other as it suits his argument, probably not by design, but because he was neither motivated nor able to make the necessary distinctions. This is not a case of the recognized linguistic use of the same term to express a variety of meanings in different contexts, but reasoning by means of a single conception with undifferentiated meanings. It could only result in confusion.

Faith is equally ambiguous in Paul. He is evidently unable to distinguish between Abraham's faith as a mere trust in God and faith as the foundation for the new being in Christ. In Rom 4:23-24 he coordinates Abraham's trust in God with faith in Christ, "It was not written only for [Abraham's] sake that [his faith] was reckoned to him [as justification], but also for our sakes to whom it will be reckoned, [we] who trust in him who raised Jesus our Lord from the dead" (author's translation). There is a transcendent factor on which Paul could rely for this coordination: God making alive what is dead by raising life from the dead bodies of Abraham and Sarah (4:17-22), and by raising Jesus from the dead (4:23-24). The meanings are nevertheless distinguishable. Abraham's trust in God in Rom 4:18-22 concerns the conception of Isaac, not the death and resurrection of Christ, but, probably relying on typological relationships, Paul transcends that distinction. There is obviously value for him in not making it. In Gal 3:8 he integrates Abraham's trust in God and faith in Christ by referring to Scripture having foreseen the justification of the Gentiles by faith in Christ as the basis for the promise to which Abraham responded by his trust in God. Inversely, in Romans 9–10 he interprets the failure of the Jews to find justification as at the same time false reliance on works of the Law and the rejection of Christ. They are two aspects of the same act, closely linked in 9:32, "[Israel who followed the Law of righteousness did not attain the Law] because it was not by faith, but through works: they stumbled against the stumbling block" (author's translation). Paul obviously did not distinguish between the manifestation of faith as faith in Christ and other manifestations of faith, such as Abraham's or, in a negative sense, the Jewish reliance on works of the Law as the rejection of faith in Christ.

The reason why Paul was unable to establish logical consistency in the relationships between these concepts is that they give expression to conceptions between which there is no logical relationship, justification by faith and justification for good works. Justification by faith relies on God's kindness, which neither depends on nor negates the believer's works, whether good or evil. Paul understands justification by faith and justification for the doing of good works as contraries, but, as I tried to show above, in a way which defies the rules of logic; they cannot be placed on a logical square. Justification by faith is contrary to justification for good works, but does not imply its negation. That justification by faith implies such a negation is the logically consistent reasoning which Paul rejects in Rom 3:8 and in 6:1, 15. Contrary to that reasoning, he maintains that justification by faith implies the doing of good works and the negation of evil, which contradicts their being contraries.

The solution that justification by faith is indeed justification of the sinner, but that from that it does not follow that the justified sinner is not expected to do good and avoid evil, agrees with Paul's reasoning in Romans 6, but does not solve the problem. Romans 2 reveals that Paul understood doing good and the avoidance of evil to have been expected of the Jew and the Gentile as well, of all human beings thus, outside the framework of faith. There is no necessary relationship between justification by faith and the doing of good works. The issue is not whether good works cannot be expected of the believer, but whether justification by faith is conditional on the doing of good works that are expected to follow, as is the case in Matthew, to whose view we will turn our attention below.

Justification of the sinner by faith and justification for good works are not related logically, but represent opposed dimensions in human existence: a social dimension in which good and evil are opposed, and an existential dimension in which life and death are opposites. The relationship between the two dimensions can be clarified by means of the following diagram.

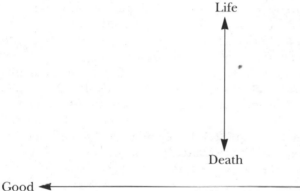

The existential opposition between life and death stands opposed to the social opposition between good and evil in such a way that what happens on the social dimension is ignored, neither affirmed nor negated, on the existential dimension. Justification by faith takes place irrespective of the point at which the believer finds herself or himself on the social plane of good and evil. In that regard the vertical two-directional arrow between life and death can be placed anywhere in relation to the horizontal arrow between good and evil. This structure with its irreconcilably opposed polar relationships represents the spectrum within which Paul's thinking takes place, but not only Paul's thinking: it is also the structure of the canon within which the books of the NT relate to each other.

In their semiotic dictionary,[20] A. J. Greimas and J. Courtés distinguish two micro-universes as the deepest level out of which meaning is generated, the one individual, which finds expression in the polarity life/death, and the other collective or social, which finds expression in the polarity culture/nature.[21] These micro-universes can be understood as the conceptual framework at the deepest level within which thought takes place. The individual micro-universe is recognizable in the existential opposition between life and death in the diagram above of the structure which underlies Paul's thinking, and the social microuniverse in the opposition between good and evil.[22] Greimas and Courtés consider these microuniverses as alternatives. What is remarkable about Paul is that his thought takes place within the framework of both alternatives.

In the NT the existential micro-universe is represented in its purest form by the Fourth Gospel, with particular clarity in 5:25, "The hour is coming, and now is, when the dead will hear the voice of the Son of God, and those who hear will live" (RSV). The author rejects the significance of what happens on the social plane of the involvement with others; attention is focused solely on the voice of the Son of God from beyond the world. The hour which was expected on the temporal, social plane of history in Jewish eschatology breaks in at every moment of time when the voice of the Son of God is heard. Hearing the voice of the Son of God, paying attention to it, effects a transformation from death to life, from an involvement in the social, historical dimension of existence in this world to incorporation into the community of the Son of God beyond this world.

Directly opposed to this view of the Fourth Gospel with its unconditional break with the social dimension of being human is Matthew's affirmation of it, formulated representatively in the statement: "Not everyone who calls me, 'Lord, Lord,' will enter into the kingdom of heaven, but whoever does the will of my father who is in heaven" (Matt 7:21). Here the unconditional appeal to the lordship of Christ is rejected. What matters is a person's behavior in the world, even as a Christian, whether or not one's deeds demonstrate active submission to the will of God.

Matthew's views are particularly interesting for our discussion because of the way he deals with issues similar to those we encounter in Paul. His understanding is the exact opposite of the view which Paul rejects in Rom 3:8 and 6:1, 15, as the logical squares below show. The mistaken view attributed to Paul misinterprets justification by faith and the doing of good works as logical contraries: diametrically opposed to that view, Matthew interprets justification by faith and the negation (absence) of good works as contraries. Matthew, it is true, does not use the expression "justification by faith," but addressing Jesus with "Lord, Lord" is semantically equivalent to having faith in Christ, and entering the Kingdom of God equivalent to justification, as, for example, in his Description of the Last Judgment (Matt 25:31-46).

Unlike in Paul's reasoning, the two views are logically consistent, but diametrically opposed to each other. Matthew's reasoning is formally similar to Paul's concerning the true meaning of justification through works of the Law in Romans 2. The First Evangelist's definition of the true meaning of faith inhrist, what it means to say, "Lord, Lord," is identical with what Paul says about

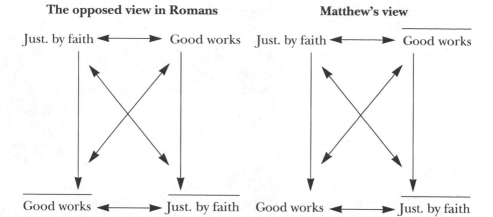

The opposed view in Romans   **Matthew's view**

the true meaning of being a Jew, for example, in his statement, "Not the hearers of the Law are just before God, but the doers will be justified" (2:13).

Actually Paul goes even further, arguing that doing what the Law requires makes the difference between Jew and Gentile irrelevant: "So, if an uncircumcised person observes the just requirements of the Law, will his [or her] lack of circumcision not be considered circumcision? And the person who is by nature uncircumcised who fulfills the Law judges you who are in the letter and through circumcision a transgressor of the Law. For not who is it in the open is a Jew, nor is circumcision in the open in the flesh, but who is it in secret is a Jew, and circumcision is of the heart, in the spirit, not the letter, of whom praise is not from human beings, but from God" (Rom 2:26-29 author's translation). Matthew does not say the same about the confession of Christ, but remains within a confessional framework: "Not *every one* who says to me, 'Lord, Lord' " (Matt 7:21*a* RSV italics mine).

It is important to note that in Matthew's logic the negation or absence of good works implies the negation of justification by faith. For Matthew there is no justification of the sinner. As in the parable of the wedding feast (Matt 22:1-14), God's invitation is directed to everyone: the king commands his servants, "invite to the wedding feast whoever you find" (v. 9*b* author's translation); and so they gathered everyone they found, "the bad and the good" (v. 10 author's translation), but the story ends with the merciless casting out of the man without a wedding garment and the warning: "Many are called, but few elect" (v. 14 author's translation). Salvation is the answer to active trust in God by doing his will. It is not earned through good works, though, but through good works, trust in God is brought to expression, as in the parable of the workers in the vineyard (Matt 20:1-15) when the workers confidently go to work in response to the owner's promise, "I will give you what is just" (Matt 20:4*c*). Matthew does not specifically negate the existential dimension of being human, but in his thought, through immersion in the doing of good works, the existential crisis of life and death becomes resolved in the social dimension of good and evil.

There is a sense in which the meaning of Matthew's presence in the canon is co-determined by the presence of the Fourth Gospel as well; inversely, what contributes to the meaning of the Fourth Gospel in the canon is the presence of Matthew as well. The Fourth Gospel is not a Gnostic writing, but if it alone were to have been representative of the NT canon there would have been little to prevent Christianity from developing into a gnosticizing, world-negating sect. On the other hand, if Matthew alone were to have been representative of the canon, Christianity may have turned out to be indistinguishable from a notable Jewish sect. One may judge a gnosticizing or Jewish sect in whatever way one wants: the point is that what gives the Christian canon its particular identity is that it includes both Matthew and John. In that way Christianity has to understand itself in terms of a structure which includes both: neither can be affirmed unconditionally because neither can be denied.

The rest of the NT canon can be understood within the same structural framework. What makes this collection of writings a canon is not a single, underlying theoretical proposition or conception, but the structure which provides for the wide range of expressions of the meaning of faith in Christ in it, each of which has to be taken into account for a Christian self-understanding. The meaning of the canon is not the cumulative meaning of all of them together, but something that arises from the fact that all of them in their contradicting and affirming interrelationships have to be taken into account, similar to what Plato wrote about metaphysics in his seventh letter: "[On these matters] one cannot speak as about others that can be learned, but through the constant engagement with the subject itself, and living with it, suddenly, as when light flares up when flint strikes iron, it is born in the spirit, already nurturing itself" (Ep. VII, 341 C5-D2).

What is significant about Paul is that in him the full range of the tension in the canon comes to expression. He may be regarded as *the* canon, not *a* canon, in the canon. In the sense of Claude Lévi-Strauss, he was not a positive, philosophical-theological thinker, but a mythical thinker, or, in the sense of Gottfried Martin, from the point of view of the contradictory formulations, his thought appears as a confusion, but from the point of view of his experience of Christ to which the contradictory formulations give expression, they represent the richness of his thought.

Chapter Twelve / THE PERSISTENCE OF APOCALYPTIC THOUGHT IN NEW TESTAMENT THEOLOGY

Charles D. Myers, Jr.

Since 1960, when Ernst Käsemann declared apocalyptic to be "the mother of all Christian theology,"[1] apocalyptic has occupied a prominent place in discussions about the theology of the New Testament. Of course, Käsemann did not initiate these discussions. Earlier in the twentieth century, Albert Schweitzer had pointed out the necessity of understanding Jesus and Paul in terms of first-century Jewish apocalyptic eschatology.[2] Keenly aware that NT thought was bound up with the first-century apocalyptic worldview, Rudolf Bultmann refused to dismiss apocalyptic outright, as so many previous interpreters had done, but instead proposed that apocalyptic be existentially reinterpreted, or "demythologized," into terms intelligible to twentieth century persons.[3] But Ernst Käsemann, in his essay entitled *"Die Anfänge christlicher Theologie"* (1960),[4] asserted in no uncertain terms the centrality of apocalyptic in NT thought, and thereby elevated to prominence what had for too long been seen as peripheral and nonessential. In so doing, Käsemann fueled the fire of debate[5] and prompted further study[6] that has lasted for more than three decades.

But rather than rehearsing all aspects of the considerable discussion about apocalyptic, the present essay will attend primarily to the impact of apocalyptic on NT thought. Such a focus seems most appropriate in a volume of essays dedicated to J. Christiaan Beker, who has contributed in a most significant way to the debate about apocalyptic's influence on the thought of the apostle Paul. Before undertaking the present investigation, however, a brief definition and description of apocalyptic is in order.

Apocalyptic Defined and Described

The term "apocalyptic" is derived from the Greek word *apokalypsis,* which literally means "revelation." Because *apokalypsis* is the first word of the last book of the canonical NT, the term "apocalyptic" (or apocalypse) is used to identify the distinctive *type of literature* that the book of Revelation (or the Apocalypse of John) and other similar works represent. Apocalyptic writing flourished from about 200 BCE to about 100 CE.[7] The Old Testament book of Daniel stands close to the beginning of what might be called the Golden Age of Apocalyptic, while the book of Revelation in the NT stands near the end. In the years between the writing of these two canonical works, additional apocalypses were composed. Numerous apocryphal and pseudepigraphal works are classed as apocalypses, among them 1 (Ethiopic Apocalypse of) Enoch, 2 (Syriac Apocalypse of) Baruch, 4 Ezra, and the Apocalypse of Abraham.[8]

Although there is some discussion about whether apocalypses represent a distinct literary genre or are merely a combination of older literary forms,[9] apocalyptic writings appear to share some common literary features.[10] Characterized by their use of fantastic imagery and symbolism, apocalypses contain one or more revelations about the end of the world, mediated through a seer or other ancient worthy. Apocalypses are usually pseudonymous writings, composed under the name of an important figure who lived in an earlier day.[11] But, while apocalyptic writings look to the future, they are not merely exercises in crystal ball gazing. In most apocalypses there is a section of paraenesis or ethical instruction that grows out of the visionary revelation and is offered to the community of faith in response to the revelation.[12]

"Apocalyptic," however, does not refer only to a type of literature or literary genre. Scholars also use the term to denote a *way of thinking* or a theological perspective that finds expression in the writings identified as apocalypses. Because the specific revelation of apocalyptic thinking concerns the end of the world, apocalyptic is a form of Endtime or eschatological thinking. But apocalyptic thinking is not limited to apocalypses. Other types of literature express apocalyptic eschatology as well.

The use of the term apocalyptic to describe a particular way of thinking, it must be pointed out, is a modern scholarly construct. Nowhere in the literature of antiquity does this term ever denote a specific outlook on life or a particular worldview. Only since the nineteenth century[13] have scholars isolated in ancient literary sources a number of distinctive elements that, taken together, they dub "apocalyptic" eschatology.

One essential component of apocalyptic eschatology is historical *dualism,* which finds expression in the apocalypticist's belief in two qualitatively different and radically discontinuous eras: This Age and the Age to Come.[14] According to the apocalypticist, This Age, which is characterized by pervasive evil and universal death, will be destroyed by God who will then bring in the Age to Come,[15] where evil, suffering, and death will be no more.[16] Since God alone decides when one age ends and the other begins,[17] historical *determinism* is another hallmark of apocalyptic eschatology. The belief that God alone created both ages[18] and that all takes place according to the foreordained plan of God is the logical outgrowth of the apocalypticist's fundamental and unwavering belief in the absolute *sovereignty of God*.

The historical dualism of apocalyptic eschatology results in a decided *pessimism*[19] about the present evil age but an attitude of hope toward the future that God promises to bring.[20] That hope will be realized soon, the apocalypticist believes, for the End of This Age is *imminent*. According to the apocalypticist, the present age is fast approaching the Day of the Lord,[21] the day of final judgment, when God will give everyone what they deserve based on their actions in life[22] and inaugurate the so-called Age to Come.[23] That Day, according to the apocalyptic thinker, is imminent.[24]

Not unrelated to the features described above is *universalism,* which also characterizes apocalyptic thought. Because the apocalypticist envisions the end of the age as a cosmic event, embracing not only all those on earth but also those in heaven and in the underworld, there is a universal sense present in these writings.[25] Another distinctive trait of apocalyptic is belief in the *resurrection of the dead*. In order to execute judgment on the last day, God will need to bring all of the dead back to life.[26] Through resurrection death is destroyed, then through judgment all evil will be destroyed and all the evildoers of the present age will be punished.[27] How one acts in the present age, therefore, is all important in apocalyptic thinking.[28] Of course, the apocalypticist does not believe that human effort can alter the predetermined course of events. But undivided allegiance to God and absolute obedience to the Law, even in the midst of present adversity, can secure a future reward for the faithful.[29]

The term "apocalyptic," therefore, is applied to a literary phenomenon and to a complex of theological notions.[30] Put differently, "apocalyptic" denotes a distinctive form of writing as well as the thought expressed through such writings. With the same word being used for two different phenomena (both form and content) it is little wonder that a degree of misunderstanding has resulted. In other words, confusion over the complicated subject of apocalyptic begins with the very definition of "apocalyptic."[31]

The Impact of Apocalyptic on New Testament Thought

Because apocalyptic writings and apocalyptic thinking were present and prevalent during the life of Jesus and while most of the NT was composed, a key question in NT theology concerns the impact of apocalyptic eschatology on the thought of the NT. In other words, how essential is apocalyptic to the gospel message? Is apocalyptic so essential that its absence would necessarily distort the gospel, or is apocalyptic merely a first-century framework for NT thought that can be readily dismissed with little or no damage to the essence of the gospel?[32]

Admittedly, the impact of the apocalypse as a literary form is not great. The book of Revelation is the only complete apocalypse in the NT, and only a few other passages contain elements of the apocalypse, most notably the "Synoptic Apocalypse" in Mark 13 (and parallels). As noted earlier, however, the apocalypse is not the only type of literature that expresses apocalyptic eschatology. Thus the impact of apocalyptic thought on the NT is greater than the presence of apocalyptic writings in the NT might suggest.

J. C. Beker has contributed to the debate about the influence of apocalyptic on NT thought by arguing persuasively in *Paul the Apostle*[33] that apocalyptic has a profound impact on Pauline thought. In fact, Beker's thesis that "Paul locates the coherent center of the gospel in the apocalyptic interpretation of the Christ-event"[34] appreciates how vital apocalyptic thinking is to Paul's theological thought. And since Paul's apocalyptic eschatological perspective remains constant and relatively unchanged throughout his apostolic career, the apocalyptic dimension of Pauline thought cannot be ignored or discarded without seriously jeopardizing the Pauline gospel.

To be sure, this first century Pharisee (Phil 3:5) would have been familiar with Pharisaic apocalyptic eschatology, so Paul's encounter with the Risen Christ (Gal 1:16; 1 Cor 9:1, 15:8) merely altered and intensified the apostle's previously held apocalyptic beliefs. One significant alteration can be seen in Paul's unwillingness to use traditional terminology that distinguishes absolutely between "This (evil) Age" and "the Age to Come." Nevertheless, Paul did believe that the End of the Age was near (1 Cor 7:29, 10:11; Rom 13:11-12*a*). On that day (Rom 2:16; 1 Cor 5:5), the dead would be raised (1 Thess 4:16; 1 Cor 15:23-24; 2 Cor 4:14), and death would be defeated once and for all (1 Cor 15:25-26). That day Paul associated with the coming (literally, parousía) of Christ (1 Thess 2:19, 3:13). Thus Paul looked forward to the Parousia (1 Thess 1:10, 2:19, 3:13), believing that "the day of the Lord" would occur at any moment (1 Thess 5:1-2), most likely during his own lifetime (1 Thess 4:15, 17; 1 Cor 15:51-52). Therefore, Paul's apocalyptic thought, which was rooted in his Pharisaic background, persists throughout his apostolic career, as Beker has argued so cogently.[35]

Nevertheless, the apostle Paul and other members of the first generation were wrong about the timing of the Parousia. Christ did not return, and the End did not arrive as was expected. This embarrassing miscalculation on the part of the early Church may help to explain in part why the apocalyptic dimension of the NT has not been fully appreciated until relatively recently. Doctrines of biblical inspiration and infallibility may have encouraged overlooking or ignoring NT passages that speak about the Parousia's arrival in the near future. Errors with regard to the timing of the Parousia, however, have allowed later interpreters to question the certainty of the Parousia's arrival as well and then dismiss the Parousia altogether. In other words, because the Parousia did not occur when it was supposed to, it probably will never happen, so why consider the Parousia at all?

The apostle Paul's thinking, however, demonstrates that a change in the timing of the Parousia need not undermine the certainty of its coming. Throughout most of his career Paul believed that he would be alive at the Parousia (1 Thess 4:15, 17; 1 Cor 15:51-52). Then, during an imprisonment (probably late in his career) Paul admits that he might die before the Parousia arrives (Phil 1:20-21). Even so, Paul remains unshaken in his belief about the coming "day of (Jesus) Christ" (Phil 1:6, 10; 2:16). Paul is still "expecting a Savior, the Lord Jesus Christ" (Phil 3:20b), and he describes his present Christian existence as "the sharing of [Christ's] sufferings by becoming like him in his death" (Phil 3:10) in order to "attain the [future] resurrection from the dead" (Phil 3:11). In the very epistle where Paul acknowledges that his own demise might precede the Parousia (Phil 1:20-21), Paul continues to affirm the imminence of the End: "The Lord is near" (Phil 4:5b). Therefore, although Paul may have changed his mind about whether or not he would be alive at the Parousia, Paul never gives up hope in Christ's future return!

The reactions of other NT authors to the nonarrival of the Parousia have a direct bearing on discussions concerning the impact of apocalyptic on NT thought.[36] After all, if apocalyptic were viewed as *adiasphoros,* a nonessential feature of the faith, then the embarrassment of the delay might have caused post-Pauline authors to abandon this futuristic hope. But if apocalyptic were indispensable for NT thought, then it could not be readily sacrificed, even in the face of the delay.

The NT provides ample testimony to demonstrate that apocalyptic eschatology was not surrendered in the post-Pauline Church. To be sure, the mention of the Parousia is less frequent in the post-Pauline literature than in Paul's undisputed epistles. But these later writings do not forfeit apocalyptic eschatological hope, when it appears that the Parousia has been put off indefinitely. In the later writings of the NT the certainty of the Parousia continues to be emphasized.

While the deutero-Pauline Epistles alter some important aspects of Paul's eschatological thought, these later epistles do not deny the future coming of the Parousia. In 2 Thessalonians 2:1-11 the author departs from Pauline practice by listing events that must take place before the Parousia.[37] One of several things that must happen before the End arrives, according to 2 Thessalonians, includes the revealing of "the lawless one," whom the author is confident "the Lord Jesus will destroy with the breath of his mouth, annihilating him by the manifestation of his parousia" (2 Thess 2:8). Therefore, while the Parousia is not as imminent in this writing as it is in Paul's undisputed epistles, the author does not give up hope in the future coming of Christ (see also 2 Thess 1:7, 10).

213

Other deutero-Pauline Epistles also evidence an alteration in Paul's apocalyptic thinking without giving up on the Parousia. Colossians, for example, mentions the future coming of Christ (Col 3:4), even though some of what Paul portrays as future realities are portrayed as present realities in Colossians.[38] Ephesians also differs considerably from the eschatological thought in the undisputed Pauline Epistles.[39] But, although Ephesians avoids mentioning the Parousia per se, the author's language about "the day of redemption" (Eph 4:30) as well as "this age" in contrast to "the age to come" (1:21; see also 2:7) indicates that the Parousia still plays a considerable role in this author's thinking.

In light of the delay the Pastoral Epistles concern themselves with regulating the ongoing life of the Church. This explains, for example, the lengthy discussions about the offices of bishop (or elder) and deacon (1 Tim 3:1-13; 2 Tim 2:24-26; Titus 1:5-9). But while the Pastorals' attention to the organization and operation of the Church reveals a belief in the abiding nature of the Church, the Pastorals also evidence belief in the future Parousia (1 Tim 6:14; 2 Tim 1:18; Titus 2:13), when Jesus will be revealed as a judge (2 Tim 4:1, 8) and will grant resurrection and life to "the elect" (2 Tim 2:11-12).

The Synoptic Gospels and the Acts of the Apostles which were also written decades after the death and resurrection of Jesus and years after Christ was originally expected to return, reaffirm the future coming of Christ. In the Gospel of Mark, the earliest of the Synoptic Gospels, the Parousia is mentioned on several occasions (Mark 8:38; 13:6-7, 26-27; 14:62; see also 10:37), and the near arrival of the kingdom of God is also stressed (1:15; 9:1). The Gospel of Matthew, which was written after Mark but was literarily dependent on Mark, defers the Parousia a bit more than Mark. In Jesus' discourse concerning Endtime judgment in Matthew (chaps. 23–25), two parables are related that mention "the delay" of one who is expected to come (Matt 24:48; 25:5). The first parable, the parable of the faithful and wise servant (Matt 24:45-51), comes from the Q source, for it is also found in Luke 12:42-46 but is absent in Mark's Gospel. Here the wicked servant grows lax because of the delay and is caught unaware by the returning master. In the parable of the ten maidens (25:1-13), which is unique to Matthew's Gospel and must have come from Matthew's own M source, five foolish maidens fail to prepare properly for the possible delay of the bridegroom and are eventually denied admission to the wedding feast. Far from denying the Parousia, Matthew emphasizes the certainty of the coming Parousia and encourages his readers to be prepared for Christ's return, even though he may come later than originally expected.

The Gospel of Luke, a writing that appears to relax the sense of eschatological urgency,[40] does not forsake the certainty of Christ's coming either. Although he does not believe that the Parousia will come "at once," Luke still claims that it will come suddenly, unexpectedly, and publicly.[41] In response to the parable of the widow who pleads with the judge in Luke

18:1-6 the Lukan Jesus asks rhetorically, "And will not God vindicate his elect, who cry to him day and night? Will he delay long over them?" (Luke 18:7). Jesus then answers, "I tell you, he will vindicate them speedily . . . when the Son of man comes . . ." (Luke 18:8).

In the meantime, the delay is explained as a time for the Church to accomplish its work (see Acts 1:6-8). As the Spirit filled Jesus at his baptism and allowed him to preach, teach, and heal, so this same Spirit fills the Church on Pentecost (Acts 2) and empowers its members to accomplish all that Jesus accomplished. But this period of the Church is not unlimited. It will come to an end when Christ returns in the future (Acts 1:10-11; 3:20-21).

In the Gospels of the NT, therefore, the delay of the Parousia did not result in a complete sacrifice of eschatological hope. The one possible exception to this statement may be the Gospel of John with its distinctive feature known as "realized" eschatology. In response to the delay of the Parousia, the author of the Fourth Gospel has taken those experiences traditionally connected in apocalyptic eschatology with the last day (for example, judgment, resurrection, and eternal life) and declared them to be "realized" in the present life of the believer. Therefore, one is *already* judged by his or her response to Christ (3:18), one is brought from death to life *in the present* by faith (5:24), and to live with faith in Christ is to have eternal life *now* (17:3). As Jesus says in John 12:31, "*Now* is the judgment of this world; *now* the ruler of this world will be driven out."

But even with this emphasis on "realized" eschatology in the Fourth Gospel, John does not forfeit all future eschatological hope. On the contrary, John still talks about the dead being raised on the last day of history (6:39-40, 44, 54) when judgment will take place (5:28-29; 12:48). And John still seems to look for a future coming of Christ (14:3, 18, 28; 21:22-23). As a result, even though John's distinctive message is that Christians already experience the future in their present existence, John does not deny the future and the hope that the future brings. He simply believes that the future holds no surprises for Christians who currently enjoy the benefits of the future.[42]

The author of 1 John also preserved belief in the coming Parousia. This epistle, which was probably written to the same community addressed by the Gospel of John but composed years after the writing of the Fourth Gospel,[43] still mentions the future appearing of Christ (1 John 2:28; 3:2) on the day of judgment (1 John 4:17). And, according to the author, that day is not far off. In fact, at the present time "it is the last hour" (1 John 2:18).

Other late writings of the NT also refer to the future Parousia. The author of Hebrews sees that "the Day [is] approaching" (Heb 10:25), when Christ will "appear a second time" (Heb 9:28). In Heb 10:37 the author cites with approval a quote from Isa 26:20 (the LXX), "For yet 'in a very little while, the one who is coming will come and will not delay.' " The Epistle of James, with its practical advice and strict moral injunctions encourages readers to "be patient . . . for the parousia of the Lord is near" (James 5:8). And the Epistle of Jude admonishes readers to "look forward to the mercy of our Lord Jesus Christ" (Jude 21) on "the great Day" (Jude 6) of judgment. The author of 1 Peter mentions that "The end of all things is near" (1 Pet 4:7), which is a reference to the future "when Jesus Christ is revealed" (1 Pet 1:7, 13). Similarly, Revelation emphasizes that "the time is near" (Rev 1:3; 22:10*b*) and that it will only be "a little longer" (Rev 6:11), for "I am coming soon" (Rev 22:7, 12, 20).

Even in 2 Peter, which is believed to be the latest writing of the NT, composed perhaps in the middle of the second century CE, the delay of the Parousia remains an issue. In fact, much of the epistle is a Christian apology for the delay. Since it is now about one hundred years after the death of Christ and the Parousia has still not occurred, some have complained, " 'Where is the promise of his parousia?' " (2 Pet 3:4). In response to this question the author cites Ps 90:4 to explain that God is on a different timetable (2 Pet 3:8). Divine time does not coincide with human time. But then the author goes on to state that the delay is in fact a sign of God's forbearance, for God does not want "any to perish, but all to come to repentance" (2 Pet 3:9*b*). In spite of this lengthy delay the author does not sacrifice eschatological hope. In fact, the author continues: "But the day of the Lord will come like a thief, and then the heavens will pass away . . . and the elements will be dissolved . . . , and the earth and everything that is done on it will be disclosed" (2 Pet 3:10). In this latest writing of the NT the delay is cast in positive terms while the author continues to underscore the certainty of the Parousia's sudden and unmistakable arrival.

Therefore, none of the post-Pauline NT writings discussed above, which include the deutero-Pauline Epistles, the Synoptic Gospels and Acts, John's Gospel, Hebrews, the general Epistles,[44] and Revelation, sacrificed their belief in the coming day of the Lord, even though the historical realities seemed to contradict the imminence of Christ's return. True, the post-Pauline writings may have placed less explicit emphasis on the Parousia than did the apostle Paul. But instead of merely ignoring the belief in Christ's return, the authors of the NT attempted to explain the delay in terms of God's patience and mercy, they detailed appropriate behavior in the meantime, and they outlined the outward mission and internal structure of the Church prior to the arrival of the End.

The fact that the nonreturn of Christ did not persuade these early Christians to relinquish their future hope is a telling statement about the significance of apocalyptic eschatology in the early Church. Why did the post-Pauline authors not simply give up on the Parousia? Why did they go to such lengths to reinterpret eschatological hope in the face of the nonarrival? Perhaps the best explanation is that apocalyptic eschatological hope was crucial to the Christian faith and could not be ignored or glossed over without profoundly altering the very essence of the gospel.

The Persistence of Apocalyptic Thought

The influence of apocalyptic on the theology of the NT, however, is not limited to the relatively few texts that specifically mention the Parousia. After all, apocalyptic represents a complex of interrelated notions, and the Parousia is only one important component of this complex. A consideration of how belief in the Parousia is related to other apocalyptic notions, therefore, may help to explain the unwillingness of NT authors to sacrifice eschatological hope and belief in the Parousia. Because this relationship between the Parousia and other apocalyptic ideas is most clearly evidenced in the few apocalyptic texts found in the NT, a closer examination of these texts (especially 1 Corinthians 15, Mark 13, and the book of Revelation) may shed some light on the persistence of apocalyptic thinking in the early Church.

Apocalyptic and the Resurrection of the Dead. As noted above, one ingredient of apocalyptic eschatology is a belief in the resurrection of the dead. At the End of This Age, on the day of the Lord, it was believed that the dead would be raised, the raised judged, and the elect rewarded with life in the Age to Come. Early Christians interpreted Christ's resurrection within this schema. But whereas the resurrection of Christ signaled the beginning of the End, the continued reign of suffering and death clearly indicated that the Age to Come had not yet arrived in its fullness. The resurrection of Christ, therefore, was understood as the foundation and the assurance of the future consummation of the kingdom of God.

Christ's death and his resurrection were understood from the beginning as essential[45] but not as ultimate events. In 1 Corinthians 15 Paul argues that Christ was "the first fruits of those who have died" (literally, "have fallen asleep," 1 Cor 15:20). Because of his own apocalyptic perspective, which associated the day of the Lord with the resurrection of the dead for the purpose of judgment, Paul did not accept the resurrection of Jesus Christ as God's ultimate victory. Not until all believers were "conformed to the image of his Son, in order that he might be the first-born among many brethren" (Rom 8:29) would God's ultimate purpose be achieved. And only "at his *parousia* those who belong to Christ" (1 Cor 15:23) would "be made alive" (1 Cor 15:22). The fact that Christ was raised from the dead was a clear indication that the End was at hand and that death, "the last enemy" (1 Cor 15:26), had been dealt a fatal blow. But the continued existence of death and suffering in the world, along with the absence of any final judgment, proved that the day of the Lord was still a future event.

The book of Revelation also portrays the resurrection of Christ as the foundational but not the ultimate event. According to the vision provided in Revelation 5, Christ, "the Lamb that was slaughtered," is now enthroned in heaven. But the enthronement of Christ (that is, the child who "was snatched away and taken to God and to his throne" in Rev 12:5) resulted in war between the forces of good ("Michael and his angels," according to Rev 12:7a) and the

217

forces of evil ("the dragon and his angels," according to Rev 12:7*b*). John describes the outcome of this heavenly battle in this way: "The great dragon was thrown down, that ancient serpent, who is called the Devil and Satan, the deceiver of the whole world—he was thrown down to the earth, and his angels were thrown down with him" (Rev 12:9).

Knowing that John (as well as every other author of the Bible) believed in a multi-tiered universe, with heaven above, the flat earth situated beneath, and the underworld below the earth, the author describes the death and resurrection of Christ as a crucial but only partial victory. While heaven has been rid of all enemies of God, other parts of the created order are not. For this reason, the author concludes this passage with the admonition: "Rejoice then, you heavens and those who dwell in them! But woe to the earth and the sea, for the devil has come down to you with great wrath, because he knows that his time is short!" (Rev 12:12).

Not until the Parousia, described in Rev 19:11-21, will the forces of evil be driven from the face of the earth (Rev 19:20-21) and Satan will be confined to the underworld (Rev 20:2-3). Finally, however, even the underworld will be rid of Satan, who will be released, then "thrown into the lake of fire and sulfur, where the beast and the false prophet were" (Rev 20:10). At that time the dead will be raised for the purpose of judgment (Rev 20:13), then Death and the underworld (Hades), which has outlived its usefulness, will be "thrown into the lake of fire" (Rev 20:14).

After that, according to John, a new heaven will descend to a new earth (Rev 21:1-2) with the result that "the home of God [will be] among mortals"[46] (Rev 21:3-4). The ultimate victory of God, as described in the book of Revelation, is not realized until life in this three-tiered universe becomes life on a single plain of existence. The resurrection of Christ, therefore, is surely the vital first step in this story of salvation, but it is clearly not the final step!

New Testament authors are unwilling to forfeit eschatological hope, therefore, because to do so would invest Christ's resurrection with an inappropriate significance. If the future consummation of the Kingdom is denied, then Christ's resurrection is perceived as the extent of God's saving activity. The resurrection of Christ becomes an act of God that affects only one individual rather than an act of God that foreshadows and secures things to come for all persons. To be sure, the elimination of this futuristic element would dramatically alter the Christian faith.

Apocalyptic and the Sovereignty of God. Another important reason that NT authors did not forfeit their apocalyptic hope was due to their belief in the sovereignty of God. Although evil and suffering may appear to have the upper hand in the present, early Christians, like all good apocalypticists, were optimistic about the future. They believed that God would triumph, and those who side with him in the present will share in God's ultimate victory. But while believers would participate in the spoils of the victory, this triumph would not be achieved by human effort. Only God could achieve the ultimate victory.

The apostle Paul, for example, knew that his missionary proclamation was a necessary precondition of faith (see Rom 10:14-17). But he was also aware that faith was not the ultimate goal to which believers should aspire. Because Paul believed that "flesh and blood cannot inherit the kingdom of God, nor does the perishable inherit the imperishable" (1 Cor 15:50), he asserted that "we will all be changed" (1 Cor 15:51). Not simply the dead, but the living as well, will have to be transformed in order to inherit the kingdom of God. And will human effort bring about this change? Of course not! God is the only one who can work this miracle of re-creation. For Paul, therefore, God plays the primary role throughout the entire drama of salvation. As Paul remarks: "For those whom *he* foreknew *he* also predestined to be conformed to the image of his Son, in order that he might be the first-born among many brethren. And those whom *he* predestined *he* also called; and those whom *he* called *he* also justified; and those whom *he* justified *he* also glorified" (Rom 8:29-30; italics mine).

It is not insignificant that Paul follows the above quote with the remarkable statement, "What then are we to say about these things? If God is for us, who is against us?" (Rom 8:32). According to Paul, nothing can thwart God's purposes, not death, life, angels, principalities, things present, things to come, powers, height, depth, or anything else in all creation (Rom 8:38-39). Paul never surrendered his belief that God's will would be done, even though present circumstances (such as the unbelief of the Jews, as Paul goes on to consider in Romans 9–11) may appear to contradict that future reality.

The book of Revelation also stresses the insufficiency of human effort to bring about God's ultimate purpose. After the final judgment in Revelation 20, then a new heaven will descend to a new earth (Rev 21:1-2), with the result that God will dwell with humanity: "He will dwell with them as their God; they will be his peoples, and God himself will be with them" (Rev 21:3b-4). As stated above, the "new Jerusalem" descends to a new earth in Revelation 21. Does human effort raise the kingdom of God on earth, according to John? No, "he who sat on the throne" takes credit when he proclaims, "Behold, I make all things new" (Rev 21:5).

Moreover, the ultimate triumph of God is never in question in Revelation. Even though this work was written by one who had suffered persecution on account of his faith (Rev 1:9) to communities that have experienced persecution (Rev 2:13; 6:9-10) and will probably suffer martyrdom in the future (Rev 6:11), John does not permit such duress to call into question the sovereignty of God. In fact, John argues, the suffering of the faithful at the present time is a sure sign of God's ultimate victory. Why? Because present persecution is the direct result of Christ's exaltation. As stated above, Satan has been cast out of heaven, and "because he knows that his time is short," he seeks out the faithful on earth in order to destroy them (Rev 12:10-12).

Apocalyptic and Ethics. Contrary to common perception, apocalyptic eschatology is not interested in the future merely out of curiosity. The fact that apocalyptic writings routinely contain ethical instruction, as noted above, indicates that appropriate behavior in the present is recognized as a legitimate concern of apocalyptic. The knowledge of what will take place in the future naturally raises the question of how best to prepare for its arrival. Apocalyptic, therefore, rightfully concerns itself with present behavior. Similarly, careful examination of NT apocalyptic texts reveals that the payoff for futuristic discussion is also present action.

The apostle Paul's treatment of the future has a present payoff. Following the Apostle's extensive examination of the futuristic dimension of the faith in 1 Corinthians 15, Paul writes: "Therefore, my beloved, be steadfast, immovable, always excelling in the work of the Lord, because you know that in the Lord your labor is not in vain" (1 Cor 15:58). For Paul, an awareness of the future informed present behavior.[47] The very fact that the Corinthians did not share Paul's view of the future (see 1 Cor 15:12) may have been in large measure responsible for their factious and excessive behavior (1 Cor 1:11-13; 11:17-22).

Again, consider also the book of Revelation, which is often perceived as a vacuous attempt at crystal ball gazing. By the author's own admission, he is not simply interested in the future. John describes the future in order to encourage his readers to endure the present. In the face of persecution the author issues "a call for the endurance of the saints, those who keep the commandments of God and hold fast to the faith of Jesus" (Rev 14:12; cf. 13:10). Even though it will mean suffering and death, Christians must reject the beast and instead be wholeheartedly devoted to God. Under these conditions, being "lukewarm" will simply not do (Rev 3:16).

The "Synoptic Apocalypse" of Mark 13 is another example of how eschatological speculation is for the purpose of present behavior. This lengthy discussion describes present signs as preliminary (Mark 13:5-23) and warns against premature claims about the arrival of the Parousia. It goes on to state that the end will be an unmistakable cosmic event (Mark 13:24-27), one which is coming soon (Mark 13:28-31), but the exact time of which one cannot calculate (Mark 13:32-33). Then the chapter ends with implications for present behavior. The proper attitude during this present time is one of watchful, prayerful waiting lest one be caught unaware (Mark 13:33-36). And the entire chapter ends on a note of admonition: "Watch" (Mark 13:37; see also 13:23).

Elsewhere in the NT a close connection between the future and present behavior is also seen. Matthew's concern with being prepared for Christ's return even though he has been delayed, accounts in part for the stringent ethical injunctions in the First Gospel. Fearful that the delay of the Parousia will result in spiritual laxity, Matthew emphasizes the need to remain faithful and wholly devoted to the cause and mission of Christ during the interim. That means doing the will of God, not simply mouthing the words, for as Matthew's Jesus says, "Not everyone who says to me, 'Lord, Lord,' will enter the kingdom of heaven, but only the one who does the will of my Father in heaven" (Matt 7:21).

According to Matthew's Gospel, the present time is an important time for accomplishing the will of God. And in Matthew one thing that is clearly the will of God is a universal mission. After his resurrection Jesus commands the disciples in Galilee to "Go therefore and make disciples of all nations . . . teaching them to obey everything that I have commanded you" (Matt 28:19a, 20a), and on another occasion the disciples are told that "this good news of the kingdom will be proclaimed throughout the world, as a testimony to all the nations; and then the end will come" (Matt 24:14). In light of this considerable task the End does not appear as imminent, but the interval before the End is cast in a positive light as a time of doing God's will and teaching others to obey as well. In fact, those who do and teach others to do God's will shall "be called great in the [future] kingdom of heaven" (Matt 5:19b). Until that time, Jesus promises to be with his disciples "to the end of the age" (Matt 28:20b).

The apocalyptic dimension of faith, therefore, inspires believers to endure present hardship, motivates God's people to do God's will at the present, and provides followers of Christ with a sense of universal mission. As a result, the authors of the NT could ill-afford to eliminate apocalyptic hope, even when Christ did not return.

Conclusion. As the foregoing discussion has demonstrated, apocalyptic thinking in the NT is not limited to a few explicitly apocalyptic texts. Neither is apocalyptic thinking and its belief in the future coming of Christ limited to the writings of first generation Christians, who so fervently awaited Christ's return. Even though later generations were faced with an indefinite delay in the arrival of the Parousia, these believers did not eliminate apocalyptic expectation.

The pervasiveness and persistence of apocalyptic thought in the NT can only be explained by realizing that apocalyptic is essential to early Christian belief. Apocalyptic understood the death and resurrection of Christ as proleptic, not ultimate events; it asserted the sovereignty of God even though present conditions might appear to contradict this; and it informed the life and practice of the Church, how Christians should act and what they should be doing in anticipation of the End.

For these reasons, this dimension of the Christian faith could not be sacrificed without drastically altering all of Christian belief. Contrary to some modern interpretations, apocalyptic is not merely a "rind" that can be peeled away to get at the "core" of faith. Rather, when this dimension is removed, one finds nothing but "peelings."

Even in the face of a lengthy delay, the early Church did not sacrifice its hope in the future. Rather, Christians worked hard to reinterpret the time of the Parousia and redefine responsibilities during the interim, as they waited with confidence for God to complete what God began in Christ.

Chapter Thirteen / ANCIENT APOCALYPTIC THOUGHT AND THE NEW TESTAMENT

James H. Charlesworth

A s most biblical scholars know, Ernst Käsemann claimed that apocalyptic thought is the mother of all Christian theology.[1] Now New Testament experts tend to concur that NT theology is grounded in and defined by apocalyptic thought. What does this conclusion denote and what are its implications?

Denotation

In the attempt to comprehend the conclusion that NT theology is grounded in and defined by apocalyptic thought,[2] I have focused on five categories of observation: 1. comprehensibility; 2. eschatology, apocalypsology, messianology, and resurrection; 3. hope; 4. coherency in NT theology; and 5. Christology and apocalypsology. At the outset, however, it is important to recognize that any contention that apocalyptic thought is comprehensible and somewhat coherent demands allowing for significant variations in what should not be *prima facie* assumed to be a literary genre. We must also proceed with caution in describing coherent features, on the one hand, because extreme variety is represented by the documents called "apocalypses" in the Hebrew Bible, the NT, and especially the Old Testament Pseudepigrapha, and on the other hand, because unusual difficulties are encountered in describing, let alone defining, an apocalypse.[3] Indeed, this is a not an easy task, since we now possess not two (Daniel and Revelation)[4] but numerous apocalypses, of which the most important are the two attributed to Enoch and those now pseudonymously assigned to Zephaniah, Ezra, Baruch, and Abraham. All these Pseudepigraphical apocalypses are contemporaneous with or antedate the NT documents.[5] The literary evidence of Jewish apocalypticism extends far beyond the documents that are apocalypses, and encompasses apocalyptic writings like testaments, especially the Testaments of the Twelve Patriarchs, and hymns, notably the Psalms of Solomon.

1. *Comprehensibility*

The foundation of apocalyptic thought is the claim that meaning is not to be sought on the earth and in historical events, no matter how apparently promising. This theological position is represented, in a stunning fashion, by the author of 1 Enoch 42:1, "Wisdom could not find a place in which she could dwell; but a place was found (for her) in the heavens." Wisdom, thence, cannot be found on earth; this perspective is markedly different from the Wisdom literature, especially Proverbs, Wisdom of Solomon, Sirach, and Ahikar. Meaning and the answers to all human questions is coming—or shall come at the Endtime—only from the heavens above the earth (in which Wisdom dwells), or solely from the future.

Apocalypsology, therefore, derives from a conviction that a seer—like Enoch, Noah, Abraham, or Ezra—has received (from God or an angel, but usually through a visit to the heavens or the future) a disclosure of what is in the heavens above or what will be in the future age that is about to dawn in the present age.[6] A vivid and representative account of how an ancient Jewish author explained how Enoch went into the heavens above is found in 2 Enoch 1–3[A]. When Enoch was 365 days old[7] he was asleep on his bed, and claims to have seen "two huge men" appearing "to me, the like of which I had never seen on earth." After a description of these angels, Enoch continues to speak: "And they called [me] by my name." After bidding farewell to his sons Enoch is reputed to have said, "And they took me up onto their wings, and carried me up to the first heaven." According to this early Jewish tradition Enoch is taken physically (in the body) into the heavens. However, in an older tradition, Enoch claims to have received "a holy vision from the heavens which the angels showed me" (1 Enoch 1:2). Other traditions, such as those in the Testament of Levi 5, conflate the two, so that a reference to a vision (T. Levi 5:1)[8] is then assumed to be a physical transference (T. Levi 5:3).[9]

These two different explanations of how a seer "entered" the heavens above help us interpret and understand, exegetically and hermeneutically, Paul's description of his apocalyptic ascent into the heavens. He wishes to stress that he did so, and that it is insignificant whether he ascended "in the body or out of the body" (2 Cor 12:2-3).

The concept of two ages, well known from Rabbinics and often incorrectly attributed to post–two hundred rabbinic thought, is found in one of the most important Jewish apocalypses, 4 Ezra, which was written in the generation that had experienced the destruction of the Temple in CE 70. Note that chronology serves theology in 4 Ezra 8:1, "The Most High made this world for the sake of many, but the world to come for the sake of few" *(Hoc saeculum fecit Altissimus propter multos, futurum autem propter paucos).*[10] Apocalyptic theology, by the time of 4 Ezra, is shaped by the understanding that in the history of the cosmos there are two ages, and the second—the blessed age—is impinging on the present age.

The theologies of Jesus and Paul were formed by this apocalyptically shaped eschatological thought. On the basis of this concept of time, Jesus can proclaim the dawning (in this age) of God's Rule (the kingdom of God), and Paul can mention "the fullness of time" (Gal 4:4). Both Jesus and Paul, especially in their eschatologically grounded theologies, were thence paradigmatically influenced by the linear and teleological concept of time that had been developed in apocalyptic theology.

It is possible that Jesus inherited the concept of the Rule of God (the kingdom of God) from apocalypticism and apocalyptic writings. His theological perspective of God's Rule was adumbrated in the OT writings (notably Pss 103:19, 145:11-13; Isa 52:7), but it is much closer—because of the highly charged eschatological tone—to the Jewish apocalyptically inspired documents (viz. Dan 3:54; Sib. Or. 3:47, 3:767; T. Benj. 9:1; T. Ab. 8:3; 1QM 6:6, 12:7; Pss. Sol. 17:4; T. Mos. 10:1-15; cf. Tob. 13:2; Wis. 6:4, 10:10).[11] Of course, Jesus' creative alteration of the concept of the Rule of God must also be acknowledged, not the least of which is in the shifting of the audience from scribal schools to the outcasts of Israel, the form not of writing but of proclamation, the urgency of the present inbreaking of God's Rule on this earth and only in his mission, and the central emphasis on the Rule of God over other competing concepts.

The claim that NT theology is grounded in, and defined by, apocalyptic thought indicates that it is originally and profoundly Jewish. This insight derives from the recognition that while pseudoapocalyptic thought may be found outside Judaism, all full-blown apocalypses are Jewish.[12] The apocalypses inherit the eschatological and apocalyptic ideas, which first appear in the OT books, especially in Ezekiel 38–39, Zechariah 5–6, 9–14, and Isaiah 24–27 and 56–66.[13]

To contend that Jewish apocalyptic theology is comprehensible certainly does not mean it is systematic or possesses a coherent core.[14] The apocalypses and apocalyptic writings are often closely (but not always) tied to social crises and, hence, derive their coherency from this contingency. Apocalypsology is based on a linear and teleological view of history, but it is often intentionally circular and redundant. It is thence phenomenologically and sociologically based and that helps us understand why some texts seem ideologically and even conceptually contradictory. That is to say, the apocalypses appear because of problems faced by Palestinian Jews from the second century BCE through the second century CE, especially the loss of the land promised by God to Abraham's descendants who are now ruled harshly by pagans who denied the power, even existence of Israel's God—the only God. The apocalyptic writings thus derive from social crises and are not to be confused with philosophical, visionary treatises like Plato's *Republic*.

2. *Eschatology, Apocalypsology, Messianology, and Resurrection*

To claim that NT theology is grounded in, and defined by, apocalyptic thought includes the recognition that apocalypsology is usually but not necessarily eschatological. Some Jewish thinkers (notably the authors of 2 Baruch[15] and 2 Enoch

224

43–68) shifted a preoccupation with the End of time to the earthly importance of otherworldly visions. This recognition helps us understand the options chosen by the authors of the Gospels of Luke and John, which are contemporaneous with these apocalypses. They chose to modify the early kerygmatically based eschatology (found, for example, in Mark 9:1, and in the speeches attributed to Peter in Acts) so that an emphasis falls on the present possession of salvation, through the presence of God's Rule among the faithful (Luke 17:1, cf. John 15, 17), experienced as the presence of salvation in "being born anew" (John 3), drinking "living water" (John 4), and eating the "bread from heaven" (John 6).

This "Christian" deemphasis of futuristic eschatology (although not in the direction of apocalyptic thought) may be foreshadowed in some Jewish documents that stress apocalyptic vision over eschatology. An example may be the Angelic Liturgy (4QShirShabb, 11QShirShabb, MasShirShabb) in which there is no eschatology but an abundance of apocalyptic visions of angels, who sometimes are described as "priests" *(kōhānim)*,[16] and whose purpose is to praise the King (who is God). The purpose of this apocalyptically inspired document is not to urge one to ponder the End of time or to stress the dawning of a new age; it is to entice the reader to experience (and even for the Most Holy Ones to participate in) what is going on in the present, the praising of God by the angels.[17]

Other Jewish documents stress eschatology and are not preoccupied with a disclosure of what is in the heavens above. For example, the Testament of Levi contains apocalyptic language which describes what shall happen at the Endtime. Note T. Levi 18:2,

> And then the Lord will raise up a new priest
> to whom all the words of the Lord will be revealed.

It is this vision of the future which was so formative for the authors of the "sectarian" Dead Sea Scrolls. Acting out the words of Isaiah 40:3,[18] which they understood to refer to them, the early Qumranites literally thought they were preparing in the wilderness the Way of Yahweh. Believing that they were living at the End of time, and that the Righteous Teacher was God's chosen one who was to plant God's eternal planting, they affirmed that this priest fulfilled the promise of the vision recorded in T. Levi 18:2. Note the key words of Pesher Habakkuk; God allowed the Moreh Hassedek to know "all the mysteries of the words of his servants, the prophets" (1QpHab 7:5). It is probable that the Qumranites knew the tradition recorded in T. Levi 18:2, and they may have known it directly from this document, since a version of the Testament of Levi has been found among the Qumran Scrolls.[19]

Such apocalyptic traditions helped shape the various theologies in the NT. The Qumranic apocalyptic and eschatological development of the concept of the Holy Spirit, which is from God, probably influenced Jesus.[20] The Qumran stress on the fact that only God can make one righteous may have influenced Paul.[21] The evangelist John was influenced by the apocalyptic and eschatological dualism, and technical terms developed definitively in the Rule of the Community.[22] Under the influence of apocalypsology the author of Hebrews portrayed Jesus as the eschatological priest who is enthroned in heaven, after the order of Melchizedek.

Many of the references to the coming of the "Messiah" in Jewish literature before CE 132 (the beginning of the messianically inspired Bar Kokhba revolt) are preserved in apocalypses, namely 4 Ezra and 2 Baruch.[23] It is Jewish apocalypsology, therefore, that significantly helped to develop the concept of an eschatological figure who will be the Messiah.[24] In the Dead Sea Scrolls (viz. 1QS) the concept of the Messiah is developed not only along eschatological but also apocalyptic lines. That is, his appearance will coincide with the apocalyptic shift in ages and the destruction of Belial in the great and final war. It is surprising, however, that references to the Messiah do not appear in the War Scroll, and that little is said about what will happen with the appearance of the Messiahs of Aaron and Israel.

A little later than the Rule of the Community, which dates from sometime before 100 BCE, some Jews living in Jerusalem noted in a hymnbook their belief in the coming of the Messiah. In the Psalms of Solomon he is portrayed apocalyptically and not historically (that is in terms of *Heilsgeschichte*). Only God knows how and when *ho christos* shall appear (Pss. Sol. 17:21). And when the Messiah purges Jerusalem of the Gentiles (obviously the Romans) he will not rely on human means, "he will not rely on horse, rider, or bow," for he "will strike the earth with the word of his mouth forever" (*tō logō tou stomātos autou eis aiona;* Pss. Sol. 17:35, cf. 17:24). There can be no doubt that this concept is a significant development of the messianic ideas found in the OT (including Zechariah): it reflects the formative influence of apocalypticism.

One of the remarkable discoveries of recent research on Jewish messianology may now be mentioned. While it is impossible, on the basis of our literary evidence, to conclude that most Jews were looking for the coming of a Messiah, and while there was no checklist of what his functions should be, or what results should accompany his coming, within a decade of Jesus' crucifixion his followers enthusiastically endorsed the concept that he had been the Messiah.[25] This proclamation is remarkable because Jesus' death was not in line with postexilic messianology (there is not one Jewish text antedating 70 CE that portrays the death of the Messiah). Moreover, Jesus did nothing that was significantly or uniquely the function of the Messiah according to the theologies of early Judaism; for example, he did not drive the Gentiles out of Jerusalem as the community of the Psalms of Solomon expected.

The influence of apocalyptic theology on the earliest *kerygma*—actually, *kērygmata*—is obvious. To proclaim that Jesus is the eschatological "Messiah" is not only to inherit, but also to recast apocalyptic perspectives and ideas. Furthermore, a major innovation in early Jewish apocalypsology is the concept of resurrection. It was in the Jewish apocalypses that the concept of the resurrection of the righteous to eternal rewards (and even the unjust to punishment) after death appeared and was developed. The earliest appearance of the Jewish concept of resurrection seems to be in 1 Enoch 22, which was composed sometime before 200 BCE,[26] and which refers to three groups—"the spirits of the souls of the dead"— who will rise "on the day of judgment." A clear presentation of this concept is in Dan 12:2, which dates from around 164 BCE: "And many of those who sleep in the earth's dust shall awake (yāqîṣu), some to everlasting life, and some to shame and everlasting contempt." It is, thus, from Jewish apocalyptic theology that the followers of Jesus inherited the belief that God will raise up those who have died, especially (and sometimes only) the righteous.

The concept that God will raise the righteous from the dead is an innovation in early Jewish theology, and this breakthrough in theological sophistication was made by the Jewish apocalyptists. The proclamation that God raised Jesus up from the dead is the essence of the earliest "Christian" theology, and this claim was possible, and culturally acceptable, because of apocalypticism.[27] This fact alone would establish the position that NT theology is grounded in and defined by apocalyptic thought, since all NT theologies develop from this essential idea. The followers of Jesus, of course, would stress that what we have labeled a concept was not an "idea"; for them it was an experienced fact (whether in actual confrontation, as with Mary Magdalene, Peter, and Paul, or in a spiritual [pneumatic] experience that Jesus continued to be present, for which diverse expressions were developed).

3. Hope

The claim that NT theology is grounded in, and defined by, apocalyptic thought becomes obvious when we consider the stress on "hope" in apocalypsology. The apocalypses are not examples of "doom" literature focused on a pessimistic view; they offer a message of hope for the faithful ones on earth.

This aspect of apocalypsology is often missed because studies often myopically focus on the explanations for the origin of sin and on the indications that apocalypses appear out of social settings in which hope is lost. The apocalyptists do acknowledge that sin is pervasive. They develop both explanations for the origin of sin found in the OT: the conception that Adam is to blame (4 Ezra from Genesis 3), and the explanation that fallen angels brought sin to earth (1 Enoch 1–36 from Genesis 6). Many Jesus traditions show that he was apparently influenced by these apocalyptic reflections, since he clearly believed in Satan (and Luke records that he claims to have seen Satan fall from heaven; Luke 10:18). Paul clearly is indebted to them (viz. Romans 1).[28]

Often the social setting behind the apocalypses is one of suffering and oppression. The author of a Jewish apocalypse, and usually his community also,[29] found it problematic (and sometimes impossible) to receive hope from the historical process on this earth. We can imagine the social alienation and depravation of those who composed the apocalyptic documents; perhaps we catch a glimpse of social realities in the following words:

> Woe unto you who eat the best bread!
> And drink wine in large bowls,
> trampling upon the weak people with your might.
> Woe unto you who have water available to you all the time, . . .
> Woe unto you, O powerful people!
> You who coerce the righteous with your power, . . .
>
> (1 Enoch 96:5-8)

It is out of such suffering that apocalypsology crafts a message of hope. Suffering is not ignored; rather it is affirmed in powerful images and scenarios (at Qumran the elect and the archangels cannot defeat the evil angels; cf. 1QM). Satan appears at times more powerful than Michael; yet, it is out of suffering that apocalyptic hope is born. The apocalyptists correlated suffering and hope. Or to return to our text, 1 Enoch 96, the powerful ones are actually powerless, for their day of "destruction is coming!" (1 Enoch 96:8). Those who are now suffering, the righteous ones, receive an inviolable promise, sent from God to them through the seer: "I now swear to you, righteous ones . . . all good things, and joy and honor are prepared for and written down for the souls of those who died in righteousness" (1 Enoch 103:1-3).

This message of apocalyptic hope helps us understand the joy of the early Jesus communities in Palestine. The crucifixion was unexpected and drained the hope of Jesus' followers;[30] recall the words of Cleopas, "we had hoped . . . " (*hēmeis de ēlpizomen;* Luke 24:21).[31] Apocalyptic fervor built up in the Palestinian Jesus communities, primarily because of the apocalyptic and eschatological claim that Jesus had been raised by God. He was alive and had appeared to Mary Magdalene and the disciples. Jesus' group of Jews can only be described as apocalyptic and eschatological; in the words of Bultmann, it was

> an eschatological sect within Judaism, distinguished from other sects and trends not only by the fact that it awaits the crucified Jesus of Nazareth as the Son of Man, but especially by the fact that it is conscious of being already the called and chosen Congregation of the end of days.[32]

Indicating the importance of Jewish apocalypticism and the apocalypses for NT theology are the following concepts in this apt assessment: "eschatological sect within Judaism," "it awaits," "the Son of Man," and "conscious of being already the called and chosen Congregation of the end of days." The Palestinian Jesus movement was an apocalyptic sect; it looked back to Jesus for a perception of God's will, but more importantly, awaited with eager expectation for his return and the Endtime. The Aramaic liturgy was couched in apocalyptic language: Marana tha, "Our Lord, come!" (1 Cor 16:22).[33]

4. Coherency in New Testament Theology

To claim that NT theology is grounded in, and defined by, apocalyptic thought implies that we can talk about NT theology and have not given up on perceiving a unity within (and behind) the diverse (and often contradictory) theologies canonized in the NT.

At the outset we must be honest and acknowledge, and remain aware that there are many theologies in the documents collected into the canon. We should be leery of trying to posit a core, and surely must resist the temptation to reduce NT theology to a system or coherent whole. Then, and only then, may we go on to grasp that there is coherence and unity to the NT theologies. I venture to suggest it may well be creatively focused and expressed as follows: at the proper time in human history (which is linear, teleological, and eschatological), the Creator moves forward (not only from the past but also from the future) and earthward (from heaven) through the eschatological prophet Jesus of Nazareth, who is the risen Christ—celebrated primarily as Lord and the Son of God—to bring oneness and peace to the cosmos and to fulfill his promises grounded in the covenants with Adam, Noah, Abraham, and Moses, and rearticulated throughout history, especially through the prophets.

The fulfillment extends beyond the bounds of the promises and redefines them in a way only adumbrated in the perception of God's love found in Hosea, so that the closest followers of Jesus did not understand Jesus' message that he must suffer, be rejected, and die. New Testament theology is focused on the claims that Jesus' life and crucifixion were not meaningless, as they were to many who knew him, including Pontius Pilate and the High Priest Caiaphas, but that these were efficacious in ways not conceptually clear or coherent.[34] The proof in this belief (the *kērygmata*) developed within a generation of Jesus' death. Jesus' Jewish followers claimed to have experienced that he who was crucified was identical to the one raised by God who appeared (most notably) to Mary, Peter, the eleven (including Thomas), and Paul. It was the experience of the resurrected Jesus and the unshakable faith in God's resurrection of him from the dead that was the catalyst, not the origin, of NT theology.

The result was the conviction that Jesus would return to fulfill the Jewish hopes often associated with the Son of man and the Messiah. Hence, the NT "theologians" further developed the Jewish concept of God's righteousness,[35] which was a concern of many Jewish authors contemporaneous with Jesus, and the apocalyptic dream that the present is meaningful because of the assurance that God's promises will be—indeed are being—fulfilled, and the conviction that Jesus' divine Sonship will be revealed as God completes and establishes his will throughout the universe.

He who had made God present, and was experienced especially in the liturgies—especially the eucharist—would return "as he was taken away" (cf.

Acts 1:11). All of these thoughts are either indirectly or profoundly shaped by the apocalypsology, the apocalyptic writings, and the apocalyptically charged intellectual world of Jesus' time and the time of his earliest followers.

5. *Christology and Apocalypsology*

To claim that NT theology is grounded in, and defined by, apocalyptic thought means that Christology is profoundly indebted to Jewish apocalypsology. Christology extends to include protology and eschatology, and each of these extensions of historical thinking was developed earlier by the Jewish apocalyptists. The previous discussions indicated the obvious fact that reflections of Jesus as the Christ were shaped by the apocalyptists' ideas concerning "the Messiah." Since specialists now recognize that the apocalyptic speculations regarding the Son of man, in 1 Enoch 37–71, are not only Jewish but roughly contemporaneous with Jesus and antedate the Christologies in the NT, then it becomes clear how formative apocalyptic thought was for Christology. Some of the best experts now recognize that the Son of man is identified with the Messiah in 1 Enoch 37–71,[36] hence, what scholars once attributed to Jesus' followers is now seen to be part of the creative reflections by Jewish apocalyptists. The evangelist John inherited from Jewish apocalypsology the concept (suggested by Genesis 1) that God created the world by his word. His concept of "the Word" may be not so much his own creation as a christological development of a Jewish perception preserved in a document that has been lost. The concept of Christ as "the Voice," which is found in Revelation 1, derives from Jewish apocalypsology, since some of the Jewish apocalypses introduce the concept of a hypostatic being, an angel with wings, who is "the Voice."[37]

The portrayal of Jesus in angelic terms, and the confession by Peter that Jesus is an angel found in the Gospel of Thomas, develops out of Jewish apocalyptic speculation. We now know that numerous biblical heroes, like Adam and Jacob, were conceived to be angels by some of Jesus' near contemporaries.[38]

The Christologies preserved in the birth narratives of Matthew and Luke are obviously influenced by Jewish apocalypsology, since they give prominence to the angelology developed in the apocalypses. This link with apocalypticism is galvanized by the recognition that Jesus' miraculous birth is paralleled by the descriptions of the spectacular births of Noah and Melchizedek found in 1 Enoch and 2 Enoch.

The parousia—the *return* of Jesus as triumphant Messiah—is itself not a totally novel idea in the history of ideas; it is foreshadowed in apocalypsology. Since the Messiah was once present on earth and with Adam[39] he can be thought to *return* to earth. Hence, Jews who looked for the coming of the Messiah could speak about his return. The classic example is found in 2 Baruch 30:

> And it shall happen after these things, when the time for the coming of the Messiah has been fulfilled and he returns [Syriac: *wenehpoch*] in glory, that all who sleep in hope of him shall arise.[40]

The concept that Jesus will return as Messiah is adumbrated in the Jewish apocalypses; in these literary masterpieces we find a record of the Jewish idea that the Messiah's appearance shall be his *return* to earth. Apocalypsology, thus, is the foreground for the earliest Christologies, providing not only protological and eschatological reflections, but also stellar concepts such as the cosmologically framed belief in the return of the Messiah to this earth. It is obvious how apocalypsology helps ground and define Christology.

New Testament Christology does not come full-blown out of the mind of Judaism as Athena out of the head of Zeus, even if the incursion by Romans into Palestinian Judaism can be compared to the thunderous blow by Hephaestus. It did, however, clearly ascend out of one of the most creative and theologically sophisticated cultures human history has known, despite the penchant of many NT specialists to talk about "primitive" Christianity.

Implications

What are the implications of this consensus among NT specialists? The following reflections must be brief, not only because of the space assigned to this essay, but because we now move out of my field of concentration and into the area of the theologian *qua* theologian. If theology is to be grounded on the NT then we must acknowledge that our search for answers to our own personal problems must be honest and realistically face life as did the Jewish apocalyptists. Any possibility of considering hope must be grounded in, and intertwined with, the admission of suffering.[41] This world is unjust and full of sin. The penchant of some Jewish apocalyptists to live only in terms of an elusive world above or ahead is not attractive. That is a surrender to aimless dreaming, and misses the mark set by the "theologians" in the NT. They stressed the reality of the crucifixion. They recorded Jesus' fear and cries in the face of death (which were muted, of course, by the author of John and other thinkers). Jesus' humanity and fleshiness (John 1:14) must not be recast docetically (*pace* the author of the Acts of John). If a Christian can have hope, it is grounded first and above all in the earthiness of Jesus, the full humanity of the incarnation, and the costly suffering this entails.

Astronomers find no heavens above the earth, as described in the Enoch books, and in virtually every apocalypse. Yet they report an unfinished story of creation. This insight might be of help as we contemplate the meaning of the unfulfilled drama of salvation, encapsulated in marana tha.

The Jewish apocalyptists stimulated the NT thinkers to contemplate the full dimensions of space (the heavens and the earth) and time (from protology to eschatology). Our own reflections and penchant to be one with others theologically, as well as different and true to our own integrity, are enriched by the diversities of thought that have come to us from the beginnings of this era. If we can pray and experience the possibility that communication with our Creator is possible, then we might receive more insight into the meaning of the apocalyptic dimensions of "thy kingdom come, they will be done on earth as in heaven." Although it is unfashionable to ask God to "deliver us from the Evil One," perhaps more reflection can help us find effective language to convey for us and ours what was on target in Jesus' prayer.

In our world it is not easy to continue carrying much of the baggage of the apocalyptists. We are forced to admit that some of the words attributed to Jesus disclose that he was mistaken about the End of time.[42] We must remember that faith is always in hope; otherwise we forget the human responsibility for belief, which is naturally fragile, or minimize our bond to this oblate spheroid.

If NT theology is anchored in the confession that Jesus' death is efficacious, and in the conviction that God raised Jesus from the dead and will bring him again into this world of ours, then it is grounded in apocalyptic language and perception.[43] Many Christians find the confession and perhaps the latter part of the conviction too mythological, legendary, or archaic. They would find it easier to affirm the power of Jesus' life and message to awake a consciousness of God's presence, and to acknowledge that capriciousness is not endemic. Each can affirm, from apocalypticism, that God has the final word.

In a certain sense the goal is simple: to recover the enthusiasm of Jesus, and of his earliest followers, namely Mary Magdalene, Peter, James, John, and the author of the Odes of Solomon.[44] We need to find refired earthen vessels for the truth. We can admire how the earliest members of the Palestinian Jesus Movement, inspired by Jewish apocalyptic eschatology, experienced the presence of their risen Lord.[45] If this fire can be rekindled in the *koinōnia* and *ekklēsia* then the Spirit will be present, and the appropriate words for articulating the "good news" will appear.

Perhaps one of us, like "a creative and skillful composer," will take up the integrity of the cohesiveness of the gospel, and dispatch a word on target in our day, which will have the "emotive and communicative power" of the *euangelion*.[46] Together—called by God through his good news into the church—we can be one in this hope as we pray, employing apocalyptic words, "thy kingdom come, thy will be done on earth as it is in heaven." Finally, in the words of Beker, "the unity of the church has a *[sic]* apocalyptic foundation and a future apocalyptic horizon: amidst the powers of evil it lives in the power of the Spirit and hopes for the defeat of the powers of sin and death in God's world. . . . "[47]

PART FOUR

BIBLICAL THEOLOGY AND THEOLOGICAL PRACTICE

Chapter Fourteen / THE COHERENCE OF THE GOSPEL IN AN INCOHERENT WORLD

George W. Stroup

The Vigilant Sentry

Students and colleagues of J. Christiaan Beker know that he has often described the task of the biblical scholar to be that of the vigilant sentry who stands watch over the biblical text and protects it from those who would abuse or silence it. Among those who have proven themselves most likely to abuse the Bible are systematic and constructive theologians who willingly ignore texts or distort them in order to force them to serve as warrants for their preconceived theologies. In order that the Bible might have its own voice in the contemporary life of the church and the world, the task of the biblical scholar is to keep watch and sound the alarm when theologians misuse the Bible.

There is nothing new about Beker's understanding of the task of the biblical scholar, but in recent history it has become an increasingly difficult responsibility. Despite a growing awareness that all readers bring assumptions and preconceptions to the Bible, much theology in the last half of the twentieth century has allowed the Bible to speak only when it agrees with the ideologies and cosmologies of its interpreters.

For example, since the Enlightenment and the emergence of modern methods of historiography, the apocalyptic language of the New Testament has often been a major problem for theologians.[1] The sheer weight of history itself and the grinding regularity of each sunrise render biblical claims about the imminent end of history and the triumph of God difficult if not unintelligible. Many liberal theologians in the nineteenth century simply ignored apocalyptic and eschatological texts in the Bible, until Johnannes Weiss and Albert Schweitzer exposed their self-deception. "The real difference," Weiss wrote, "between our modern Protestant world-view and that of primitive Christianity is, therefore, that we do not share the eschatological attitude. . . . We no longer pray, 'May grace come and the world pass away,' but we pass our lives in the

235

joyful confidence that *this* world will evermore become the showplace of the people of God."[2] In their own time, Weiss and Schweitzer served as faithful sentries, sounding the alarm that liberal theologians had abused the Bible by ignoring its eschatological and apocalyptic themes.

The image of the vigilant sentry is one Beker not only espouses but practices as well. In response to those theologians in the latter half of the twentieth century who have ignored, censored, or neutered the apostle Paul's use of apocalyptic language to interpret the resurrection of Jesus Christ and the meaning of the gospel, Beker has argued that the coherent center of Paul's Gospel is "a field of meaning, a network composed of parts that interlock in a symbolic relationship" and that the content of this field of meaning "is determined by the apocalyptic act of God in the death and resurrection of Christ."[3] Theologians may be baffled by what to do with Paul's strange apocalyptic language, and they may argue that Paul's use of apocalyptic, while understandable in the first century, is no longer viable in the twentieth century, but Beker will not allow them to ignore or dismiss the apocalyptic center of Paul's interpretation of the gospel and at the same time claim that their "modern" interpretations of the gospel are consistent with Paul's.

Beker does not expect theologians simply to repeat Paul's apocalyptic language and hope that it will somehow be intelligible to people in the twentieth century. He recognizes there is no escape from the difficult but necessary task of hermeneutics. "A direct transfer of Paul's formulation of the Gospel to our situation cannot succeed."[4] The decisive issue, however, is not how best to evade Paul's troublesome use of apocalyptic language, but how contemporary biblical scholars and theologians can best interpret Paul's apocalyptic language in order that Paul's understanding of the gospel may be heard today.

Beker believes one major example of how contemporary theologians ignore or censor Pauline apocalyptic, because it does not fit easily with their preconceived notions, is that diverse array of theological proposals sometimes grouped together under the rubric of "narrative theology."[5] Theologians appear to be attracted to the category of narrative for various reasons. In the first place, narrative offers an alternative to the role played by metaphysics in classical theology and to the role played by other philosophical movements (such as existentialism, process philosophy, or Marxism) in contemporary theology.[6] A second motive is that the category of narrative provides one way to articulate the larger, coherent message of the biblical canon. While historical criticism focused attention on the context in which biblical texts were written, it also led to historical and sociological rather than theological interpretations of the text. The use of literary criticism by some narrative theologians and the emergence of different forms of canonical criticism has led to a rediscovery of the theological themes in the Bible. What troubles Beker, however, is that recent attempts at narrative theology seem to give little or no attention to the importance of apocalyptic in the interpretation of the Gospel.[7]

Beker's reservations about narrative theology deserve careful consideration. He raises at least three important issues. In the first place, do narrative theologians assume that personal and communal identity must have unity and coherence? Are there not some lives that are so filled with chaos, suffering, and evil that no unity or coherence can be given to them without denying the reality of chaos, suffering, and evil? And insofar as narrative theologians ignore the reality of chaos, suffering, and evil, do they not impose a false unity and coherence on life and on the Bible, do injustice to both life and the Bible, ignore the biblical theme of God's apocalyptic triumph, and invite the rebuke of Beker's vigilant sentry?

Second, do narrative theologians assume that not only life, but the Bible itself, has a unity and coherence, and, if they do, what kind of coherence is it?[8] Is there an inherent conflict between the commitment of narrative theologians to the unity and coherence of the Bible on the one hand and Pauline apocalyptic on the other? In stressing the unity and coherence of the Bible does narrative theology exclude the eschatological and apocalyptic dimension of the gospel?[9]

Finally, do narrative theologians confuse the categories of unity and coherence and in so doing bring premature closure to both life and the gospel? It may be that there is an important difference between arguing that there is a coherence to both life and the gospel as opposed to a unity. One interpretation of "coherence" would suggest something like the reconciliation of different and perhaps even contradictory events, while "unity" might be understood to mean not the reconciliation, but the dissolution and even the denial of contradiction. In other words, do narrative theologians compound their mistakes about the unity and coherence of both life and the Bible by suggesting that the Bible provides a unity that denies life's experience of evil? It may be that for people who live lives that are marked by unrelieved suffering and evil, the good news of the gospel cannot be a false unity that denies the reality of their suffering, but only an apocalyptic trust in the sovereignty of God and God's promise in God's good time "to wipe away every tear."[10] The latter might be a theological coherence that does not affirm an existential unity in life experience. To what extent, however, do narrative theologians assume there is both unity and coherence in life and in the Bible and in so doing fail to appreciate the apocalyptic horizon in the Bible?

The Unity and Coherence of Life

Many philosophers and theologians are attracted to the category of narrative because they believe that the question of Christian identity, for both individuals and communities, has become acute in the latter half of the twentieth century.

Furthermore, they recognize that identity has a necessary relation to narrative, memory, and the anticipation of the future. The identity question is at least twofold. In the first place, how are personal and communal identity to be understood in the midst of a world that is increasingly aware of its diversity and pluralism? Second, how are personal and communal identity to be constructed when many of those resources that traditionally helped form and establish identity—such as institutions, symbols, and myths—have become at best suspect or at worst nonfunctional?

Some theologians have returned to claims by Augustine and John Calvin that knowledge of self and knowledge of God are reciprocally related. In Calvin's words it is true both that "the knowledge of ourselves not only arouses us to seek God, but also, as it were, leads us by the hand to find him" and that "man never achieves a clear knowledge of himself unless he has first looked upon God's face."[11] Personal and communal identity, therefore, are for Christians inseparable from what they claim to know (or in Christian language "what has been revealed to them") about that holy mystery they call "God." The issue then becomes What do Christian claims about God's grace, mercy, and judgment have to do with those narrative events that are constitutive of the identity of persons and communities? It is one thing to talk about God's grace and judgment as abstract theological concepts. It is something else to be able to talk about what God's grace and judgment mean in the particular context of one's personal and communal life. Reciprocally, personal and communal identity can and should be subjected to psychological and sociological analysis, but it is also important that they be constructed and interpreted from the perspective of Christian faith.

If knowing God and knowing self are, as Augustine and Calvin suggest, reciprocally related, how do we know God and how do we have self-knowledge? Many narrative theologians have been influenced by H. Richard Niebuhr's distinction between external and internal history and by his claim that "Faith cannot get to God save through historic experience as reason cannot get to nature save through sense experience."[12] Knowledge of God is revealed at that juncture where external history becomes a part of the internal history of individuals and communities. And insofar as internal history, in both its personal and communal expressions, assumes the form of a narrative, then the use of narrative is not accidental but necessary for the articulation of Christian identity.[13]

The contemporary crisis in Christian identity might be described as the hermeneutical incoherence between the external history of Christian faith and the internal histories of individuals and communities. In response to that crisis, some philosophers and theologians have suggested that the task is to reconstruct personal and communal identity by means of the gospel.[14] Of course, that response assumes not only that a coherence between the gospel and life is possible, but that there are second and third senses of coherence in both personal and communal identity on the one hand and in the gospel on the other. What if either personal or communal identity is so filled with chaos, suffering, and evil that it cannot be said to "cohere"? Does the incoherence of life itself mean that the coherence of the gospel cannot and must not be imposed on life, lest it distort and misrepresent the reality of human experience?

There does seem to be widespread, but by no means unanimous, agreement that personal and communal identity are hermeneutical constructions of the coherence of life. Most recent work on narrative seems to agree with Alasdair MacIntyre's claim that "all attempts to elucidate the notion of personal identity independently of and in isolation from the notions of narrative, intelligibility and accountability are bound to fail."[15] In response to the question as to what constitutes the unity of an individual life, MacIntyre writes, "The answer is that its unity is the unity of a narrative embodied in a single life. . . . The unity of a human life is the unity of a narrative quest."[16] Parenthetically, it is important to note that MacIntyre and others working with the narrative structure of personal identity often seem to use the terms "unity of life" and "coherence of life" synonymously. It is not necessarily the case, of course, that coherence entails unity.

MacIntyre does not ignore the reality of incoherence and radical change within life. In an article on the relation between epistemological crises, dramatic narrative, and the philosophy of science, he acknowledges that a significant epistemological crisis is resolved "by the construction of a new narrative which enables the agent to understand *both* how he or she could intelligibly have held his or her original beliefs *and* how he or she could have been so dramatically misled by them."[17] Although this observation leads MacIntyre to an appropriate acknowledgment of the provisionality of all narratives or "master stories," he continues to assume that each new narrative that emerges out of the ashes of epistemological crises will be characterized by progress and unity. "What is carried over from one paradigm to another are epistemological ideals and a correlative understanding of what constitutes the progress of a single intellectual life."[18] What MacIntyre does not consider is the possibility of an epistemological crisis so severe that it can be resolved only by a narrative that gives up unity for the sake of faith in a God of apocalyptic coherence.

While there is considerable agreement about the narrative shape of personal identity, there is significant disagreement as to whether the coherence of life is entirely a narrative construction, for example, a coherence constructed by the narrator, or whether there is some sense in which the coherence resides in the events themselves and the relation between events. For example, Louis Mink has argued , "Stories are not lived but told. Life has no beginnings, middles, or ends; there are meetings, but the start of an affair belongs to the story we tell ourselves later, and there are partings, but final partings only in the story."

There is no coherence in the events of life itself; rather, the construction of narrative out of the events of life is an artistic exercise.[19]

In what was perhaps the first significant attempt by a contemporary theologian to reflect on the significance of narrative for theology, Stephen Crites argued that "the formal quality of experience through time is inherently narrative."[20] Contrary to Mink and White, Crites seems to believe that narrative is not simply a construction imposed on events but that there is a tension to experience that demands the tenses of language. Following Augustine, Crites argues that the three modalities of past, present, and future are correlative to one another in every moment of experience; determine the inner form of any possible experience; and as a "tensed unity" already have "an incipient narrative form."[21]

Furthermore, Crites describes three dimensions to the narrative quality of experience.[22] First, there are sacred stories, stories that "cannot be fully and directly told, because they live, so to speak, in the arms and legs and bellies of the celebrants."[23] These stories form consciousness and as such are only indirectly available to consciousness. Second, there are mundane stories, stories that are told, that are directly seen and heard, that are fully accessible to consciousness, and, most important, stories that define "the objective horizon of a particular form of consciousness."[24] These mundane stories are "among the most important means by which people articulate and clarify their sense of that world."[25] And finally the third dimension to the narrative quality of experience is the temporal form of experience itself, what Crites describes as "the tensed unity" of the three distinct modalities of past, present, and future in every moment of experience.

It is not clear that Crites uses "unity" and "coherence" as synonymously as does MacIntyre. For example, one of Crites's theses in regard to the unity of past, present, and future is that "the tensed *unity* of these modalities *requires* narrative forms both for its expression (mundane stories) and for its own sense of the meaning of its internal *coherence* (sacred stories)."[26] In other words, the unity of temporal experience requires the internal coherence of sacred stories. The relationship between the three modalities of past, present, and future, which Crites describes as a "unity," is both an ontological and an existential statement about time and not necessarily synonymous with the internal coherence of a narrative of sacred story or the coherence between that sacred story and, to use Crites's categories, any particular mundane story. Events in a plot can cohere and still be disjointed and unresolved in a way that the relations between past, present, and future cannot. Crites's thesis seems to be that the unity in temporal experience requires the internal coherence in sacred story, but here unity and coherence may mean quite different things.

Leaving aside the issue of whether there are such things as preconscious sacred stories, is there a necessary relation between the unity of temporal experience and the coherence of those stories which are constitutive of human identity? At a philosophical level, one might argue the intrinsic relation between past, present, and future. That is, each modality implies and requires the others. However, at an existential level, at the level of lived experience and existential meaning, some lives are characterized only by radical fissures that cannot be unified. The issue may be whether there is any sense in which these fissures in life can be made to be unified.

In our time, these fissures are most evident in the struggle in contemporary Judaism to come to terms with the Holocaust. What does the reality of the Holocaust mean for present and future Jewish faith? For some Jewish thinkers, the reality of the past, the reality of the Holocaust, means that faithful Jews must give up their faith in the God of the covenant in order not to blaspheme the suffering of those who perished in the Holocaust and in order to protect unborn generations who must learn to rely upon one another and not upon God. For other Jewish thinkers, most notably Emil Fackenheim, the history of Israel's covenant experience with God has a commanding authority that compels it not to forsake its faith in the living God of the present and the future for two reasons. In the first place, Hitler must not be given in the present and the future a victory that was denied him in the past, and, second, while God was not present in the Holocaust and there was absolutely nothing that was redemptive or salvific about the suffering of those who perished in the Holocaust, "The Voice of Auschwitz commands Jews not to go mad. . . . The Jew of today can endure because he must endure, and he must endure because he is commanded to endure."[27]

Fackenheim does not argue that there is some kind of hidden unity to the Jewish experience of the Holocaust. Nor does he argue that the Holocaust is an "epistemological crisis" that requires a new narrative whose coherence can make sense out of (for example, unify) the Holocaust with the rest of Jewish faith and history. The contemporary Jew is left with a personal and communal narrative of radical disunity, a narrative of contending fragments, a narrative in which any sense of coherence must be found finally either in madness or in the mystery of God, but a narrative that must be told nonetheless.

How would MacIntyre and Crites respond to Fackenheim? To use Crites's categories, what happens to personal and communal identity when a chasm separates mundane from sacred story? MacIntyre acknowledges at least a version of the problem of existential incoherence, but because of his almost exclusive reliance on a category of tradition that is oriented entirely to the past seems to have no basis for resolving it:

> When someone complains—as do some of those who attempt or commit suicide—
> that his or her life is meaningless, he or she is often and perhaps characteristically
> complaining that the narrative of their life has become unintelligible to them,
> that it lacks any point, any movement towards a climax or a *telos*. Hence the point

of doing any one thing rather than another at crucial junctures in their lives seems to such a person to have been lost.[28]

MacIntyre seems to assume that personal identity (and perhaps communal identity as well) requires a unified narrative. He does not allow for the possibility that some lives cannot be unified, and, from a Christian perspective, can be said to "make sense" only in the context of that apocalyptic narrative that is resurrection faith.

Incoherence in the Jesus Story

Narrative theologians who work within the context of Christian faith should recognize that there is incoherence in those narratives that are constitutive of the gospel. Insofar as the Gospels in the NT attempt to answer the question of Jesus' identity, they do so by means of stories that recognize the fissure that separates Jesus' ministry from his passion and death. Perhaps the primary example is the so-called little apocalypse of Mark 13 (with its parallels in Matthew 24 and Luke 21).

Both biblical scholars and literary critics have pointed out that within the larger context of Mark's Gospel chapter 13 is, in several senses, a significant disruption. In the first place, the plot or movement of Mark's story is disrupted by Jesus' apocalyptic discourse.[29] While the narrative has been slowly picking up momentum as events rush to their climax in Jerusalem, chapter 13 brings the plot to a temporary, but extended pause unlike any other in Mark's version of the Jesus story. Second, not only is there a pause in the plot, but chapter 13 puts the reader in a different relationship to the story. As Marxsen points out, 13:14 (with its parenthetical "let the reader understand") addresses the reader more directly than any other text in Mark, and "This not only marks a literary caesura, but also a break in the life of the reader who is led, as it were, from present to future."[30]

Mark 13, therefore, serves several purposes. First, it points to a disruption, an incoherence if you will, in the Jesus story itself. The passage from Jesus' teaching and ministry to the events of his arrest, trial, death, and resurrection will not be an easy one for either the disciples and the other characters in Mark's story or for the reader to understand. Second, the transition for the reader from faith in Jesus Christ to the practice of discipleship will be no less easy. As Norman Perrin so eloquently put it, "Mark's purpose is to catch the attention of his readers and lead him [sic] from Galilee through Caesarea Philippi to Jerusalem and the empty tomb, and to the realization that he, the reader, is being challenged to discipleship in the context of the prospect of the coming Jesus as Son of Man."[31] Third, Mark's Gospel tells the reader that not only is there incoherence in the Jesus story and in the reader's call to discipleship, but that finally there is disruption and incoherence in Christian hope itself, because only after "those days," after "that suffering" (13:24), will the elect be gathered "from the ends of the earth to the ends of heaven" (13:27).

Mark's Gospel is anything but an uninterrupted storyline. Chapter 13 suggests that the story which gives Jesus his identity is a disrupted plot. As Frank Kermode has observed,

> Scholars speak of the gospel as recording the end-in-the-process-of-realizing-itself. But the end is not yet, and it says that also. It stands at the moment of transition between the main body of history and the end of history; and what it says has a powerful effect on both. In this respect, as I've said, the "little apocalypse" of Chapter 13 is a model of the whole; before it stands a narrative of obscure organization; after it comes the well-formed and completive Passion story. So the gospel stands between past and immediately future time, establishing a continuity which makes sense only in terms of that which interrupts it.[32]

Without entering the debate about the historicity of chapter 13, whether it represents the words of the historical Jesus or is a later insertion,[33] an important literary and theological issue that bears on the questions we have been discussing is why Mark breaks the rhythm of his narrative with chapter 13 and what his purpose is in doing so. Mark introduces the language of apocalypse here, between his account of Jesus' ministry and the beginning of Jesus' passion, Kermode argues, because it "is the great literary vehicle of the moment of epochal transition, the period that is interposed between the past and the imminent end," and as such it is "the largest of his intercalations, in fact, an analepsis that is certainly homodiegetic, an incursion of the future, properly terrible, properly ambiguous, into a narrative which proleptically shapes and sanctifies it."[34]

Mark introduces "an incursion of the future" at precisely this point in the Jesus story because the narrative has reached a moment of crisis, and it is crisis that provides the occasion for and sometimes requires apocalypse.[35] The crisis is threefold. In the first place, despite Jesus' predictions of his passion in 8:31-32, 9:30-32, and 10:33-34, the reader cannot move from chapters 1–12 to chapters 14–16 without concluding that the narrative is tragedy, and there is no basis in tragedy for the call to discipleship that is so central to Mark's Gospel. Chapter 13 tells the reader that the relation between Jesus' ministry and his passion cannot be understood from within the story itself, but that its final meaning can be understood only from outside the story—that is proleptically, or in Kermode's words "as an incursion of the future." It is in this unstated, proleptic, yet necessary sense that Mark's Gospel, even if it does end at 16:8, presupposes the apocalyptic act par excellence of God's resurrection of Jesus from the dead.

Second, Mark tells the reader that he or she cannot move from chapters 1–12 to chapters 14–16 and avoid the conclusion that the Gospel is fundamentally tragic without an awareness that the incoherence in the story is finally resolved in the apocalyptic activity of God. Consequently, the conclusion drawn by one recent commentator—that the coming of God's kingdom in Mark 13 "has nothing to do with triumphalism; it comes from below, in solidarity with the human family in its dark night of suffering"[36]—is not only wrong, but fundamentally wrong. In Mark's Gospel, as in Paul's, the incoherence in the Jesus story is irresolvable apart from the triumph of God in raising Jesus from the dead. Otherwise, "we are of all people most to be pitied" (1 Cor 15:19).

Third, Mark uses chapter 13 to tell readers that if they respond to Jesus' call to discipleship, a sign that "all these things are about to be accomplished" (13:4) will be that their lives also will be filled with chaos, suffering, and evil, for "they will hand you over to councils; and you will be beaten in synagogues; and you will stand before governors and kings because of me, as a testimony to them" (13:9). Mark warns the reader ("Let the reader understand" 13:14) that the suffering that comes with discipleship will not end in "those days," for "in those days there will be suffering, such as has not been from the beginning of the creation that God created until now, no, and never will be"(13:19). It is only "after that suffering," when the Son of Man will come on clouds with great power and glory, that the angels will gather his elect from the four winds (13:26-27). In other words, neither that particular suffering to which Jesus' disciples are called nor the suffering that will come "in those days" will be resolved prior to God's final, apocalyptic act.

In Mark's Gospel, therefore, there is considerable evidence that any interpretation of the Jesus story or the story of Jesus' followers that does not acknowledge the reality of disruption and incoherence is contradicted by the biblical witness. Mark 13 occurs where it does in the Jesus story not primarily because of the content of Jesus' apocalyptic discourse, but because the fissure in the Jesus story cannot be overcome within the story itself.[37] In this sense, it is fitting that Mark's Gospel ends at 16:8, because this so-called "shorter ending," as well as Mark 13, tells the reader that the ending to the gospel story is outside of and from beyond the story.

The Coherence of the Gospel

As we have seen, some narrative theologians do suggest that Christian identity (both personal and communal) is characterized by unity and coherence. It is not clear, however, what they mean by these terms. When Crites writes about unity he seems to have in mind the structural relationship between the three modes of temporality. MacIntyre, on the other hand, often describes personal identity as a "unity," and his comments about suicide imply that the meaning (or lack thereof) to a life is a matter of its "intelligibility." A life is intelligible if it is unified, and it is unified if it "has a point" and if it moves "towards a climax or *telos*."[38] From the point of view of Mark 13, however, the Jesus story does not have its climax and *telos* within the story, except proleptically.

Narrative theologians, therefore, need to learn from the biblical story in general and Mark's Gospel in particular that personal identity does not necessarily require a unified life story, if "unity" means the resolution of incoherence. The incoherence in Mark's Gospel between chapters 1–12 and 14–16 is not resolved within the story itself, but only outside of and beyond it. In this latter sense, there can be a coherence of sorts to personal identity, but it is not a coherence of unity, not a coherence that requires the unification or resolution of contradictions, not a coherence that denies the reality of the existential experience of disruption, incoherence, and meaninglessness, but a coherence that acknowledges the incoherence of life and finds its completion in that which transcends it and "makes all things new."

On the other hand, narrative theologians must never cease reminding "apocalypticists" that the gospel story cannot be reduced simply to Jesus' crucifixion and resurrection. Chapter 13 does not give the reader permission to ignore the first twelve chapters of Mark's Gospel and to pay attention only to the last two. The Jesus who is executed and whose final identity as the Christ lies outside the story is also the Jesus who casts out demons and who eats with sinners. Just as it would be a mistake to reduce the Gospel to a description of Jesus' ministry, so too it would be an equally unfortunate mistake to separate the final advent of Jesus Christ from those narratives that detail the nature of his ministry.

Apocalyptic is central to the Christian gospel and it has some obvious implications for how Christians construct and understand the narratives that give them their personal and communal identities.

First, if those narratives Christians use to articulate their personal identity were unified and coherent, in the sense that they had no loose ends and nothing was left unresolved, they would be a-theistic narratives, a-theistic in that they are self-contained and require nothing beyond themselves for their completion. Such a conclusion would mean that the final identity of individuals and communities has little or nothing to do with their relation to God.

Second, Mark's Gospel and Pauline apocalyptic enable Christians to be utterly realistic about the reality of suffering and evil. The Gospel does not ask Christians to deny the reality of suffering and evil nor does it invite cynicism and apathy as an appropriate response. The Gospel affirms the reality of evil by making it a central character in the Jesus story. After all, prior to Jesus' crucifixion it is only the demons in Mark's Gospel who recognize Jesus for who he truly is. And Jesus' death in the stories of the Gospels is a real death. Whatever it is that the Gospels have to say about the reality of Jesus' resurrection in no way mitigates the reality of his death.

On the other hand, unlike so much of the liberal theology that reigns in the latter half of the twentieth century, the gospel does not affirm that suffering and evil are defeated prior to God's final apocalyptic act. While contemporary liberal theology repeatedly locates the triumph of God within history—in movements of social justice, in the struggle for gender equality, in the liberation of the oppressed—these events in the Gospels are but signs (to be sure, real and true signs, but still only signs) of God's final triumph and not that triumph itself. To confuse the former with the latter is to practice a cruel hoax on those who yearn for God's true justice, as has been recognized by Christian realists from Paul to Augustine to Reinhold Niebuhr.

Third, the apocalyptic horizon to the biblical story is finally an important theological statement that the meaning to human existence cannot be found in human existence itself, but is ultimately rooted in God. More so than any other theme in the biblical story, Pauline apocalyptic affirms not only the transcendent otherness of God but also the transcendence of human identity and destiny. The latter, of course, presupposes the reality of the former. Over against everything in contemporary society that insists that the meaning to human life is to be found within life itself, Pauline apocalyptic is a reminder and a promise that the final meaning to life—when we see "face to face"—is an eschatological and apocalyptic event.

Finally, biblical apocalyptic serves the indispensable hermeneutical function of reminding narrative theologians that there must always be a degree of openness to every "reading" of those narratives that are most important to Christian identity—both narratives in the Bible and those narratives Christians use to articulate their sense of who they are and what they are about in the world. To bring closure prematurely to the interpretation of these "texts," would be both unfaithful and an act of idolatry, because to do so would be to fix and thereby absolutize meaning somewhere other than in the final activity of God.

That is not to say that Christians have no clue as to where their story with God is headed. Jesus' ministry, death, and resurrection provide both a clue and a promise to the direction of that story. They do not, however, exhaust the meaning to that narrative. It is of overriding hermeneutical importance that when Paul describes the final activity of God, especially in 1 Corinthians 15, he can do so only by means of metaphor and the language of poetry. Surely something is being said here about God and human destiny that must be said, but something that can be said only inadequately and provisionally.

Chapter Fifteen / "FEMINIST" THEOLOGY AND BIBLICAL INTERPRETATION

Katharine Doob Sakenfeld

In the development of biblical theology in recent decades, and especially in Old Testament theology, the issue of unity and diversity and the issue of the authority of scripture have been much in evidence. J. Christiaan Beker has worked hard at these issues in his writings, not just with respect to the Pauline corpus, but also for the larger collection of biblical writings.[1] These same themes of unity/diversity and authority have characterized much of "feminist" theology, particularly as it has sought to relate itself to the Bible. In feminist interpretation, the theoretical and practical consideration of the Bible takes place with special attention to contexts of suffering and struggle; suffering and struggle have been a part of Professor Beker's life and writing as well.[2] Thus it is an honor to dedicate this essay to my longtime colleague and friend. The essay offers an orientation to key issues in the current discussion and concludes with a concrete example by which readers are invited into the process of feminist biblical interpretation for the church.

Preliminary Definitions

It should be emphasized at the outset that so-called "feminist" theology is characterized by great diversity.[3] There is not even agreement on the definition of the term "feminism." One definition broad enough to be accepted by a wide spectrum of conscientized women is that of Letty Russell: "Feminism is advocacy of women. It is not, therefore, *against* men, but only *for* the needs of women, needs that cannot be met without changes in the lives of both men *and* women. . . . It represents a search for liberation from all forms of dehumanization on the part of those who advocate full human personhood for all. . . . This means that men can also be feminists if they are willing to advocate for women."[4]

The concept of advocacy is basic to this definition and finds wide acceptance. Very recently I presented a definition of feminism much like this to a group of male church leaders; they all initially found it innocuous. "Is that all there is to feminism?" one queried. They were all in favor of liberation from dehumanization. But advocacy involves concreteness as much as an abstract principle. When I asked whether their local congregations would consider calling a woman pastor they were very dubious that any "competent" women pastors existed. Thus questions immediately arise concerning what constitutes a "form of dehumanization," what therefore "liberation" would look like in specific instances, who gets to decide such questions and how, as well as what role men may play in the process. In any local context it is a great challenge to articulate the relationship between "full personhood for all" and the particular needs of women; the challenge is greatly multiplied when set in a global perspective.

Russell's definition does not make use of the terms "androcentrism" or "patriarchy." Since the advocacy of feminism is usually understood to be in response to these two phenomena, however, a comment about their definitions is needed. Androcentrism means looking at the world through the lens of a male or man's point of view. Sometimes this perspective is conscious, but more often it is not. An old library catalog subject heading epitomizes this viewpoint: "man, including woman." Androcentrism is evident in the generic English language usage of "he" (meaning "he or she") and in any literature or scholarship that regards males as the paradigmatic human beings.[5]

Definitions of patriarchy have been more debated. Some feminists insist that this term should be used in a purely descriptive fashion, to refer to a system of "gender hierarchy" that may manifest itself in very different ways in different times and cultures.[6] Much feminist literature, however, including literature concerned with relating feminism to the Bible, uses the term patriarchy to describe a world order in which men are in control at the top of a pyramid of power. In that pyramid, as we experience it in the twentieth century, there are "graded subjugations" among men of different races and economic status, with women and children below men within any grouping.[7] Among feminists who emphasize the importance of ecology as part of feminist concern, the pyramid is sometimes expanded to include animals below all human beings and plants at the very bottom.[8] In such usage, patriarchy is understood not as a neutral term but as systemic oppression that needs to be overcome by advocacy. The relationship of race, sex, and class factors within patriarchy, and whether one of these can be shown to be a root cause, continues to be debated; but it is agreed that these three factors are intertwined within the system.

Overview

In the context of a volume on biblical theology, I have chosen to develop the theme of unity and diversity among "feminists" into two parts, moving from alternative hermeneutical theories within "feminist" Christian faith to diversity in actual biblical interpretation by "feminists." The presentation is limited to writers who have not found "feminism" and the Judeo-Christian heritage to be ultimately contradictory. Nevertheless it should be remembered that this view is not accepted by all feminists who have lived and studied the Judeo-Christian tradition.[9] The basic question is how much can Christian doctrine and biblical interpretation change and still be considered "Christian." Change in church teaching is hardly a new phenomenon, and there is a range of theologies within global Christianity today. Can there be a Christian understanding of God and of Jesus Christ that is nonpatriarchal? Can the Bible still speak to people who are aware of its pervasive patriarchy and androcentrism? My own answer and that of many Christian feminists across the globe is still "yes" to both questions; but these questions are not easy ones.

Part One of this essay considers selected aspects of diversity among those within the Christian tradition who seek to relate the biblical text to advocacy for women. This diversity is apparent not just in methods used to analyze biblical texts but more important in interpretive (hermeneutical) theory about how these ancient texts should be related to contemporary concern for the wholeness of all persons, particularly women. Focal questions are language about God and the role of experience in relation to the Bible.

Differences in "feminist" theory have until recently been visible primarily in the literature by economically comfortable North Atlantic white women, because these women have had privileged access to the educational systems and publishing structures that are interested in such theoretical issues. Voices of those women doubly or triply marginalized (by race or ethnic group and by economic condition) are just beginning to be published in book forms and in academic journals;[10] discernment of how their varying contexts inform their theoretical work will be important to clearer discernment of the influence of context in the writings of all women.

Recognition of the importance of differing contexts has led many women who are not North Atlantic whites to reject "feminist" as an umbrella term and to turn instead to the use of terms such as "womanist" theology to refer to black American women's work, *"mujerista"* theology to refer to the work of Hispanic women (with recognition of the existence of many different contexts among these women), and "Asian women's" theology for work done in Southeast and East Asia (again with recognition of many national and regional subgroupings). African women are also beginning to publish work out of their context. North Atlantic white women are increasingly recognizing the significance of these distinctions, although efforts to overcome our unconscious ethno- and geo-centrism often fall short of what is needed.

This situation creates a caution for the use of the words "feminism" and "women" in this essay and in any discussion of our topic. Some effort must be made to counter the implicit hegemony of white women's work in using the term "feminism"; at the same time care must be taken not to lump together all "women of color." In this essay I have tried to use adjectives to modify "feminism" and "women" at many places in order to keep myself and readers aware of this problem. Yet my white perspective probably has kept me from noticing other places where qualifying adjectives are needed. I have used quotation marks at some points as a further reminder; readers might consider putting both words in quotation marks at every point, to assess for themselves the danger of inappropriate generalizations.[11]

In Part Two, the essay turns to the Bible itself and presents differing interpretations of individual biblical passages offered by women (and "feminist" men) who are living and studying the Bible in very different contexts. It is often not through theory, but rather through encountering surprising interpretations of actual texts from perspectives of those most different from ourselves that we begin to comprehend the importance of experience and advocacy in our own turning to the Bible as a resource for faith.

Part One

Among those feminists who remain within the Judeo-Christian tradition, there is great diversity of method and perspective in dealing with the biblical witness. I have chosen two critical topics for review: the question of language about God, and the role of experience in biblical interpretation. Each of these theological themes is related in its own way to the problem of biblical authority.

Language About God

It is possible to meet Russell's definition of feminism focused on advocacy for women in the midst of wholeness for all people without special attention to God language. Yet because of the Christian claim that human beings are created in God's image, the content of God language has become an important issue for many "feminist" thinkers, especially for those who hold to the importance of language as a force that not only reflects reality but also functions to shape reality. The problem stems, of course, from the preponderance of male/masculine language about God in the Bible (especially "King" and "Father") and the use of the grammatically masculine pronoun "he" to refer to God in biblical Hebrew and Greek. These factors have led to a long tradition of Christian art in which the deity is portrayed as male; the idea that the Christian God is male is reinforced in popular theology by the male gender of Jesus as God incarnate.

Despite the language of the Bible, church theologians from earliest times have insisted that the God of the Christian faith is beyond male and female. How to bring this theological reality to experiential awareness is the challenge that many "feminist" Christians are posing. The problem of pronouns varies from language to language. The work of many women and men writing in English shows that it is possible to revise sentence structures so that no pronouns are used to refer to the deity. Many other languages (for example, Indonesian, Korean) lack gender-specific pronouns, so the problem familiar to English speakers does not arise. Nonetheless, because of the prevalence of male/masculine imagery the word "God" is experienced as male by Christian believers in both kinds of language systems, even when the usage of pronouns in English or similar languages is eliminated.

Various strategies are being employed by those who seek to emphasize that God is indeed beyond male and female. The simplest (and least controversial from the standpoint of biblical authority) is the supplementation of popularly used male/masculine imagery for God with other biblical imagery, both female/feminine and inanimate.[12] Mother language generates discomfort among many, however, even though it is clearly found in the OT. Debate heightens when imagery not explicitly biblical is added to the list. A hymn entitled "Dear Sister God" by Brian Wren,[13] and the proposal of Sallie McFague that God be spoken of with models of Lover and Friend[14] are often labeled non-Christian, even by people who have for years sung "What a Friend We Have in Jesus" or "Jesus Lover of My Soul." The controversy highlights the importance of considering more than the bare words in any discussion of imagery about God.

Still more objection arises when the English pronoun "she" is used for God. Most writers do this to unmask the unconscious assumption that the word "God" refers to a male being (similarly to the way that the English words neurosurgeon or fighter pilot are usually still "heard" as referring to men), but the jarring effect of the "she" word often is misunderstood as proclaiming a female deity in opposition to biblical witness.

Whether one may use nonbiblical imagery, indeed whether one can even change the proportions of emphasis within the scope of biblical imagery, depends upon one's understanding of how the Bible functions in the community of faith. If the Bible is understood as a repository or databank of verbally correct information about God, then its words and grammatical structures should limit our own. If, however, the Bible is viewed as establishing a trajectory for Christian living, a trajectory that the continuing community checks and rechecks by reference to the Bible, then its authority functions quite differently. Under this view theologians and liturgists not only may but should consider new imagery for God, imagery that is meaningful for their own times and places as well as consonant with the full witness to God in the biblical material.

Diversity of context must also be considered in continuing discussions of God language. Susan Thistlethwaite points out, for instance, that father language for God seems to be much more a problem for white feminists than for black women writers. She notes that in black churches there is proportionally greater emphasis on the terms Spirit and Lord, so that father language is "already mediated" and trinitarian imagery is more strongly present.[15] Thistlethwaite also notes that among battered women and incest victims, some have a religious background that needs to hold onto the father-god on the road to healing, while others do well to let go of this imagery. As the debate about God language continues, such cultural and personal differences must be remembered; this issue should not be used as a sole criterion in assessing people's commitment to advocacy for women. Thistlethwaite's examples point us to our second main topic within Part One.

Experience in Biblical Interpretation

Feminist theology is frequently criticized for replacing scriptural authority with the authority of personal experience. This criticism masks the complexity of the discussion about the role of experience among feminist theologians, as well as the role of experience in theology generally. Elizabeth A. Johnson is among many who argue cogently that "consulting human experience is an identifying mark of virtually all contemporary theology, as indeed has been the case at least implicitly with most of the major articulations in the history of Christian theology."[16] Thus the question is not *whether* to "consult experience," but rather *how* to name or describe human experience and *how* to assess its proper contribution. What follows is but a sampling of positions, representing some of the range of proposals on this issue.

Elisabeth Schüssler Fiorenza makes one of the strongest claims for the importance of beginning with women's experience, specifying their "experience in their struggle for liberation" as the basis for assessing "oppressive or liberating dynamics of all biblical texts." Jesus' freedom to challenge his own received tradition for the sake of human wholeness ("the sabbath was made for humankind . . . ," Mark 2:27) is offered as a model, along with an appeal to established principles within Roman Catholic tradition. This approach is coupled for Fiorenza with understanding the Bible itself as a "historical prototype rather than as a mythical archetype."[17] Although she gives a priority to experience that is uncomfortable for many, it is a particular kind of experience, one that evokes the liberation theology theme of the hermeneutical privilege of the oppressed.

By contrast to Fiorenza, within the evangelical wing of American Protestantism feminists such as Letha Dawson Scanzoni and Nancy A. Hardesty continue to insist on the Bible as the first source for theology. Yet they also expect that tradition, experience, and reason will come into play in the interpretation of Scripture.[18]

Ada María Isasi-Díaz explains that for historical reasons the Bible plays a very limited role in the lives of Hispanic women. She points out that *mujerista* theology centers on communal praxis oriented to questions of physical and cultural-historical survival. In this setting Isasi-Díaz insists that the Bible must be used "as authoritative"; but the Bible is to be tested by Hispanic feminist praxis.[19]

Clarice Martin describes womanist theology as emerging from "African-American women's historical struggles against racial and gender oppression, as well as against the variegated experiences of classism." These factors are "constitutive elements in their conceptual and interpretive horizon and hermeneutics . . . " Such experiences of oppression, "like all human experience, affect the way in which women and men code and decode sacred and secular reality."[20] While the precise relationship between the Bible and experience is not spelled out in theoretical terms here, Martin goes on to show graphically how the differences in context and standpoint between slave apologists and the slaves themselves led to radically opposing interpretations of biblical teaching about slavery. She concludes with an emphasis on the importance of "amplifying marginalized voices" who speak out of a "hermeneutics of suspicion, resistance, liberation and hope. . . . "[21]

Letty Russell writes of experience as "a source" of theology. "Experience is by no means the only source for Christian theology. But neither is it simply an added-on afterthought." For Russell, the experiences of very diverse peoples of both past and present must be taken into account in doing theology. Such experiences are "an invitation to expand our understanding of how God's Word is believed and lived out in many different societes and in many different parts of the world. . . . It is an invitation to look at how faith is shaped by life and how it can grow, change, and deepen as the contexts of life and learning shift."[22]

An example of some Asian women's approach to the role of experience appears in a paper prepared by the EATWOT (Ecumenical Association of Third World Theologians) Women's Collective in the Philippines. The paper begins with individual women's stories of oppression, moves to a more general analysis of women's situation in the Philippines, considers the general heritage (precolonial and Christian colonial) of the Filipino people and what might be reclaimed, then attempts to incorporate that material into a theological process of struggle, reflection, and commitment to the poor. In this process theological and biblical reflection seeks to underline the "liberative message" of scripture and tradition and "expose their patriarchal contents." The paper is careful to recognize that all contexts have "biases" and that "communal endeavor" is required.[23]

Toward the end, the Filipino women's paper sets forth the following tentative principle: "we interpret and judge texts, events and realities as in accordance with God's design when they (1) promote the authentic personhood of women, (2) foster inclusive communities based on just relationships, (3) contribute toward genuine national sovereignty and autonomy, and (4) develop caring and respectful attitudes not only among human beings but towards the rest of creation as well."[24]

In reading the Filipino essay I was at first taken by surprise by the inclusion of national sovereignty in a "feminist" principle; I was not used to thinking about that as a part of "feminism." My surprise (and subsequent recognition of the appropriateness of this theme in the Philippines, and similarly the appropriateness of the theme of national reunification among feminists in Korea) illustrates a potential weakness in the category of experience in white feminist theory. Various groups of women of color have observed that white women in an act of unconscious racism describe their experiences as if they applied to all women.[25] The development of biblical analyses and theologies done from the standpoint of women in contexts of double and triple oppression is essential first of all for the integrity of these women; awareness of their work may also help white, first world feminists to discover their racist, colonialist, and economically privileged blind spots. Honoring diversity of experiences and development of these so-called local theologies may appear to lead to fragmentation; but it is only when *all* women gain a clearer sense of their distinctive and diverse identities that commonalities can be constructively considered.[26]

G. Stroup has put forward two further criticisms of the way in which most feminists use the category of experience. According to Stroup, either the Bible is actually the hidden criterion by which a principle of evaluation is established, or else the community declares its experience inaccessible to others and thus not subject to correction by the Bible itself or by others' interpretation of the Bible.[27] It is my own view that both criticisms are overdrawn when the larger scope of the authors' work is taken into account.

Russell, for example, describes Bible study as a "spiral" model of action and reflection. In studying a text, people are asked to consider what experience of their own informs their view of the text, what context might have caused the production of the text, and what someone from a disadvantaged group might ask about the text. Community discussion of the intersections of these three responses then leads both to further questions and to clues for faithful Christian living. People come back to study the text again after trying to incorporate these insights.[28] Further development of this spiral method insists on the importance of being in solidarity of action with the disadvantaged, not just discussing them theoretically as groups "out there."[29] The evaluative function of the biblical witness is made explicit here, and the process is deliberately designed to render the community correctable.

Just as attention to our own contexts may lead us to be critical of the Bible and church tradition, so also we are enabled to hear criticism of our own actions and worldviews as the biblical text is interpreted by others. What is new, to reiterate, is that feminists propose listening especially to interpretations from those on the margins (particularly women) rather than from those in the center. Although canonization of the biblical material was controlled by those in the center, first in Judaism and then in Christianity, the Bible as a whole is full of testimony to the model of listening, especially to those speaking from the margins. Much of prophecy, for example, criticizes the establishment. The poetry of Job criticizes the establishment's theological correlation between good works and divine reward. Ecclesiastes models the freedom to raise radical doubts about theological "conventional wisdom." Jesus repeatedly challenges establishment Judaism. Peter challenges the leaders in Jerusalem to incorporate Gentiles into the early Church. It is through such attention to the unlikely edges of diversity that the larger truth of who God is may be discerned.

Part Two

We turn now to illustrations of ways in which women from different cultural, racial, and economic contexts are reading biblical texts. Nearly every biblical story about a woman has been treated by someone around the globe from a "feminist" perspective, as have many passages on themes such as forgotten imagery for God, or economic and political justice. It is my impression that womanists and women from third world countries have written more frequently than white North American feminists on passages about the latter theme; this is hardly surprising given the maelstrom of economic and political upheaval in which many of these women live. As R. Weems points out, the choice of focal texts as well as the interpretation offered will be affected by context.[30]

Weems's point is well illustrated by my experience in Korea and in the Philippines with the story of Jael as recounted in the Song of Deborah (Judges 5). This story of the woman who drove a tent peg into the head of General Sisera is much appreciated by women whom I met in these countries. They are not skittish about the use of force to achieve justice and compare Jael's action to save her people with heroines of resistance to the Marcos regime in the Philippines or the Japanese forces in Korea. I commented to a Korean women's group studying this text[31] that it seemed to me that many white, economically comfortable women in North America (including myself) were very ill at ease with this story and tended to avoid it; I attributed this attitude to the lack of armed conflict on American soil in recent memory and the continuing influence of the Victorian tradition of the "gentlewoman" who should be protected by a man and not engage in violence. I then posed the question, How might the Korean women's understanding enable people like me to engage this text and hear a word of God? The answer came back quickly from the far end of the table: "If you North American women would recognize that your place in this story is that of Sisera's mother, waiting for her conquering son to come home and supposing that he is delayed by violating more women and collecting more booty . . . ,[32] *then* you would understand this story." It was for me a moment of truth. For all my practice in recognizing myself as an Egyptian rather than a Hebrew in the Exodus narrative, for all my verbalizing of my complicity as a U. S. resident in first world colonialism and world economic hegemony, I had not really learned. Probably I will need to be taught again and again. The encounter made real for me once again that authority of scripture is an "event" in which God addresses us through a community gathered around the text, especially through voices from the margin.

I choose the story of Ruth for a more extended example because a wide variety of "feminist" perspectives on this biblical book is available for comparison. Weems reminds us that with this story, as with any text, readers may have multiple contexts from which they engage in reading the Bible. "For example, Christian African American women belong to at least four communities of readers: American/Western, African American, female, and Christian. . . . An African American woman [reading Ruth may] focus predominantly on Ruth the woman, Ruth the foreigner, Ruth the unelected woman, Ruth the displaced widow, or, perhaps, Ruth the ancestress of the King of Israel, King David, to name a few."[33] The goal of reviewing women's interpretations of Ruth, therefore, is to show how varied these readings are, without making any mechanical ties between context and interpretation and without presuming that all women in a given country or culture adhere to a single interpretation. The interpretations presented come from North America and from Asia. Those from Asia are not based on published material, but are my reports of actual Bible study meetings (each about two hours in length) in which I took part as a visitor in the spring of 1993.

The first of the Asian Bible studies was done by Filipino women.[34] Two themes emerged from their conversation. First, this group highlighted the importance of solidarity among poor women to work for change in their condition. They focused on Ruth and Naomi standing together, with first one, then the other taking initiative for change.[35] Second, the story of Ruth was related to the problem of prostitution. A woman pastor present had been approached by a fourteen-year-old girl from a destitute family in a poverty stricken rural village. A "recruiter" had invited this child to go as a "dancer" to a foreign country and the girl had decided to accept. She hoped to win the notice of a rich foreign man who would marry her and support her family in the Philippines. To her pastor she offered the role model of Ruth, who put herself forward sexually to a rich man in order to gain economic security for herself and her mother-in-law. Where the teenager got this interpretation of Ruth (from the recruiter? from her family? from other girls?) was not known, nor was it clear whether she knew she would almost surely be forced into prostitution after leaving home. Since sex-tourism as a structural evil is high on the list of advocacy concerns of many Filipino women, this story struck a nerve. The participants in this study then struggled to assess the tensions between these two themes. Could they reconcile their appreciation of Ruth's and Naomi's efforts toward change with their recognition of the socioeconomic setting that led to the need for dependence on a rich male, and a hungry child's rationalization of a life of prostitution?

A few weeks later I met with several groups of women in Myanmar (Burma).[36] A group of older laywomen with daughters-in-law expressed their delight with Ruth's concern for Naomi; they suggested that God rewarded her self-sacrifice by allowing her to become an ancestor of King David. They were troubled, however, by the scene at the threshing floor. Despite their familiarity with the tradition of levirate marriage, they suggested that the OT moral standard was not really in accord with the will of God—women should not tempt men sexually.

A group of young unmarried women expressed their nervousness that too much would be expected of them as future daughters-in-law because of Ruth's example. Ruth should be admired because she struggled for survival, but women of today should find their own ways of struggle, not follow her example either with regard to her mother-in-law or with regard to Boaz.

A third group gave attention to the theme of solidarity between Ruth and Naomi as poor women. Their attention centered, however, on different ways by which women may be left without men (in their situation, imprisonment of suspected male dissidents) and the resulting economic displacement that leads to migration of women to areas of different language and customs.

A gathering of Japanese women expressed ambivalence about Ruth.[37] On the one hand, they could imagine that Ruth and Naomi had a certain freedom of action typical of Japanese women many centuries ago, and as Japanese women they were interested to explore historical-cultural parallels. On the other hand, as Christian women they expressed strong distaste for the story, explaining that it was much used by male church leaders as biblical warrant for completely self-sacrificing devotion of daughter-in-law to mother-in-law, a cultural tradition they sought to challenge.

Again in Taiwan women expressed differing responses.[38] In a hallway during a refreshment break one vented her rage at the handing over of baby Obed to his grandmother Naomi and the Bethlehem women's proclamation that "a son has been born to Naomi" !(Ruth 4:16-17). This scene underscored for her her cultural tradition in which all rights for upbringing of children were given to the paternal grandmother; the mother did not even eat meals with the children, but had to eat with the family servants. By contrast, one paper presenter suggested ways in which Naomi's actual treatment of her daughter-in-law was much better than that typical of culture in Taiwan; she had even organized a mothers-in-law group in her church to teach kinder treatment of daughters-in-law with the example of Naomi as a biblical model. Consideration, in a second paper, of the contrast between peaceful village life in the book of Ruth and the war and devastation of the book of Judges led to conversation about ecojustice and the politics of polluted rice paddies. The theme of poverty and economic structures proved of interest to many participants, but it was I as the visitor who introduced this theme. Generally, the cultural issue of family relations among women seemed to dominate the participants' perspective and to leave them, at best, ambivalent about Ruth as a model for conscientized women's living.

Womanist Renita Weems, writing on the North American scene for the African-American religious women's community,[39] lifts up yet other aspects of the story, thinking about the relationship between Ruth and Naomi in rather different categories. She suggests that once the husbands were dead, "Naomi and Ruth could never return [to] their former relationship to one another: mother-in-law and daughter-in-law. . . . They would have to give friendship a chance. . . . Ruth's pledge was to Naomi, the woman."[40] Weems's retelling of the story emphasizes the themes of recovery from the grief, learning how to relate as women in mutual respect for differences, and the importance of maintaining friendships with women alongside of relationships with men.

Israeli Jewish writer (living in North America) Esther Fuchs argues that Ruth is regarded as a heroine in Israelite tradition because of her "voluntary and active support of the patriarchal institution of the levirate, which insures the patrilineage of a deceased husband." Ruth is "self-seeking, . . . fighting for her *own* benefit and security . . . by giving birth to a son."[41] Fuchs suggests that Ruth complies precisely with Israelite patriarchal expectations by following her mother-in-law, and that her character is portrayed by the narrator in a way that reflects and promotes male prejudices and desires (though the narrator presents her actions as her own desires, not any sacrifice of freedom). For Fuchs the purpose of the story is to describe to ancient women and men how an ideal woman should think and act. One may infer that Fuchs does not find in the Ruth of this patriarchal ideology any traits to be praised or emulated by contemporary women seeking to challenge patriarchal culture.

A study that is by now widely known is Phyllis Trible's presentation of Ruth as "A Human Comedy."[42] As a white North American Christian feminist she uses literary and rhetorical analysis to assess the story. She views the underlying motive for much of the action as the need for the daughters-in-law to find husbands; this theme enunciated by Naomi in her farewell speech to Ruth and Orpah carries through the following chapters. Trible highlights Ruth's choice to follow Naomi as commitment to an old woman rather than to a marriageable man; "there is no more radical decision in all the memories of Israel."[43] Trible gives the title "All's Well that Ends Well" to her presentation of Ruth 4, in which the decisions at the town gate culminate in the marriage of Ruth and Boaz and the birth of the boy Obed. The story ends in "wholeness and wellbeing. . . . the brave and bold decisions of women embody and bring to pass the blessings of God."[44]

A final North American interpretation is jointly authored by a white woman and a white man teaching in Protestant seminaries. Danna Nolan Fewell and David Miller Gunn[45] find a high degree of self-interest rather than altruism in many of the actions of the characters, including Naomi's efforts to send away her daughters-in-law and Ruth's insistence (against Naomi's wishes) on accompanying her mother-in-law. So also Boaz contrives the encounter at the gate to make himself appear noble in the eyes of the Bethlehemites for doing what he wanted to do anyway, marry the foreign woman by whose beauty and character he was already smitten. The conclusion of the narrative raises for Fewell and Gunn the painful issues of surrogate motherhood as Naomi is handed the baby Obed as a son and heir.[46]

A further search, especially if done cross-culturally in other languages and in nonacademic publications, might well turn up more instances of interpreting Ruth from a feminist perspective. The preceding examples have been set down one after another with deliberate omission of any observations of comparison or contrast among them. In keeping with a "feminist" approach to biblical interpretation that values experience, struggle, the biblical text, and interpretations from various kinds of margins, readers are invited to finish the work of this essay by entering into their own conversations with the text of Ruth, with their own communities of faith, and with these interpreters of Ruth from around the world. At the same time, all are invited to find places of communal praxis, of active solidarity with those more marginalized than themselves. For in the end, authority of scripture is an "event," something to be experienced more than argued; authority of scripture is an "event" of God's Spirit in which encountering the Bible in a diverse, struggling, hoping-against-hope community of faith does, against all odds, bring forth life out of the midst of death.

Chapter Sixteen / BIBLICAL THEOLOGY AND SOCIAL ETHICS

Walter Wink

No consistent or thoroughgoing social ethic has ever been developed out of the New Testament alone. Biblically based social ethics have fared far better when they were grounded in the Old Testament. The Exodus and the fulminations of the prophets provide powerful images, precedents, and criteria for ongoing social protest and action, though in practice it has been black preaching or base community Bible studies that have actually shaped history, not systematic treatments by scholars in the remote fastness of their university studies.

But the NT has not seemed to provide the raw materials for a powerful social ethic. The Sermon on the Mount has, to be sure, played a significant role in the peace church witness since the Reformation, but that witness has been confined to a tiny segment of the Church and virtually quarantined by the mainline churches. Jesus' teachings on love and his vision of the coming reign of God have fertilized recurrent renewal movements and experimental communities, but provide few guidelines for transferring these insights to the life of institutions or the rough-and-tumble of politics.

This odd lack of concern for politics as we understand it has been traced to the almost total absence of a political culture in Jesus' Palestine. A tiny priestly oligarchy managed the day-to-day rule of Judea, and a despotic client-ruler, Herod Antipas, presided over Galilee. In neither case was regular citizen action and involvement permitted. Rome fixed all the parameters of political life, and against them there was virtually no appeal, apart from delegations to the Emperor and episodic nonviolent demonstrations of stunning effectiveness.

Perhaps one reason Jesus never spoke of voter registration drives and institutional reform was that there were no channels for democratic political action. But he does teach nonviolent direct action (Matt 5:38-42; Luke 6:29-30).[1] What we have taken as an absence of politics was, in fact, a different kind of politics, the only kind of politics possible under a dominant empire or oligarchy or autocratic state: the politics of nonviolent action.

In his teaching about nonviolence, Jesus was endorsing and elaborating on a form of resistance already discovered and used by his own Jewish contemporaries. Daniel and his companions were the great exemplars of the nonviolent action. In Jesus' entry into Jerusalem, his demonstration in the Temple, and his manner of dying, the man from Nazareth incarnated nonviolence. The Church faithfully continued his nonviolent way, refusing military service and rejecting armed retaliation even when savagely persecuted. Though it failed to maintain the radicality of Jesus' relationships with women, or to resist the slide back into hierarchical social structures and legalism, the Church doggedly persisted in the nonviolent way that Jesus taught for three centuries. And it focused its nonviolent resistance on idolatry of the emperor, at the cost of many martyrdoms.

The Church clearly understood its vocation to be one of nonviolent resistance to the divinization of the state. That fact alone should provide plenty of grist for a NT social ethic. I want to return to this issue of the Church's vocation later on, but first we need to recover another major component of the biblical witness essential for a social ethic: the principalities and powers, which for brevity I will simply call the Powers.[2]

In the past the Powers have been treated as spiritual beings flying in the sky, looking for some hapless mortal to leap upon and possess. Satan, the demons, angels, gods, the elements of the universe—these were the spooky and sinister beings of Christian superstition that the Enlightenment ruled out as inadmissible. Besides, many Christians themselves were fed up with attempts by clergy to frighten them and their children into compliance with arbitrary rules of behavior by means of these morbid creatures. So the Powers went into eclipse. Like Puff the Magic Dragon, indeed, like dragons and sea serpents and the Loch Ness monster, spiritual powers ceased for many people to be believable.

More recently, the Powers have been reinterpreted by some liberation theologians as the institutions, structures, and systems that encompass human life and so often oppress it. We are at least vaguely familiar with this possibility through the expression, "The Powers That Be." Here popular language is far in front of much of church theology. But the Powers are scarcely reducible to *just* institutions, structures, and systems, for they are described by the NT as being both visible *and invisible,* both earthly *and* heavenly (Col 1:16). What then is this invisible surplus of meaning? What is this heavenly dimension of earthly powers?

I have tried to provide an answer to these questions in a trilogy I have written on the Powers.[3] My hypothesis, put briefly, is that the Powers are the simultaneity of an outer, physical manifestation, and an inner, spiritual reality. Corporations, governments, churches, schools, clubs, gangs, and families have external concretions or visible characteristics (a building, membership rolls, staff, a budget, a sales territory or area or domain), and a withinness or interiority (a corporate personality, a family system, a spirit, a collective culture, with an accompanying symbol system, sets of rules and expectations, sanctions, and legitimations).

Perhaps I can make myself clearer by a series of images:

The Ancient Worldview

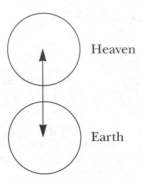

This is the worldview reflected in the Bible. In this conception, everything earthly has its heavenly counterpart, and everything heavenly has its earthly counterpart. Every event is thus a simultaneity of both dimensions of reality. There is nothing intrinsically sacrosanct about this imagery. It was shared not only by the writers of the Bible, but also by Greeks, Romans, Egyptians, Babylonians, Assyrians, Sumerians—indeed, everyone in the ancient world, and it is still held by large numbers of people in Africa, Asia, and Latin America. It is a profoundly true picture of reality.

The Gnostic Worldview

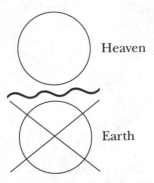

In this worldview, the goodness of the created order is denied. Only the spiritual is true. Earthly life is a mistake, and is presided over by imperfect and evil Powers. Creation *was* the Fall. Something of the same picture would fit some forms of Eastern religions, except that they would see the world not as evil but as illusion.

The Materialistic Worldview

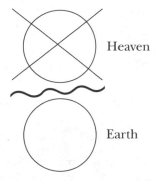

There is no heaven, no spiritual world, no God, no soul; nothing but material existence and what can be known through the five senses and reason. This view became prominent in the Enlightenment, but is as old as Democritus (ca. 460–ca. 370 BCE).

The Evangelical Worldview

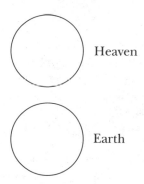

In reaction to the Enlightenment, evangelical Christianity invented the "supernatural" realm. Acknowledging that this supersensible realm could not be known by the senses, theologians conceded earthly reality to modern science and preserved a privileged "spiritual" realm immune to confirmation or discon- firmation—at the cost of an integral reality and the simultaneity of heavenly and earthly aspects of existence.

An Integral Worldview

Emerging from a confluence of sources, especially the new physics, this worldview sees everything as having an outer and an inner aspect:

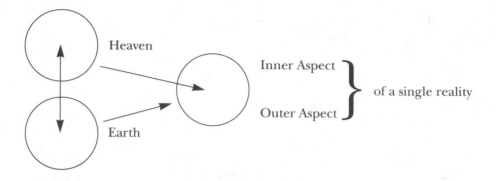

It attempts to take seriously the spiritual insights of the ancient or biblical worldview by positing a withinness or interiority in all things, but sees this inner spiritual reality as inextricably related to an outer concretion or physical manifestation. It is no more intrinsically Christian than the ancient worldview, but it is far more adequate than anything since.

The integral worldview that is emerging in our time takes seriously all the aspects of the ancient worldview, but combines them in a different way. Both images are spacial. The idea of heaven as "up" is a natural, almost unavoidable way of indicating transcendence. But few of us in the West, who have been irremediably touched by the Enlightenment, can actually think that God, the angels, and departed spirits are somewhere in the actual sky, as most ancients did (and some people today still do—including atheists. Remember the glee of the Soviet cosmonauts in announcing to the world that they had encountered no angels in space?).

The image of the spiritual as "withinness" is not, however, a flat, limited, dimensionless point. It is a within coterminous with the universe—an inner realm every bit as rich and extensive as the outer realm. The psychologist Carl Jung spoke of this rich inner dimension as the collective unconscious, meaning by that, a realm of largely unexplored spiritual reality linking everyone to everything. The amazement of mystics at the discovery of this realm within is matched only by the amazement of the physicists upon discovering that the "final" building block of matter, the atom, is in fact invisible, patterned energy.

My argument is that what people in the world of the Bible experienced and called "principalities and powers" was in fact real. They were discerning the actual spirituality at the center of the political, economic, and cultural institutions of their day. The spiritual aspect of the Powers is not simply a "personification" of institutional qualities that would exist whether they were personified or not. On the contrary, the spirituality of an institution exists as a real aspect of the institution even when it is not perceived as such. Institutions have an actual spiritual ethos, and we neglect this aspect of institutional life at our peril.

The spiritual dimension of the Powers is invisible, however, and can only be known by means of projection. In NT times, people did not read the spirituality of an institution straight off its outer manifestations. Instead, they projected the *felt* or *intuited* spiritual qualities out onto the screen of the universe, and perceived them as cosmic forces reigning from the sky.

In the ancient worldview, where earthly and heavenly reality were inextricably united, this view of the Powers worked effectively. But modern Westerners are, on the whole, incapable of maintaining that worldview. What we encounter instead is fundamentalist treatments of the Powers as demons in the air, wholly divorced from their concretions in the physical world, or liberal denials that this spiritual dimension even exists.

What is necessary is to complete the projection process by *withdrawing* the projections and recognizing that the spiritual force that we are experiencing is emanating from actual institutions or systems or structures. Visitors to Nazi Germany in the late 1930s spoke of the palpable evil in the "air," of a pervading "atmosphere" that hung over the entire land, full of foreboding and menace. Those who leave South Africa remark on the sense of an enormous weight of anxiety and tension that drops off their shoulders as the plane leaves South African airspace. People who remember the assassination of President John F. Kennedy will still recall a feeling of darkness over the face of the nation that lasted for days. These "spirits" were real, but they were not independent operatives from on high; they were the actual spirituality of the nations involved, and the sheer intensity of evil rendered them palpable.

The relevance of the Powers for a biblical social ethic should by now begin to be clear. Any attempt to transform a social system without addressing its spirituality is doomed to failure. For example, in the book of Revelation, John is commanded by the risen Christ to write seven letters to the *angels* of seven churches in western Asia Minor; not to the people in these churches, but to the angels of the churches. Why? Because the angel represents the Church as a totality. It is its corporate personality, its spirituality, its ethos, encompassing both the visible and invisible dimensions of the Church, including all its people. Leaders and members may come and go, but there is something that persists over time, that in fact draws similar new people to replace those who leave, thus guaranteeing that the new people will continue to manifest the same general spirit.

The angel is not something separate from the people; it *is* the people as a single entity in their spiritual aspect. But the angel also reflects the church's building, its goals, its history, conflicts, wounds, and sacrifices. Anyone who tries to change a church simply by getting rid of a minister or changing the makeup of the governing board will soon discover the truth of the French maxim that runs, "The more things change, the more they stay the same." Only by addressing the spirituality *and* its concretions can the total entity be transformed, and that requires a kind of spiritual discernment and praxis that the materialistic ethos in which we live knows nothing about.[4]

There is nothing mystical or mysterious about all this. Anyone who has moved from one corporation to another knows how different they are. IBM and Gulf+Western have totally different felt gestalts, and their corporate personalities have the effect of a gyroscope, maintaining the system in equilibrium despite all the institutional turnover and crises that beset it. Canada and the United States, despite their virtual visual identity, have altogether different national "angels" (see Daniel 10 for this concept) that distinguish them sharply, especially on the issue of public violence.[5]

If social structures are made up of more than simply this dictator and his army or that pastor and her church, but have a discrete spirituality as well, then attempts at social change will need to address both the outer forms and the inner spirit. Nothing permanent is achieved by removing President Nixon from office if nothing is done to alter the imperial American presidency. The office has its own momentum through time that almost requires certain behaviors. The presidency determines, as much as it is determined.

The NT's understanding of the Powers is clear but extremely subtle. It avoids the two extremes of divinizing the status quo, and demonizing it. It asserts unequivocally that the Powers are created in, through, and for Christ, through whom they receive coherence (Col 1:16). This means that institutions and social structures are not human inventions that can be dispensed within the New Creation. They are integral to human existence in any conceivable form it might take. They are constituent parts of God's good creation, and exist to serve the humanizing purposes of God declared in Jesus. However derelict from their created intent they become, they nevertheless belong to the One in and through and for whom they were created, and cannot exist for one moment, even in gravest iniquity, apart from Christ.

This truth is even recognized by the secular states of today, which betray by their very titles a recognition that they exist merely to serve the higher good: the "Ministry of Education," the "Ministry of Agriculture," the "Armed Services." Their constitutions, however much they violate them in practice, show that they know full well that the only justification for their existence is to foster human rights, economic security, justice, and plenty for all, administered equally and without bias. No nation lives up to these ideals; but the fact that they have them reflects their inchoate recognition that the nation is not an end in itself, but serves the higher good of humanity.

But in fact, what we see is institutional life become idolatrous. Nations, businesses, hospitals, and universities all tend to put their own survival and advancement above the human purposes of the One in and through and in whom they exist. This idolatry issues in the demonic. It is significant that the biblical myth speaks nowhere of God creating the demons. They are good angels, fallen. When a corporation makes profit the highest good, it becomes idolatrous, and that false worship of money leads it into behaviors that will be destructive of other companies, its own personnel, and of the values upon which the public welfare depends for a decent quality of life.

Demonic institutions or states thus embody a diseased spirituality that cannot be exorcised simply by firing a manager or deposing a ruler (though this might become the *occasion* through which the diseased spirituality might be addressed). As Eph 6:12 puts it, "our struggle is not against enemies of blood and flesh, but against the rulers, against the authorities, against the cosmic powers of this present darkness, against the spiritual forces of evil in the heavenly places." Implicit in this statement is the recognition that, at a spiritual level, the most important battleground is not the one presented by the visible aspects of the organization with which we are struggling, but rather the invisible force that is indifferent to the personnel that serve it and is ready to dispense with them any time such betrayal would serve its interests.

The institutions of the Roman world of the first century were experienced as suprahuman, remote, and overwhelmingly powerful. They demanded, and received, worship as divine. But their sovereignty was maintained by violence, and the "peace" they imposed on the world was a peace based on violence. To one with eyes to see from a perspective outside the imperial spell, the empire was part of a total domination system, a "dominion of darkness" (Col 1:13). Most people could not see this. Jesus' crucifixion marked the great exposure of the delusional system that had been spun to keep humanity complicit with its own oppression. On the cross, Col 2:15 asserts, God exposed the rulers and authorities and made a public example of them, triumphing over them through Jesus.

The Gospels provide no explanation for Jesus' execution. None of the charges pressed by the authorities stand up. The Powers could not reveal their real reasons for killing Jesus, for to do so would have been an admission that there was a system beyond their system, an authority beyond their authority, a power beyond their powers. Jesus had to die because he revealed to the world the lie that was named truth, and disclosed the truth of God's inbreaking alternative order.

Jesus' death was no different from that of any other rebel who dared to challenge the Powers that dominate the world. But something went awry with Jesus. The rulers scourged him with whips, but with each stroke of the lash their own illegitimacy was laid open. They mocked him with a robe and a crown of thorns, spitting on him and striking him on the head with a reed, ridiculing him with the ironic ovation, "Hail, King of the Jews!"—not knowing that their acclamation would echo down the centuries as accurate. They stripped him naked and crucified him in humiliation, all unaware that this very act had stripped them of the last covering that disguised the towering wrongness of the whole way of living that their violence defended. They nailed him to the cross, not realizing that with each hammer's blow they were nailing up, for the whole world to see, the *mene, mene, tekel, u-pharsin* by which the Domination System would be numbered, weighed in the balances, found wanting, and finally terminated (Dan 5:25-28).

What killed Jesus was not irreligion, but religion itself; not lawlessness, but precisely the Law; not anarchy, but the upholders of order. It was not the bestial but those considered best who crucified the one in whom the divine Logos was visibly incarnate. And because he was not only innocent, but the very embodiment of true religion, true law, and true order, this victim exposed their violence for what it was: not the defense of society, but an offense against God.

Paul paradoxically asserts that it was not through the resurrection that the Powers were unmasked, but through the Cross:

> And you, who were dead in trespasses and the uncircumcision of your flesh, God made alive together with him, having forgiven us all our trespasses, having canceled the charge which stood against us with its legal demands; this he set aside, nailing it to the cross. Unmasking the principalities and powers, God publicly shamed them, exposing them in Christ's triumphal procession by means of the cross. (Col 2:13-15)[6]

The very Powers that led him out to Golgotha in their triumphal procession were in fact stepping into a divinely set trap. "The devil saw Jesus as his prize, snapped at the bait, and was pulled out of the water for all to see" (Luther). Only it was not really a trap since nothing was hidden.[7] As a result, it is the Powers themselves who are now paraded, captive, in God's triumphal procession. The Cross marks, not the failure of God, but of violence.

As a revelatory event, the Cross exposed evil where one had always looked for good: in the guardians of the faith of the people. It exposed, as well, humanity's complicity with the Powers, its willingness to trade increments of freedom for installments of advantage. The Cross shows us that we are now free to resist the claim of any finite thing as absolute, or of any subsystem to be the whole.

The Cross also reveals humanity's rebelliousness against God, its hatred of limits on greed, its boundless appetite for consumption, its fury at not being God.[8] And it reveals as well God's infinite patience and love, God's unconditional pardon. If human beings killed the One who fully embodied God's intention for human life; killed not innocuously but deliberately, in order to blot out God's claim on their lives; and if, despite their having thus tried to evacuate God from the universe, God still loved them, then nothing can separate us from the love of God. But if God is that loving, then there is no need to try to appease God, or earn God's love by doing good. And if God loves us unconditionally, there is no need to seek conditional love from the various Powers who promise us rewards in return for devotion.

The Cross thus reveals that God has forgiven our sins. Sin, understood moralistically, is just one more delusion by which the Powers—specifically, religious systems—paralyze us with guilt. But sin, as Paul saw with such awesome clarity, is not the infraction of moral codes; for these too are Powers, are relative, and change from culture to culture and age to age. Sin is the failure to be authentic. But our authenticity is not just something we surrender without a fight; it is also stolen from us by the Powers. Before we reach the age of choice, our choices have already been chosen for us by a system indifferent to our uniqueness. We are born into a world that teaches inauthenticity, duplicity, and self-concealment.

And yet we are responsible not only for what we do but for what has been done to us. The Cross frees us to acknowledge the ways we have missed our lives. It invites us to die to that old system and be born again to a new. It enables us to abandon the ephemeral quest for freedom from one Power by means of another Power. It enables us to recognize that we cannot save ourselves, that deliverance must come from outside the Domination System, that

> The stronger we are the sooner all is over;
> It is our strength with which they gobble us up.[9]

It shocks us awake to the depth of our complicity in our own unraveling, and it frees us for the possibility of authentic living.

Jesus lived authentically. That is perhaps the single greatest source of his attractiveness. The powers loathe authenticity. They reward conformity, obedience, docility. Corporations and bureaucracies prefer predictable behavior. But the Cross reveals Powers unable to make Jesus be what they wanted him to become, or to cease being who he was. Here was a person able to live out to the fullest what he felt God's will to be. His freedom was labeled demonic, his sensitivity to God's prompting, arrogance, his response to human needs, unlawful. He chose to die rather than compromise with violence.[10] The Powers threw at him every weapon in their arsenal. But they could not deflect him from the path he and God were blazing. Because he lived thus, we too can dare to walk that path.

Because they could not kill what was alive in him, the Cross also revealed the impotence of death. Death is evil's final sanction. The fear of death is what so long kept Eastern Europeans and Palestinians complicit in the face of tyrannous regimes. When they faced their fear, they became free. The brave have always known this. What the Cross adds is the promise of resurrection. Not only is one free from the constraint of fear, but one can believe that truth, justice, and God will certainly and finally triumph.

Jesus' truth could not be killed. The massive forces arrayed against the truth are revealed to be puny against the force of a free human being. The Chinese student who stood alone before a column of tanks for an eternity of minutes in

269

Tiananmen Square graphically displayed this power. The stunning collapse of Soviet and Eastern bloc Communism is a breathtaking reminder that ours is a moral universe, and that no evil can forever hold dominion.

Today the Powers are raging because they are naked. As the Sesotho proverb says, "the horse kicks hardest when it is about to die." The problem is that many innocent people will be kicked by the dying horse. The Resurrection affirms that *nothing* can prevent the final triumph of righteousness. The days of oppression are numbered.

Those who are freed from the fear of death are, as a consequence, able to break the spiral of violence. On the cross, Jesus voluntarily took upon himself the violence of the entire system. "When he was reviled, he did not revile in return; when he suffered, he did not threaten; but he trusted him who judges justly" (1 Pet 2:23). The Cross is the ultimate paradigm of nonviolence. It reveals, as René Girard aptly notes, that there is no longer any distinction possible between legitimate and illegitimate violence.[11] Through the Cross, God is revealing a new way, occasionally tried before, but now shown to be capable of consistent, programmatic embodiment.

Jesus' nonviolent response mirrored the very nature of God, who reaches out to a rebellious humanity through the Cross in the only way that would not abridge our freedom. Jesus' crucifixion was the agony of undergoing and tolerating human freedom to resist God. Had God not manifested divine love toward us in an act of abject weakness, one which we experience as totally noncoercive and nonmanipulative, the truth of our own being would have been forced on us rather than being something we freely choose.

Likewise, as Tillich put it, Jesus sacrifices everything in him and of him that could bring people to him as an overwhelming personality. Instead, he brings them to that in him which is greater than both he and they.[12] "For us this means that in following him we are liberated from the authority of everything finite in him, from his special traditions, from his individual piety, from his rather conditioned world view, from any legalistic understanding of his ethics. Only as the crucified is he 'grace and truth' and not law."[13] By this act of self-emptying, Jesus meets us, not at the apex of the pyramid of power, but at its base: "despised and rejected by others," a common criminal, the offscouring of all things.

As the Crucified, Jesus thus identifies with every victim of torture, incest, or rape; with every child terrified in the crossfire of enemy patrols; and with every single one of the forty thousand children who die each day of starvation. In his cry from the cross, "My God, my God, why have you forsaken me?" he is one with every doubter whose sense of justice overwhelms his capacity to believe in God; with every mother or father who cradles the lifeless body of a courageous son or daughter; with every Alzheimer's patient slowly losing her or his mind. In Jesus we see the suffering of God with and in God's people.

The Cross is God's victory in another, unexpected way: in the act of exposing the Powers for what they are, Jesus nevertheless submitted to their authority as instituted by God. Jesus' way of nonviolence preserves respect for the rule of law even in the act of resisting oppressive laws. By submitting to the authority of the Powers That Be, Jesus acknowledged their necessity but rejected the legitimacy of their pretentious claims. He submitted to the legally constituted authorities, but in so doing relativized, de-absolutized, and de-idolized them, showing them to be themselves subordinate to the whole. As such they are subordinate to the one who subordinated himself to them. Therefore, according to the Epistle to the Ephesians, God has

> enthroned Jesus at God's right hand in the heavenly realms, far above all government and authority, all power and dominion, and any title of sovereignty that commands allegiance, not only in this age but in the age to come. God has put everything in subjection beneath his feet.[14]

In our struggles with the Powers, consequently, we do not have to "make" the Cosmic Christ their Lord. We do not have to install Christ as the System of the systems. That is what the Cosmic Christ already *is*. We simply have the privilege of calling attention to that fact. The Powers, despite every attempt to deny it, are indissolubly linked to the whole and cannot exist for a single moment, even in their idolatry, apart from the whole. And it was in the event of the Cross that this truth became manifest.

The Cross is also God's victory over the Powers because, in this event, the Christ-principle, which was incarnated and humanized in Jesus, was made universal, and was liberated to become the archetype of humanness for all who are drawn to him. Jesus not only fulfilled the Law and the prophets of the Jews; he also fulfilled the myths of the pagans. He not only lived out the inner meaning of the old covenant, lifting it to a new plane; he also lived out, in the daily pattern of his life, teaching, and in an exemplary way, in his death and resurrection, the pattern of dying and rising known to myths around the globe. What these myths depicted as the necessary course of personal and social development, Jesus demonstrated as an actual human possibility. In so doing, his own history became mythic, universal. By historicizing the myths he mythicized his history. Jesus' death on the cross was like a black hole in space that sucked into its collapsing vortex all the meanings of the universe, until in the intensity of its compaction there was an explosive reversal, and the stuff of which galaxies are made was blown out into the universe. So Jesus as the Cosmic Christ became the universal human, and as such, the bearer of our own utmost possibilities for living.

Killing Jesus was like destroying a dandelion seed-head by blowing on it. It was like shattering a sun into a million points of light.

The Cross was, we might even say, a liberation of God. It stripped off from God all notions of God as the hierarchical apex of the pyramid of power. If Christ "emptied" himself of all grasping after equality with God (Phil 2:6), should not God be emptied as well? If love demands 'self-giving, if worship requires self-offering, should not God be given, be offered as well? If the gospel calls us to relinquish our preening arrogance, our lust for power, our manipulation of persons and things for ends unrelated to the whole—then shall not God also abandon that vaunted omnipotence, that unruffled heavenly calm, that blessing of the status quo so often ascribed to "him"? And is this not what happens at the Cross?

On the cross, does not Jesus unmask God? Is it not the case that the "God" of most religions, including Christianity, has all too often been conceived as a veritable tyrant? As the ultimate oppressor? It is true that in God's service is perfect freedom, but for many it has been a hellish slavery. *That* "God," who is nothing more than a projection of kingship onto the cosmos; *that* "God," who is nothing more than the summary of all the rules, obligations, hang-ups, repressions, threats, recriminations, and blame of a given society; *that* "God," who is nothing more than an idol of human fabrication, dies with Jesus on the cross. In *that* "God's" place is a new revelation of God, continually lost through the twisted reasonings and idolatrous regressions of alienated humanity: the God of Abraham, Moses, and the prophets, born again, saved—from us—on the cross!

Through the Cross, God has broken the unconscious, compulsive capacity of the Powers to manipulate us into idolatry. Unmasked and exposed, they only continue to have whatever power we choose to give them. Not only has their evil been revealed, but the Powers themselves will be reconciled. As Col 1:20 puts it, "Through him [Christ] God was pleased to reconcile to himself all things, whether on earth or in heaven, by making peace through the blood of his cross." The repetition of "whether on earth or in heaven" is clearly a flashback to verse 16, where the Powers are explicitly described as being "in heaven and on earth." God will neutralize their evil (1 Cor 15:24)[15] and place them under Christ's feet (1 Cor 15:25). The very Powers which were created in, through and for Christ (Col 1:16), and which have fallen to such depths of apostasy and violence, will be redeemed.

The image in the book of Revelation says it best: the nations (which one would have thought were utterly annihilated in the great judgment scene of Revelation 20) nevertheless come marching into the Holy City, bearing the unique gifts of their cultures: "The nations will walk by its light, and the kings of the earth will bring their glory into it" (Rev 21:24); and the leaves of the tree of life in the New Jerusalem will be "for the healing of the nations" (22:2).

In all this the Church has a unique and indispensable task, and here I want to return to my earlier comment about vocation. The Church has many functions, to be sure, but in reference to the Powers it is explicitly to unmask their idolatrous pretensions, to disenthrall their victims, to identify their dehumanizing values, and to strip from them the mantle of respectability. The Church's charter in its struggle with the powers is published in Eph 3:10—"that through the church the wisdom of God in its rich variety might now be made known to the rulers and authorities in the heavenly places." This statement enshrines a riddle, however: how is the *Church,* an earthly institution, supposed to carry out a revelatory task in reference to the Powers if they are in *heaven?*

If our working hypothesis is correct, then "the heavenlies" *(ta epourania)* are not off at the edge of space somewhere, but in our very midst as the *interiority* of earthly institutions, systems and structures. The task of the Church, then, is to practice a ministry of disclosure to the spirituality or withinness of these Powers.

In the immediate context of Ephesians, the mystery that has been revealed to the world through the cross of Jesus is that the basis of racial and ethnic enmity has now been dissolved. Jew and Gentile are now one in Christ. The Church's task is to make this new fact known to the ruling powers "in the heavenlies," that invisible layer of culture where racism is so deeply imbedded. To root out racism requires new outer arrangements, and the Church provided that: a fellowship of equals growing together into a "holy temple" (Eph 2:21). But just as crucial was the eradication of the *spirit* of racism, and that could only be countered by the message of the gospel.

Those who have devoted their lives to social struggle may be mystified and even a bit uneasy about talk of changing the spirituality of the Powers as an integral part of the resistance effort. They have seen all too many Christians limit their efforts to perfunctory prayers for general betterment of the situation. It is important to stress that the issue is not either/or, but both/and; the effort to change structural arrangements must also include attention to changing the spiritual gestalt that may even survive our changes and undermine them.

All our organizing, letter-writing, petitioning, political work, demonstrating, civil disobedience campaigns, fasting and prayers move to this end: to recall the Powers to the humanizing purposes of God revealed in Jesus. We are not commissioned to create a new society; indeed, we are scarcely competent to do so. We are not "building the Kingdom," as an earlier generation liked to put it. We simply lack the power to force the Powers to change. We faithfully do all these things with no illusions about our prospects for direct impact. We merely prepare the ground and sow; the seed grows of itself, night and day, until the harvest. And God will—this is our most profound conviction—bring the harvest.

This does not mean that our opposition, pitiful as it usually is, is irrelevant. Far from it! The Church is to be like a bulldog that sinks its teeth into an elephant's leg. It cannot bring the elephant down, but it can so distract the elephant's attention that the beast fails to notice the elephant trap and plunges in.

As Bill Moyer points out, every oppressive regime regularly oversteps itself. Hubris is the very essence of their lust for power; the dictators Marcos of the Philippines and Pinochet of Chile themselves called the "snap" elections that

273

proved their downfall. But unless there is a group of people prepared to capitalize on these "trigger events," nothing comes of them. A trigger event, according to Moyer, is the synchronous coincidence of a prepared opposition and a public outrage that creates citizen awareness and indignation.[16]

The antinuclear energy movement in the U.S. faithfully built up a constituency, and exercised all available forms of democratic intervention, referenda, injunctions, and so on. But it was incapable of stopping the increase of nuclear reactors. Already 260 were operating, ordered, or under contract by 1974. It was the disaster at Three Mile Island in 1979 that galvanized public resistance and rang the death knell of the nuclear industry.

But a similar disaster occurred at the Fermi reactor in Alabama in 1966, and the fact was suppressed from public knowledge. There was no movement of protest to which information about *that* disaster might be leaked, and the public attitude was still one of misbegotten trust. Trigger events are wasted when the people are not prepared to capitalize on them. Wisdom's little ironies must be met by Wisdom's children, ready to press into the opened breach.

Churches, however, are seldom organized as social change movements. They are made up of people of all political persuasions, and are usually incapable of mounting even the simplest protest *if it involves conflict*. Earlier I mentioned the fact that the early churches did *not* engage in even the political activities that would have been open to them. But they did do one thing consistently well, something that we, with our politicized consciousness, might not regard as political in the least. They proclaimed Jesus as Lord (Caesar, emperor, ruler). This seemingly innocuous action brought down on the Church, in increasing waves of intensity, the full wrath of the Roman Empire. To say Jesus is Lord was to relativize Rome. To all effects it de-divinized it. And what the empire needed more than anything, more even than military might, was the aura of divine legitimation provided by the worship of Roma and the emperor's *genius* (and often the emperor himself). That simple affirmation cost thousands of Christian lives over three turbulent centuries. The Church made known to the principalities and powers in the heavenly places the manifold wisdom of God, and the empire could not tolerate it.

Others may join hands with us in the daily discipline of resisting evil. But there is one thing the Church, and it alone, is commissioned to do, and that is to remind the Powers whose they are. Psalm 29:1-2 shows how this is done. The psalmist cries out to the Powers That Be:

> Ascribe to Yahweh, O heavenly beings,
> Ascribe to Yahweh glory and strength.
> Ascribe to Yahweh the glory of God's name;
> worship Yahweh in holy array. (author's translation)

Here the principalities and powers in their spiritual manifestation—that is, the spirituality of earthly institutions, structures, and systems—are being called upon by the people of God to abdicate all pretensions to absoluteness, ultimacy, and divinity, and to offer praise and worship to the true God. Praise is the homeostatic principle of the universe. It preserves the harmoniousness of the whole by preventing usurpation of the whole by its parts. Praise is the ecological principle of divinity whereby every creature is subordinated to its organic relationship to the Creator. *Praise is the cure for the apostasy of the Powers.*

The command expressed in the Psalm is not issued by God, however, but by us! In all simplicity, this is finally the task of the Church vis-à-vis the Powers: to remind the Powers that God alone is worthy of worship. This may seem to some to be the last indignity: the reduction of social action to worship. But it is nothing of the sort. For the spirituality of the Powers is not off somewhere in the sky, but at the very core of the institutions that make up our world. This does mean, however, that social action will increasingly take on the form of liturgies, and liturgies will be increasingly located in the entrances of military plants and corporate headquarters.[17]

The uniqueness of the Church's vocaton vis-á-vis the Powers does not mean that Christians should not join in coalitions with others not of our faith. But it does suggest that the gospel is something more than liberals at worship. It does challenge us to fashion forms of protest and social transformation that take into account the spiritual reality we are up against. It cautions us against sacrificing the integrity of the gospel for short-term political goals. And it gives us a hope that cannot be destroyed by the failure of any proximate goal: the vision of the final redemption of the Powers in the coming Reign of God.

Chapter Seventeen / FRAGMENTS OF AN UNTIDY CONVERSATION: THEOLOGY AND THE LITERARY DIVERSITY OF THE NEW TESTAMENT

Luke Timothy Johnson

The literary diversity of the New Testament is an obvious fact whose dimensions become more apparent as sustained literary-critical attention is given to these earliest Christian writings. Gospels not only differ from letters, and letters from apocalypses, but one Gospel differs from another Gospel in literary structuring, tone, and emphasis; one letter of Paul differs from another in conventional type, mode of argumentation, and rhetorical style.

For the critic who reads the NT primarily for the evidence it provides of first century Hellenistic literature, such diversity is only delightful, particularly since the NT is so generically unstable, borrowing, reshaping, and shedding forms as it goes. For the historian who reads the NT for evidence of early Christian mores or social settings, literary diversity is a difficult but not insurmountable roadblock to be negotiated. Rhetoric must be taken into account before a text can be treated as a source of information.

For those who want to use the NT in theology, however, the literary diversity of the writings is a serious problem. It is so, above all, for the one who defines theology in terms of an ecclesial, that is, a communal and faith defined process for which the *literal* meaning of the text is an essential component, and who thinks of the NT writings as discrete literary compositions whose diverse genres and rhetorical conventions demand consideration for any responsible reading. Literary diversity is only apparent to those who can see the writings as a whole; a factor only for those who read them with the expectation of hearing not only their human author's voice, but in some fashion, God's Word.

This essay is being written by one for whom the difficulty posed by the literary diversity of the NT is real. Before trying to explicate the problem more fully or suggesting a way in which the problem may be seen as providing a possibility for creative theology, it is appropriate to acknowledge that my problem is not everyone's problem. There are other ways of thinking about the NT as a source for literary interpretation or as a resource for theology.

And even before that, a salutary reminder to myself and to my reader: academic exercises such as this one are simply that, academic. People who write essays on hermeneutics are like librarians who worry about the books being properly shelved, or grammarians who fuss over the correct use of verbs. We do no great harm so long as we remember how marginal our efforts must always remain, so long as we do not confuse our library regulations with the business of reading and research, or think of our grammatical rules as either creating or constraining poetic genius.

The pertinence of the reminder? Hundreds of millions of people all about us look to the Bible as a source of power and authority. They incense it, swear by it, parade it around in processions, anoint it, bow before it, sing from it, pound on it, lay it on wounds of head and heart. Sometimes they even read it. Few of these people know or care what academicians or theologians think about them or their use of the Holy Book.

Such richly imaginative uses of the Bible offer the student of religion more interesting material than the hermetic discussions of librarians and grammarians. And so natural, long-standing, and pervasive is this unruly conversation swirling about the scripture that theologians might begin to learn some lessons from it. The first is modesty about our own efforts; we can observe the conversation and even have a small voice within it, but we cannot control it. The second is a change in attitude: all of this untidy, unmanageable discourse about and with the Bible need not be (as the educated are prone to think) perversity; it may be, indeed, the Spirit's preferred way of finding a space for its freedom.

The topic for the present essay, however, is theology: a small, highly specialized, but not necessarily well defined fragment of that larger and more interesting conversation. People who do theology have at least this in common: they locate the *authority* of the text in its *being read*. Does this seem too obvious? Perhaps, but it makes a useful distinction from all those religious uses of the Bible which are fundamentally talismanic.

Sometimes the talismanic use of the Bible is obvious, as when we swear on the book, or incense it. Sometimes it is more subtle. Is it "theology" to extract a handful of verses, arrange them in a set of propositions, and apply them to every circumstance without ever actually *reading* them? In any case, I take it as axiomatic that theology in the proper sense is interested in the Bible as a text to be read and not as an object to venerate. How the Bible (and specifically the NT) is to be read, however, and how that reading is to function within the limited exercise called theology is not at all clear.

Theology and the Individual Reader

Patristic theologians did not perceive the literary diversity of the NT as a major difficulty. To some extent we may wonder whether they perceived it at all. Certainly, disagreements between the evangelists on questions of fact concerning Jesus' ministry were attacked by educated opponents of Christianity such as Porphyry, requiring sustained rebuttal and the construction of Gospel harmonies. Certainly, theological differences between Paul and his opposition provided the occasion for theological discriminations such as that of Marcion. But these cavils were based not so much in specifically *literary* diversity as in the perception of conflict at the historical or religious level. Sorting through such issues was the business of polemicists.

For the ordinary work of theology carried on in homilies, catechisms, edifying discourses, commentaries, letters, and disputations, the literary diversity of the NT writings scarcely was noticed. Yes, sophisticated readers like Origen knew and appreciated the conventions of their own literature, and could even acknowledge the presence of a genre, as Origen does in his *Commentary on the Song of Songs* when he calls it an Epithamalium. But the formal recognition has no real impact on his reading.

The general patristic neglect of the literary elements deriving from a human author's choices and intentions is rooted in a number of shared presuppositions concerning the source and nature of scripture. Everyone agreed, for example, that the real and ultimate author of all the NT was the Holy Spirit; even when not explicitly stated, belief in divine inspiration was axiomatic. This conviction obviously relativized the significance of literary diversity and its corollary, authorial intention.

Belief in inspiration was accompanied and abetted by an imaginative construal of the scripture as a collection of divine oracles. Patristic writers took it for granted that each verse of scripture had its own revelatory value, and was in effect much like an oracle delivered at Delphi, demanding yet enabling interpretation without reference to its immediate literary (literal) context. What appears to us as random proof texting or a completely atomistic focus was not unprincipled. It was based on an appreciation of the scripture as a collection of divine oracles *(logia),* not as a collection of literary *compositions* whose message was communicated as a whole by means of intertextual signals.

Another shared premise was that the reading of these oracles was governed by the *regula fidei* and the teaching authority of the community. Irenaeus's greatness lay in his perception that the orthodox understanding of scripture could stand against the wild vagaries of Gnostic interpretation only by steadily and equally maintaining the three legs of the canon of scripture, the rule of faith, and the apostolic succession. Irenaeus's own steadfast adherence to a literal/historical reading of both Testaments, however, had its own problems and was not universally followed. More frequently the ecclesial context provided a normative range of acceptable readings for those who preferred the more "spiritual" readings made available by allegory.

The sense of scripture as a loose collection of oracles, each of which could be independently interpreted, was controlled by an ecclesial consensus (at least in fundamentals), resting on the synergy of bishop, canon, and creed. Yet the shared framework gave theologians great freedom in their reading of the text. Origen was the boldest, most imaginative orthodox theologian of all. But before he delved into his more arcane speculations, he patiently laid out the universally accepted elements of faith to which he also assented. He thereby felt himself free to build a system of readings erected on an anthropological analysis: the threefold meaning of scripture at the literal/historical, moral, and allegorical levels, corresponded to and was legitimated by the threefold constitution of humans as body, soul, and spirit.

Origen's allegorical approach came to dominate the theological appropriation of the NT. Its triumph was partly due to the historical fact that rival approaches (like Theodore of Mopsuestia's) were marginalized by heretical associations and geographical/cultural isolation. But the main reason for its victory was its admirable flexibility and comprehensiveness. If the deepest religious (theological) meaning of *every* text is to be found in its nonliteral, spiritual meaning, then the issue of literary diversity is bypassed entirely: the deep calls out to the deep, the spirit in the text speaks to the spirit in the reader.

Even the greatest admirers of Origen and of the allegorical approach must also recognize the costs of his victory. Theology in his mode is not only a highly intellectual and elitist activity (Origen sometimes has a hard time keeping his contempt for the "literalists" under control), it is also, in principle, private and individualistic. The framework of canon, church, and creed is indeed assumed and even affirmed, but it is not *engaged*. It is the individual reader's body, soul, and spirit that is addressed by the text, and addresses it in return. The church as church figures as an allegorical trope, but not as the reader nor as the one challenged to transformation. Allegory cannot build a community, cannot bring a community's experience into the process of reading, cannot—by the very nature of its method—have a reading *in common*. The more directly and individually the text is read, in fact, the more a communal sense of the text tends to disappear.

The consequence (as Reformation critics saw) was a distortion of both "scripture" and "tradition." The common life of the community could become progressively rote and rigid, because insufficiently challenged by the prophetic power of the scriptural texts. At the same time and for the same reason, the reading of the scripture in sermon and commentary could become progressively random and fanciful. Allegorical readings could have great beauty and even power, but the connection between the reading and the text was sometimes difficult to detect. And as theology itself became a purely scholastic, scientific enterprise to be carried out by an individual scholar in the social context of the University, rather than by the preacher in the social context of the liturgical community, the patristic habit of proof texting was carried even further in elaborate collections of *loci communes* in support of dogmatic propositions.

The Reformation offered incisive criticism, but no solution. Indeed, by kicking out one leg of the tripod, that of the Church, the principle of *sola scriptura* only made the theological appropriation of the NT more problematic. Yes, allegory was vigorously rejected in favor of the literal meaning. But allegory alone was not the problem! The basic *premise* of allegory, that the vivifying power of scripture is to be found in the reading *by an individual* was, if anything, made even more explicit by the Reformation. The word of God spoke directly to the heart of the individual without mediation.

The principle of free interpretation based on the literal sense led directly if paradoxically to the remarkable fragmentation of Protestantism into thousands of disputing parties. Why? Because the literal sense is directed to the practical life of communities, not to the imagination or spirituality of individuals. The literal sense begs to be translated into action, practice, and structure. But if each person is free (indeed obliged) to determine that literal sense as guided without intermediary by the Spirit, then division on the basis of different readings must quickly and inevitably follow. It seems impossible to combine a theology based on the literal sense, the principle of free individual interpretation, and a unified church.

Not that desperate measures to combine them have been lacking. Both the efforts of the Tübingen School and of the Biblical Theology Movement can be seen as attempts to root theology in something "objective"—whether it be the reconstituted reality called "history," which in proper Hegelian style is itself regarded as the vehicle of theology—or in some ineluctable quantity extracted from the text (though not exactly "in the text" either) that can gain universal assent, such as "Salvation History." The corrosive acid of postmodern criticism, however, has revealed how loosely glued these measures in fact always were. The more we seriously try to do "history," the less plausible appears its use for the distinct mode of knowing called theology.

The recent collapse of "biblical theology" in its classic form was the collapse of a sustained attempt to ground theological consensus on an objective understanding of the text without explicit appeal to the authority of church or creed. In the aftermath, we can observe a more general flight from every sort of authority except that of the individual reader. The authority of the community is absent, the authority of the creed is not determinative, and now even the authority of the text (as some sort of historically verifiable entity) is abandoned. What remains is the principle of free interpretation, rooted in the subjectivity of the individual reader. What remains, in other words, is chaos.

However fanciful the flights of Origen and his allegorical successors, and however much their individualistic readings eroded the sense of canon, church, and creed, they never explicitly abandoned them. There always existed, therefore, at least the possibility of conversation between various theologies and strategies of reading. The difference between Origen and contemporary proponents of reader-response theories is the deliberate abandonment of any coherent community code of conduct and convictions as a context, much less a guide, to reading. As I understand the intellectual fashion called postmodernism (at least in its literary manifestation of deconstructionism), the collapse of all such normative/alienating structures of meaning is celebrated. The literary critic and the theologian use the text primarily as the occasion for self-referential reflection. The pertinence of the *literal* meaning for theology is the resistence it offers to subjective manipulation. But if the point of all reading is to celebrate such subjective manipulation, then the literal meaning is otiose.

I am indeed painting with a coarsely bristled brush! Please do not stumble over all these *obiter dicta*. I know as well as you how much they need qualification, debate, at least footnotes! But if I paused to support all these assertions, I would need a monograph, and still not get to my own thesis. I therefore beg your indulgence for all these historical generalizations and too tidy compartmentalizations. My purpose in these remarks has not been to disqualify any sort of reading or for that matter any mode of doing theology. It is possible, I am sure, to define theology in terms of an individual's thinking about God, or as an indvidual thinker's attempt to interpret the world in terms of faith in God. One could also, on the basis of such a definition, make a pretty fair argument that some contemporary literary criticism has as much of a religious, and perhaps even theological character, as does the biblical interpretations of Origen, or of the (also highly arbitrary) biblical construals of a Barth or Bultmann.

My purpose instead has been to emphasize that for all the individualistic, subject-based strategies of reading, the literary diversity of the NT is no real problem, since the literal meaning itself is at best only a secondary consideration. But just the opposite is the case in the model of theology I will speak of next.

Theology as the Articulation of the Faith of the Church

Another way of defining theology is as an ecclesial activity, as the articulation of the faith of the church. Since even this definition is capable of multiple understandings, some clarification is required. The most efficient procedure may be to focus on the separate terms.

By church, I do not mean an organization but a living organism. I mean a local community gathered on the basis of the Word of God and committed to Jesus as Lord. The first proper locus of theology is not the classroom but such a community. The life of this community requires explication, because it is there that the experience of God (everywhere else real but implicit) is brought to explicit expression. The main business of theology is not speculative and theoretical, but practical and prudential. It is to discern the word of God in the lives of humans. Pastoral theology is not the retail outlet for nuggets of truth about God refined in the crucible of philosophical analysis. If, in fact, theology

281

has to do not alone with ideas but with faith in the living God, pastoral or practical theology is the research arm of theology.

By faith, then, I do not mean simply the framework of belief expressed by the creed, although the creed is part of the normative framework structuring the church's activity. The creed defines and offers inexhaustible possibilities for depth, but does not by itself enliven. Faith, in the proper sense, is rather the response of the human spirit to the call of God in the world, a response of belief, trust, obedience, and loyalty within the specific circumstances of worldly structures and activities. The subject of theology is the living God who presses implicitly on us in our every encounter with the world. And since God's activity (most fundamentally in the gift of creation renewed at every moment) always precedes us, theology must always be an open-ended, constantly changing response to that initiative.

The definition of theology as faith seeking understanding remains perennially valid. Living faith seeks to understand the Living One to whom it responds. It thereby also seeks to understand itself and the implications of being so called and so gifted. Theology articulates faith in at least three ways. First, it gives voice to faith. Theology tends the symbols of the story of faith and thereby keeps alive the possibility of that story's continuation. Second, theology articulates faith by disclosing its internal structure, how various aspects of the response to God fit together. Third, it searches out the connections between this most fundamental response to our shared gift of existence, and our other comprehensive understandings of reality.

Theology, so understood, is essentially an ecclesial activity. By this I mean not only that it takes place within the social setting of the church and is given normative shape by the canon and the creed, but also that it is an activity that is undertaken by all the members of the church. The theological task is implied by the very life of faith itself. Every Christian is called to seek an understanding of his or her response of faith, every Christian is called to the act of discernment of God's activity in the world and within the community. The church is not simply a set of symbols with reference to which a theologian works. The church is the place within which the activity called theology makes sense, as all the faithful seek articulation and understanding of their common life in the Spirit.

For this activity to take place, the work of God in the Spirit is presumed, and is in fact the premise that generates theology in the first place: human lives are intersected by the power and presence of God in the world. Furthermore, theology presumes that God's power and presence are truly *experienced* in the lives of humans, not always explicitly, clearly, or unambiguously, but truly. In defeat, depression, despair, and death as much as in triumph, success, hope, and healing are lives touched by the merciful and mighty one. But how can those diverse experiences be raised to the level of ecclesial discernment? Theology seeks to give voice to these implicit experiences through *narratives of faith,* which progressively reach toward a community narrative of God's work.

In the speaking and hearing of such narratives, the community as such is addressed by the work of the Holy Spirit in the present instance, is called to response, and is challenged afresh to a decision in favor of God's work, and thereby to a new interpretation of its life of faith. I am not by any means suggesting that the experience of God in the world is accessible for casual perusal. These matters require careful attention and delicate diagnosis. The process of discernment is risk-filled, and never self-validating. The interpretation of the present moment in terms of God's activity is perilous, prone to error and false prophecy, and at the very least requires constant renewal and revision. But such discernment, such interpretation of God's word as speaking through the fabric of human lives is the absolutely fundamental and necessary task of theology. Without it, there is no subject matter.

The Normative Role of Scripture

I am therefore defining theology first of all as a reading of the *texts of human lives* in a continuing process of self-revelation by the Living God, rather than as, first of all, a reading of the *texts of scripture* as a record of a past and finished revelation. This raises the question of the normative role of the scripture generally, and for Christian theology in particular, of the NT. How do the scriptural texts function within this understanding of theology? Have they lost their normative authority, or are they seen to exercise it in a different way?

The ecclesial process of discerning and articulating God's word in contemporary life requires as an essential component the discernment and articulation of God's Word in the scripture. The community does not regard the NT simply as an interesting if haphazard congeries of historical vignettes, or as a compelling anthology of literary insights, or as a classic collection of community customs. It acknowledges it as the canon of scripture, and with that acknowledgment, confesses as well that in some fashion these texts have prophetic authority for the church in every age and place: they do not only have a meaning in the past, they have a significance for the present.

Implicit in the recognition of the NT as prophetic is the acknowledgment of these writings as "inspired by God." But in contrast to the ancient appreciation of divine inspiration, this ecclesial model for theology insists that the full implications of human authorship be taken into account in any reading. The confession of divine inspiration, in other words, is not a theory of literary composition, but an attribution of authority; not a reason to bypass consideration of literary structure and authorial intentionality, but an invitation to do so.

Functionally, the attribute of inspiration means that the church does not seek to subsume these texts into its own agenda, make them its own possession, and reduce them to ideology. It means that these texts are regarded as "other," addressing the present circumstances of the community with the same voice (albeit in a different mode) as the narratives of the experience of God among the faithful.

As the church discusses, debates, and makes decisions pertinent to the meaning and the demands of God's kingdom for its own place and time, the texts of the NT provide the symbolic framework for the discernment of God's Word in the world, the language and perceptions that *enable* the church to discern the work of the Holy Spirit and distinguish it from the realm of the demonic and destructive. But by themselves the texts of the NT do not exhaust the possibilities of God's action; rather, they are continually opened to new dimensions of meaning, constantly reinterpreted in light of the astonishing things God does in the world. Neither the experience of God in the community as expressed through narratives of faith, nor the text of scripture is a *norma non normata;* both are essential moments in a dialectic of experience and interpretation that constantly characterizes the living faith community.

The *authority* of the NT within this process can be understood in three distinct yet related ways. First, the NT is an authority because it "authors" a certain kind of identity both for individuals and above all for communities. It is at this level, above all, that the church relies on its "inerrancy," its truth-telling. When it comes to shaping an authentic and distinctive messianic identity in the world, the texts of the NT taken together can be trusted. They do not deceive. A second meaning of authority is that the NT "authorizes" individuals and communities in a number of ways; that is, it empowers them to exercise their freedom as children of God. One of the most important ways it does this is by providing in its own process of reinterpreting Torah in light of a crucified and raised Messiah, the model for the church's continuing reinterpretation even of these texts in light of God's continuing work in the world. A third way the NT is an authority is that it provides a set of "authorities" *(auctoritates)* for the debate and discernment of the church on the widest possible variety of issues pertinent to its life in the world.

For the texts of the NT to exercise their authoritative functions within the community as part of a continuing process of theological reflection, it is necessary that they be engaged at the literal level. I recognize that the term "literal" is itself scarcely unequivocal, and can mean different things. Here is what I mean by it: at the most basic level I mean the text in its most publicly available form, the text as it comes to us most as "other," and at least shaped by our individual preconceptions and preconstruals. I mean the text as the mediator of ecclesial identity through the successive historical realizations of the church from its earliest times. In short, I mean the diverse compositions of the canon taken in all their literary diversity and historically conditioned symbols. It is in this form that the text can address the church as "other" than itself, and become part of a dialogical process involving many voices, instead of being another element in our individual or communal stream of consciousness.

We have come at last to the precise problem presented to this understanding of the theological task by the literary diversity of the NT. On the one hand, the historically and linguistically conditioned meaning of the text is imperative for the NT to speak to us *as* other, and to be available to the discernment of all. And for the text to mediate the identity of an entire community, it can only be through the literal (functionally, the commonly available) reading of it. On the other hand, the very "otherness" of the text is fragmented and differentiated. The literary diversity of these writings seems to preclude the community's hearing any single voice it can heed and obey.

Problem or Possibility?

I have used the expression "untidy conversation" to characterize theology in the church. I suggest that the untidiness is not cause for dismay but for celebration. I will suggest as well that the problems presented by the literary diversity of the NT writings actually turn out to be openings to new possibilities. But to state this is to call for a sort of mental conversion, a letting go of certain idolatrous closures to embrace the freedom God offers us.

We must let go of any fantasy concerning the church as a stable, predictable, well-regulated organization. If the church is truly the place in the world where the experience of God is brought to the level of narrative and discernment, then the church will always be disorderly, a family living under stress, because it will, as a community, always be in transition between partial closure and openness, between the idolatry of institutional self-preservation and the obedience of faith in the living God. We must let go of the desire for theology to be a finished product of complete conceptual symmetry. If theology is in fact the attempt to understand living faith, then it must always be an unfinished process, for the data continues to come in, as the Living God persists in working through the lives of people and being revealed in their stories.

We must also let go of any pretense of closing the NT within some comprehensive, all-purpose, singular reading which reduces its complexity to simplicity. Whether we call it NT Theology, or Narrativity, or Existential Hermeneutics, or something else, we must recognize our attempts to reduce multiplicity to unity, to nail down some central, single, encompassing meaning in the NT that is also and above all portable, as attempts precisely at closure! We seek a stable package of meaning that we can then apply to other situations or fit within our systematic theological constructs, so that, ideally, we need never really read the texts again!

A conversion to an understanding of church, theology, and the reading of scripture which is appropriate to faith in the Living God is one that is fully committed (though never fully realized because the inertia of idolatry always pulls us backward) to the risk-filled, tricky, and unpredictable freedom of the

Spirit. We celebrate (with understandable trepidation) the fact that the church is inevitably and properly a community that is unstable, that must always make up its identity as it goes along, that is always experiencing conflict, because conflict is simply one of the faces of discernment in a community context. We rejoice (with some misgivings) in the fact that theology can never be packaged and distributed as a product, but must always remain a fragmented and fragile process, always trying to catch up with the One who constantly precedes our thought in action. We abandon (with considerable fear) the longing for a singular fixed understanding of the NT that is not open to further revision, deepening, and extension, but recognize that its texts are a world in which we must continue to dwell, whose contours we must always reexamine each morning, whose faces are always changing, whose voices can still surprise.

By no means, however, are we thereby cast adrift in formless subjectivism. It is as a *community* that we commit ourselves to these perceptions, and as a community we are bound by any number of constraints that govern and give shape to the messy project of interpreting faith in the Living God. And if we are a real community that meets together, and not simply an abstraction called church, then our search for meaning is not absolutely and dangerously free-floating. We share the life of a historical community with specific traditions of belief and behavior, and with specific instruments and procedures for making decisions and exercising authority. Our identities are shaped by our patterns of ritual and the use of scripture within worship and sacrament. Our discernment of God's word in the narratives of faith enunciated within the assembly is guided by the rule of faith that we share as part of our heritage. The texts we engage as part of our communal conversation about the nature and demands of God's activity among us are finite. As the canon of scripture, they are also part of the tradition handed down to us. We have more than enough structure to allow some spontaneity.

It is an essential aspect of the church's historical tradition, in fact, that the canon is made up of discrete literary compositions. Too seldom has theology appreciated this remarkable fact. The process and ratification of canonization over the first three centuries institutionalized the literary diversity of the Christian scripture. The temptation offered by Tatian to replace the messiness of four separate Gospels by a single coherent harmonized life of Jesus was rejected. The temptation offered by Marcion to reject theological plurality in favor of a (simplified) Paulinism was even more emphatically rejected. Nor was anyone ever terribly concerned about what happened to the authority of the NT in translation; versions proliferated merrily and without hesitation because of the conviction (implicit to be sure) that in the NT God's Word was to be found not in the life of Jesus or in a theology or in the transformative power of the Greek language, but *in and through the diverse literary compositions as such.*

The contemporary appreciation of the literary and rhetorical diversity of the NT could not, then, be more in tune with the implicit logic of the canonizers.

In this respect, not Origen with his construal of scripture as a set of *logia* inspired by God but we with our construal of the canon as a collection of compositions written by human authors, are closer to the tradition that shapes authentic Christian identity. It is *as* self-contained literary compositions each with its own internal integrity, that the writings *most resist* our manipulation, and therefore most challenge our individual and communal preconceptions.

But we are also obliged to deal more explicitly with the full implications of this literary diversity. The more we study the Gospels in literary terms, for example, the more we become aware how profoundly their message, their "voice" is embedded in their overall literary structure. No one schooled in the literary analysis of the Gospels could assert that Mark and Matthew were really "saying the same thing." Likewise the more we take seriously the multiple rhetorical conventions operative in the epistolary literature, the less willing we are to think of Galatians and Romans as "basically making the same point." Still less are we willing to talk about the "teaching of the Synoptic Gospels," or the "theology of Paul," and quite rightly, for we are aware that by seeking such systematization, we lose more than we gain; we lose precisely the nature and quality of the voice enunciated by each of these compositions.

We are coming to appreciate with specific and detailed clarity how each NT composition speaks, not as the repository of early sources or of historical data, not as a set of truthful propositions about the reality of God and the world, but as a coherent, intricately and intentionally contrived literary composition, whose structure and rhetoric is not a disposable surface effect but the very vehicle of meaning. The failure to produce a really convincing "Theology of the NT" in recent years may, in fact, derive in part from the implicit recognition that the reduction of literary multiplicity to theological unity comes at too great a cost.

But how difficult it would seem to deal theologically with this literary diversity! No progress will be made, however, if we think that the answer lies in creating smaller portable packets, such as "the theology of Luke-Acts" or "the theology of Mark," for if these are smaller abstractions, they are still abstractions. But then how arduous is trying to work our way through all the hurdles to quick and easy appropriation posed by an entire literary composition? What part of it do we focus on? Whose reading do we accept? Must we become experts in literary criticism in order to be theologians? Don't we find ourselves in a hopeless regressive debate over the meaning of the text without ever getting to the task of theology? These are the questions of people who think of theology as an academic discipline! And if we think of theology as an academic enterprise, then yes, the issues become hopelessly entangled. Then the direct appropriation of the NT in its literary diversity would be endlessly arduous, complex, and confusing.

But what if we think of theology first of all as an ecclesial process of discernment? Then it is the most natural thing in the world to read through an entire Gospel together as a community, paying the closest attention to the way it elicits our own narratives of faith, how it challenges our own words, as it unfolds in its literary integrity. Will there be many and even conflicting readings? Of course there will be, as many as there are members of the church taking part. And are these multiple readings a problem? No, because they are not essays in a book on hermeneutics, or academic contributions to the science of reading, but are all part of a fluid, ongoing, dialogical, open process of discernment, rooted in, and guided by, the Gospel itself, not as an abstraction but as a voice that speaks to each one of us and to us all with power. The same is, if anything, even more true of reading Paul's letters, or the book of Revelation, or the other epistolary literature of the NT.

Only within this *communal* process of reading and discernment, in fact, do these writings come to life as they were intended to from the beginning. The writings of the NT were not composed for private readership, after all, or for individual interpretation. They were composed as documents written for *communities*. They were intended to be read aloud, and to be interpreted in preaching, and to be open to the discernment of all. They are therefore best fitted not to the transformation of individual lives, but to the edification of communities. This is why they were written and it is the work they do best.

In the give-and-take of communal reading and interpretation, the texts of the NT are encountered as they were meant to be encountered. The dangers of subjectivity and distortion are reduced, for the process of discernment is open and public. The voice of each writing is heard in its own terms with minimal manipulation exercised by excerption or packaging. The literal meaning of the text is finally freed for its work within a community for the building up of that community's identity and holiness. And as the community reads different texts from the NT, it begins to learn that these many voices help to shape many legitimate ways of living out that identity, that within the broad consensus of community commitment, a healthy diversity of life is actually authorized by the NT itself. It may begin to learn, as well, the ways in which the NT does not speak directly or explicitly to its situation, but must be cracked open by the experience and insights gained by the Spirit's working in the church.

I am suggesting, of course, that the irreducible literary diversity of the NT canon resists the efforts of the academician-theologian to systematize and thereby ossify the texts, but that this same literary diversity opens itself to the doing of theology within the community of faith as an essential part of the discernment of God's Word in the world. Is this cause for dismay? Only if we think being a librarian is more important that reading books, or that being a grammarian is more significant that writing poetry. And it still remains possible for those of us who are academic theologians also to "take and read" within in the community of faith.

I cannot resist also making, in conclusion, a highly polemical remark about the contemporary Academic Captivity of the Church. Those interested in doing theology within the context of the church would provide the greatest service not by learning ever more elaborate theories of reading (which ultimately are ways in which we resist the otherness of the text), but by learning the languages, the symbolic worlds, and the literary conventions of the biblical world, so that these texts can, in fact, resist our ever more aggressive attempts at using them for our own ends.

ABBREVIATIONS

AB	Anchor Bible
AnBib	Analecta biblica
Bib	*Biblica*
CBC	Cambridge Bible Commentary
CBQ	*Catholic Biblical Quarterly*
ExpTim	*Expository Times*
HBT	*Horizons in Biblical Theology*
ITC	International Theological Commentary
Int	*Interpretation*
IDB	*Interpreter's Dictionary of the Bible* (4 vols., Nashville: Abingdon Press, 1962; Supplementary Volume, 1976)
JAOS	*Journal of the American Oriental Society*
JBL	*Journal of Biblical Literature*
JSNT	*Journal for the Study of the New Testament*
JSNTSup	Journal for the Study of the New Testament, Supplement Series
JSOT	*Journal for the Study of the Old Testament*
JSOTSup	Journal for the Study of the Old Testament, Supplement Series
OBT	Overtures to Biblical Theology
OTL	Old Testament Library
RB	*Revue biblique*
SB	Sources bibliques
SBT	Studies in Biblical Theology
SJT	*Scottish Journal of Theology*
SJOT	*Scandanavian Journal of the Old Testament*
TBü	Theologische Bücherei
TRE	*Theologische Realenzyklopädie*

TS	*Theological Studies*
USQR	*Union Seminary Quarterly Review*
VT	*Vetus Testamentum*
VTSup	Vetus Testamentum, Supplements
ZAW	*Zeitschrift für die alttestamentliche Wissenschaft*

NOTES

Introduction

1. Rudolf Smend, *Die Mitte des Alten Testaments*, Theologische Studien 101 (Zürich: EVZ-Verlag, 1970), provides a history and critical assessment of such proposals in Old Testament theology, where they have predominated.

2. Elsie Anne McKee has described the way in which Calvin's biblical exegesis led him to revise subsequent editions of his *Institutes*. See her essay "Exegesis, Theology, and Development in Calvin's Institutio: A Methodological Suggestion," *Probing the Reformed Tradition: Historical Studies in Honor of Edward A. Dowey Jr.*, ed. E. A. McKee and B. G. Armstrong (Louisville: Westminster/John Knox Press, 1989), 154-73.

3. Pim Valkenberg, "Readers of Scripture and Hearers of the Word in the Mediaeval Church," *The Bible and Its Readers* (*Concilium* 1991/1), ed. Wim Beuken, Sean Freyne, and Anton Weiler (Philadelphia: Trinity Press International, 1991), 47-57.

4. John W. Rogerson, *W. M. L. de Wette, Founder of Modern Biblical Criticism: An Intellectual Biography*, JSOTSup 126 (Sheffield: JSOT Press, 1992).

5. *Lehrbuch der christlichen Dogmatik*, 2 vols. (Berlin: Reimer, 1831).

6. Hermann Gunkel, "Biblische Theologie und biblische Religionsgeschichte: I des AT," *RGG*, 2nd ed. (1931), 1089-91; William Wrede, "The Task and Methods of 'New Testament Theology'," *The Nature of New Testament Theology*, ed. Robert Morgan, SBT 2/25 (London: SCM Press, 1973). Wrede's essay was first published in 1897. The differences between Gunkel and Wrede are more significant than their joint appearance in this note will suggest.

7. Gunkel, *Reden und Aufsätze* (Göttingen: Vandenhoeck & Ruprecht, 1913), 24-25.

8. Heiki Räisänen, *Beyond New Testament Theology* (London: SCM Press, 1990), 137.

9. Jon D. Levenson explains why Biblical Theology has been a Christian affair, in "Why Jews Are Not Interested in Biblical Theology," *Jews and Christians in Biblical Studies: The Hebrew Bible, the Old Testament, and Historical Criticism* (Louisville: Westminster/John Knox Press, 1993), 33-61.

10. For his part, Wrede was unconcerned even to exercise a veto. He would do his disinterested work, and "how the systematic theologian gets on with its results and deals with them that is his own affair" (*The Nature of New Testament Theology*, 69).

11. Gerhard von Rad, *Old Testament Theology*, 2 vols. (New York: Harper & Row, 1962, 1965).

12. Rudolf Bultmann, *Theology of the New Testament*, 2 vols. (New York: Scribner's, 1955) and various essays such as "Das Problem einer theologischen Exegese des Neuen Testaments," *Zwischen den Zeiten* 3 (1925), 334-57; ET, "The Problem of a Theological Exegesis of the New Testament," *The Beginnings of Dialectical Theology*, ed. James M. Robinson (Richmond: John Knox Press, 1968), 236-56 and those found in *Glauben und Verstehen*, 4 vols. (Tübingen: J. C. B. Mohr, 1933–1965); vol. I translated as *Faith and Understanding* (London: SCM Press, 1969).

13. Elisabeth Schüssler Fiorenza, "Feminist Hermeneutics," *ABD* 2:783-91, quoting from 783. Social interests and moral commitments are front and center in the essays collected as *The Bible and the Politics of Exegesis*, ed. David Jobling, Peggy L. Day, and Gerald T. Sheppard (Cleveland: Pilgrim Press, 1991).

14. On this and related matters see A. K. M. Adam, "Biblical Theology and the Problem of Modernity: Von Wredestrasse zu Sackgasse," *Horizons in Biblical Theology* 12 (1990), 1-18.

15. *Fragmented Women: Feminist (Sub)versions of Biblical Narratives* (Philadelphia: Trinity Press International, 1993), 11, n. 8., and generally; David Tracy, *Plurality and Ambiguity: Hermeneutics, Religion and Hope* (San Francisco: Harper & Row, 1987).

16. Thomas Tracy, *God, Action, and Embodiment* (Grand Rapids: Eerdmans, 1984), 74-83, quoting from 75.

17. See Rolf Knierim, "The Task of Old Testament Theology," *Horizons in Biblical Theology* 6 (1984), 25-57.

18. Brevard Childs, *Biblical Theology in Crisis* (Philadelphia: Westminster Press, 1970), 95.

1. Biblical Theology in the Patristic Period

1. J. N. D. Kelly, *Early Christian Doctrines*, rev. ed. (New York: Harper & Row, 1978), 87-88.

2. On this process, cf. note 6 below.

3. H. G. Liddell and R. Scott, *A Greek-English Lexicon*, rev. and aug. (Oxford: Clarendon Press, 1968), 790b, citing Plato, *Republic*, 379a.

4. Alongside more traditional treatments of the history of doctrine such as Kelly's, the student of this process today needs to consider radically different approaches such as W. Bauer, *Orthodoxy and Heresy in the Earliest Christianity*, trans. from the German 2nd ed. by R. Kraft, G. Krodel, et al. (Philadelphia: Fortress Press, 1971).

5. The essential introduction to the Greek and Latin materials in English is Johannes Quasten, *Patrology*, vols. 1-3 (Utrecht: Spectrum, 1950, 1953, 1960; rep. 1975), v. 4, Angelo di Berardino et al., ed. and trans. Placid Solari (Westminster, Md.: Christian Classics, 1986); vol. 3 is well supplemented by Frances M. Young, *From Nicea to Chalcedon: A Guide to the Literature and Its Background* (Philadelphia: Fortress Press, 1983). For the oriental traditions in addition to the works listed by Quasten, 1, 8-9, on Syriac Christian literature, cf. Sebastian Brock, "An Introduction to Syriac Studies," in *Horizons in Semitic Studies: Articles for the Student*, ed. J. H. Eaton (Birmingham, 1980); supplemented by the bibliographies of Brock in *Parôle de l'Orient* 10 (1981–82), 291-412 and 14 (1987), 289-360; and on Coptic literature, cf. Tito Orlandi, "Coptic Literature," in *The Roots of Egyptian Christianity*, ed. Birger A. Pearson and James E. Goehring (Philadelphia: Fortress Press, 1986), 51-81; and especially for the Coptic Gnostic materials, cf. *The Gnostic Scriptures*, a new translation with annotations and introductions by Bentley Layton (New York: Doubleday, 1987), with bibliography, 463-66.

6. For a comprehensive view of allegorical exegesis in antiquity, cf. Jean Pépin, *Mythe et Allégorie: Les origines grecques et les contestations judéo-chrétiennes*, 2nd ed. (Paris: Études Augustiniennes, 1976). On developments among the Middle and neo-Platonic writers and their contemporaries, cf. Robert Lamberton, *Homer the Theologian: Neoplatonist Allegorical Reading and the Growth of the Epic Tradition*, The Transformation of the Classical Heritage 9 (Berkeley: University of California Press, 1986). On the Jewish and Christian use of allegory, cf. Pépin, *Mythe et Allégorie*, esp. 215-516; Lamberton, 44-54, 78-82; R. M. Grant, *The Letter and the Spirit* (New York: Macmillan, 1957); C. K. Barrett, "The Interpretation of the Old Testament in the New," *Cambridge History of the Bible*, ed. R. Ackroyd and C. F. Evans, 3 vols. (Cambridge: Cambridge University Press, 1970–73), 1:377-411, esp. 377-85, 408-10; and R. C. Hanson, "Biblical Exegesis in the Early Church," *CHB* 1:412-53, esp. 416-17, 435, 443-53; and M. F. Wiles, "Origen as Biblical Scholar," *CHB* 1:454-89, esp. 466-67; R. M. Grant with David Tracy, *A Short History of the Interpretation of the Bible*, 2nd ed. (Philadelphia: Fortress Press, 1984), esp. 19, 49, 52-72; Karlfried Froehlich, *Biblical Interpretation in the Early Church* (Philadelphia: Fortress Press, 1984), esp. 5-8, 15-16.

7. Pépin, *Mythe et Allégorie*, 104.

8. On this strand of allegorical exegesis, cf. Pépin, *Mythe et Allégorie*, esp. 97-98, 103-4, 121-33, 141-43, 152-55, 181-88, 232-33, 239-43, 291-307, 317-23.

9. For Stoic cosmology and cosmogony, cf. David E. Hahm, *The Origins of Stoic Cosmology* (Columbus: Ohio State University Press, 1977), esp. ch. v, "Cosmobiology," ch. vi, "The Cosmic Cycle" and ch. vii, "Epilogue: The Definition of Nature and the Origins of Stoic Cosmology,"

136-215; and Michael Lapidge, "Stoic Cosmology," in John M. Rist, ed., *The Stoics* (Berkeley: University of California Press, 1978), 161-85.

10. The following section is extracted with minor changes from my article, K. E. McVey, "The Use of Stoic Cosmogony in Theophilus of Antioch's *Hexaemeron*," in *Biblical Hermeneutics in Historical Perspective: Studies in Honor of Karlfried Froehlich on His Sixtieth Birthday,* ed. M. S. Burrows and Paul Rorem (Grand Rapids: Eerdmans, 1991), 32-58, esp. 46-49.

11. The phraseology is Robert B. Todd's in "Monism and Immanence: The Foundations of Stoic Physics," in Rist, 137-60, esp. 139. Similarly, Lapidge suggests one should think of "one primal substance with two aspects, one active, one passive" (p. 164, citing SVF 1.87, 2.308, 313).

12. For "inert" rather than the more usual "unqualified" or "qualityless," cf. Todd, 140-41.

13. Lapidge notes this as the first of two stages, 166, cf. Hahm, 76.

14. Cf. Todd, 143-46; Lapidge, 165-66; Hahm, 57-90.

15. This is the second stage according to Lapidge, 166; for the arrangement and the phrase quoted, cf. Lapidge, 177. This is Zeno's arrangement; for Chrysippus's modification, cf. note 18 below.

16. Cf. SVF 1.102 and its citation and discussion by Todd, 143-44; also Hahm, 76-78.

17. Lapidge, esp. 163-66, Hahm, esp. 43-48, 60-78.

18. Cf. SVF 1.102 and SVF 2.579, as cited and discussed by Lapidge, 166-67.

19. For this translation of SVF 1.171, cf. Hahm, 200; further on Zeno's definition of nature, cf. Todd, 143-48, 154-55 and Hahm, 200-8.

20. Todd, 148-55, esp. 149.

21. Todd, esp. 150, 153.

22. Lapidge, 168-80. The spirit may permeate only the sublunar world, producing either a needed link or a problematic break in Stoic monism; cf. Todd, 150-55.

23. Diog. Laer. 7.139 = SVF 2.644; Lapidge, 178-80, cf. Hahm, 150; this does not, however, mean that it is "situated above and around the four elements" as I had surmised (cf. McVey, 48). As we shall see below, his view is more complex.

24. Lapidge, 172-76, Hahm, 136-84, esp. 164-74.

25. Lapidge, esp. 176.

26. Hahm, 185-99.

27. Both in Lapidge, 180-85, but only reproduction in Hahm, 194.

28. Cf. Hahm, esp. 79-82, 211-12; also Pépin, 125-31.

29. Cicero, de deor. nat. I.15.41 and Philodemus, de piet. fr. 13-14, H. Diels, *Doxographi Graeci,* 4th ed. (Berlin: de Gruyter, 1879; rep. 1965), 547-48.

30. Cf. Hahm, 61-63, and Lapidge, 166.

31. Theog. 921-23. Hesiod, *Theogony,* ed. M. L. West (Oxford: Clarendon Press, 1966) (henceforth = West, text and comment), 145-46; ET, Hesiod, *Theogony* and *Works and Days,* trans. M. L. West (Oxford: Oxford University Press, 1988) (henceforth = West, trans.), 30.

32. Dio Chrysost. Or. 36. 55-57, SVF 2.622; for the text with an English translation, cf. *Dio Chrysostom,* trans. J. W. Cohoon and H. Lamar Crosby, Loeb Library (Cambridge, Mass.: Harvard University Press, 1940). The passage is actually a description of the re-creation of the universe after the conflagration, as an examination of its fuller context shows. Since each repetition must match in every respect its antecedent, however, it is legitimate to use this as a description of the primordial cosmic generation. Cf. also, Hahm, 57-90, esp. 61. For further witnesses to the allegorical interpretation of the marriage of Zeus and Hera as well as to its portrayal in painting, cf. also SVF 2.1061-75, and the comments of Pépin, 454.

33. *Theogony* 886-90. West, text and comment, 144-45; West, trans., 29.

34. West, text and comment, 401. For its portrayal in Greek art, cf. Arthur B. Cook, *Zeus: A Study in Ancient Religion,* III.I (Cambridge: Cambridge University Press, 1940), 662-726; for the analogous story of the birth of Dionysus from the thigh of Zeus, its role in art and literature, and its relation to the rite of adoption, ibid., 79-95. Within biblical tradition the extraction of Eve from Adam's side in Gen 2:21-23 represents this sort of male usurpation of the primordial female capacity to give birth. For further parallels outside of the Greco-Roman world, ibid., 95-98, n. 3.

35. *Theogony* 924-29. West, text and comment, 146; West, trans., 30, with modifications to the translation of the first line *[autos d' ek kephalēs glaukoida geinat' Athenēn]*—"he himself" for "by himself" and "gave birth to" for "fathered"—to show more clearly that the content of this passage does not necessarily conflict with *Theogony* 886-90. There is a scholarly consensus, however, that the last lines of the *Theogony* are not Hesiod's; West [text and comment, 397-99, esp. 399] holds that

the poet who completed the poem as it stands also "remodelled the end [as composed by Hesiod = lines 901-29], but following the outlines of the original." I have also translated *ou philotēti migeisa* in line 927, left out by West. My changes to his translation make clear that Hera's solitary production of Hephaestus is explicitly stated in the text while Zeus's production of Athena seems to be the delayed result of his earlier swallowing of Metis, not strictly a solitary act.

36. Galen, de plac. Hipp. et Plat. III.8.3-4; cf. SVF 2.908. Critical text with English translation: *Galen on the Doctrines of Hippocrates and Plato*, edition, translation, and commentary by Phillip de Lacy, 2 v., Corpus Medicorum Graecorum (Berlin: Akademie Verlag, 1978).

37. Galen, de plac. Hipp. et Plat. III.8.10-18; de Lacy's English translation here; cf. SVF 2.908, also H. G. Evelyn-White, trans., *Hesiod, The Homeric Hymns and Homerica*, Loeb Library (Cambridge, Mass.: Harvard University Press, 1967), 146-49, and the insightful discussion of this fragment by Carl Curry, "The Theogony of Theophilus," *Vigiliae Christianae* 42 (1988), 318-26, esp. 322-24.

38. The essential content of this fragment is confirmed and supplemented by another preserved by Philodemus, de piet. fr. 15-16 = SVF 2.910 and Diels 549-50. Further on the allegorical interpretations of Athena's birth, cf. Cook, III.I, 726-39, Pépin, *Mythe et Allégorie*, 98-103, 123, 163-66, 337, 349, 397-98, 423, 452. For the portrayal in Greek art of the emergence of Athena from the crown of Zeus's head, sometimes with the brutal assistance of Hephaestus, cf. Cook, III.I, 662-81.

39. Galen, de plac. Hipp. et Plat. I.2, ET, de Lacy. More extensively on Galen's philosophical stance, cf. Michael Frede, "On Galen's Epistemology," in *Galen: Problems and Prospects*, ed. Vivian Nutton (London: Wellcome Institute for the History of Medicine, 1981), 65-86, and Paul Moraux, "Galien comme philosophe: la philosophie de la nature," in Nutton, 87-116.

40. Justin, Apol. I.64 = SVF 2. 1096. A fuller excerpt with Greek text is cited below at n. 55.

41. According to Arius Didymus, cf. SVF 2.642; pace Lapidge, who dismisses this report as a textual corruption (Lapidge, 179).

42. For the technical distinction in Stoic philosophy, cf. Max Pohlenz, *Die Stoa: Geschichte einer geistigen Bewegung*, 4th ed. (Göttingen: Vandenhoeck & Ruprecht, 1970), 39-40, 185.

43. Ps-Cl. Hom. 6. 7.5 8.1. Bernhard Rehm, ed., and J. Irmscher, *Die Pseudoklementinen*, I: *Homilien*, GCS (Berlin: Akademie Verlag, 1953), 109.16-22. Although included by Kern as an Orphic (rather than Stoic) fragment (cf. Otto Kern, *Orphicorum Fragmenta* [Berlin: Weidmann, 1922], fr. 57), much of this appears to be at least taken over from earlier Stoic interpretation; cf. Pépin, *Mythe et Allégorie*, esp. 396-403. In its current setting it provides the allegorical interpretation of Appion, an Alexandrian grammarian, whose views are then refuted by Clement in the following sections (Ps.Cl. Hom. 7.11-25). It is close to the form of the allegory Origen attributes to Celsus, since here he assumes that Athena, not Metis, is to be identified as *phrónēsis: Hina de kai tropologetai kai legētai phronēsis einai hē Athēna* (c. Cels. VIII.67, Paul Koetschau, ed., *Origenes Werke*, v. 2, GCS (Leipzig: J. C. Hinrichs, 1899), 283.9-10.

44. For example, cf. Harry A. Wolfson, *The Philosophy of the Church Fathers*, I: *Faith, Trinity, Incarnation*, 2nd rev. ed. (Cambridge, Mass.: Harvard University Press, 1964), 192-231; Pohlenz, 412-13, Kelly (cited in n. 2), 18-19, 96, 99-100; Robert M. Grant, *Gods and the One God* (Philadelphia: Westminster Press, 1986) (= Grant, *Gods*), 88, 130.

45. Most strongly argued by Wolfson, 223-24, but cf. also Pohlenz, 373-75, Kelly, 10, 96, and Robert M. Grant, *Greek Apologists of the Second Century* (Philadelphia: Westminster Press, 1988) [= Grant, *Apologists*], 170.

46. Autol. II.10 and II.22. Theophilus of Antioch, Ad Autolycum, ed. and trans. Robert M. Grant, *Oxford Early Christian Texts* (Oxford: Clarendon Press, 1970) (= Autol.); cf. Grant, *Apologists*, 169-71.

47. *Echōn oun ho theos ton heautou logon endiatheton en tois idiois splagchnois egennēsen auton meta tēs heautou sophias exepeuxamenos pro ton olōn.* Autol. II.10. Grant's trans. with one change "by the aid of" rather than "together with" for *meta*.

48. Gustave Bardy, *Théophile d'Antioche: Trois Livres à Autolycus*, trans. J. Sender, SC 20 (Paris: Cerf, 1949), 38-45, esp. 44, vs. Grant, *Apologists*, 169-71, and Nicole Zeegers-Vander Vorst, "La Création de l'Homme (Gen 1, 26) chez Théophile d'Antioche," VC (1976), 258-67, esp. 258-60.

49. Autol. II.10; cf. II.22.

50. Autol. II.18; cf. II.15.

51. Autol. I.7 vs. II.13.

52. Autol. II.10 vs. II.22.

53. Apol. 1.33.6; cf. the discussion in Grant, *Apologists*, 60-61.

54. Grant, *Apologists*, 108-9.

55. Just. Dial. 61.3, 126.1, Athenag. Leg. 10.4.

56. *kai ten Athēnan de homoiōs ponēreuomenoi thygatera tou Dios ephasan, ouk apo mixeōs, all', epeide ennoēthenta ton theon dia logou ton kosmon poiesai egnōsan, hōs ten protēn ennoian ephasan ten Athēnan hoper geloiotaton hēgoumetha einai, tes ennoias eikona parapherein thēleion morphen.* Apol. I. 64.5. Greek text: Edgar J. Goodspeed, *Die ältesten Apologeten* (Göttingen: Vandenhoeck & Ruprecht, 1914; rep. 1984), 73-74.

57. Grant, *Apologists,* 169-71; again, id., *Gods,* 129-30. According to his translation (cf. n. 47 above) both Logos and Sophia are brought forth. I prefer to translate with Sophia as the means by which Logos is brought forth, since it is an acceptable reading and it makes the parallel with Chrysippus more evident.

58. Curry (cited in n. 37).

59. Psalm 44:2a (= Ps 45:1 RSV), *Exēpeuxato hēkardia mou logon agathon.* Psalm 109:3 (= Ps 110:3b-c, RSV), *meta sou arche en hēmera tes dunameos sou, en te lamprotēti ton hagiōn. ek gastros pro heōsphorou exegennēsa se.*

60. Cf. the discussion at n. 37 above.

61. McVey, cited in n. 10 above.

62. This point is further reinforced by the similar use of these psalms by Justin (Dial. 38 and 76) and Tertullian (Adv. Herm 18.6, Prax. 7.1, Marc. 2.4.1); cf. Grant, *Apologists,* 169; id., *Gods,* 130.

63. Further on this point, cf. McVey, 43-46.

64. For an overview of Philo's use of allegory with respect to the figure of Wisdom, cf. Burton L. Mack, "Weisheit und Allegorie bei Philo von Alexandrien," *Studia Philonica* 5 (1978), 57-105; for spousal and birth imagery and the parallel with Isis, cf. id., *Logos und Sophia: Untersuchungen zur Weisheitstheologie im hellenistischen Judentum,* Studien zur Umwelt des neuen Testaments 10 (Göttingen: Vandenhoeck & Ruprecht, 1973), esp. 155-58; and cf. John M. Dillon, *The Middle Platonists* (Ithaca, N.Y.: Cornell University Press, 1977), esp. 163-64.

65. Cf. D. W. Bossuet, *Jüdisch-Christlicher Schulbetrieb in Alexandria und Rom: Literarische Untersuchungen zu Philo und Clemens von Alexandria, Justin und Irenäus,* Forschungen zur Religion und Literatur des Alten und Neuen Testaments 23 (Göttingen: Vandenhoeck & Ruprecht, 1915), 7-43, esp. 14; Pépin, "Remarques sur la théorie de l'exégèse allégorique chez Philon," in *Philon d'Alexandrie,* R. Arnaldez, C. Mondesert and J. Pouilloux, eds. (Paris: Éditions du CNRS, 1967), 131-67, esp. 131-33; also Pépin, *Mythe et Allégorie,* esp. 221-41; and David M. Hay, "Philo's references to other Allegorists," *Studia Philonica* 6 (1979–80), 41-75; cf. also, Richard Goulet, *La Philosophie de Moïse: Essai de reconstitution d'un commentaire philosophique préphilonien du Pentateuque,* Histoire des Doctrines de l'Antiquité Classique 11 (Paris: J. Vrin, 1987), esp. 27-89. Since it is not feasible to give a thorough discussion of this issue here, I will merely state my view without attempting to substantiate it: Pépin's modification of Bossuet seems most convincing to me. Although Hay provides the most systematic and thorough discussion of all Philo's direct references to other allegorists, he does not explain the prominence of Stoic materials sufficiently, nor does he respond adequately to his own account of Terian's observations, 67-68, n. 39.

66. Further on Philo's use of mythological materials, cf. Pierre Boyancé, "Écho des exégèses de la mythologie grecque chez Philon," in Arnaldez et al., *Philon,* 169-88; and J. Dillon, "Ganymede as the Logos: Traces of a Forgotten Allegorization in Philo," *Studia Philonica* 6 (1979–80), 37-40; and Yehoshua Amir, "The Transference of Greek Allegories to Biblical Motifs in Philo," in *Nourished with Peace, Studies in Hellenistic Judaism in Memory of Samuel Sandmel,* ed. Frederick E. Greenspahn, Earle Hilgert, and Burton L. Mack, Scholars Press Homage Series (Chico, Calif.: Scholars Press, 1984), 15-25, esp. 20-24.

67. de ebr. 30-31. *Philo,* ed. and trans. F. H. Colson and G. H. Whitaker, Loeb Library (New York: G. Putnam's Sons, 1930), III, 332-35; my trans. here. Note that Philo quotes a variant on the LXX text of Prov 8:22: *ho theos ektesato me prōtistēn ton heautou ergōn* rather than the LXX: *kyrios ektisen me archeon hodon autou eis erga autou.* Although Bossuet discussed the cosmogonic allegory of other passages (Bossuet, 15-43) and other aspects of this treatise (Bossuet, 83-98), he did not focus on this section and its cosmogonic import since Philo does not mention "physical men" or "physical" interpretation here. For further references and some discussion of recent scholarship pertaining to this passage, cf. D. T. Runia, *Philo of Alexandria and the 'Timaeus' of Plato* (Amsterdam: Vrije Universiteit Boekhandel, 1983), 2 vols., esp. 1:245-48.

68. ebr. 33, Colson's trans. here. Similarly in de fug. 109: *patros men theou, hos kai ton sumpantōn esti pater, mētros de sophias, di' hes ta hola elthen eis genesin.* Again, in deter. 54, God as Father begot

the world, and through Wisdom as Mother it was completed: *ean de porrō ton logon apo nou kai aisthesēos apagagon patera men ton gennesanta kosmon, mētera de ten sophian, di 'hes apetelesthē to pan, times axioses, autos eu peise.* In deter. 115-18 to interpret Deut 32:13 Philo introduces Wisdom as the mother who feeds her offspring from her breast: *sophūn theou . . . autē gar hoia metēr ton en kosmo genomenētas trophas ex heautes euthys enegke tois apokyētheisin.* deter. 116.

69. de fuga 50-51, Whitaker's trans. here. Cf. quaest. in Gen IV. 97. Dillon has noted two other places in which Philo alludes to Athena's birth, without mentioning her name, opif. 100 and leg. all. 1.15, cf. Dillon, Ganymede (cited in n. 67), 38.

70. virt. 62.

71. quaest. in Gen IV. 97; trans. of R. Marcus; cf. opif. 100 and leg. all. 1.15.

72. de fuga 52.

73. For example, leg. alleg. 43-45. Cf. Runia, esp. v. 1, 31-39, 355-58.

74. For example, cf. John Carmody, *Holistic Spirituality* (New York: Paulist Press, 1983).

75. Cf. Sallie McFague, *Models of God: Theology for an Ecological, Nuclear Age* (Philadelphia: Fortress Press, 1987), esp. 69-78.

3. Facing Janus: Reviewing the Biblical Theology Movement

1. Jon Levenson, *The Hebrew Bible, the Old Testament, and Historical Criticism* (Philadelphia: Westminster/John Knox Press, 1993), xiv.

2. William Irwin, "A Still Small Voice . . . Said, What Are You Doing Here?" JBL 78 (1959), 3.

3. Jeffrey Stout, *Ethics After Babel: The Languages of Morals and Their Discontents* (Boston: Beacon Press, 1988), 164.

4. "Integration and Integrity in New Testament Studies," *Christian Century* (May 13, 1992), 516.

5. Often, during the time we were colleagues at Princeton Theological Seminary, Beker enjoyed catching me out in these sorts of conversations. Even so, he taught me much about the task of biblical scholarship through those conversations and by the friendship he afforded me. I wish here to thank him.

6. Here Beker likely would join with the claims made by Karl Barth in response to the critics of his Romans commentary. Barth argues: "As one who would understand I must press forward to the point where insofar as possible I confront the riddle of the subject matter and no longer merely the riddle of the document as such, where I can almost forget that I am not the author, where I have understood him so well that I let him speak in my name, and can myself speak in his name. I know that these sentences will bring me another severe reprimand but I cannot help myself." Karl Barth, Foreword to "The Epistle to the Romans" in *The Beginnings of Dialectical Theology*, ed. James M. Robinson (Richmond: John Knox Press, 1968), 93. Like Barth, Beker grants the necessity of utilizing critical tools and taking the results into account. Nevertheless he refuses to consider that the end of exegesis.

7. Here the inaugural address of Johann Philip Gabler is taken to be the initial statement of that need. To be sure, Gabler laid out a program and its difficulties in a succinct and important manner. Whether the solution he proposed is still viable in an age that questions his philosophical grounding of universals is open to question. For a careful delineation of the issues see Hendrikus Boers, *What Is New Testament Theology?* (Philadelphia: Fortress Press, 1979), and Ben Ollenburger, "Biblical Theology: Situating the Discipline," in *Understanding the Word* (Sheffield, JSOT Press, 19), 37-62. Ollenburger's further remarks on the usefulness of Gabler's program for contemporary theological interpretation of the Bible can be found in this volume, pages 81-103.

8. This is expressed classically by Van Harvey in *The Historian and the Believer*. Harvey's argument is made more precise in "The Ethics of Belief Debate Reconsidered," in *The Ethics of Belief Debate*, ed. Gerald D. McCarthy, AAR Academy Series 41 (Atlanta: Scholars Press, 1986). For a perceptive discussion of the issues involved with this discussion see the essay by William Beardslee, "Truth in the Study of Religion," in *Truth, Myth, and Symbol* (Englewood Cliffs, N.J.: Prentice-Hall, 1962), 61-75.

9. The arguments about how this translation are to take place are articulated well, but differently by David Tracy, *The Analogical Imagination: Christian Theology and the Culture of Pluralism* (New York: Crossroad Publishing, 1986), 3-46 and George Lindbeck, *The Nature of Doctrine: Religion and Theology in a Postliberal Age* (Philadelphia: Westminster Press, 1984). The debate between the revisionist and postliberal perspectives articulated by Tracy and Lindbeck is discussed well in *The Modern Theologi-*

ans: An Introduction to Christian Theology in the Twentieth Century, ed. David F. Ford (Oxford: Basil Blackwell, 1989).

10. Asked to comment on the enterprise of Biblical Theology, Gerhard Ebeling started with a history of the term's use. He concluded that it often arose in relation to an unacceptable dominance of ecclesiastical or dogmatic control of critical inquiry. Gerhard Ebeling, "The Meaning of 'Biblical Theology,' " *Word and Faith,* trans. by James W. Leitch. (Philadelphia: Fortress Press, 1963), 84. In *The Promise and Practice of Biblical Theology* (Minneapolis: Fortress Press, 1992), John Reumann characterized Biblical Theology in this way: "There were times in the 1950s and 1960s when people spoke of biblical theology as the Cinderella of theological studies and as a beacon for ecumenical advance, especially in the form of heilsgeschichte (salvation history) or in the theology of the Second Vatican Council, as mysterium salutis. But again and again the claims of its practitioners, for example, members of the American 'biblical theology movement' of the 1950s were reduced to cinders and ashes. Terms such as crisis, demise, and rebirth figured in descriptions of this confused and changing scene. Each time the death certificate for biblical theology has been displayed, signs of new life have appeared. Like the ancient, legendary phoenix or like a Transylvanian vampire— depending on one's perspective—biblical theology rises again" (p. 1).

11. I have used the term as convenient shorthand. There was never an organized movement of scholars. The term was coined by Brevard Childs in *Biblical Theology in Crisis* (Philadelphia: Westminster Press, 1970), 9. It is simply a shorthand to point out the particular form of protest that arose in the United States. The issues were present elsewhere as one would expect since they are part of the hermeneutical issues that pervade all attempts to appropriate the past.

Childs's use of the phrase is rejected by James Smart in *The Past, Present, and Future of Biblical Theology* (Philadelphia: Westminster Press, 1979), 10-12. Smart's reaction is an overreaction prompted by his confusion of the questions that biblical theologians were trying to answer with the answers that group of scholars provided. Childs recognized the multifaceted nature of the movement but still was able to see enough similarities to justify the term. Childs's depiction of this group of scholars has more to do with the common manner in which they attempted to answer the questions than with the fact that the questions are ever present. See the comments of James Barr, "The Theological Case Against Biblical Theology," in *Canon, Theology and Old Testament Interpretation: Essays in Honor of Brevard Childs,* ed. Gene M. Tucker, David L. Petersen, and Robert Wilson (Philadelphia: Fortress Press, 1988), who characterizes Smart's response as "crusty and ill-tempered."

12. One could argue this fairly easily in terms of a seminary situation, but it is also an issue for those who teach in nonseminary settings. See on this, Jon Levenson's argument that even historical analysis is not necessarily a good reason for keeping the practice of these disciplines within an academic setting. The point is that the justification of teaching religious texts in the academy is not so much contingent on adopting the methods of the natural sciences as it is on showing the reasons why these texts are valuable in the ongoing efforts of the academy as an institution of education. Simply stating that these texts were influential in Western culture is not a satisfying argument unless education is only about that culture.

Levenson argues: "That the cultures of the Jews and of the Christians have been enormously influenced, indeed shaped, by the Bible for the past two millennia (more in the case of the Jews) cannot be gainsaid. But why should the history of those two very different but related cultures be privileged over the history of Indian, Chinese, or, for that matter, the African-American culture? And why, a dean might justly ask (and some doubtless do), should we devote a second appointment to the history of the Bible as scripture when we lack even one appointment in the history of the scriptures and classics of most of the world's other religious traditions? To answer with the claim that the Bible is a foundational document of *our* culture is to imply more cultural homogeneity than many believe to be warranted. What is worse, it is to make a claim of normativity that is at odds with the historicistic methods [practitioners] continued to endorse." Jon Levenson, "Historical Criticism and the Fate of the Enlightenment Project," in *The Hebrew Bible, The Old Testament, and Historical Criticism,* 109.

13. Throughout his career Beker has struggled with the arguments raised by the Movement and with the way the movement has proceeded to put those arguments forth. In his inaugural address at Princeton Theological Seminary he rejects academic forms of Biblical Theology outright; "Biblical Theology in a Time of Confusion" *Theology Today* 25 (1968), 185-94. But in "Reflections on Biblical Theology," *Interpretation* 24 (1970), 303-20 that position is softened somewhat. Interestingly enough Beker argues in this article that a hookup between the apocalyptic mentality of biblical authors with modern mentality is an impossibility (p. 316). Later, in *Paul's Apocalyptic Gospel: The*

Coming Triumph of God (Philadelphia: Fortress Press, 1982), he suggests that this apocalyptic framework cannot be eliminated and so attempts to show why it must be hooked up to modern sensibilities (p. 84). Here is an instance of just how difficult and slippery the relationship of critical inquiry to modern interpretation can be.

14. Luke T. Johnson, "The Crisis in Biblical Scholarship," *Commonweal* 70:21 (Dec. 3, 1993), 18.

15. Minear made an early plea for Biblical Theology in "Wanted: A Biblical Theology," *Theology Today* 1 (1944), 47-59. His own attempt followed in *Eyes of Faith: A Study in the Biblical Point of View* (Philadelphia: Westminster Press, 1946), where he incorporated Kierkegaard's existential categories for understanding biblical stances. H. H. Rowley was a British biblical scholar, but his article "The Relevance of Biblical Interpretation," *Interpretation* 1 (1947), is an early argument for the biblical theological mode of interpretation, and his *Unity of the Bible* was an early mainstay of the movement.

16. Stamping a false unity on the biblical texts was a failing of the Movement, and to argue that all the interpreters included under the rubric Biblical Theology Movement held the same views and made the same interpretive moves would be to make the same kind of mistake. There were significant differences in the answers that each interpreter proposed but also a sufficient family resemblance among them to justify the term *movement* and to present representative voices. Synthetic overviews of the Movement are presented by Childs in *Biblical Theology in Crisis* and James Barr in "Biblical Theology," *IDB* Supplement, 104-11. Barr lists eight characteristics of the Movement. These are: (1) opposition to the influence of philosophy and philosophical theology on biblical studies; (2) an opposition to the oversystematic approach of dogmatic theology which was imposed on the biblical material; (3) a contrast of Hebrew and Greek thinking; (4) an emphasis on the unity of the Bible; (5) a word study approach to the biblical languages; (6) insistence on a contrast between the Bible and its environment; (7) an understanding of revelation through history; and (8) the idea that biblical study be oriented to theological concerns.

17. Others could have been chosen. For example, for most biblical studies students in the United States the movement is associated with Oscar Cullmann's *Christ and Time* (Phialdelphia: Westminster Press, 1950), and Bultmann's critique of it, or G. Ernest Wright's *The God Who Acts: Biblical Theology as Recital* (Chicago: Alec R. Allenson, 1952). Wright's work is perhaps the most characteristic of the Movement's idea of revelation through history and the interpreter's consequent task. In some ways Wright is the best known of the biblical theologians. Others may have been more significant as thinkers, but Wright's verve and accessible prose made him an important voice in the Movement. Wright's phrase "the God Who Acts" has achieved the status of pithy formulation and is often used without sense of its initial context. When criticism of the Movement arose it was Wright who responded. He continued to reflect on the nature of Biblical Theology well after its heyday had passed. However, Wright's positions are also some of the most extreme and so received the most critical attention. Chief of these critics was James Barr, who in a number of works dismantled Wright's arguments. When Barr lists the characteristics of the Biblical Theology Movement and its foibles, it is Wright's arguments that form the core of his attention. It is just this extreme manner of arguing both in stating the case and in the critiques that it engendered that make Wright less helpful for the purposes of this essay.

18. John H. Hayes and Frederick Prussner, *Old Testament Theology: Its History and Development* (Atlanta: John Knox Press, 1985), 210.

19. Childs, *Biblical Theology in Crisis,* 19-22.

20. In effect, without entering into the debate directly, the movement was attempting to mediate the consequent forms of the inherited debate between Adolf von Harnack and Karl Barth. That correspondence is discussed in H. Martin Rumscheidt, *Revelation and Theology: An Analysis of the Barth-Harnack Correspondence of 1923* (Cambridge: Cambridge University Press, 1972) and in Robinson, ed., *The Beginnings of Dialectical Theology.*

21. Childs, *Biblical Theology in Crisis,* 17.

22. So says John A. Mackay in an editorial introducing the first issue of *Theology Today.* In "Editorial: Our Aims," Mackay argued that the present world situation of confusion and crisis made "theology the most important study in which men can engage as they make their pilgrimage from one era to another, and from this world to the world to come." *Theology Today* 1 (1944), 3. Both *Theology Today* and *Interpretation* were inaugurated at this time, and both strove to incorporate critical biblical scholarship with theological interpretation. Incidentally, both periodicals were tied to Presbyterian seminaries and reflected the concerns of the Reformation movement for this integration.

23. G. Ernest Wright, "The Christian Interpreter as Biblical Critic," *Interpretation* 1 (1947), 145.

24. H. H. Rowley, "The Relevance of Biblical Interpretation," *Interpretation* 1 (1947), 3.

25. Irwin, 4. Irwin makes other points about the excess of the Biblical Theology Movement's claim to transcend previous failures including a confusion of the task of the biblical interpreter with the theologian and allowing religious presuppositions to play inappropriate roles in determining the meaning of the Bible. His strongest objection however, is the failure to respect the theological efforts of previous historical critics. Consider these remarks: "It is sometimes said that the critical age erred in that it stopped just where it was ready to begin. When all the historical orientation was done and the literary questions dealt with (which too often meant analysis into absurd snippets), there still remained the Bible in all its greatness and transforming power. Such a charge may be fitting, if leveled against second—or was it third?—generation critics, mere camp followers like myself, who came on the field of battle to strip the slain but were often troubled only remotely by the agony of soul extracted from the protagonists. But when directed toward the great figures of the movement, the charges merely declare an ignorance of the history of our common activity" (p. 11).

26. Henry J. Cadbury, "The Peril of Archaizing Ourselves," *Interpretation* 3 (1949), 332-33. The reply from G. Ernest Wright is hardly as delicate or elegantly stated. See "The Problem of Archaizing Ourselves," *Interpretation* 3:450-59.

27. As Childs points out, not all the biblical theologians agreed on how history was the means of revelation. In fact the positions on this varied greatly. Minear, as we will see, stands out as someone who agrees with the general idea but who has an entirely different understanding of history. See Childs, *Biblical Theology in Crisis*, 39-44.

28. This is a fundamental premise of *The God Who Acts: Biblical Theology as Recital* and the reason for the subtitle.

29. Paul Minear, *Eyes of Faith*, 291.

30. Minear, *Theology Today*, 47.

31. Ibid., 48. The observations are parallel to those of Johnson noted above.

32. Ibid. Minear's position is remarkably close to Levenson's observation that Jewish and Christian scholars find great agreement as long as they ignore the fact that they are Jews and Christians. As he states it, "to the extent that Jews and Christians bracket their religious commitments in the pursuit of biblical studies, they meet not as Jews and Christians, but as something else" (Levenson, 84). This something else is a sort of religious neutrality carved out by historical analysis. However, never "should a method that studiously pursues neutrality be mistaken for the key to a genuine and profound dialogue between two great religious communities" (Levenson, 84). Levenson's point is well expressed in these comments by Richard Rorty, "A conviction which can be justified to anyone is of little interest. 'Unflinching courage' will not be required to sustain such a conviction." Beliefs of this type are "the sort of beliefs that nobody wants to argue about because they are neither controversial nor central to anyone's sense of who she is or what she lives for." Richard Rorty, *Contingency, Irony, and Solidarity* (Cambridge: Cambridge University Press, 1989), 47.

33. Paul Minear, *Theology Today*, 49.

34. Ibid.

35. Ibid. Note the deliberate use of Kierkegaard's title.

36. Ibid., 49-50.

37. Ibid., 50.

38. Ibid., 50-51.

39. Ibid., 54.

40. Ibid.

41. Ibid.

42. Ibid., 55.

43. Ibid.

44. Ibid.

45. Ibid., 56.

46. Ibid., 57.

47. Ibid., 51.

48. Ibid., 58.

49. Here Ben Ollenburger's statement on the nature and location of Biblical Theology are pertinent. Ollenburger suggests that Biblical Theology would be understood better as an activity rather than a genre of literature and that a natural place for that activity is within a church setting. "Biblical Theology: Situating the Discipline," 51-54.

50. Here too there is an analogy with Elisabeth Schüssler Fiorenza's call to decenter biblical scholarship. See "Biblical Interpretation and Critical Commitment," *Studia Theologica* 43 (1989), 5-18 and her presidential address to the SBL, "The Ethics of Interpretation: De-Centering Biblical Scholarship," JBL 107 (1988), 3-17.

51. Wright's formulation is more caustic than Rowley's but it captures the thrust of his argument. "Protestant scholarship of the last three generations has largely been laboring under the delusion of its objectivity. . . . Failure to realize this fact and openly confess it has resulted in a particular myopia which has kept the biblical scholar from understanding the part his own theology has played in shaping his conclusions. Hence it has been quite easy for him, not only to make his own presuppositions the basis for understanding the relevance of the Bible, but also to read them into the literature itself in such a way as to make it their buttress and support" (Wright, *Interpretation*, 148-49).

52. Commenting on the previous generation's efforts, Wright charged that "the higher critics have not actually been concerned with real exegesis and interpretation because their central interest has not been theological, whereas the Bible is primarily a theological book. Furthermore, when the critics have dealt with Biblical Theology, they have done so by means of value judgments, presuppositions, and perspective which are totally unbiblical since they refuse to take seriously the Bible's own point of view. Their idol, it is claimed has been objectivity and dispassionate search for truth, but their presuppositions have betrayed them into a subjectivity which is simply unable to come to grips seriously with many of the primary affirmations of biblical faith" (Wright, *Interpretation*, 143).

53. Rowley, 4. G. E. Wright is much less polite. Criticizing the same scholars, he writes: "Protestant liberalism, however, in continued reaction against biblical and theological conservatism has shown striking symptoms of fixation and a surprising lack of self-criticism. Consequently, its biblical scholarship during the present century has exhibited a dullness and sterility which always appears when self-criticism is missing. In fact, it is scarcely an exaggeration to say that in the OT field particularly the dominant scholarship has consisted in a series of appendixes and footnotes to the work of Julius Wellhausen and his associates." G. Ernest Wright, *Interpretation* 1 (1947), 142-43.

54. Rowley, 4. Just as Rowley notes the ease with which the shortcomings of the previous generation can be recognized, so it is the case with the shortcomings of his own. The lesson here is not, however, to remark on the hubris of the previous generation but to point out the need for respectful engagement by the present one. Nor is it to hone in on the inadequacy of their expressions. Rather "to move forward," subsequent generations would need to understand what sort of questions prompted these expressions and to know why their predecessors thought that these were good ways to speak. As easily as we see the foibles of our predecessors, our own successors spot ours. To recognize the contingent nature of our own formulations ought to remain a high priority when we assess the work of those who precede us. See Richard Rorty's wry discussion of the need for this ironic liberality. *Contingency, Irony, and Solidarity*, 73-95.

55. Rowley, 5.

56. Ibid.

57. Ibid.

58. Ibid., 6.

59. Ibid.

60. So too Wright, who maintains the distinction is to be found in two ways: (1) "The Bible is entirely different from any other sacred literature and almost an offense to the normal expectations and desires of the human mind. For one thing, its God is so utterly different from the normal gods of the human race from the earliest of times until the present." (2) "In the polytheisms and naturalistic religion the emphasis is utterly different. God is not set over against man and creation; there is instead a concentration on harmony for the sake of comfort and security." And "yet in the Bible a profound disharmony exists. God is set over against his world in judgment, and man is seen in need of salvation, for his life is a history of rebellion against his Lord." Wright, *Interpretation*, 145-46. In *The God Who Acts* he argues that this distinction is also found in Israel's understanding of history.

61. Rowley, 8.

62. Ibid., 9.

63. Ibid., 11.

64. The issues of the question are focused in the different positions taken by revisionists and postliberals. A helpful discussion of the issues is that of Mark Wallace, "Can God Be Named Without Being Known?: The Problem of Revelation in Thiemann, Ogden, and Ricoeur," *JAAR* 59 (1991), 281-308.

65. David Kelsey notes this when he discusses Wright's understanding of biblical authority in *The Uses of Scripture in Recent Theology* (Philadelphia: Fortress Press, 1975), 37-38. He also notes the irony of Wright's methods for analyzing scriptures. Though Wright called for a recognition of the narratives as narrative, the mode of biblical literature as narration plays no role in Wright's use of scripture. In the end, despite his protest, Wright returns to the propositional form of theology that he argued was inappropriate.

66. Childs, *Biblical Theology in Crisis*, 34.

67. J. Stout, "What Is the Meaning of a Text?," *New Literary History* 14 (1982), 1-12.

68. Wright, *God Who Acts*, 38-46.

69. Ibid., 50-58.

70. Childs, *Biblical Theology in Crisis*, 40-41.

71. Oddly enough, given the demise of the Movement, Barr's criticisms of the Movement have continued and become a constant portion of his scholarly activity. The initial criticisms are found in *The Semantics of Biblical Language* (Oxford: Oxford University Press, 1961) and in his inaugural lecture at Princeton Theological Seminary entitled "Revelation Through History in the Old Testament and in Modern Theology," *Princeton Seminary Bulletin* 56 (1963), 4-14. They continued in *Old and New in Interpretation* (New York: SCM Press and Harper & Row, 1966) and *The Scope and Authority of the Bible* (Philadelphia: Westminster Press, 1980).

72. Childs, *Biblical Theology in Crisis*, 71.

73. Ibid., 72.

74. Wright, "Revelation and Theology," in *The Old Testament and Theology* (New York: Harper & Row, 1969), 46-48. Wright attempts a sort of rebuttal, but it is not substantive. In the end it is an apology by way of negation. He argues that "Just because the viewpoint being attacked is full of difficulties and inadequacies does not necessarily mean that it is entirely wrong" (49).

75. Langdon Gilkey, "Cosmology, Ontology, and the Travail of Biblical Language," *Journal of Religion* 41 (1961), 194-204. Gilkey's arguments were prefigured by Winston L. King, "Some Ambiguities in Biblical Theology," *Religion in Life* 27 (1957–58), and James Branton's lead article "Our Present Situation in Biblical Theology" in *Religion in Life* 26 (1956–57), 5-18.

76. Ibid., 194.

77. Ibid., 195.

78. Ibid.

79. Ibid., 196.

80. Ibid.

81. Ibid., 200.

82. Childs, *Biblical Theology in Crisis*, 65.

83. Gilkey's arguments still hold power, and the question remains a dilemma for theologians of any stripe. See Owen Thomas, ed., *God's Activity in the World: The Contemporary Problem* (Chico, Calif.: Scholars Press, 1983); Ronald Thiemann, *Revelation and Theology: The Gospel as Narrated Promise* (Notre Dame: Notre Dame University Press, 1985); and Peter Hodgson, *God in History: Shapes of Freedom* (Nashville: Abingdon Press, 1989), for continued discussions of the difficulties involved in clarifying the nature of the question and its proposed solutions.

84. Elisabeth Schüssler Fiorenza, "The Ethics of Interpretation," 15-16.

85. Childs, *Biblical Theology in Crisis*, 91.

86. Ebeling, *Word and Faith*, 89-90, 96.

87. Stout, *Ethics After Babel*, 165.

88. In some ways this is a form of Lessing's gap, in others not. For a helpful discussion of Lessing's ditch and its various forms, see Gordon Michalson, Jr., *Lessing's Ugly Ditch: A Study of Theology and History* (University Park: Pennsylvania State University Press, 1985).

89. Krister Stendahl, "Biblical Theology, Contemporary," *IDB* 1:418-32; reprinted as "Biblical Theology: A Program," in *Meanings: The Bible as Document and as Guide* (Philadelphia: Fortress Press, 1984), 11-44.

90. Ebeling, 80.

91. Ben Ollenburger, "What Krister Stendahl 'Meant'—A Normative Critique of 'Descriptive Biblical Theology,' " *Horizons in Biblical Theology* 8 (1986), 61-98.

92. Stout, *Ethics After Babel*, 163.

4. Old Testament Theology: A Discourse on Method

1. I have described something of Old Testament theology's diversity up to 1930, in "From Timeless Ideas to the Essence of Religion: Method in Old Testament Theology before 1930," *The Flowering of Old Testament Theology*, ed. Ben C. Ollenburger, Elmer A. Martens, Gerhard Hasel, Sources for Biblical and Theological Study 1 (Winona Lake: Eisenbrauns, 1992), 3-19. In the same volume, Elmer Martens ("The Multicolored Landscape of Old Testament Theology," 43-57), and Gerhard Hasel ("The Future of Old Testament Theology: Prospects and Trends," 373-83), point to the diversity both among current theologies and among proposals about what OTT should become. In this essay I will use the traditional Christian terms "Old Testament" and "Old Testament theology," not in order to cause needless offense, but to be clear what I am talking about. On the point, see Jon D. Levenson, "Theological Consensus or Historicist Evasion? Jews and Christians in Biblical Studies," *Hebrew Bible or Old Testament,* ed. Roger Brooks and John J. Collins (Notre Dame: Notre Dame University Press, 1990), 109-45, esp. 135-43.

2. Henning Graf Reventlow, *Problems of Old Testament Theology in the Twentieth Century* (Philadelphia: Fortress Press, 1985; the German original was published in 1982); John H. Hayes and Frederick Prussner, *Old Testament Theology: Its History and Development* (Atlanta: John Knox, 1985); John Goldingay, *Theological Diversity and the Authority of the Old Testament* (Grand Rapids: Eerdmans, 1987); Jesper Høgenhaven, *Problems and Prospects of Old Testament Theology* (Sheffield: JSOT Press, 1988); Gerhard Hasel, *Old Testament Theology: Basic Issues in the Current Debate,* 4th ed. (Grand Rapids: Eerdmans, 1991); Ollenburger, Martens, & Hasel, *Old Testament Theology,* 1992. See also Manfred Oeming, *Gesamtbiblische Theologien der Gegenwart,* 2nd ed. (Stuttgart: Kohlhammer, 1987).

3. Among the most helpful discussions of method is Wolfgang Richter's, in *Exegese als Literaturwissenschaft* (Göttingen: Vandenhoeck & Ruprecht, 1971), 9-19, 187-90.

4. Hendrikus Boers, *What Is New Testament Theology?* (Philadelphia: Fortress Press), 37. Boers provides a superb summary and analysis of Gabler's proposal (23-38). The only easily accessible text of Gabler's is his inaugural address at the University of Altdorf, in 1787. John Sandys-Wunsch and Laurence Eldredge have provided an English translation and helpful commentary, in "J. Gabler and the Distinction Between Biblical and Dogmatic Theology," *SJT* 33 (1980), 133-58. Gabler's address, "An Oration On The Proper Distinction Between Biblical and Dogmatic Theology and the Specific Objectives of Each," as translated by Sandys-Wunsch and Eldredge, is now reprinted in Ollenburger, Martens, and Hasel, *Old Testament Theology,* 493-502 (my references to Gabler's "Oration" will cite this edition). Otto Merk, *Biblische Theologie des Neuen Testaments in ihrer Anfangszeit* (Marburg: Elwert, 1972), quotes extensively from Gabler's other writings; his book is the most comprehensive treatment of Gabler. Hans Frei gives a brief but rich account of Gabler and his context in *The Eclipse of Biblical Narrative* (New Haven: Yale University Press, 1974), 156-74, 245-66.

5. Compare, or contrast, Gabler's metaphor of stripping *(entkleiden)* an idea of its clothing *(Einkleidung)* with Naomi Schor's metaphor of striptease as an interpretive alternative to rape ("Fiction as Interpretation/Interpretation as Fiction," *The Reader in the Text: Essays on Audience and Interpretation,* ed. Susan R. Suleiman and Inge Crosman [Princeton: Princeton University Press, 1980], 165-82, esp. 181-82).

6. Merk, *Biblische Theologie,* 100, 101.

7. Gabler sketches this rationale already in his "Oration," 493-502, esp. 499-500.

8. For Gabler, the history of biblical literature is plotted on the history of humankind's enlightenment. Merk (*Biblische Theologie,* 137) speaks of a "stufenweise Entwicklung mit der ihr verbundenen stufenweisen Aufklärung"—a development by stages joined to an enlightenment by stages (see also 84).

9. Merk discusses Gabler's distinctions between *auslegen* and *erklären,* in *Biblische Theologie,* 69-81.

10. Merk (*Biblische Theologie,* 97), quoting from Gabler's comments in the *Journal für theologische Literatur* of 1802. Gabler seems to limit Biblical Theology's aims to providing a *foundation* for Dogmatic Theology; in that respect, it has an apologetic function. Theology based upon it "will . . . be made more certain and more firm, and there will be nothing further to be feared for it from the most savage attack from its enemies" ("Oration," 496-97).

11. Merk, *Biblische Theologie,* 105, and note 313.

12. I have discussed some of the reasons why in "Biblical Theology: Situating the Discipline," *Understanding the Word: Essays in Honor of Bernhard W. Anderson,* ed. James T. Butler, Edgar W. Conrad, and Ben C. Ollenburger, JSOTSup 37 (Sheffield: JSOT Press, 1985), 37-62.

13. Boers, *New Testament Theology*, 25-26.

14. Gabler, "Oration," 497-98.

15. L. F. O. Baumgarten-Crusius observed already in 1828 that historical study of the Bible and Biblical Theology emerged together (*Grundzüge der biblischen Theologie* [Jena: Frommann, 1828] 4). See Ollenburger, "Timeless Ideas," 3-4.

16. Quoted in Rudolf Smend, "Nachkritische Schriftauslegung," *Parrhesia: Karl Barth zum achtzigsten Geburtstag* (Zürich: Evangelischer Verlag, 1966), 221. A century later, Wilhelm Wrede said much the same thing ("The Task and Methods of New Testament Theology," *The Nature of New Testament Theology*, ed. Robert Morgan [London: SCM Press, 1973], 68-116, see esp. 69-70). Wrede's essay was first published in 1897, and included the adjective "so-called" before "New Testament Theology."

17. Merk, *Biblische Theologie*, 53.

18. Wolfhart Pannenberg, *Theology and the Philosophy of Science* (Philadelphia: Westminster Press, 1976), 355-56, 372-77.

19. Gabler agreed with Immanuel Kant on the latter point, but insisted that Kant's indifference to textual, historical scholarship resulted in allegorical interpretation. See Merk, *Biblische Theologie*, 58-68; Ollenburger, "Biblical Theology," 44-46. Kant remarks on the matter in *Religion Within the Limits of Reason Alone* (New York: Harper & Brothers, 1960), see esp. 9-10, 100-3.

20. Bauer, *Theologie des Alten Testaments* (Leipzig: Wygand, 1796).

21. In this regard, see Alasdair MacIntyre, "Epistemological Crises, Dramatic Narrative, and the Philosophy of Science," *The Monist* 60 (1977), 453-72. Perhaps the most powerfully revisionist enquiry to date is that of Gerhard von Rad, the first volume of whose *Old Testament Theology* locates itself historically (or by means of dramatic narrative, in MacIntyre's sense) in relation to previous inquiries *Old Testament Theology*, 2 vols; New York: Harper, 1962–65, 1. 105-28. Equally revisionist, but in contrary directions, are the proposals of John J. Collins ("Is a Critical Biblical Theology Possible?" *The Hebrew Bible and Its Interpreters*, ed. W. H. Propp, Baruch Halpern, and D. N. Freedman [Winona Lake: Eisenbrauns, 1990], 1-17), and Friedrich Mildenberger (in the section " 'Biblical Theology' as Symptomatic for the Problem of Scholarly Interpretation of the Bible," *Theology of the Lutheran Confessions* [Philadelphia: Fortress Press, 1986], 212-21).

22. *Theologie des Alten Testaments* (2 vols.; Stuttgart: W. Kohlhammer, 1991–92). Numbers following in the text refer to pages in the first volume of Preuss's work.

23. Philadelphia: Westminster Press, 1957, 9 (first German edition, 1935).

24. New York: Harper, 1958, 11 (first French edition, 1955).

25. Atlanta: John Knox Press, 1978, 12 (first German edition, 1972). In his book's first two sentences, Zimmerli stipulates more expansively: "Any 'Old Testament theology in outline' must . . . lead readers to bring together in their own minds the diverse statements the Old Testament makes about God, who wishes to be known not as a manifold God but as the one Yahweh" (p. 10).

26. Atlanta: John Knox, 1982, 9 (first German edition, 1978).

27. Werner E. Lemke, "Is Old Testament Theology an Essentially Christian Theological Discipline?" *HBT* 11 (1989), 59-71, quoting from 67.

28. This is not to deny the extensive reflection behind the OT theologies of, for example, Zimmerli, Westermann, and Preuss (see, for example, Zimmerli, *Studien zur alttestamentlichen Theologie und Prophetie: Gesammelte Aufsätze 2*, TBü 19 [Munich: Chr. Kaiser, 1974]; Westermann, *Erträge der Forschung am Alten Testament: Gesammelte Studien 3*, TBü 73, ed. Rainer Albertz [Munich: Chr. Kaiser, 1984]; Preuss, *Das Alte Testament in christlicher Predigt* [Stuttgart: Kohlhammer, 1984]).

29. Wilhelm Vatke, *Die biblische Theologie wissenschaftlich dargestellt*. Volume I: *Die Religion des Alten Testaments* (Berlin: Bethge, 1835); J. C. K. von Hofmann, *Der Schriftbeweis*, 2 vols. (Nördlingen: Beck, 1952–56). For a summary, see Ollenburger, "Timeless Ideas," 6-15.

30. Johann C. F. Steudel, *Vorlesungen über die Theologie des Alten Testaments*, ed. G. F. Oehler (Berlin: Reimer, 1840); Eduard K. A. Riehm, *Alttestamentliche Theologie*, ed. Karl Pahncke (Halle: Strien, 1889). In what follows I am drawing extensively on Walther Zimmerli, "Biblische Theologie: Altes Testament," *TRE* 6 (1980), 426-55.

31. James Barr, *The Scope and Authority of the Bible* (Philadelphia: Westminster Press, 1980), 45 (the italics are his). Barr adds: "It is deeper-lying because it goes back to a time before the rise of many critical questions properly so-called; it goes back to questions about the literal and the grammatical sense of which the middle ages, in Judaism as well as in Christianity, were aware and which came to expression in the Reformation" (ibid.). Barr is right, but the power to differentiate

between the historical sense and any version of the literal sense, which the nineteenth century acquired in vast measure, changed the nature of the questions.

32. With rare exceptions, the OT theologies produced in the latter half of the century were published posthumously. Zimmerli suggests that this was mainly because OT scholars had grown insecure in venturing proposals about the OT as a whole, in view of the many critical questions that were up in the air ("Biblische Theologie I: Altes Testament," 433). The dead don't have to read reviews of their books.

33. "Ziele und Methoden der Erklärung des Alten Testamentes," *Reden und Aufsätze* (Göttingen: Vandenhoeck & Ruprecht, 1913), 11-29; "The 'Historical Movement' in the Study of Religion," *ExpTim* 38 (1926-27), 532-36.

34. "The History of Israelite-Jewish Religion and Old Testament Theology," in Ollenburger, Martens, and Hasel, *Old Testament Theology,* 20-29 (German original, 1926).

35. "Does Old Testament Theology Still Have Independent Significance Within Old Testament Scholarship?" in Ollenburger, Martens, and Hasel, *Old Testament Theology,* 30-39, quoting from 36 (German original, 1929).

36. Many of these matters are taken up in David J. A. Clines, Stephen E. Fowl, Stanley E. Porter, eds., *The Bible in Three Dimensions* (JSOTSup 87; Sheffield: JSOT Press, 1990), 357-77. See also the important work by Mark G. Brett, *Biblical Criticism in Crisis? The Impact of the Canonical Approach on Old Testament Studies* (Cambridge: Cambridge University Press, 1991). On feminism and Biblical Theology see Phyllis Trible, "Five Loaves and Two Fishes: Feminist Hermeneutics and Biblical Theology," *TS* 50 (1989), 279-95 (reprinted in Ollenburger, Martens, and Hasel, *Old Testament Theology,* 445-64); Mary H. Schertz, "Biblical Theology and Feminist Interpretation: A Dinosaur at the Freedom March?" *So Wide a Sea: Essays on Biblical and Systematic Theology,* ed. Ben C. Ollenburger (Elkhart, Ind.: Institute of Mennonite Studies, 1991), 65-78. On Judaism and OTT see Jon D. Levenson, "Why Jews Are Not Interested in Biblical Theology," *Judaic Perspectives on Ancient Israel,* ed. Jacob Neusner, Baruch A. Levine, and Ernest S. Frerichs (Philadelphia: Fortress Press, 1987), 281-307; Rolf Rendtorff, "Toward a Common Jewish-Christian Reading of the Hebrew Bible," in Brooks and Collins, eds., *Hebrew Bible or Old Testament,* 89-108.

37. To be fair to Preuss, his initial definition does not entirely beg the question. Subsequently, he offers reasons in favor of a systematic theological summary of the OT: it enhances comparisons with the NT, the evaluation of the OT in Christian theology, and the use of the OT in preaching and in religious instruction (p. 23).

38. For example, von Rad points to "the surprising convergence—indeed the mutual intersection—which has come about during the last twenty or thirty years between introductory studies and Biblical theology" (*Old Testament Theology,* vol. 1, v). See also Rolf Rendtorff, who refers to von Rad, in "Theologie des Alten Testaments: Überlengungen zu einem Neuansatz," *Kanon und Theologie: Vorarbeiten zu einer Theologie des Alten Testaments* (Neukirchen-Vluyn: Neukirchener Verlag, 1991), 1, 10. On what I mean by "material," see section I. It may bear pointing out that I do not oppose "critical" to either "constructive" or "normative."

39. Childs, *Old Testament Theology in a Canonical Context* (Philadelphia: Fortress Press, 1986); Gottwald, "Literary Criticism of the Hebrew Bible: Retrospect and Prospect," *Mapping of the Biblical Terrain: The Bible as Text* (ed. Vincent L. Tollers and John Maier; Lewisburg, Pa.: Bucknell University Press, 1990), 27-43. David J. A. Clines has explored the general issue helpfully, in "Reading Esther From Left to Right: Contemporary Strategies for Reading a Biblical Text," *The Bible in Three Dimensions,* 31-52.

40. Peter Dirksen makes this claim, in "Israelite Religion and Old Testament Theology," *SJOT* 2 (1990), 96-100, see 99.

41. *A Theology of the Old Testament* (Garden City, N.Y.: Doubleday, 1974), 15.

42. Dirksen, "Israelite Religion," 100. An argument similar to Dirksen's was made earlier by R. N. Whybray, in "Old Testament Theology: A Non-existent Beast?" *Scripture: Meaning and Method,* ed. Barry Thompson (Hull: Hull University Press, 1987), 168-80. Both Whybray and Dirksen define OTT in ways that make it impossible, and both take this as exposing OTT, rather than their own definitions, as nonsense. Whybray goes Dirksen one better by making the history of Israelite religion impossible as well: he assigns it a concern for "the Old Testament as a whole," with the task of discovering " 'what made the ancient Yahwist tick' " (p. 174).

43. Quotations in this paragraph are from "Israelite Religion," 100.

44. Ibid., 97-98.

45. Preuss says that it is "the noblest and most important task of Old Testament scholarship" (*Theologie des Alten Testaments*, vol. 1, 1). Cf. A. H. J. Gunneweg's criticism of some forms of this claim, in " 'Theologie' des Alten Testaments oder 'Biblische Theologie'?" *Sola Scriptura: Beiträge zu Exegese und Hermeneutik des Alten Testaments* (Göttingen: Vandenhoeck & Ruprecht, 1983), 228-34, esp. 234. Heinz Schürmann simply denies the claim, in "Bibelwissenschaft unter dem Wort Gottes: Eine selbstkritische Besinnung," *Christus Bezeugen: Für Wolfgang Trilling* (Freiburg: Herder, 1990), 11-42, 19.

46. *Theologie des Alten Testaments* (Tübingen: J. C. B. Mohr [Paul Siebeck], 2nd ed., 1947), v (italics mine). My copy of Köhler's book is a gift of Edward Dowey, Köhler's former student and Chris Beker's friend and colleague. A good part of my theological education was gained during lunchhour discussions with Dowey and Beker, rare scholars and teachers both.

47. *Literary Theory: An Introduction* (Minneapolis: University of Minnesota Press, 1983), 210. Eagleton suggests that "strategic" considerations should govern the choice of methods and theories. I will argue that, in the case of OTT, considerations of strategy should be constituent in the method itself. What we *should* want to do is open to debate, including moral debate.

48. I have taken the term and some of the ideas surrounding it from Heinz Schürmann, "Bibelwissenschaft unter dem Wort Gottes," 16-17. Schürmann refers espressly to Kant.

49. *Critique of Pure Reason*, trans. F. Max Müller (Garden City, N.Y.: Doubleday, 1966), 426 (A 643-47/B 561-75).

50. Ibid., 437 (A 663-66/B 691-94). The italics are Kant's. F. Strawson offers pertinent criticisms of Kant's notion of regulative ideas, in *The Bounds of Sense* (London: Methuen, 1966), 159-61, 223-26.

51. See most recently, *The World of Biblical Literature* (New York: Basic Books, 1992).

52. *Old Testament Theology*, vol. 1, 105. Manfred Oeming describes von Rad's proposed conjunction between theology and historical criticism as the "innere Tragik" of von Rad's theology (*Gesamtbiblische Theologien*, 73).

53. Pannenberg expects from Biblical Theology "a theology of the formation of the Judaeo-Christian tradition" (*Theology and the Philosophy of Science*, 386), which is the sort of thing OTT could do best if it followed von Rad (from whom Pannenberg learned). For Frei, see especially his essay, "The 'Literal Reading' of Biblical Narrative in the Christian Tradition: Does It Stretch or Will It Break?" *The Bible and the Narrative Tradition*, ed. Frank McConnell (Oxford: Oxford University Press, 1985), 36-77.

54. "The Theological Case Against Biblical Theology," *Canon, Theology, and Old Testament Interpretation: Essays in Honor of Brevard S. Childs*, ed. G. M. Tucker, D. L. Petersen, and R. R. Wilson (Philadelphia: Fortress Press, 1985), 10. Barr apparently disposes of this material quite well. See his *Biblical Faith and Natural Theology: The Gifford Lectures for 1991* (Oxford: Clarendon Press, 1993).

55. *Problems and Prospects*, 88. Høgenhaven concludes from this canonical status of the OT that it "should be read for what it is—the national literature of an ancient Near Eastern people" (ibid.). It is unclear, in this case, what "canonical status" means, or that it means anything at all.

56. Barr, *Scope and Authority*, 45.

57. "Das Problem einer theologischen Exegese des Alten Testaments," *Zur Neugestaltung des theologischen Studiums* (Göttingen: Vandenhoeck & Ruprecht, 1935), 61-69. The quote is from 67-68, as translated in Reventlow's *Problems of Old Testament Theology*, 18, from which I have taken it.

58. "Exegesis and Dogmatic Theology," *Theological Investigations* (vol. 5; London: Darton, Longman & Todd, 1966), 67-93, quoting from 71-72. Paul Hanson illustrates something of Rahner's point by reiterating something like Lindblom's. Hanson criticizes Jürgen Moltmann and Hans Küng, not for clumsy dabbling, but for attending too little to "Hebrew Scripture." He blames this relative inattention on the failure of biblical scholarship "to produce background studies on which we have every reason to believe theologians like Küng and Moltmann would have gladly drawn had such studies existed. This observation provides the challenge to which the present work responds" (*The People Called: The Growth of Community in the Bible* [San Francisco: Harper & Row, 1986] 521). Hanson's diagnosis and his proposed cure are questionable; nonetheless, Hanson provides a relatively full discussion of the aims of his inquiry, of its strategy (its regulative ideas and constitutive principles), and of the material on which he conducts it (ibid., 519-46).

59. "Is a Critical Biblical Theology Possible?" (see note 20), quoting from 15. Collins speaks of biblical rather than of OT theology, but the difference is not crucial to the points under discussion. Numbers following in the text refer to the pages of Collins's article, which Gerhard Hasel discusses, in Ollenburger, Martens, and Hasel, *Old Testament Theology*, 374-76.

60. There is a confusion here between (a) the relation of a text's genre to *its* truth claim, and (b) the truth claims *we* can make for a text. Collins commits himself to (b), but there is meager limit

on truth claims we can make for or about a text, regardless of its genre. It is clear from his subsequent comments (p. 10) that Collins has (a) in mind. While Collins cites Meir Sternberg for support on this point, they seem to argue in opposite directions. Sternberg would charge Collins with misidentifying "history writing with historical truth and, correspondingly, of reading postulates with the reader's beliefs" (*The Poetics of Biblical Narrative: Ideological Literature and the Drama of Reading* [Bloomington: University of Indiana Press, 1985] 33, and see 29).

61. It is unclear what Collins means by this "last claim," or by the "bedrock of certainty" that theologians have sought in the genre "history." Perhaps he has in mind George Ernest Wright, to whom he refers earlier, and whose "biblical archaism" he claims "is a product of twentieth-century positivism" (10-11).

62. In the examples he cites, Collins says that "we may *suspect* that we are dealing with ideological rhetoric rather than theological truth" in the conquest accounts (13), and that "We can *understand*" how accounts of creation and the Maccabean martyrs' expectation of reward after death fostered and strengthened certain attitudes (13-14, italics mine). These fall short of establishing a social function, even if they are plausible suggestions (and in case "ideological rhetoric" and "theological truth" are mutually exclusive).

63. In the ellipses, Collins refers for support to Jon Levenson, whose point is at odds with his own. Levenson's point is that Israel's "historical orientation," in which it saw "the hand of God lying behind events," was the basis of its covenantal self-understanding (Levenson, *Sinai and Zion: An Entry Into the Jewish Bible* [Minneapolis: Winston Press, 1985] 41-42). Levenson does say that, for Israel, the recitation of history is "subordinate" to law, and that it is "prologue" to the enduring "mutual relationship between unequals that is the substance of covenant" (p. 45). But "observance of the Mosaic Torah" as "the vehicle of and the sign of just that relationship" (Levenson) is vastly different from taking Israel's historical orientation, and thus its assertions about God, only as "rhetorical devices to motivate behavior" (so Collins). If the assertions are only rhetorical devices, there is no relationship, and thus no observance—only regulated conduct. The difference is definitive.

64. People of no confession or faith seem not to engage in biblical or OT theology. Some, like Bruno Bauer, lose their faith after engaging in it; others, like G. C. Kaiser, come to faith in the process. It's dangerous business in any event.

65. "Five Loaves and Two Fishes," esp. 288-89. Numbers following in the text refer to pages of Trible's article. I am unsure whether Collins would include "literary analysis" (Trible's term) under historical criticism, or whether the latter has a more limited extension. See Richter's comments on the inadequacy, the imprecision, of the term "historical criticism" (*Literaturwissenschaft*, 17-18).

66. Collins claims that critical Biblical Theology is incompatible with "confessional theology," because the latter "is committed to specific doctrines on the basis of faith." Yet he proposes to accept uncritically a theory of "biblical religion" holding that "myth and cult are supporting devices to regulate the conduct that is at the heart of the religion" ("Critical Biblical Theology," 13, 14). It is not obvious that confessional theology would be less pervious to a critical Biblical Theology than that theory would be. Collins apparently assumes that Biblical Theology could play only a foundational role in relation to confessional theology; in fact, he assigns it a critical role, on the theory that confessional statements are rhetorical devices to motivate behavior. In relation to that theory, his Biblical Theology remains wholly uncritical.

67. "The Historical Jesus and the Theology of the New Testament," in *The Glory of Christ in the New Testament: Studies in Christology*, ed. L. D. Hurst and N. T. Wright (Oxford: Clarendon Press, 1987), 187-206, quoting from 198. Heikki Räisänen refers to similar statements of Morgan's, in *Beyond New Testament Theology* (London: SCM Press, 1991), 76-77. M. H. Goshen-Gottstein makes a similar claim, but more cautiously, in speaking of "Tanakh Theology" ("Tanakh Theology: The Religion of the Old Testament and the Place of Jewish Biblical Theology," *Ancient Israelite Religion: Essays in Honor of Frank Moore Cross*, ed. Patrick D. Miller, Jr., Paul D. Hanson, and S. Dean McBride [Philadelphia: Fortress Press, 1987] 617-44; see esp. 629-30, 640 n. 43).

68. Hermann Diem, *Dogmatics* (Philadelphia: Westminster Press, 1959), 301.

69. Nicholas Lash, "What Might Martyrdom Mean," *Theology on the Way to Emmaus* (London: SCM Press, 1986), 90. Lash's essay, "Performing the Scriptures," in the same volume (37-46), treats this theme more extensively. In both of these eloquent and provocative essays, Lash speaks as if the NT is exhaustive of "the Scriptures."

70. Manfred Oeming, "Unitas Scripturae: Eine Problemskizze," *JBTh* 1 (1986), 48-70, esp. 66-68. I have explored this point further in two essays, "Isaiah's Creation Theology," *Ex Auditu* 3 (1987),

54-71; "We Believe in God . . . Maker of Heaven and Earth: Metaphor, Scripture, and Theology," *HBT* 12 (1990), 64-96.

71. *Real Presences* (Chicago: University of Chicago Press, 1989), 155. Numbers following in the text refer to pages of Steiner's book.

72. I here emphasize this definition of canon, aware that a canon is also susceptible of the definition Steiner gives of a syllabus: it is "established over time . . . , represents cultural, social, pedagogic choices which aim at a more or less stable consensus . . . , is instinct not only with aesthetic but also with political and political-economic motives and valuations" (p. 184). For Steiner, a canon is personal; I have extrapolated to the communal.

73. The kind of relation they can have depends on how biblical and dogmatic (or systematic) theology are conceived; the same is true of OTT. See my essay, "Biblical and Systematic Theology: Constructing a Relationship," *So Wide a Sea,* 111-45. Cf. Claus Westermann, "Das Alte Testament und die Theologie," *Erträge der Forschung am Alten Testament,* 9-26.

74. Wolfhart Pannenberg, *Systematic Theology: Volume 1* (Grand Rapids: Eerdmans, 1991), 16-17.

75. "A Rabbinic Pragmatism," *Theology and Dialogue: Essays in Conversation with George Lindbeck,* ed. Bruce D. Marshall (Notre Dame: University of Notre Dame Press, 1990), 213-48, quoting from 232.

76. See especially vol. 6, *The Old Covenant* (Edinburgh: T & T Clark, 1990).

77. *New Testament Theology,* 95. He makes this comment in response to Ernst Käsemann's claim, which he quotes, that "the history and exegesis of the NT . . . exercise a function in the life of the Church" (p. 94).

5. New Testament Theology

1. Cf. the title of Hanz Conzelmann's collected essays, *Theologie als Schriftauslegung* (Munich: Chr. Kaiser, 1974), and the successive Prefaces of Karl Barth's *The Epistle to the Romans* (2nd ed. 1921; ET, London: Oxford University Press, 1933). Eg., ix: "My sole aim was to interpret Scripture."

2. The best short analysis and critique is James Barr's article "Biblical Theology" in *IDB* Supplement, 104-11. See also Brevard S. Childs, *Biblical Theology in Crisis* (Philadelphia: Westminster Press, 1970).

3. William Wrede, *Über Aufgabe und Methode der sogenannten neutestamentlichen Theologie* (Göttingen: Vandenhoeck & Ruprecht, 1987); reprinted in G. Strecker, ed., *Das Problem der Theologie des Neuen Testaments* (Darmstadt: Wissenschaftliche Buchgesellschaft, 1975); ET in R. Morgan, *The Nature of New Testament Theology* (London: SCM Press, 1973), 68-116.

4. In this key methodological essay of 1925, Bultmann called the discipline "theological exegesis." But he accepted the more usual (though still ambiguous) label NTT. Bultmann's later notion of "preunderstanding" is crucial for the present argument that the characteristic mark of NTT is the interpreter's theological preunderstanding.

5. Rudolf Bultmann, *Theologie des neuen Testaments* (Tübingen: J. C. B. Mohr (Paul Siebeck), 1948-53), 599; ET, *Theology of the New Testament,* 2 vols. (London: SCM Press, 1952–55), 2:251.

6. For example, Hans Conzelmann, *Grundriss der Theologie des Neuen Testaments* (Munich: Chr. Kaiser, 1967; ET, *Outline of the Theology of the New Testament,* New York: Harper & Row, 1969); Karl Hermann Schelkle, *Theologie des Neuen Testaments* (Dusselldorf: Patmos-Verlag, 1968-76, 4 vols., in 5; ET, Collegeville, Minn.: Liturgical Press, 1971-78); Werner G. Kümmel, *Die Theologie des Nenen Testaments nach seiner Hauptzeugen Jesus, Paulus, Johannes* (Göttingen: Vandenhoeck & Ruprecht, 1969; ET, Nashville: Abingdon Press, 1974); George E. Ladd, *A Theology of the New Testament* (Grand Rapids: Eerdmans, 1974); Eduard Lohse, *Umwelt des Neuen Testaments* (Göttingen: Vandenhoeck & Ruprecht, 1974); Leon Goppelt, *Theologie des Neuen Testaments* (Göttingen: Vandenhoeck & Ruprecht, 1975–76; ET, 2 vols., Grand Rapids: Eerdmans, 1981–82); Donald Guthrie, *New Testament Theology* (Downers Grove, Ill.: Inter-Varsity Press, 1981); John Reumann, *Variety and Unity in New Testament Thought* (New York: Oxford University Press, 1991). Cf. Ernst Käsemann, *Der Ruf der Freiheit* (1968, 5th ed. 1972; ET, New York: Oxford University Press, 1969); Luke Timothy Johnson, *The Writings of the New Testament* (Philadelphia: Fortress Press Press, 1986); Eduard Schweizer, *Theologische Einleitung in das Neues Testament* (Göttingen: Vandenhoeck & Ruprecht, 1989; ET, Nashville: Abingdon Press, and London: SPCK, 1991)—which are virtually NTTs. Jeremias called his account of *The Proclamation of Jesus* (New York: Scribner's, 1971) NTT. This can be criticized as a category mistake, but in view of Jeremias's own theology confirms the connection between NTT and the modern scholar's beliefs.

7. Heikki Räisänen, *Beyond New Testament Theology* (London: SCM Press, 1991), xi-xiii.

8. Since Räisänen (p. xviii) acknowledges the necessity of theological or some other type of "critically actualizing" interpretation of exegetes' historical work (!) it might seem odd that he should call his valuable book *Beyond New Testament Theology*. The reason for this loaded phrase appears in his concluding remarks which show (138-41) that he personally wants to move beyond the ecclesial theology of traditional Christianity, on the more enlightened position of a Gordon Kaufman. To his credit that does not distort his excellent presentation of the history of NTT. But a more neutral title might have been "Away from NTT!"

9. See Otto Merk, *Biblische Theologie des Neuen Testaments in ihrer Anfangszeit* (Marburg: Elwert, 1972).

10. J. Gabler, *Oratio de iusto discrimine theologiae biblicae et dogmaticae regundisque recte utriusque finibus* (1787); German translation (1831) reprinted and set in context by Merk and G. Strecker; English translation and commentary in J. Sandys-Wunsch and J. Eldridge, *SJT* 33 (1980), 133-58.

11. Best articulated by Krister Stendahl's article "Biblical Theology, Contemporary," *IDB* 1:418-32; reprinted as "Biblical Theology: A Program," in *Meanings: The Bible as Document and as Guide* (Philadelphia: Fortress Press, 1984), 11-44, and followed by Räisänen. The most sophisticated development is by Klaus Berger, *Hermeneutik des Neuen Testaments* (Gütersloh: Gütersloher Verlagshaus, 1988).

12. Stendahl's essay was directed against the "Biblical Theology Movement" which often did less than justice to the otherness of the text. A far more self-critical use of the conflation model is found in Bultmann and his school. In comparison the two-stagers have (until Berger) paid too little attention to the question of preunderstanding.

13. From the first use of the phrase as the name of a discipline in W. J. Christmann's *Teutsche Biblische Theologie* (1629), through S. Schmidt's *Collegium Biblicum* (1671), down to the survival of this unhistorical proof-text approach in the exegetically responsible Enlightenment theologian G. T. Zachariä, *Biblische Theologie, oder Untersuchung des biblischen Grundes der vornehmsten theologischen Lehren*, 4 vols. (Göttingen, 1771–86). Cf. Gerhard Ebeling "The Meaning of 'Biblical Theology'" in *Word and Faith*, translated by James W. Leitch (Philadelphia: Fortress Press, 1963), 84. Also Hans-Joachim Kraus, *Die Biblische Theologie. Ihre Geschichte und Problematik* (Neukirchen-Vluyn: Neukirchener Verlag, 1970), and all three articles on "Theology" in *The Anchor Bible Dictionary*, 6 vols. (New York: Doubleday, 1992), vol. 6.

14. For example, C. Haymann, *Biblische Theologie* (1708), and A. F. Büsching, *Gedanken von der Beschaffenheit und dem Vorzug der biblische-dogmatischen Theologie vor der alten und neuen scholastischen* (1756).

15. I suggested how this might be done in "The Historical Jesus and NTT," in *The Glory of Christ in the New Testament: Studies in Christology*, ed. L. D. Hurst and N. T. Wright (Oxford: Clarendon Press, 1987), 187-206. In addition to introducing historical information about Jesus and his teaching in a critical presentation of the theology of each evangelist it would be wise to add a historical sketch of Jesus in an appendix, to make clear that the Christ of faith and NTT is none other than the man from Nazareth, crucified and vindicated and become the focus of Christian faith in God. For a more robust approach see Leander E. Keck, *A Future for the Historical Jesus* (Nashville: Abingdon Press, 1971; London: SCM Press, 1982). Also A. Lindemann, "Jesus in der Theologie des Neuen Testaments," in *Jesus Christus in Historie und Theologie*, ed. Georg Strecker (Tübingen: J. C. B. Mohr [Paul Siebeck], 1975), 27-57.

16. As Bultmann recognized in "Zur Geschichte der Paulus-Forschung," *Theologische Rundschau* N.F. 1 (1929). Reprinted in K. H. Rengstorf, ed., *Das Paulusbild in der neueren deutschen Forschung* (Darmstadt: Wissenschaftliche Buchgesellschaft, 1964). See Baur's *Paulus* (1845; ET, 1875); *Die kanonischen Evangelien* (1847; reprinted Aalen, 1988), *Vorlesungen über neutestamentliche Theologie*, ed. F. F. Baur (1864; reprinted Darmstadt: Wissenschaftliche Bushgesellschaft, 1973).

17. His idealist interpretation of Spirit in Paul was falsified by Gunkel in 1888, and his Kantian view of Jesus' teaching by J. Weiss in 1892.

18. As Bultmann insisted against Barth in his review of the latter's *Römerbrief* (2nd ed.) in *Christliche Welt* 26 (1922). Reprinted by Jürgen Moltmann, ed., *Anfänge der dialektischen Theologie* (Munich: Chr. Kaiser Verlag, 1966); ET in James M. Robinson, ed., *The Beginnings of Dialectical Theology* (Richmond: John Knox Press, 1968). See the continuing conversation in Barth's Preface to the third edition (1922) and Bultmann's essay on "Karl Barth, *The Resurrection of the Dead*" (1926) in *Faith and Understanding* I (London: SCM Press, 1969).

19. It might be thought tasteless. Alan Richardson was much mocked for calling Bultmann's NTT "heretical" in *An Introduction to the Theology of the New Testament* (London: SCM Press, 1958),

14. The judgment may have been mistaken, but it credits Bultmann with writing confessional theology, not merely theological scholarship or history of ideas.

20. Not entirely, as Conzelmann, *An Outline of the Theology of the New Testament* (London: SCM Press, 1969), xvi, observed. Placing "The development towards the early church" *after* the Johannine theology is said to reflect the Protestant theory of decline into Catholicism. But the Fourth Gospel may not have been the fourth.

21. In the Foreword to his second edition of the *Lehrbuch* (1911), vol. 1, x-xii.

22. Gerd Theissen, *Psychological Aspects of Pauline Theology* (Philadelphia: Fortress Press, 1987), is thus far more persuasive than the old psychologizing accounts of Paul's conversion. L. T. Johnson, *The Writings of the New Testament* also shows the theological and hermeneutical value of such a conceptuality.

23. Cf. C. A. Bernoulli, *Die wissenschaftliche und die kirchliche Methode in der Theologie* (Tübingen: J. C. B. Mohr [Paul Siebeck], 1897) and Troeltsch's sense of its importance (*GGA* 1898).

24. Bornkamm, *Jesus of Nazareth* (ET, London: SCM Press, 1961), 21.

25. See David Way, *The Lordship of Christ* (Oxford: Clarendon Press, 1991).

26. Like Schlatter he interpreted most of the NT theologically, but his interpretation of what he dubbed "early catholicism" was as critical as his interpretation of the Fourth Gospel. His own standing ground, or "canon within the canon" was Paul, understood as insisting on the "justification of the ungodly."

27. E. P. Sanders, *Paul and Palestinian Judaism* (Philadelphia: Fortress Press, 1977), marks a watershed. See also Heikki Räisänen, *Paul and the Law* (Tübingen: J. C. B. Mohr [Paul Siebeck], 1983; 2nd ed. 1987), and Francis Watson, *Paul, Judaism and the Gentiles* (Cambridge: Cambridge University Press, 1986). Neil Elliott, *The Rhetoric of Romans*, JSNTSup 45 (Sheffield: Sheffield Academic Press, 1990), takes the discussion in other new directions.

28. For example, Friedrich Buchsel, *Theologie des Neuen Testaments* (Gutersloh: C. Bertelsmann, 1935); Ethelbert Stauffer, *Die Theologie des Neuen Testaments* (Gutersloh: C. Bertelsmann, 1941; ET, New York: Macmillan, 1955); Martin Albertz, *Die Kirche Jesu Christi und ihre dienst nach dem Neuen Testament* (Berlin: Haus und Schule, 1949–57); Frederick C. Grant, *An Introduction to New Testament Thought* (New York: Abingdon-Cokesbury Press, 1950); Max Meinertz, *Theologie des Neuen Testaments* (Bonn: Hanstein, 1950); J. Bonsirven, *Theologie du Novean Testament* (Paris: Aubier, 1951; ET, Westminster, MD: Newman Press, 1963); Oscar Cullmann, *Heil as Geschichte: heilsgeschichtliche Existenz im Neuen Testament* (Tübingen: J. C. B. Mohr [Paul Siebeck],1965; ET, *Salvation in History*, New York: Harper & Row, 1967).

29. Käsemann emphasizes this ecclesial aim in "The Problem of a NTT," *NTS* 19 (1972–74), 235-45, which the present essay follows, while recognizing the legitimacy of nontheological interests in the NT. M. G. Brett, *Biblical Criticism in Crisis* (Cambridge: Cambridge University Press, 1991), stresses this interpretative pluralism.

30. This approach was developed further by H. Schlier in *Grundzüge einer paulinischen Theologie* (Freiburg: Herder, 1978), 9-24, but has not been followed. Kümmel's title, *The Theology of the New Testament According to Its Major Witnesses; Jesus-Paul-John,* is less illuminating.

31. As Nils A. Dahl noted in is brilliant review article in *Theologische Rundschau* 22 (1954); ET in *The Crucified Messiah* (Minneapolis: Augsburg, 1974), 112.

32. The ecclesial context of theology and hence NTT has to be understood quite loosely in a largely post-Christian culture. The boundaries are blurred, even in academic theology, and judgments about the faith of individuals would be impertinent as well as irrelevant. All that is needed to write theology and NTT is an intention to speak of God from the standpoint of some religious tradition and community. To call this "confessional" sounds too committed; to call it merely "hypothetical" sounds frivolous.

33. The phrase "canon within a canon" refers to a negative criterion found within the wider canon of scripture.

34. Barth sensed a whiff of this in his recovery of Luther's Pauline interpretation (*Romans,* 13) and Käsemann was willing to "break a lance" for Marcion in *Das Neue Testament als Kanon* (Göttingen: Vandenhoeck & Ruprecht, 1970), 355-56, 408-9. Bultmann's lack of positive theological apprecia-tion for the OT is notorious, as were Schleiermacher's and Harnack's.

35. Thus Georg Strecker, *Das Problem der Theologie des Neuen Testaments* (Darmstadt: Wissen-schaftliche Buchgesellschaft, 1975), 29, thinks a NTT should begin with Paul. This priority follows from his historical position and theological weight, but it also happens to suit the supposed correspondence of his theology with Lutheranism. The idea of shaping NTT purely from a historical perspective thus looks like a Lutheran bombshell, now defused by a more accurate understanding of Paul.

36. By assigning vol. 1 to *Die Geschichte des Christus* and including Paul in vol. 2, *Die Theologie der Apostel*. A similar disposition of the material was normal in the nineteenth century and is followed by Goppelt. It was only within Bultmann's sphere of influence that historical models reflecting Luther's theology became prominent.

37. Cf. Hayden White, *Metahistory* (Baltimore: Johns Hopkins University Press, 1973) and several works of Paul Ricoeur.

38. Notably on the historical Jesus, but cf. also Käsemann on John.

39. Cf. James D. G. Dunn, *Unity and Diversity in the New Testament: An Enquiry in to the Character of Earliest Christianity* (Philadelphia: Westminster Press, 1977); *Jahrbuch für Biblische Theologie* I: *Einheit und Vielfalt Biblischer Theologie* (Neukirchen: Neukirchener Verlag, 1986); John Reumann, *Variety and Unity*.

40. So Bultmann, *Faith and Understanding* (London: SCM Press, 1969), 86, 93, 280-81.

41. See H. Clavier, *Les Variétés de la Pensée Biblique et le Problème de son Unité* (Leiden: E. J. Brill, 1976); G. F. Hasel, *New Testament Theology: Basic Issues in the Current Debate* (Grand Rapids: Eerdmans, 1982); Henning Graf Reventlow, *Problems of Biblical Theology in the Twentieth Century* (Darmstadt: Wissenschaftliche Buchgesellschaft, 1983; ET, Philadelphia: Fortress Press, 1986).

42. This is recognized by Hans Hübner's return to the old title in his *Biblische Theologie des Neuen Testaments, I: Prolegomena* (Göttingen: Vandenhoeck & Ruprecht, 1990), and F. Mildenberger's return to De Wett's title (1813), in his *Biblische Dogmatik: Eine Biblische Theologie in dogmatischer Perspektive, I: Prolegomena* (Stuttgart: W. Kohlhammer, 1991). See also Merk, *Biblische Theologie des Neuen Testaments*, and "Biblische Theologie II Neues Testament," *TRE* 6 (1980), 455-77.

6. Historical-Critical Method, Theology, and Contemporary Exegesis

1. One may gain an interesting insight into this debate by comparing Brevard Childs's "Interpretation in Faith: The Theological Responsibility of an Old Testament Commentary," *Int* 18 (1964), 432-49, with James Barr's "Exegesis as a Theological Discipline Reconsidered and the Shadow of the Jesus of History," *The Hermeneutical Quest: Essays in Honor of James Luther Mays on His Sixty-fifth Birthday*, ed. Donald G. Miller (Allison Park, Pa.: Pickwick Publications, 1986), 11-45.

2. "Scripture, Consensus, and Community," *The World: A Journal of Religion and Public Life* 23/4 (1988), 16.

3. Ibid., 5-6.

4. A critique of this method has been a persistent theme in his work throughout his career. See his comments, for example in "Interpretation in Faith: The Theological Responsibility of an Old Testament Commentary," *Int* 18 (1964), 432-49; *Biblical Theology in Crisis* (Philadelphia: Westminster Press, 1970), 141-42; *The Book of Exodus: A Critical, Theological Commentary* (OTL; Philadelphia: Westminster Press, 1974), xiii-xvi; *Introduction to the Old Testament as Scripture* (Philadelphia: Fortress Press, 1979), 39-41; *The New Testament as Canon: An Introduction* (Philadelphia: Fortress Press, 1984); and *Old Testament Theology in a Canonical Context* (Philadelphia: Fortress Press, 1985), 17. Moreover, these major works represent only a partial sampling of what Childs has written on this topic, as one can easily see from his bibliography published in *Canon, Theology, and Old Testament Interpretation: Essays in Honor of Brevard S. Childs*, ed. Gene M. Tucker, David L. Petersen, and Robert R. Wilson (Philadelphia: Fortress Press, 1988), 329-36.

5. Though addressing broader issues, James Barr has offered a trenchant critique of both Childs's negative theological assessment of the traditional historical-critical approach and of the theological value of Childs's own canonical approach. See Barr's "Exegesis as a Theological Discipline Reconsidered and the Shadow of the Jesus of History," 11-45; and his "The Theological Case Against Biblical Theology," *Canon, Theology and Old Testament Interpretation*, ed. Gene M. Tucker, David L. Petersen, and Robert R. Wilson (Philadelphia: Fortress Press, 1988), 3-19.

6. *From Sacred Story to Sacred Text: Canon as Paradigm* (Philadelphia: Fortress Press, 1987), 78-79. Barr's scathing review of this volume in *Critical Review of Books in Religion 1988: A Cooperative Venture of the Journal of the American Academy of Religion and the Journal of Biblical Literature*, ed. Beverly Roberts Gaventa, 137-41, is worth noting, particularly his comments on 139: "Able as Sanders may be in telling us what he thinks, nothing that he says about other people's thoughts or about trends in scholarship can be relied on. And this is no incidental remark, but bears upon the whole validity of the canonical criticism movement: its most powerful arguments, as I have said elsewhere, consisted in attacks on the faults of previous scholarship; and, if previous scholarship is as badly

misrepresented as it is in this volume, then the entire case for canonical criticism becomes all the weaker."

7. Walter Wink, *Transformation: Toward a New Paradigm for Biblical Study* (Philadelphia: Fortress Press, 1973), 1, 4, 15.

8. This has been a recurring theme among adherents of a literary approach to the Bible, and, at least in the form presented by Hans Frei, *The Eclipse of Biblical Narrative: A Study in Eighteenth and Nineteenth-Century Hermeneutics* (New Haven: Yale University Press, 1974), has exercised a major influence on "Narrative Theology."

9. "Scripture, Consensus, and Community," *This World: A Journal of Religion and Public Life* 23/4 (1988), 5-24. Fuller documentation of his views expressed here may be found in his book, *The Nature of Doctrine* (Philadelphia: Westminster Press, 1984).

10. Ibid., 6.

11. Lindbeck, "Scripture, Consensus, and Community," 7. According to Childs, "The term 'canonical text' denotes that official Hebrew text of the Jewish community which had reached a point of stabilization in the first century AD, thus all but ending its long history of fluidity" (*Introduction to the Old Testament as Scripture*, 100). Thus "the Masoretic text is not identical with the canonical text, but is only a vehicle for its recovery" (ibid.). In fact, "there is no extant canonical text" (ibid.). All that Childs means by these reservations, however, is that one must make some very minor textual corrections to the Masoretic text in order to recover the canonical text.

12. Childs's attempt to deal with this difficulty (*Introduction to the Old Testament as Scripture*, 659-71), can hardly be considered adequate. Cf. James Barr's critique in "Childs' Introduction to the Old Testament as Scripture," *JSOT* 16 (1980), 12-23.

13. "Scripture, Consensus, and Community," 7.

14. Barr points out how little is actually known about the community of the time of the canonizers and how in Childs's work that community may amount to no more than "an imaginative construct formed out of his (Childs's) own ideas about the centrality of canon" (*JSOT* 16 [1980] 21).

15. "Scripture, Consensus, and Community," 7.

16. Claus Westermann, following Gerhard von Rad, tried to construe OTT in historical categories, but he had to admit that Wisdom simply had no place in this schema (*Theologie des Alten Testaments in Grundzügen* [Göttingen: Vandenhoeck & Ruprecht, 1978] 7). The "historical" construal of much of the other nonnarrative OT literature in his outline also seems forced, and a simple switch from "history" to "narrative" as the controlling category will not ease this fit in the slightest.

17. *Introduction to the Old Testament as Scripture*, 325.

18. Cf. Barr's comment: "Canon, meaning recognition as regulative scripture, may have conflicted with canonical form, in the sense of the guidance given by the total literary form of a work; for fixation as scripture could mean, and probably often did mean, that the sense for the total literary form was lost and meaning was seen in individual word-groups and locutions. The sense for the total literary form of a text was there in central OT times, and we have it also in modern times; it is not so certain that it was there in the late canonizing and supposedly canonically guided community" (*JSOT* 16 [1980] 18).

Even for the central OT times the possibility must remain open that the total literary form of some works suggested to the competent reader that he or she was dealing with a mere collection of discrete units more or less haphazardly arranged.

19. For a fuller discussion of these glosses see my commentary, *Nahum, Habakkuk, and Zephaniah: A Commentary* (OTL; Louisville, Ky.: Westminster/John Knox Press, 1991), 115-17. Such glosses correspond to what Barr calls "anti-hermeneutic" changes in the text (*JSOT* 16 [1980] 18).

20. E. A. Speiser, *Genesis* (AB 1; Garden City, N.Y.: Doubleday, 1964), 91-94.

21. Harry L Eichler, "Another Look at Nuzi Sisterhood Contracts," *Essays on the Ancient Near East in Memory of Jacob Joel Finkelstein*, ed. Maria de Jong Ellis, Memoirs of the Connecticut Academy of Arts and Sciences, 19 (Hamden, Conn.: Archon Books, 1977), 45-59; A. Skaist, "The Authority of the Brother at Arrapha and Nuzi," *JAOS* 89 (1969), 10-17.

22. On this point Childs is also quite critical of Lindbeck's program, *The New Testament as Canon: An Introduction*, 545.

23. For a detailed discussion of this point, see my article, "Isaiah and His Children" *Biblical and Related Studies Presented to Samuel Iwry*, ed. Ann Kort and Scott Morshauser (Winona Lake, Ind.: Eisenbrauns, 1985), 193-203, especially 200-1.

24. Barr, "Exegesis as a Theological Discipline Reconsidered and the Shadow of the Jesus of History," *The Hermeneutical Quest: Essays in Honor of James Luther Mays on His Sixty-fifth Birthday,* ed. Donald G. Miller (Allison Park, Pa.: Pickwick Publications, 1986), 22-23. Note also his elaboration of this point on 23-24: "In other words, the apparent reluctance of the commentary to address directly the theological and ethical questions of the present day is not necessarily a fault; nor is it a consequence of a "historical" orientation that refuses to face modern problems. It is, on the contrary, a decision perfectly seriously grounded in theological principle, in the fact that theological consequence does not follow directly from the text itself but only from its interaction with other texts and with pre-existing theological tradition. Since the nature of that tradition is highly variable, it is a perfectly responsible theological decision that the commentary cannot handle all the possibilities of theological consequence but must concentrate on providing and discussing the evidence of the text itself, within its own environment, the impact of which evidence upon the theological assumptions forms the core of theological exegesis."

7. Standing on God's Promises

1. J. Christiaan Beker, "Paul's Letter to the Romans as Model for a Biblical Theology: Some Preliminary Observations," in *Understanding the Word: Essays in Honor of Bernhard W. Anderson,* ed. James T. Butler, Edgar W. Conrad, and Ben C. Ollenburger, JSOTSup 37 (Sheffield: JSOT Press, 1985), 359-67.

2. See further my essay, "Abraham, the Friend of God," *Interpretation* 42 (1988), 353-66.

3. Here the use of "nation" *(goy)* instead of "people" *('am)* may reflect the nationalism of the Davidic era, when this story was given written form.

4. Hans Walter Wolff, "The Kerygma of the Yahwist," in *The Vitality of Old Testament Traditions,* ed. Walter Brueggemann and H. W. Wolff (Atlanta: John Knox Press, 1975), 49-50.

5. For an illuminating discussion of Paul's use of this passage, along with Hab 2:4, see the essay by J. C. Beker, cited in note 1.

6. Moshe Weinfeld, "The Covenant of Grant in the Old Testament and in the Ancient Near East," *JAOS* 90 (1970), 184-203.

7. Wendell Berry, *The Gift of Good Land: Further Essays Cultural and Agricultural* (San Francisco: North Point Press, 1982), 167-281.

8. Ibid., 169.

9. Ibid., 170.

10. See H. L. Strack and Billerbeck, *Kommentar zum Neuen Testament aus Talmud und Midrasch,* vol. 3 (Munich, 1926), 209. This view is based, for instance, on an interpretation of Gen 14:19-20. Taking the verb *qānā* to mean "acquire" rather than "create," Abraham is blessed by God, the Possessor of heaven and earth, the upper and lower spheres of the cosmos. Another rabbinical view is based on Gen 28:14, where it is said that the promise to Jacob—that his descendants will spread out to the four compass points—will be fulfilled in the days of the Messiah.

11. Rosemary Radford Ruether, *Gaia & God: An Ecofeminist Theology of Earth Healing* (San Francisco: Harper, 1992), 215.

8. Creation and Covenant

1. Gen 14:19, 22; Pss 115:15; 121:2; 124:8; 134:3. Cf. the many instances where the verbs *qānā* and *'āsa* are used with other particular aspects of Yahweh's creations. The participle *bōrē'*), "Creator" is not used in this particular construction, but it appears in similar formulations referring to God as creator of the earth or the heavens (Isa 40:18; 42:5; 45:18; 65:17). On extrabiblical references to God as creator of the earth *(qōnēh 'ares),* see D. Miller, "El, The Creator of Earth," *Bulletin of the American Schools of Oriental Research* 239 (1980), 43-46.

2. Deut 7:9; 1 Kgs 8:23 (=2 Chr 6:14); Dan 9:4; Neh 1:5; 9:32, cf. Deut 7:12.

3. The development of federal theology out of Reformation thought has been described in detail recently by D. A. Weir, *The Origins of the Federal Theology in Sixteenth-Century Reformation Thought* (Oxford: Clarendon Press, 1990).

4. Robert C. Dentan, *Preface to Old Testament Theology* (New York: Seabury Press, 1963), 16.

5. Hans Frei, *The Eclipse of Biblical Narrative* (New Haven: Yale University Press, 1974), 46.

6. W. Eichrodt, *Theology of the Old Testament,* 2 vols. (Philadelphia: Westminster Press, 1961-67).

7. Eichrodt, *Theology of the Old Testament*, vol. 1, 14.

8. G. E. Wright, *God Who Acts: Biblical Theology as Recital*, "Studies in Biblical Theology," 8 (London: SCM Press, 1952), 55.

9. Ibid., 103.

10. L. Perlitt, *Bundestheologie im Alten Testament*, WMANT, 36 (Neukirchen-Vluyn: Neukirchener Verlag, 1969).

11. For a review of these works, see R. A. Oden, Jr. "The Place of Covenant in the Religion of Israel," *AIR*, 429-47. Cf. Miller, "Israelite Religion," *The Hebrew Bible and Its Modern Interpreters*, ed. by Douglas A. Knight and Gene M. Tucker (Philadelphia: Fortress Press, 1985), 222-23.

12. W. Zimmerli, "The Place and Limit of the Wisdom in the Framework of the Old Testament Theology," *Studies in Ancient Israelite Wisdom*, ed. J. Crenshaw (New York: KTAV, 1976), 314-26. For further elaboration of this thesis, see H.-J. Hermisson, "Observations on the Creation Theology in Wisdom," *Israelite Wisdom*, ed. J. G. Gammie, W. A. Brueggemann, W. L. Humphreys, J. M. Ward (Missoula, Mont.: Scholars Press, 1978), 43-57 [reprinted in *Creation in the Old Testament*, ed. B. W. Anderson (Philadelphia: Fortress Press, 1984), 118-34].

13. In *Creation in the Old Testament*, ed. B. W. Anderson, 102-17. This essay appeared in its longer original form as "Schopfung, Gerechtigkeit und Heil," *ZTK*, 70 (1973), 1-19.

14. G. von Rad, "The Theological Problem of the Doctrine of Creation," *The Problem of the Hexateuch and Other Essays* (New York: McGraw-Hill, 1966), 131-43.

15. Ibid., 111.

16. W. Brueggemann, "A Shape for Old Testament Theology, I: Structure Legitimation," *CBQ*, 47 (1985), 40 [reprinted in W. Brueggemann, *Old Testament Theology: Essays on Structure, Theme, and Text* (Minneapolis: Fortress Press, 1992), p. 15].

17. Ibid., 41 [*Old Testament Theology*, 16].

18. Ibid., 36-42. See his comment on 42: "Creation theology readily becomes imperial propaganda and ideology" [*Old Testament Theology*, 16].

19. "A Shape for Old Testament Theology II: Embrace of Pain," *CBQ*, 47 (1985), 398 [reprinted in W. Brueggemann, *Old Testament Theology*, 25].

20. J. Levenson, *Creation and the Persistence of Evil: The Jewish Drama of Divine Omnipotence* (San Francisco: Harper & Row, 1988), 135.

21. In *Creation and the Persistence of Evil*, 135, Levenson expresses these variant forms of a single ideal as follows: "As persuasive as the treaty analogy is, it should be noted that much the same pattern can be detected in mythic literature, such as the *Enuma elish* and its Canaanite and Israelite parallels: the gods willingly and gladly accept the kingship of their heroic savior, grant him the right to determine the destinies, and redefine themselves as his servitors. It is this act of voluntary heteronomy that, by establishing his kingship and ensuring their survival, works to the benefit of both lord and liege. There is, of course, a vast formal difference between the covenant and the combat myth. The first originates in the world of diplomacy, the second in cult. But when the language of diplomacy is transposed into theology, YHWH replacing the emperor, and the language of cult is substantially historicized, people (largely) replacing gods, the convergence is remarkable."

22. Ibid., 135-36.

23. F. M. Cross, *Canaanite Myth and Hebrew Epic: Essays in the History of the Religion of Israel* (Cambridge, Mass.: Harvard University Press, 1973), 3-75.

24. On the epithet of "creator of (heaven) and earth" see D. Miller, "El, The Creator of Earth." An eighth-century inscription has been found in Jerusalem with the words [ ] *qn rs*, probably to be translated "[El] creator of earth." It is not surprising that such an epithet, which surely in this time was applied to Yahweh, should be found in Jerusalem where Genesis 14 also seems to locate it.

25. See Cross, *Canaanite Myth and Hebrew Epic*, 28, n. 84 and 39. Cross reads "god of the covenant," but "El of the covenant" is more likely inasmuch as this is a hymn to El. Linguistically, either reading is possible.

26. Ibid., 60-75.

27. Exodus 15:16 ("until the people whom you created pass by"); Deut 32:15-18.

28. Cross, *CMHE*, 89-90.

29. R. Rendtorff, " 'Wo warst du, als ich die Erde gründete,' Schöpfung und Heilsgeschichte," and " 'Bund' als Strukturkonzept in Genesis und Exodus," *Kanon und Theologie: Vorarbeiten zu einer Theologie des Alten Testaments* (Neukirchen-Vluyn: Neukirchener Verlag, 1991), 94-112 and 123-31. [ET " 'Where Were You When I Laid the Foundation of the Earth?' Creation and Salvation History," and " 'Covenant' as a Structuring Concept in Genesis and Exodus," *Canon and Theology: Overtures*

to an Old Testament Theology, OBT (Minneapolis: Fortress Press, 1993), 92-113, 125-34.] The second essay appeared first in English as " 'Covenant' as a Structuring Concept in Genesis and Exodus," *JBL,* 108 (1989), 385-93. Reference here is to the earlier English form of the essay.

30. " 'Covenant' as a Structuring Concept," 386.

31. Referring to Childs, Rendtorff (" 'Covenant' as a Structuring Concept," 386) says at the beginning: "Indeed, 'the witness of the whole,' that is, the text as we have it before us, in my view, should be the first and main subject of our theological interpretation of the Hebrew Bible."

32. See his essay "Theologie des Alten Testaments: Uberlegungen zu einem Neuansatz," *Kanon und Theologie,* 9-12. [ET, "Old Testament Theology: Some Ideas for a New Approach" in *Canon and Theology,* 10-16.] Rendtorff regards Childs's own OTT as more "systematic" than "canonical," presumably because of his ignoring of the canonical structure of the OT in his organization.

33. " 'Wo warst du . . . ,' " 109 [*Canon and Theology,* 109].

34. " 'Covenant' as a Structuring Concept," 393.

35. " 'Wo warst du . . . ,' " 108-9 [*Canon and Theology,* 108-9].

36. Ibid.

37. Similar notes are sounded in Jer 5:21-25 where the astonishing assertion is made that Israel's sin disturbs the very order of creation, and in 14:19-22 the direct connection of remembering the covenant and reference to rain that only God can bring shows again how the Noah covenant is foundational for the relation between God and Israel (" 'Wo warst du . . . ',"110-11 [*Canon and Theology,* 110-12]).

38. "Of course, a number of diachronic problems remain. Nevertheless, the meaning of the composition we have before us is clear" (" 'Covenant' as a Structuring Concept," 389; cf. n. 11).

39. E.g., B. W. Anderson, *Creation Versus Chaos,* 2nd ed. (Philadelphia: Fortress Press, 1987), 43-77, a work for which Brueggemann wrote the Foreword and which probably has exercised some influence on his own thinking on this topic; and W. J. Dumbrell, *Covenant and Creation* (Nashville: Thomas Nelson Publishers, 1984).

Most recently Terence Fretheim has written a commentary on the book of Exodus in which he has vigorously pursued the thesis that it "is shaped in a decisive way by a creation theology." God's work in creation, he claims, "provides the basic categories and interpretive clues for what happens in redemption and related divine activity." He sets this forth in four points:

1. A creation theology provides the *cosmic purpose* behind God's redemptive activity on Israel's behalf.

2. God's redemptive activity is set in terms of a *creational need.*

3. God's redemptive activity is *cosmic in its effects.*

4. God's calling of Israel is given *creation-wide scope.*

Exodus (Interpretation; Louisville: John Knox Press, 1991), 13-14.

40. "The Redemption of Nature," *Princeton Theological Seminary Bulletin,* 10 (1989), 94.

41. Ibid., 96.

42. Brueggemann, "Trajectories," 184. He sees an inherent social conservatism in process theology.

43. von Rad, "The Theological Problem of the Doctrine of Creation." While the essay was originally published in Germany in 1936, it was given as a paper at the OT international congress in Germany in 1935. See Rendtorff, " 'Wo warst du . . . ,' " 95.

44. Barth set forth his own perspective on this matter in his *Church Dogmatics,* (Edinburgh: T & T Clark), esp. paragraphs 41 (vol. 3/1), 45 (vol. 3/2), and 48 (vol. 3/3). E. David Willis-Watkins has summarized his position as follows: "Barth argues that covenant is the presupposition of creation. Out of God's boundless love, God wills to be for another and to give another life-in-relation. Out of nothing except this unbounded gracious love, God created for this relationship. The creation sagas in Genesis are taken over from common creation myths and rewritten to make one central thing clear: this is how the God whom we have experienced as deliverer and covenant maker went about creating. The reworked creation stories, and the narratives of deliverance and successive covenants, are primarily proclamations of who God is and who therefore we are to be as a people. Belonging to this God means that we, too, share in his own ongoing purposive activity in (and often over against) unfolding events. The courses of events, like the hills and trees and luminaries, are there to testify to the steadfast love of this particular—the one true and living—God." ("Creation and Human Creativity," *The Princeton Seminary Bulletin,* 10 [1989], 106-7.)

45. "Against the attempts of this time to amalgamate theology and church with National Socialist ideology over the 'creation,' von Rad denied to 'Old Testament creation faith' any autonomy and consequently subordinated it to 'election faith.' That move had its justification at that time; it was a matter of securing and holding firm the center of faith, that for neither Israel nor the church had this been 'creation.' " R. Albertz, *Weltschöpfung und Menschenschöpfung. Untersucht bei Deuterojesaja, Hiob, und in den Psalmen* (Stuttgart: Calwer Verlag, 1974), 174 (The passage is quoted in Rendtorff, " 'Wo warst du . . . ,' " 97 [*Canon and Theology*, 95-96]).

46. See the language of Gen 1:28 reflected several times in Exodus 1 and the summary statement of T. Fretheim: "God's redemptive activity is set in terms of a *creational need*. The fulfillment of God's creational purposes in the growth of Israel is endangered by Pharaoh's attempted subversion thereof. If Pharaoh succeeds in his antilife purposes at that point at which God has begun to actualize the promise of creation (1:7-14), then God's purposes in creation are subverted and God's creational mission will not be able to be realized. God's work in redemption, climaxing in Israel's crossing of the sea on 'dry land,' constitutes God's efforts at re-creation, returning creation to a point where God's mission can once again be taken up." (*Exodus* [Interpretation; Louisville: John Knox Press, 1991], 13.)

47. See his *Sinai and Zion* (San Francisco: Harper & Row, 1987). In the more recent study, *Creation and the Persistence of Evil*, 10-13, Levenson has some suggestive comments on the Noachic covenant.

48. The terminology "all flesh" (Gen 6:12, 13, 17, 19; 7:15, 16, 21; 8:17; 9:11, 15, 16, 17) and "living creature" (Gen 9:10, 12, 15, 16; cf. 1:20 and 2:19) in the Flood story refer to both human and animal life.

49. Rendtorff, " 'Wo warst du . . . ,' " 111 [*Canon and Theology*, 112]. I have expanded on his point to some degree.

50. See Job 38:8-11; 41:1-8 [Heb 40:25-32]; and Ps 104:6-9.

51. Levenson, *Creation*, 17.

52. Cf. Deut 32:8-9.

53. *Genesis 12-50: Regenerating the Generations of Heaven and Earth* (International Theological Commentary; Grand Rapids: Eerdmans), in press. Janzen points out.how the blessings to Abraham, "[I] will make you exceedingly numerous" (or "multiply you exceedingly"—v. 2), and "I will make you exceedingly fruitful" (v. 6), and the blessing to Sarah, "I will bless her . . . I will bless her" (v. 16) are all brought together—echoing the priestly blessing of Gen 1:28a—in the blessing to Ishmael, to which is added the echo of the promise to Abraham in Gen 12:2: "I will make [him] a great nation."

54. See Exod 33:9–34:10; Neh 9:17, 31-32; Ps 103:8,18, and *passim;* 111:4-5; Ps 145:8, which makes it clear that this covenantal character is "over all that he has made." Cf. Isa 54:1-10 with its climactic promise of a covenant of peace and its *Leitwort* of "compassion," *(rhm)*. On the use of forms of *rhm* in the exilic period, see W. Brueggemann, "At the Mercy of Babylon: A Subversive Rereading of the Empire," *JBL*, 110 (1991), 3-22 [reprinted in W. Brueggemann, *A Social Reading of the Old Testament: Prophetic Approaches to Israel's Communal Life*, ed. P. D. Miller (Minneapolis: Fortress Press, 1994), 111-33].

55. So the covenant of peace in Ezek 24:25-31; 37:24-28.

56. See J. L. Mays, *Amos* (The Old Testament Library; Philadelphia: Westminster Press, 1969).

9. A Shattered Transcendence?

1. J. Maxwell Miller and John H. Hayes (*A History of Ancient Israel and Judah* [Philadelphia: Westminster Press, 1986], 416) write: "The fall of the city and the exile of its citizens marked a watershed in Judean history and have left fissure marks radiating throughout the Hebrew Scriptures. The 'day of judgment' heralded in prophetic announcements had not just dawned, it had burst on Judah with immense ferocity."

2. See the data summarized by Miller and Hayes, *A History of Ancient Israel and Judah*, 416-36, and John Bright, *A History of Israel* (Philadelphia: Westminster Press, 1981), 343-72.

3. Daniel L. Smith, *The Religion of the Landless: The Social Context of the Babylonian Exile* (Bloomington: Meyer Stone, 1989).

4. See Jacob Neusner, *Understanding Seeking Faith: Essays on the Case of Judaism* (Atlanta: Scholars Press, 1986), 137-41 and *passim*, and Paul Joyce, *Divine Initiative and Human Response in Ezekiel* (JSOTSup 51; Sheffield: JSOT Press, 1989), 12-17.

5. See the analysis of Richard Elliott Friedman, *The Exile and Biblical Narrative* (Chico, Calif.: Scholars Press, 1981) on the two great narrative responses to the crisis of exile.

6. See Peter R. Ackroyd, *Exile and Restoration* (OTL; Philadelphia: Westminster Press, 1968), Ralph W. Klein, *Israel in Exile* (OBT; Philadelphia: Fortress Press, 1979), Enno Janssen, *Juda in der Exilszeit* (Göttingen: Vandenhoeck and Ruprecht, 1956), and Paul Joyce, *Divine Initiative and Human Response in Ezekiel.*

7. The reality of exile may have led some to despair, but not in the community that generated the text. Elaine Scarry, *The Body in Pain: The Making and Unmaking of the World* (New York: Oxford University Press, 1985) has shown how speech counters the dismantling of personhood. In parallel fashion I submit that text counters despair, both as text-making and text-reading. The exilic community was intensely engaged in text-making and text-reading as a counter to despair.

8. I take this to be a widely accepted judgment. James Sanders, *Torah and Canon* (Philadelphia: Fortress Press, 1972) has argued this case effectively. Canon criticism, he writes, "begins with questions concerning the function of those ancient traditions which were viable in the crucifixion-resurrection experience of the sixth and fifth centuries B.C. and which provided the vehicle for Judaism's birth out of the ashes of what had been. . . . But if one's interest is rather in the actual history of how the Bible came to be, what events gave rise to the collecting of the materials actually inherited, and why these traditions were chosen and not others, then two main historical watersheds impose themselves. The Bible comes to us out of the ashes of two Temples, the First or Solomonic Temple, destroyed in 586 B.C., and the Second or Herodian Temple, destroyed in A.D. 70" (pp. xix, 6). See the discerning statement by Donn F. Morgan (*Between Text and Community: The "Writings" on Canonical Interpretation* [Minneapolis: Fortress Press, 1990]) on the canonical power of the exilic experience.

9. This is the essential dynamic of von Rad's two volume OTT. See Gerhard von Rad, *Old Testament Theology II* (New York: Harper & Row, 1965), 263-77 and *passim*, and Paul D. Hanson, "Israelite Religion in the Early Postexilic Period," *Ancient Israelite Religion* ed. Patrick D. Miller, Jr., et al. (Philadelphia: Fortress Press, 1987), 485-508.

10. For a careful review and assessment of the contribution of Wellhausen and his dominant paradigm, see the essays in Douglas A. Knight, ed., *Julius Wellhausen and His Prolegomena to the History of Israel Semeia* 25 (1983).

11. It should be possible to acknowledge some crucial discontinuity between ancient Israel and emergent Judaism without a judgment of inferiority. But to assert discontinuity without "bootleg-ging" inferiority requires an important break with the assumptions of the Wellhausen paradigm. Hanson, "Israelite Religion in the Early Postexilic Period," has enunciated the discontinuity without suggesting inferiority.

12. Peter R. Ackroyd, *Continuity: A Contribution to the Study of the Old Testament Religious Tradition* (Oxford: Basil Blackwell, 1962) reprinted in *Studies in the Religious Tradition of the Old Testament* (London: SCM Press, 1987), 3-16; "Continuity and Discontinuity: Rehabilitation and Authentica-tion," *Tradition and Theology in the Old Testament,* ed. Douglas A. Knight (Philadelphia: Fortress Press, 1977), 215-34, reprinted in *Studies in the Religious Traditions,* 31-45; "The Temple Vessels: A Continuity Theme," VTS 23 (1972), 166-81, reprinted in *Studies in the Religious Tradition,* 46-60; and "The Theology of Tradition: An Approach to Old Testament Theological Problems," *Bangalore Theological Forum* 3 (1971), 49-64, reprinted in *Studies in the Religious Traditions,* 17-30.

13. Intertextuality, as reflected in the work of Michael Fishbane, provides a powerful way to maintain a flexible continuity in contexts of discontinuity.

14. Ackroyd, "Continuity: A Contribution," *Studies in the Religious Tradition,* 15.

15. Such a statement makes no assumptions about inspiration, revelation, or authority. I refer to such "theological realism" in terms of the claims made by the text itself. The ground for such a claim is of course theological, but in the first instant, it can be heeded on the grounds of the text as a "classic" which requires our attendance.

16. On such an understanding of the text, see Dale Patrick, *The Rendering of God in the Old Testament* (OBT; Philadelphia: Fortress Press, 1981). This approach understands theology as dramatic rendering and proceeds by bracketing out metaphysical questions.

17. On the notion of "covenantal discourse," see Harold Fisch, *Poetry with a Purpose: Biblical Poetics and Interpretation* (Bloomington: Indiana University Press, 1988), 118-31. The gain of Fisch's assertion is that it takes seriously the claim of the text itself without excessive historical-critical reservation. See Fisch's "Theological realism" concerning the Psalms (pp. 108-14).

18. On the question of continuity and discontinuity, see Ernst Käsemann, "Blind Alleys in the 'Jesus of History' Controversy," *New Testament Questions Today* (London: SCM Press, 1969), 23-65; Ernst Fuchs, *Studies of the Historical Jesus* (SBT; Naperville: Alec R. Allenson, 1964), 11-31; and James D. G. Dunn,

Unity and Diversity in the New Testament: An Inquiry into the Character of Earliest Christianity (Philadelphia: Westminster Press, 1977). See Professor Beker's theological discussion of the question, *Paul the Apostle: The Triumph of God in Life and Thought* (Philadelphia: Fortress Press, 1980), 192-208.

19. J. Christiaan Beker, *Suffering and Hope: The Biblical Vision and the Human Predicament* (Philadelphia: Fortress Press, 1987).

20. For the purposes of my argument, it cannot be insisted upon too strongly that the mode of God's self-presentation is dramatic, and that we are witnessing the character of God through a drama. The warrant for such a mode of discourse is that the text itself proceeds in this way.

21. On the several theological resources from the Exile which give different voice to God, see the works of Ackroyd and Klein cited in n. 6, and Friedman in n. 5.

22. A. D. H. Mayes, "Deuteronomy 4 and the Literary Criticism of Deuteronomy," *JBL* 100 (1981), 23-51, supported by the argument of G. Braulik, has made a strong case for the literary unity and coherence of the passage. See Norbert Lohfink, *Höre Israel! Auslegung von Texten aus dem Buch Deuteronomium* (Dusseldorf: Patmos Verlag, 1965), 87-120; and G. Braulik, *Die Mittel deuteromischer Rhetorik* (AnBib 68; Rome: Biblical Institute Press, 1978).

23. See Frank M. Cross, *Canaanite Myth and Hebrew Epic* (Cambridge, Mass.: Harvard University Press, 1973), 274-89, and Richard D. Nelson, *The Double Redaction of the Deuteronomistic History* (JSOTSup 18; Sheffield: JSOT Press, 1981).

24. See Hans Walter Wolff, "The Kerygma of the Deuteronomic Historical Work," *The Vitality of Old Testament Traditions* by Walter Brueggemann and Hans Walter Wolff (Atlanta: John Knox Press, 1975), 96-97.

25. Phyllis Trible, *God and the Rhetoric of Sexuality* (OBT; Philadelphia: Fortress Press, 1978), 31-59.

26. On the double movement, see Zech 1:15-17 and Isa 60:10-14. The former text has important parallels to our text. On the "hidden face" of God, see Samuel E. Balentine, *The Hidden God: The Hiding of the Face of God in the Old Testament* (New York: Oxford University Press, 1983), esp. 148; and Lothar Perlitt, "Die Verborgenheit Gottes," *Probleme biblischer Theologie*, ed. Hans Walter Wolff (München: Christian Kaiser Verlag, 1971), 367-82.

27. On the double theme in Jeremiah, see J. Lust, " 'Gathering and Return' in Jeremiah and Ezekiel," *Le Livre de Jeremaie*, ed. M. Bogaert (Leuven: Leuven University Press, 1981), 119-42; and Thomas M. Raitt, *A Theology of Exile: Judgment and Deliverance in Jeremiah and Ezekiel* (Philadelphia: Fortress Press, 1977).

28. Hans Frei (*The Identity of Jesus Christ: The Hermeneutical Bases of Dogmatic Theology* [Philadelphia: Fortress Press, 1975]) holds a magisterial view of the single story of God focused on Jesus Christ. That single and magisterial story necessarily asserts the profound and universal continuity. Against such a claim of any "great story," see the protest of Jean Francois Lyotard, *The Postmodern Condition: A Report on Knowledge* (Minneapolis: University of Minnesota Press, 1984). See the judicious comments of William C. Placher, *Unapologetic Theology: A Christian Voice in a Pluralistic Conversation* (Louisville: Westminster/John Knox Press, 1989), 156 and *passim*, concerning a "universal" story and the Christian narrative.

29. John Calvin, *Commentary on the Book of the Prophet Isaiah* (Grand Rapids: Baker Book House, 1979), 140.

30. Kornelis H. Miskotte, *When the Gods Are Silent* (New York: Harper & Row, 1967), 405. See also Karl Barth, *Church Dogmatics* 2/1, #30 (Edinburgh: T & T Clark, 1957), 372-73.

31. Cf. for example, Exod 33:5; Isa 26:20, 47:9; Ps 30:6; Lam 4:6.

32. Cf. 1 Cor 15:52.

33. Miskotte, *When the Gods Are Silent*, 405. Miskotte understands that the move from abandonment to compassion happens only through God's deep pathos, that is, through "the breaking of his own heart." Westermann, *Isaiah 40-66, a Commentary* (OTL: Philadelphia: Westminster Press, 1969), is not as explicit, but alludes to the same reality: "A change has come over God. He ceases from wrath, and again shows Israel mercy" (p. 274). In his comment, however, Westermann speaks of the way Israel's "heart throbbed," but does not draw God's heart into the trouble in the same way.

34. Much of the Noah-flood story is from P, and therefore from the Exile. Thus it is not unexpected that that flood narrative should be on the horizon of this exilic poet.

35. For example, the "again" ('*od*) of Isa 54:9 is clearly reminiscent of the same word in Gen 9:11, with the same intention.

36. Bernhard W. Anderson, "From Analysis to Synthesis: The Interpretation of Genesis 1–11," *JBL* 97 (1978), 23-29, has shown that Gen 8:1 is the pivot of the Flood narrative, for instance, when

God remembers Noah. In the structure of the narrative, that decisive *remembering* is preceded by God's *forgetting* of Noah. In the same way, in Isaiah 54, God's act of compassion is preceded by a real act of abandonment. Thus the analogy of our text to that of the Flood narrative applies to the entire dramatic structure of the narrative.

37. On "covenant of peace" see Bernard F. Batto, "The Covenant of Peace: A Neglected Ancient Near Eastern Motif," *CBQ* 49 (1987), 187-211.

38. For that reason, this text does not need an ʿod of reassurance. That is, this text entertains no discontinuity, and therefore there is no need for reassertion and new promise.

39. In Isa 54:9-10, the claim for the future is based on ʿod.

40. On the late dating of vv. 35-37, see Robert Carroll, *Jeremiah, A Commentary* (OTL; Philadelphia: Westminster Press, 1986), 115-16, and William L. Holladay, *Jeremiah 2* (Hermeneia; Minneapolis: Fortress Press, 1989), 199. Holladay dates the text to the time of Nehemiah. My argument, however, is that in doing theology, one must move beyond such critical judgment to take the realistic assertion of the text. Such a posture, I suppose, is one of "second naivete."

41. Such "common theology" necessarily interprets exile simply as punishment in a sharper system of retribution. On "common theology," see Norman K. Gottwald, *The Tribes of Yahweh* (Maryknoll, N.Y.: Orbis Books, 1979), 667-91, and Walter Brueggemann, "A Shape for Old Testament Theology, I: Structure Legitimation," *CBQ* 47 (1985), 156-68.

42. The new resolve of God in our texts is not unlike the new resolve of God in the Flood narrative (Gen 8:20-22, 9:8-17). In the Flood narrative no reason is given for that new resolve, as none is given here.

43. Critically, the changes can be explained by the identification of distinct literary sources. Such distinctions, however, often violate the intention of the final form of the text, which is the proper material for doing Biblical Theology.

44. Jürgen Moltmann, *The Crucified God* (New York: Harper & Row, 1974), has most powerfully insisted upon this dialectic of crucifixion and resurrection, refusing to let the Resurrection overcome or nullify the centrality of the Crucifixion in the story of God's life.

45. On getting from Friday to Sunday, George Steiner, *Real Presences: Is There Anything in What We Say?* (London: Faber & Faber, 1989), 231-32, concludes with a pathos-filled statement: "There is one particular day in Western history about which neither historical record nor myth nor Scripture make report. It is a Saturday. And it has become the longest of days. We know of that Good Friday which Christianity holds to have been that of the Cross. But the non-Christian, the atheist, knows of it as well. That is to say that he knows of the injustice, of the interminable suffering, of the waste, of the brute enigma of ending. . . . We know also about Sunday. To the Christian, that day signifies an intimation, both assured and precarious, both evident and beyond comprehension, of resurrection, of a justice and a love that have conquered death. If we are non-Christians or non-believers, we know of that Sunday in precisely analogous terms. . . . The lineaments of that Sunday carry the name of hope (there is no word less deconstructible).

"But ours is the long day's journey of the Saturday. Between suffering, aloneness, unutterable waste on the one hand and the dream of liberation, of rebirth on the other. In the face of the torture of a child, of the death of love which is Friday, even the greatest art and poetry are almost helpless. In the Utopia of the Sunday, the aesthetic will, presumably, no longer have logic or necessity. The apprehensions and figurations . . . which tell of pain and of hope, of the flesh which is said to taste of ash and of the spirit which is said to have the savour of fire, are always Sabbatarian. They have risen out of an immensity of waiting which is that of man. Without them, how could we be patient?"

Steiner's poignant statement from outside the Christian faith (as a Jew) is paralleled from inside the Christian community by Nicholas Lash. Lash, *Easter in Ordinary: Reflections on Human Experience and the Knowledge of God* (Charlottesville: University Press of Virginia, 1988) writes: "In a fascinating section of *What Is Man?*, Buber distinguishes between 'epochs of habitation and epochs of homelessness.' Whether we like it or not, ours is an epoch of homelessness. . . . But homelessness is the truth of our condition, and the 'gifts of the spirit,' gifts of community and relationships, forgiveness and life-giving, are at least as much a matter of promise, of prospect, and of the task that is laid upon us, as they are a matter of past achievement or present reality" (pp. 216, 268).

Both Steiner and Lash voice the discontinuity and affirm that our current habitation is in the homelessness between. The OT moment of exile is indeed one long Saturday, which afterward may seem to have been "a moment."

46. Moltmann, *The Crucified God*, underscores the abandonment which overrides every claim of transcendence. Thus "The Fatherlessness of the Son is matched by the Sonlessness of the Father" (p. 243).

47. Lyotard, *The Post-Modern Condition* insists that there are only concrete narratives and claims in communities of testimony. The reality of Israel's struggle with God requires the giving up of every universal. See his appeal on 40 to a figure from Wittgenstein, that a town consists of many little houses, squares, and streets. See the remarkable argument by Stephen Toulmin, *Cosmopolis: The Hidden Agenda of Modernity* (New York: The Free Press, 1990), 31-32, and *passim.*

48. See Richard L. Rubenstein, "Job and Auschwitz," *USQR* 25 (Summer 1970), 421-37.

49. Emil Fackenheim, *To Mend the World: Foundations of Future Jewish Thought* (New York: Schocken Press, 1982), has most eloquently characterized our new, post-Holocaust theological situation which requires theology to lower its voice back to more concrete claims which are brought to speech only in communities of hurt and risk.

50. Beker (*Suffering and Hope,* 91) concludes: "Finally, a biblical theology of hope allows us to be realistic and honest about the poisonous reality of death and dying in our world. . . . And so the biblical vision still offers a promissory word in the face of suffering due to the power of death." Beker's final affirmation is rooted exactly in the testimony of exiles who discern God making promises to exiles, in exile, beyond exile.

10. Wisdom Literature and Experience of the Divine

1. For example, see Sally McFague, *Models of God: Theologies for an Ecological, Nuclear Age* (Philadelphia: Fortress Press, 1977); R. S. Sugirtharajah, ed., *Voices from the Margin: Interpreting the Bible in the Third World* (Maryknoll, N.Y.: Orbis Books, 1991); Cain Hope Felder, ed., *Stony the Road We Trod: African American Biblical Interpretation* (Minneapolis: Fortress Press, 1991).

2. *Interpreting the Pentateuch* (Old Testament Studies 4; Collegeville, Minn.: Liturgical Press, 1990). McEvenue builds on the interpretive theories of Bernard Lonergan. See *Method in Theology* (London: Darton, Longman, and Todd, 1972). See also John J. Collins, "Is a Critical Biblical Theology Possible?" *The Hebrew Bible and Its Interpreters,* ed. William Henry Propp, et al. (Winona Lake, Ind.: Eisenbrauns, 1990), 12-14.

3. Loretta Dornisch, "Symbolic Systems and the Interpretation of Scripture: An Introduction to the Work of Paul Ricoeur," *Semeia* 4 (1975), 1-22.

4. See Werner G. Jeanrond, *Text and Interpretation as Categories of Theological Thinking* (New York: Crossroad, 1988), 74-75.

5. Ibid., 72-103.

6. Gale A. Yee, "The Author/Text/Reader and Power: Suggestions for a Critical Framework for Biblical Studies," a paper presented at the Annual Meeting of the Catholic Biblical Association, Washington, D.C., 1992; Collins, "Is a Critical Biblical Theology Possible?," 14.

7. See also McEvenue, *Interpreting the Pentateuch,* 10-14.

8. On levels of meaning in texts, see Jeanrond's discussion, *Text and Interpretation,* 80-81.

9. A point long made by Roland E. Murphy, "Wisdom and Creation," *JBL* 104 (1985), 3-11; *The Tree of Life: An Exploration of Biblical Wisdom Literature* (New York: Doubleday, 1990), 113; and by James L Crenshaw, "The Human Dilemma and the Literature of Dissent," *Tradition and Theology in the Old Testament,* ed. Douglas A. Knight (Philadelphia: Fortress Press, 1977), 235-58.

10. Carole R. Fontaine, "Proverbs," *The Women's Bible Commentary,* ed. Carol A. Newsom and Sharon Ringe (Louisville: Westminster/John Knox Press, 1992), 147-51.

11. "Le peuple juif et les nations a partir de l'Ancien Testament," *Pontificium Concilium pro dialogo inter Religiones* 77 (1991), 43-61; and see James L. Crenshaw, *Old Testament Wisdom: An Introduction* (Atlanta: John Knox, 1981), 209.

12. Beauchamp, "Le Peuple juif et les nations," 46-47.

13. Alexander DiLella, "Conservative and Progressive Theology: Sirach and Wisdom," *Studies in Ancient Israelite Wisdom,* ed. James L. Crenshaw (New York: KTAV, 1976), 401-26.

14. Jan van Braght, "Theology of Religions and the Christian Tradition," a paper presented to the Faculty of the Maryknoll School of Theology, Maryknoll, N.Y., December, 1991.

15. Hans-Jürgen Hermisson, "Observations on the Creation Theology in Wisdom (1978)," *Creation in the Old Testament,* ed. Bernhard W. Anderson (IRT 6; Philadelphia: Fortress Press, 1984), 118-34.

16. See my essays, "Job and the Collapse of Relationship," *The Wisdom Literature* (Message of Biblical Spirituality 5; Collegeville, Minn.: Liturgical Press, 1988), 86-113, and " 'With My Own Eyes': A Feminist Hermeneutical Revision of the Book of Job," *Continuum,* forthcoming; and Martin

Buber, "A God Who Hides His Face," *The Dimensions of Job,* ed. Nahum N. Glatzer (New York: Schocken Books, 1969), 56-64.

17. But see, for example: É. Bonnard, "De la Sagesse personifée dans l'Ancien Testament à la Sagesse en personne dans le Nouveau," *La Sagesse de l'Ancien Testament,* ed. M. Gilbert, Editions Duculot (Gembloux: Leuven University Press, 1979), 117-49; Paul Ricoeur, *Essays on Biblical Interpretation,* ed. Lewis S. Mudge (Philadelphia: Fortress Press, 1980), 88.

18. Claudia V. Camp, in *Wisdom and the Feminine in the Book of Proverbs,* Bible and Literature 11 (Sheffield: JSOT Press/Almond Press, 1985), 23-68, provides an excellent survey of scholarly estimates of Wisdom that I do not repeat here.

19. J. Blenkinsopp, "The Social Context of the Outsider Woman in Proverbs 1–9," *Bib* 72 (1991), 457-73.

20. *Wisdom and the Feminine.* That Woman Wisdom symbolizes historical women is also the position of A. H. DeBoer, "The Counselor," *Wisdom in Israel and in the Ancient Near East* (VTSup 3; Leiden: E. J. Brill, 1960), 42-71.

21. "Wisdom Mythology and the Christological Hymns of the New Testament," *Aspects of Wisdom in Judaism and Early Christianity,* ed. Robert Wilken (Notre Dame: University of Notre Dame Press, 1975), 17-41.

22. A phrase adopted from Hans Conzelmann, "The Mother of Wisdom," *The Future of Our Religious Past,* ed. James M. Robinson (New York: Harper & Row, 1964), 230-43. Schüssler Fiorenza's proposal resembles that of Burton L. Mack's "Wisdom Myth and Mythology," *Int* 24 (1970), 46-60.

23. "Proverbs IX: A Suggested Ugaritic Parallel," *VT* (1975), 298-306.

24. *Hellenism and Judaism: Their Encounter in Palestine in the Early Hellenist Period* (Philadelphia: Fortress Press, 1974), 153.

25. Claudia V. Camp, "The Female Sage in the Biblical Wisdom Literature," *The Sage in Ancient Israel and the Ancient Near East,* ed. John G. Gammie and Leo G. Perdue (Winona Lake, Ind.: Eisenbrauns, 1990), 185-203, acknowledges that in the Greek books Wisdom is not an ordinary woman but God's "throne partner." See C. Larcher, *Études sur le Livre de la Sagesse* (Paris: Gabalda, 1969), 329-414.

26. Carol Newsom, "Woman and the Discourse of Patriarchal Difference: A Study of Proverbs 1–9," *Gender and Difference in Ancient Israel.* ed. Peggy L. Day (Minneapolis: Fortress Press, 1989), 42-59; Camp, *Wisdom and the Feminine;* Carole R. Fontaine, "Proverbs," *Harper's Bible Commentary* (San Francisco: Harper & Row, 1988), 501-3.

27. Paul Ricoeur, "The Metaphorical Process," *Semeia* 80 (1975), 80.

28. The NAB is an exception.

29. J. Kugel, *The Idea of Biblical Poetry; Parallelism and Its History* (New Haven and London: Yale University Press, 1981).

30. Robert Alter, *The Art of Biblical Poetry* (New York: Basic Books, 1985).

31. *Ruhi* and *debāray* do not appear to be synonymous in Isa 59:21 either.

32. Pss 78:2, 19:2, 59:7, 99:4, 119:121, 145:7; Prov 15:2, 18:4; but see Eccl 10:1.

33. *Ntn* in Isa 42:1, Ezek 36:27, and 37:14; *'sq* in Isa 44:3; *spk* in Joel 3:1 (2:28 English), 3:2 (2:29 English), and Ezek 39:29; and see Zech 12:10.

34. Roland E. Murphy ("Wisdom's Song: Proverbs 1:20-33," *CBQ* 48 (1986), 456-601 doubts the divine associations of spirit because the rebuking nature of Wisdom's speech in v. 24 contradicts the nonthreatening quality of God's pouring out of the spirit in Isa 44:3.

35. William McKane, *Proverbs: A New Approach* (OTL London: SCM Press, 1970), 212.

36. A rhetorical question that parallels 1:20 draws attention to the immediacy and urgency of her invitation. Verses 2-3 continue the parallel with 1:20-21, locating Wisdom's speech in the midst of the city, and verses 4-5a echo her invitation to the simple in 1:22. Again Wisdom resembles a prophet whose mouth utters truth (v. 7) or a sage from whose lips come what is right (vv. 6-9), and again she offers her invitation to a universal audience. She urges all people *(bene 'ādām)* to "hear her instruction" (v. 4b).

37. See Bernhard Lang, *Wisdom and the Book of Proverbs: An Israelite Goddess Redefined* (New York: Pilgrim, 1986).

38. André Barucq, *Le Livre de Proverbes,* (SB; Paris: Gabalda, 1964), 88.

39. Bruce Vawter, "Prov 8:22: Wisdom and Creation," *The Path of Wisdom: Biblical Investigations* (Wilmington: Background Books, 1986: 161-77). In Proverbs the primary meaning of *qānāh* is "to acquire" or "to possess" (1:5; 4:5; 4:7, 3 times; 16:16; 17:16; 18:15, 22; 19:8 and possibly 15:32). In 23:23 and 20:14 *qānāh* probably means "to buy." Elsewhere in the Hebrew Bible, *qānāh* can mean "to create" (Gen 14:14, 22; Deut 32:6; Ps 139:13) and in Gen 4:1 "to give birth."

40. See, for example, R. B. Y. Scott, *Proverbs/Ecclesiastes* (AB 18; Garden City, N.Y.: Doubleday, 1965), 69.
41. Aletti, "Proverbs 8:22-31: Etude de Structure," *Bib* 57 (1976), 25-37; Yee, "An Analysis of Prov 8:22-31 According to Style and Structure," *ZAW* 94 (1982), 58-66.
42. *Wisdom in the Book of Proverbs*, 65.
43. McKane's translation (*Proverbs*, 223) emphasizes her activity. "I was beside him as his confidant, I gave him pleasure daily."
44. Michael David Coogan, "Canaanite Origins and Lineage: Reflections on the Religion of Ancient Israel," *Ancient Israelite Religion*, ed. Miller, et al. (Philadelphia: Fortress Press, 1987, 115-24) believes she may be God's consort.
45. R. N. Whybray, *The Book of Proverbs* (CBC; Cambridge: Cambridge University Press, 1972), 54. Whybray argues that pillars were merely a feature of palaces of the period.
46. R. B. Y. Scott, *Proverbs/Ecclesiastes* (AB 18; Garden City, N.Y.: Doubleday, 1965), 76.
47. Ibid.
48. Lang, *Wisdom and the Book of Proverbs*, 90; and Fontaine, "Proverbs," *The Women's Bible*, 148.
49. McCreesh, "Wisdom as Wife: Proverbs 31:10-31," *RB* (1985), 25-46. Camp (*Wisdom and the Feminine*, 186-207) notices the same evidence but interprets it somewhat differently.
50. McCreesh, ibid., 46.

11. Paul and the Canon of the New Testament

1. J. Christiaan Beker, *Paul the Apostle: The Triumph of God in Life and Thought* (Philadelphia: Fortress Press, 1980).
2. Ibid., 15.
3. *Unity and Diversity in the New Testament: An Inquiry into the Character of Earliest Christianity* (London: SCM Press, 1977), 369.
4. "Der Sinn der neutestamentlichen Christologie," *ZThK* 54 (1957), 341-77; repr. in Herbert Braun, *Gesammelte Studien zum Neuen Testament und seiner Umwelt* (Tübingen: J. C. B. Mohr [Paul Siebeck], 1962, 241-82; ET "The Meaning of the Christology of the New Testament" (by Paul J. Achtemeier), *JTC* 5 (1968), 89-127; also, "Die Problematik einer Theologie des Neuen Testaments," *ZThK* 58 (1961), 3-18; repr. in *Gesammelte Studien*, 325-41; ET, "The Problem of a Theology of the New Testament" (by Jack T. Sanders), *JTC* 1 (1965), 169-83; repr. in Thomas J. J. Altizer, ed., *Towards a New Christianity* (New York: Harcourt, Brace, 1967), 201-15.
5. "Der Sinn der neutestamentlichen Christologie," *ZThK*, 373; *Gesammelte Studien*, 277.
6. "Sackgassen im Streit um den historischen Jesus," *Exegetische Versuche und Besinnungen* (Göttingen: Vandenhoeck & Ruprecht), vol. 2, 1964, 44; ET (by W. J. Montague), "Blind Alleys in the 'Jesus of History' Controversy," *New Testament Questions of Today* (London: SCM Press, 1969), 38.
7. *Einleitung in die allgemeine Metaphysik* (Köln 1961), 146; see also, *Allgemeine Metaphysik. Ihre Probleme und ihre Methode* (Berlin: Walter de Gruyter & Co, 1865), 330-32; ET, *General Metaphysics: Its Problems and Its Method* (London: Allen & Unwin, 1968), 331-32.
8. "[wir verstehen] unter Dialektik einen Standpunkt und eine Disziplin. Insofern die Dialektik einen Standpunkt bedeutet, verstehen wir darunter die Überzeugung, da einander widerstreitende Sätze zugleich wahr sein können und da beide als wahr erwiesen werden können. Insofern die Dialektik eine Disziplin bezeichnet, verstehen wir darunter diejenige Disziplin, die sich die Untersuchung möglicher Widersprüche zum Thema macht. Sie wird also die Widersprüche aufsuchen und herausstellen. Sie wird die einander widerstreitenden Sätze beweisen, und sie wird schlielich die Bedeutung der Widersprüche und die Gründe ihres Auftretens untersuchen" (*Algemeine Metaphysik*, 322; ET., 323).
9. "The Structural Study of Myth," *Journal of American Folklore* 78 (1955), 428-44; repr. in *Structural Anthropology* (New York: Basic Books, 1963; paperback ed., Garden City, N.Y.: Doubleday, 1967), 202-28; translated with additions and modifications as, "La structure des mythes," *Anthropologie structurale* (Paris: Plon, vol. 1, 21974), 226-66.
10. "La structure des mythes," 254-55. The original English is slightly different; see "The Structural Study of Myth," 227. The modifications are obviously intended as clarifications of his intended meanings.
11. "La structure des mythes," 255. The original English is formulated slightly differently. See "The Structural Study of Myth," 227.

12. *To dē philosophō kai tauta malista timōnti pasa . . . hosa akinēta kai kekinēmena, to hon te kai to pan sunamphotera legein* (Soph 249, c10-d4).

13. Albert Camus, *Le Mythe de Sisyphe* (Paris: Gallimard, 1942); repr. in *Essais* (Paris: Gallimard, 1965), 117-18; ET, *The Myth of Sisyphus* (New York: Vintage Books, 1955), 21.

14. Ibid., 135; ET, 37.

15. Ibid., 120-21; ET, 23.

16. Ibid., 125; ET, 28.

17. Ibid., 121; ET, 24.

18. Ibid., 125; ET, 28; cf. above page.

19. The distinction was first clearly recognized by E. Sanders, *Paul and Palestinian Judaism: A Comparison of Patterns of Religion* (Philadelphia: Fortress Press, 1977); also *Paul, the Law, and the Jewish People* (Philadelphia: Fortress Press, 1983). Independently of Sanders it was also recognized by Roman Heiligenthal, *Werke als Zeichen, Untersuchungen zur Bedeutung der menschlichen Taten im Frühjudentum, Neues Testament und Frühchristentum* (WUNT 9; Tübingen: J. C. B. Mohr [Paul Siebeck] 1983).

20. *Sémiotique: dictionnaire raisonné de la théorie du langage* (Paris: Hachette, 1979); ET., *Semiotics and Language* (Larry Crist, Daniel Patte, et al.; Bloomington: Indiana University Press, 1982).

21. See the entries "Micro-univers," and "Sémantique fondamentale," ET, "Micro-universe," and "Semantics, Fundamental."

22. In the NT there are also cases where the social universe comes to expression at a more abstract level in the opposition between good and bad. The opposition between good and evil is a specific case of the more general opposition between good and bad, which includes, for example, the aesthetic opposition between beautiful and ugly. So Paul, in 1 Cor 11:3-15, when he makes a final (bourgeois!) appeal to the aesthetic distinction between good and bad taste to resolve what he takes to be the religious-ethical issue of the veiling of women: "Judge for yourselves: Is it proper for a woman to pray to God unveiled? And does nature itself not teach you that it is degrading for a man to have long hair, but if a woman has long hair it becomes her?" (1 Cor 11:13-15a).

12. The Persistence of Apocalyptic Thought in New Testament Theology

1. Käsemann's comment was first published in his article entitled, "Die Anfänge christlicher Theologie" in *ZTK* 57 (1960), 162-85. An English translation, entitled "The Beginnings of Christian Theology," is printed in *New Testament Questions of Today* by Ernst Käsemann (Philadelphia: Fortress Press, 1969), 82-107.

2. Albert Schweitzer, first in *Skizze des Lebens Jesu* (1901), then in *Von Reimarus zu Wrede. Eine Geschichte der Leben-Jesu-Forschung* (1906; 2nd ed., 1913). The English translation entitled *The Quest of the Historical Jesus. A Critical Study of Its Progress from Reimarus to Wrede* (1910) was based on the first German edition of 1906. The initial draft of Schweitzer's *Die Mystik des Apostels Paulus* was completed in 1906, but due to a number of personal delays, the manuscript was not published until 1929. The English translation of this work was entitled, *The Mysticism of Paul the Apostle*, and was issued in 1931. In 1911, however, Schweitzer published as a separate monograph what was originally intended to be the introduction to *Mystik*, namely, *Geschichte der paulinischen Forschung* (in English, *Paul and His Interpreters*).

3. First proposed by Rudolf Bultmann in his 1941 essay entitled, "Neues Testament und Mythologie: Das Problem der Entmythologisierung der neutestamentlichen Verkündigung." The English translation of this important article, "New Testament and Mythology: The Problem of Demythologizing the New Testament Proclamation," along with several scholarly responses to Bultmann's thesis, is available in *Kerygma and Myth: A Theological Debate*, ed. H. W. Bartsch (London: SPCK, 1953), 1-44.

4. Käsemann followed up this 1960 article with two subsequent articles: "Zum Thema der christlichen Apokalyptik" in *ZTK* 59 (1962), 257-84, and "Paulus und der Frühkatholizismus" in *ZTK* 60 (1963), 75-89. All three articles on the centrality of apocalyptic in the NT are reprinted in translation in Käsemann's *New Testament Questions of Today* (Philadelphia: Fortress Press, 1969).

5. Some of this early debate is captured in *Journal for Theology and the Church* 6 (1969), which was devoted entirely to the topic of "Apocalypticism."

6. The International Colloquium on Apocalypticism, which was held in Uppsala, August 12–17, 1979, is merely one example of this kind of further study. The proceedings of this conference were published under the title, *Apocalypticism in the Mediterranean World and the Near East*, ed. David Hellholm (Tübingen: J. C. B. Mohr [Paul Siebeck], 1983).

7. While apocalypses flourished in the period from 200 BCE on, the roots of apocalyptic writing are surely earlier. The so-called "Isaiah Apocalypse" of chaps. 24–27, along with Joel 2, Zechariah 9–11, 12–14, and Ezekiel 38–39 are examples of earlier apocalyptic writings. Paul Hanson in *The Dawn of Apocalyptic: The Historical and Sociological Roots of Jewish Apocalyptic Eschatology* (Philadelphia: Fortress Press, 1975) argues that 2 Isaiah (chaps. 40–55) is "proto-apocalyptic" and Trito-Isaiah (chaps. 56–66) is "early apocalyptic." Speaking about the origin of this type of writing Hanson states: "The apocalyptic literature of the second century [BCE] and after is the result of a long development reaching back to pre-exilic time and beyond, and not the new baby of second-century foreign parents" (*The Dawn of Apocalyptic*, 6).

8. *The Old Testament Pseudepigrapha*, vol. I: *Apocalyptic Literature and Testaments*, ed. J. H. Charlesworth (Garden City, N.Y.: Doubleday, 1983) contains 19 apocalypses (such as, 1 Enoch, Sibylline Oracles, 4 Ezra, Apocalypse of Elijah) and 6 testaments (such as, Testaments of the Twelve Patriarchs, Testament of Abraham, Testament of Moses). Also included in some lists are 1 Baruch, Apocalypse of Moses (or the Life of Adam and Eve), Book of Jubilees, and Ascension of Isaiah. Discovered among the Dead Sea Scrolls are some previously known apocalypses (Daniel, 1 Enoch, and Jubilees) and some previously unknown apocalyptic works (the War Scroll [1QM], the Thanksgiving Psalms [1QH], and the Description of the New Jerusalem [5Q15]). For a more complete listing of Qumran materials that evidence apocalyptic features and a discussion of some of that material, see D. S. Russell, *The Method and Message of Jewish Apocalyptic: 200 BC–AD 100* (OTL; Philadelphia: Westminster Press, 1964), 38-48.

9. Gerhard von Rad in *Old Testament Theology*, vol. II (ET; New York: Harper & Row, 1965), 301-15, asserts that apocalyptic writing is merely a mixture of well-known literary forms rather than a decidedly new literary genre.

10. Lists of characteristics, not each of which is found in every apocalyptic writing, are found in numerous works. See, for example, Klaus Koch's *The Rediscovery of Apocalyptic* (ET by M. Kohl; London: S.C.M., 1972), 23-28; Philip Vielhauer's "Introduction [to Apocalyptic in Early Christianity]" in *New Testament Apocrypha*, ed. E. Hennecke and W. Schneemelcher, trans. R. McLachlan Wilson, 2 vols. (Philadelphia: Westminster Press, 1965), 2:582-87; and D. S. Russell's *Jewish Apocalyptic*, 104-39.

11. By attributing their works to an ancient patriarch or prophet or other holy biblical figure, the apocalypticist achieves two goals: this pseudonym lends the work an antiquity as well as an authority that it otherwise would not have. The one apocalypse that is not composed under a pseudonym is Revelation. There is no reason to doubt that this work was composed by one whose name was John (Rev 1:1, 4; 22:8) who is a "brother" of those addressed (1:9*a*) and who calls himself a preacher and a prophet (19:10, 22:8-9). But it is unlikely that the John of Revelation is either the Apostle John (the brother of James and a son of Zebedee) or the author of the Fourth Gospel.

12. Vielhauer notes in his "Introduction" (in *NT Apocrypha* II, 587) that "all Apocalypses included paraenesis, both exhortations to repentance and conversion in view of the imminent end and of judgment, and also paraenesis in the form-critical sense of the word, i.e. traditional ethical exhortations in the form of maxims and series of aphorisms which are sometimes arranged thematically."

13. Friedrich Lücke in *Versuch einer vollständigen Einleitung in die Offenbarung des Johannes, oder allegemeine Untersuchungen über die apocalyptische Literatur überhaupt und die Apokalypse des Johannes insbesondere* (Bonn: Weber, 1832) is generally credited with being the first to use the word "apocalyptic" not only to identify a distinctive type of literature but also the type of thought that is expressed through apocalyptic writings.

14. The doctrine of the Two Ages is seen in the often cited remark, "For this reason the Most High has made not one world but two" (4 Ezra 7:50). The radical discontinuity between the two ages finds expression in Daniel's vision of the four beasts who "came up out of the sea" (Dan 7:2-8) in contrast to the image of the so-called son of man who is portrayed as "coming with the clouds of heaven" (Dan. 7:13-14). See also the contrast between the present and the future age in 2 Bar 44:8-15.

15. Reference to the destruction of the present age is made in the statement, "For, behold, the days are coming, that all that has been will be taken away to be destroyed, and it will become as though it had not been" (2 Bar 31:5). But the end of This Age is merely the beginning of the Age to Come: "The first heaven shall depart and pass away; a new heaven shall appear; and all the powers of heaven shall shine forever sevenfold" (1 Enoch 91:16).

16. This new age is eternal, "for the God of heaven will set up a kingdom that shall never be destroyed . . . it shall stand forever" (Dan 2:44). Moreover, "there is a time that does not pass away. And that period is coming which will remain forever" (2 Bar 43:11-12). Similarly, 4 Ezra says, "This

present world is not the end . . . But the day of judgment will be the end of this age and the beginning of the immortal age to come, in which corruption has passed away" (7:112).

17. In 4 Ezra 6:1-6 the Lord asserts, "At the beginning of the circle of the earth, before the portals of the world were in place, and before the assembled winds blew, and before the rumblings of thunder sounded . . . then I planned these things, and they were made through me and not through another, just at the end shall come through me and not another."

18. God's creation of This Age as well as the Age to Come is stated in 4 Ezra 8:1, "The Most High made this world for the sake of many, but the world to come for the sake of the few."

19. Pessimism about the present age is sometimes expressed through the image of the irreversibility of old age. This is seen in 4 Ezra, where the created order is described as "already . . . aging and passing the strength of youth" (4 Ezra 5:55), and again in the comment, "For the age has lost its youth, and the times begin to grow old" (4 Ezra 14:10). Similarly, it says in 2 Bar 84:10 that "the youth of this world has passed away, and the power of creation is already exhausted. . . . " (84:10).

20. Future hope finds expression in the unusual description of 2 Bar 29: "The earth will also yield fruits ten thousandfold. And on one vine will be a thousand branches, and one branch will produce a thousand clusters, and one cluster will produce a thousand grapes, and one grape will produce a cor of wine. And those who are hungry will enjoy themselves. . . . " (vv. 5-6a).

21. According to 4 Ezra 4:26-27, Ezra is told, "If you are alive, you will see, and if you live long, you will often marvel, because the age is hastening swiftly to its end. For it will not be able to bring the things that have been promised to the righteous in their appointed times, because this age is full of sadness and infirmities."

22. See 2 Bar 83:4-9, which says that "The end of the world will then show the great power of our Ruler since everything will come to judgment" (83:7) and everyone will get what they deserve. See also the judgment scene described in 4 Ezra 7:33-38 when "recompense shall follow" judgment. That "recompense" involves either "the pit of torment" or "the place of rest," "the furnace of Hell" or "the Paradise of delight" depending on one's actions in the present age.

23. According to 4 Ezra, " . . . the day of judgment will be the end of this age and the beginning of the immortal age to come. . . . " (7:112).

24. Although the end is near, the apocalypticist waits impatiently for its arrival. As a result, a common refrain in apocalyptic literature is the question, "How long . . . ?" See Dan 8:13, 12:6; 4 Ezra 4:33, 6:59. When Ezra asks for some specifics about the date of the end (4 Ezra 4:44-52), in particular, whether or not he will be alive when in comes (4 Ezra 4:51), he is only told generally that "the quantity [of time] that has passed was far greater [than the quantity of time remaining]" (4 Ezra 4:50).

25. Notice that the lamentation of Ezra in 4 Ezra 7:62-69 is for all of humanity ("the human race," in 7:65) and not specifically for any one nation. Similarly, Ezra laments over the fate of the descendants of Adam in 4 Ezra 7:116-126.

26. See Dan 12:1-2, where it is stated that "at that time . . . many of those who sleep in the dust of the earth shall awake, some to everlasting life, and some to shame and everlasting contempt." 2 Baruch devotes several chapters to the idea of resurrection of the dead. First, Baruch asks God, "In what shape will the living live in your day?" (49:2). God responds, "For the earth will surely give back the dead at that time" (50:2), and then goes on to describe the resurrection body in chap. 51.

27. According to 4 Ezra 7:37-38, "Then the Most High will say to the nations that have been raised from the dead, 'Look now, and understand whom you have denied, whom you have not served, whose commandments you have despised! Look on this side and on that; here are delight and rest, and there are fire and torments!' Thus he will speak to them on the day of judgment."

28. This explains the presence in most apocalyptic writing of extensive ethical instruction. In 1 Enoch, for example, the paraenesis frames the central section of the work (chaps. 2–5 and then again in chaps. 91–105, 108).

29. The story of Shadrach, Meshach, and Abednego in the fiery furnace in Daniel 3 as well as Daniel being thrown to the lions in Daniel 6 illustrate the apocalyptic belief that obedience to the Law of God would result in adversity. This contrasts with the Deuteronomic perspective (seen in Deuteronomy 28), which equated righteousness and obedience to God with material abundance and physical health. Whereas in the Deuteronomic perspective one obeyed the commandments of God *in order to avoid* suffering, in apocalyptic one obeys *in spite of* suffering, knowing that the present situation of the faithful would be reversed in the near future, when the Lord would end this age and usher in the Age to Come.

30. Vielhauer in his "Introduction" (in *NT Apocrypha* II, 582) writes: "By means of the word 'Apocalyptic' we designate first of all the literary genre of the Apocalypses, i.e. revelatory writings which disclose the secrets of the beyond and especially of the end of time, and then secondly, the realm of ideas from which this literature originates."

31. For a fuller discussion of this problem of definition, see Richard E. Sturm, "Defining the Word 'Apocalyptic': A Problem in Biblical Criticism," in *Apocalyptic and the New Testament*, ed. J. Marcus and M. L. Soards (JSNTSup 24; Sheffield: JSNT Press, 1989).

32. James D. G. Dunn, in *Unity and Diversity in the New Testament: An Inquiry into the Character of Earliest Christianity* (Philadelphia: Westminster Press, 1977), poses this key question in the following manner: "to what extent is apocalyptic integral to Christianity, so that without it Christianity becomes something qualitatively other than that movement which began in Palestine nineteen and a half centuries ago?" (p. 310).

33. J. Christiaan Beker, *Paul the Apostle: The Triumph of God in Life and Thought* (Philadelphia: Fortress Press, 1980).

34. J. C. Beker, *Paul the Apostle*, 18.

35. See two subsequent works by J. C. Beker, *Paul's Apocalyptic Gospel: The Coming Triumph of God* (Philadelphia: Fortress Press, 1982) and *The Triumph of God: The Essence of Paul's Thought* (Philadelphia: Fortress Press, 1990), which is a translation into English of a German translation and abridgment of *Paul the Apostle* (1980) entitled *Der Sieg Gottes* (Katholisches Bibelwerk, 1988).

36. For example, the very fact that "the parousia of Christ never took place as the New Testament expected" leads Rudolf Bultmann, in "New Testament and Mythology" (in *Kerygma and Myth: A Theological Debate*, ed. H. W. Bartsch [New York: Harper, 1961]), to conclude that "The mythical eschatology [of the New Testament] is untenable" (p. 5).

37. After Paul has written in 1 Thessalonians that "concerning the times and the seasons, brothers and sisters, you do not need to have anything written to you. For you yourselves know very well that the day of the Lord will come like a thief in the night" (1 Thess 5:1-2), it seems odd that Paul would go on in 2 Thess 2:1-11 to describe all that must take place before the End! This passage in 2 Thessalonians is best understood as the work of a later author who is concerned with explaining why the End has not yet occurred.

38. According to Colossians, God "*has* transferred [past tense] us to the kingdom of his beloved Son" (1:13), whereas Paul speaks of one's participation in the "kingdom of God" (not "kingdom of the Son") in the future (1 Cor 15:50). Moreover, through baptism Christians have not only died with Christ, but they have also risen with him, according to Col 2:12-13, 3:1. But in Paul the emphasis is on dying with Christ; the rising with him is still in the eschatological future (Rom. 6:1-2, 1 Thess 4:14-15).

39. In Eph 1:20-23 Christ is already enthroned above all cosmic powers (cf. 1 Cor 15:25-28), and Christians have been made alive and are enthroned with Christ, according to Eph 2:5-7 (cf. Rom 6:4).

40. In Luke 21:8, for example, Jesus warns his disciples not to be led astray by those who say, "the time is at hand! Do not go after them." Remembering that "the time is at hand!" is the very essence of the message in Paul's writings, as well as in Mark (for example, 1:15) and elsewhere in the NT, Luke now asserts that this is the message of false prophets! Similarly in Luke 19:12-27 Jesus tells the parable of the pounds to refute the mistaken notion "that the kingdom of God was to appear immediately" (19:11).

41. Joseph A. Fitzmyer in *The Gospel According to Luke I-IX: Introduction, Translation, and Notes* (The Anchor Bible 28; Garden City, N.Y.: Doubleday, 1981) concludes his discussion on "Lukan Salvation-History and Eschatology" (pp. 18-22) with this observation: "As I see it, the parousia may not be as imminent for Luke as for some other NT writers, but it is still for him a reality to be expected, which will come suddenly and unpredictably" (p. 21).

42. For a succinct discussion of the eschatology of the Fourth Gospel, see Robert Kysar, *John, the Maverick Gospel* (Atlanta: John Knox Press, 1976), 86-93.

43. For a discussion of the historical setting of the Johannine epistles and their relationship to the Fourth Gospel see Raymond Brown, *The Community of the Beloved Disciple* (New York: Paulist Press, 1979), 93-144.

44. Of the seven general epistles, only 2 and 3 John fail to refer to the coming Parousia. In fact, 2 and 3 John are the only post-Pauline writings in the NT that do not mention the Parousia either explicitly or implicitly. Nevertheless, these two epistles are the shortest writings included in the NT, and their brevity and consequently their limited scope probably explain why the Parousia is not considered in either of them.

45. From the outset of the Christian movement the death and resurrection were central affirmations of faith. In 1 Cor 15:3-5 Paul introduces a brief creedal statement with the remark that this is "of first importance." That creed emphasizes the death and resurrection of Christ. Considering that Paul wrote these words into the early 50s, reminding the Corinthians of a tradition that Paul had delivered to them in the late 40s and which Paul himself had received perhaps as early as the mid-30s, then the death and resurrection of Christ were essential to the Christian faith from the beginning.

46. Literally "with men" *(meta anthrōpon)*. The NRSV rendering of this phrase as "among mortals" is misleading. The translators of the NRSV are to be commended for the masterful way in which they eliminated in an unobtrusive manner much of the so-called "masculine-biased language" found in the Bible and in previous English translations. Their inclusive translation of Rev 21:3, however, is unfortunate, because it actually distorts the meaning of this particular text. At this time, in the drama of Revelation, those "mortals" among whom God will dwell are in fact immortal! Death has already been destroyed (Rev 20:14), along with all those whose names are not written in the book of life (Rev 20:15). Those who remain are informed that "Death will be no more" (Rev 21:4).

47. According to Paul the nearness of the End does not absolve believers of their present responsibilities. It is noteworthy that merely a few verses prior to Paul's comment concerning the nearness of the Parousia—"the night is far gone, the day is near" (Rom 13:12a)—Paul urges the Romans to live up to their present financial obligations: "Pay to all what is due them—taxes to whom taxes are due, revenue to whom revenue is due . . . " (Rom 13:7a). For a discussion of the differences between "taxes" *(phoros)* and "revenue" *(telos)*, as well as an excellent treatment of the historical background of Rom 13:1-7, see "Christians and Governing Authorities," which is chapter v in Victor Paul Furnish's *The Moral Teaching of Paul: Selected Issues*, 2nd ed., rev. (Nashville: Abingdon Press, 1985), 115-39.

13. Ancient Apocalyptic Thought and the New Testament

1. E. Käsemann, "Die Anfänge christlicher Theologie," *TTK* 57 (1960), 162-85; ET, "The Beginnings of Christian Theology," in *Apocalypticism*, ed. R. W. Funk, trans. J. W. Leitch (New York: Herder, 1969), 17-46.

2. In this essay I shall attempt to be true to the refined definitions: apocalypticism denotes the social world and the social matrix of the apocalypses, which are the literary products (indeed masterpieces) of pre-Rabbinic Judaism. In German "Apokalyptik" is a noun, in English it can only properly be an adjective. There are two problems with this widely accepted improvement in nomenclature for studying the heart of early Jewish thought: such categories can mislead students into thinking that the apocalypses can be studied without learning apocalypticism, and more important, there is no umbrella concept for all of them (as "apocalyptic" once denoted); hence, apocalypsology may be suggested as the comprehensive term and the noun to denote the cultural sophistication and intellectual breakthrough reflected in the apocalypses.

3. See the discussions on D. Hellholm, ed., *Apocalypticism in the Mediterranean World and the Near East: Proceedings of the International Colloquium on Apocalypticism* (Uppsala, August 12–17, 1979) (Tübingen: J. C. B. Mohr [Paul Siebeck], 1983).

4. The claim that neither of these is really an apocalypse fails to understand that our definition of what an "apocalypse" is derives from the assumption that these two documents are apocalypses. G. Boccaccini concludes that Daniel does not "belong to the apocalyptic tradition of thought." See his *Middle Judaism: Jewish Thought, 300 B.C.E. to 200 C.E.* (Minneapolis: Fortress Press, 1991), 159-60.

5. Each of these apocalypses is translated and introduced in the first volume of J. H. Charlesworth, ed., *The Old Testament Pseudepigrapha*, 2 vols. (Garden City, N.Y.: Doubleday, 1983–1985). All quotations from the apocalypses and Pseudepigrapha are according to those in *OTP*, unless otherwise noted.

6. We need to think more about the social crises caused by—or causing—the attributing of *all truth* to an individual not prominent in the shaping of social institutions and the biblical canon. If Moses and Ezra were leading figures in this process, and highly revered by the cultus, then to attribute knowledge of God's will to another, like Enoch, may well reflect opposition to the social institutions, like the Temple and the Pharisaically controlled synagogue.

The individuals who wrote the Enoch Apocalypses, and the communities behind them, both of which certainly postdate 250 BCE, certainly rejected the honor and glory attributed *solely* to Moses. Before 200 BCE, and continuing until the time of Hillel, they may have embodied a polemic against the Mosaic Books (the Pentateuch of the Hebrew Bible). Such speculations are prompted by passages such as the following one which antedates 200 BCE: "I Enoch, I saw the vision of the end of everything *alone;* and *none* among human beings will see as I have seen" (1 Enoch 19:3; italics mine). It is also instructive to contemplate why Moses is not mentioned, or alluded to, in the recitation of the history of God's dealings with his people; the Exodus from Egypt is described but "the Lord of the sheep" is not Moses by God (cf. 1 Enoch 89). According to 2 Enoch 47:2, which may date from the end of the first century CE, the books of Enoch are superior to all others. That indicates that those who revered them considered them superior to all the books in the Hebrew Bible.

7. The author clearly alludes here not only to Genesis 5 but also advocates the solar calendar which he, and his community, had stressed was linked with God's liturgical calendar (as in Jubilees and in the Qumran Scrolls).

8. TLevi 5:1, "At this moment the angel opened for me the gates of heaven and I saw the Holy Most High sitting on the throne."

9. TLevi 5:3, "Then the angel led me back to the earth."

10. A. F. J. Klijn, *Der Lateinische Text der Apokalypse des Esra* (Texte und Untersuchungen 131; Berlin: Akademie-Verlag, 1983), 56.

11. See my "The Historical Jesus in Light of Writings Contemporaneous with Him," *ANRW* (1982) II.25.1, 451-76.

12. For a discussion of Egyptian, Babylonian or Akkadian, Persian, and Greek and Latin apocalyptic works, and a guide to texts and translations, see Charlesworth, *The New Testament Apocrypha and Pseudepigrapha: A Guide to Publications, with Excursuses on Apocalypses* (American Theological Library Association Bibliography Series, no. 17; Metuchen, London: Scarecrow Press, 1987), 54-55.

13. See my discussion in "Folk Traditions in Jewish Apocalyptic Literature," *Mysteries and Revelations: Apocalyptic Studies Since the Uppsala Colloquium,* ed. J. J. Collins and J. H. Charlesworth (Journal for the Study of the Pseudepigrapha Series Supplement Series 9; Sheffield: Sheffield Academic Press, 1991), 91-113.

14. The attempt to make the apocalypses coherent and comprehensible to Post-Enlightenment scholars led many biblical specialists, like R. H. Charles, to emend and rearrange such masterpieces as 1 Enoch and the Apocalypse of John (see his commentaries on these books).

15. While the author of 4 Ezra is so distraught about the loss of the Temple and the destruction of Israel by the Romans that he cannot articulate a coherent answer to the perplexing problems he sees, the author of 2 Baruch tends to stress that the answers to human problems do not reside in the heavens and the future as much as in the Torah (the Law given to Moses): "But only prepare your heart so that you obey the Law, and be subject to those who are wise and understanding with fear" (46:5).

16. C. Newsom offers the opinion that only in ShirShabb are the "angels" called "priests." See Newsom, *Songs of the Sabbath Sacrifice: A Critical Edition* (Harvard Semitic Studies 27; Atlanta: Scholars Press, 1985), 26.

17. Newsom rightly states that "the cycle of the Sabbath Shirot is a quasi-mystical liturgy designed to evoke a sense of being present in the heavenly temple." *Songs of the Sabbath Sacrifice,* 59.

18. The early members of the Qumran group certainly inherited an interpretation of Isa 40:3 which signaled its importance, as we can see clearly from the indention of this verse in 1QIsa[a]. They understood this verse to mean, "A Voice cries, 'In the wilderness prepare the Way of Yahweh.' "The priests who began the Qumran movement withdrew from the Temple to live in the *wilderness.* They thought of themselves as members of the Way. Isaiah was one of the most important books for the development of Qumran theology. The Qumranites left us not only two large scrolls of Isaiah but also two major commentaries on Isaiah.

19. For the text of 4QTestLevi[a] see J. T. Milik, *The Books of Enoch* (Oxford: Clarendon Press, 1976), 23. Also, see Milik's article in *RB* 62 (1955), 328-406.

20. I was surprised to make this discovery; it is presented in the first chapter of *Jesus and the Dead Sea Scrolls* (New York: Doubleday, 1992), see esp. 20-22.

21. See the articles in J. Murphy-O'Connor and J. H. Charlesworth, eds., *Paul and the Dead Sea Scrolls* (New York: Crossroad, 1990). Also, see K. Stendahl and J. H. Charlesworth, eds., *The Scrolls and the New Testament* (New York: Crossroad, 1991).

22. These thoughts are presented by numerous scholars in my *John and the Dead Sea Scrolls* (New York: Crossroad, 1990).

23. See my "The Concept of the Messiah in the Pseudepigrapha," *ANRW* (1979) II.19.1; 188-218.

24. See the numerous studies in Charlesworth, et al., eds., *The Messiah* (Minneapolis: Fortress Press, 1992).

25. Some of Jesus' earliest followers (at first) proclaimed that Jesus would return as the Messiah; so Jesus was *messias designatus* (Acts 2:36 may suggest that Jesus had not been the Messiah but was so designated at the resurrection; if so, one needs to examine the links between such ideas and the concept of the exaltation of Enoch as Messiah in 1 Enoch 37–71). See such discussions by Charlesworth, Black, and VanderKam in *The Messiah*.

26. 1 Enoch 1–36 is one of the earliest sections of the Enoch corpus. An Aramaic fragment of this Book of Enoch (4QEn[a]) was found in Qumran Cave IV; it dates paleographically from the first half of the second century BCE. The original composition must antedate this copy. See J. T. Milik, *The Books of Enoch*, p. 22, see Plates I-V.

27. The thought was transmitted in Jewish writings which cannot be labeled apocalyptic; for example, it was highlighted in I-IV Maccabees and recited through the Amidah (the 18 Benedictions) in the synagogues.

28. It is instructive to note that in the margins to the Greek of Romans 1 are references to 1 Enoch *(bis)*, 2 Baruch, 4 Ezra, TMos, TJos, and 2–4 Maccabees.

29. The apocalypses are not theological treatises like Philo's allegorical volumes; they are expressions of anguish in troubled times. They are works by an individual who is giving expression to the frustrations and dreams of his own group, or community.

30. As Chris Beker states, "When Jewish Christianity emerged out of Judaism, it had to come to terms with the problem of a crucified Messiah. Its polemic with Judaism could not be fruitful unless the death of the Messiah was accounted for." Beker, *Paul the Apostle: The Triumph of God in Life and Thought* (Philadelphia: Fortress Press, 1980), 202.

31. If this story is not authentic, the loss of hope is one element in it that is authentic, as we know from the multiplicity of other indications of the disenchantment of the disciples, and the historical plausibility for it.

32. Bultmann, *Theology of the New Testament*, trans. K. Grobel, 2 vols. (New York: Scribner's, 1951), 1:42.

33. Beker rightly states that the "petition 'Maranatha' (1 Cor 16:22; Rev 22:20; Didache 16) expresses the fervent eschatological longing that is aroused by the resurrection and the gift of the Spirit." *Paul the Apostle*, 202.

34. As E. Käsemann stated, apocalypsology "first made historical thinking possible within the realm of Christianity. For just as it sees the world as having a definite beginning and a definite end, so too it sees history as moving unrepeatably in a definite direction, linked by a succession of clearly distinguishable epochs." Käsemann, "The Beginnings of Christian Theology," 34.

35. Against a stellar list of experts Beker shows that Romans 9–11 is an integral part of Romans, and that the gospel in Romans is "the revelation of the righteousness of God." Beker, "Romans 9–11 in the Context of the Early Church," *Princeton Seminary Bulletin, Supplementary Issue,* No. 1 (1990), 40-55. Beker also rightly calls for a reassessment of the theocentric nature (coherence) of NT, on the basis of which not only an appreciation of the Jewish antecedents of Christology can be insightfully digested, but an honest dialogue with present-day Judaism becomes meaningful (54-55).

36. See the reflections by J. VanderKam, M. Black, and myself in *The Messiah*.

37. See my "The Jewish Roots of Christology: The Discovery of the Hypostatic Voice," *SJT* 39 (1985), 19-41.

38. See my "The Portrayal of the Righteous as an Angel," *Ideal Figures in Ancient Judaism: Profiles and Paradigms,* eds. J. J. Collins and G. W. E. Nickelsburg (SCS 12; Chico, Calif.: Scholars Press, 1980), 135-51.

39. See, for example, not only the Rabbinic traditions but the TAdam.

40. My translation is based on S. Dedering, "Apocalypse of Baruch," *Vetus Testamentum Syriace* IV.3 (Leiden: E. J. Brill, 1973), 16.

41. Beker rightly warns that "a biblical theology of hope allows us to be realistic and honest about the poisonous reality of death and dying in our world. We are not compelled to dress it up with spiritualistically benign colors or to mask it as if its satanic destructiveness carries, after all, a lovely face." Beker, *Suffering and Hope: The Biblical Vision and the Human Predicament* (Philadelphia: Fortress Press, 1987), 90-91.

42. Bultmann boldly claimed: "Of course, Jesus was mistaken in thinking that the world was destined soon to come to an end." *Primitive Christianity in Its Contemporary Setting,* trans. R. H. Fuller (New York: World, 1956), 92. We might be able to point to Jesus traditions that suggest he was more perceptive, but we would have to confront the possibility that these may not derive from Jesus, and the certainty that some of his sayings were incorrect (viz. Mark 9:1). This insight does not clash

against any Christian dogma, but in fact frees us from creating a perfect Jesus, one that fits our imagination but is unhistorical.

43. Once again I agree with Beker: "Paul's apocalyptic gospel instills in us a new conviction and a new vision: the conviction that the triumph of God is in his hands alone and so transcends all our chronological speculations, and the vision that God's coming triumph will transform all our present striving and sighing (Rom 8:17-39) into the everlasting joy of his glory." Beker, *Paul's Apocalyptic Gospel: The Coming Triumph of God* (Philadelphia: Fortress Press, 1982), 17.

44. I am thinking in particular of the joy the odist expressed as he or she contemplated the coming of the promised Messiah; note, for example, Ode 41:3-4,

"We live in the Lord by his grace,
and life we receive by his Messiah.
For a great day has shined upon us,
and wonderful is he who has given to us of his glory."

45. See the numerous reflections in W. H. Gloer, ed., *Eschatology and the New Testament: Essays in Honor of George Raymond Beasley-Murray* (Peabody, Mass.: Hendrickson, 1988).

46. Obviously, my words are indebted to the challenging reflections of Beker in *Heirs of Paul: Paul's Legacy in the New Testament and in the Church Today* (Minneapolis: Fortress Press, 1991), 128.

47. Beker, " 'Paul's Theology' Consistent or Inconsistent?" *NTS* 34 (1988), 364-77, quoting from 376.

14. The Coherence of the Gospel in an Incoherent World

1. For a classic statement of the problems involved in the relation between faith and history see Van Austin Harvey, *The Historian and the Believer: The Morality of Historical Knowledge and Christian Belief* (Toronto: The Macmillan Company, 1966). For a discussion of the problem of history and eschatology see Carl E. Braaten, *History and Hermeneutics*. Volume II in "New Directions in Theology Today" (Philadelphia: Westminster Press, 1966), esp. 160-79.

2. Johannes Weiss, *Jesus' Proclamation of the Kingdom of God*. Eds., Richard H. Hiers and D. Larrimore Holland in "Lives of Jesus Series," ed. Leander E. Keck (Philadelphia: Fortress Press, 1971), 135. The use of the pejorative phrase "primitive Christianity," of course, represents a significant value judgment.

3. J. Christiaan Beker, *The Triumph of God: The Essence of Paul's Thought*, trans. Loren T. Stuckenbruck (Minneapolis: Fortress Press, 1990), 19. So too, "The apocalyptic field of meaning, determined and modified by the Christ-event, constitutes the decisive coherent center of Paul's thought," 115. Beker first argued that the theme of apocalyptic is not peripheral but a part of the coherent center of Paul's theology in his book *Paul the Apostle: The Triumph of God in Life and Thought* (Philadelphia: Fortress Press, 1980), 135-81. *The Trumph of God* is a 1990 English translation of the 1988 German text *Der Sieg Gottes*, and is important because in it Beker modifies and clarifies his interpretation of the categories of coherence and contingency which are central to his argument in *Paul the Apostle* (1980). See Beker, *The Triumph of God*, 117-25.

4. J. Christiaan Beker, *Paul's Apocalyptic Gospel: The Coming Triumph of God* (Philadelphia: Fortress Press, 1982), 106.

5. For a brief description of narrative theology, see George W. Stroup, "Narrative Theology" in Donald W. Musser and Joseph L. Price, eds., *A New Handbook of Christian Theology* (Nashville: Abingdon Press, 1992), 323-27.

6. Whether narrative theologians can evade the metaphysical issues that traditionally have confronted theologians remains to be seen. For an excellent discussion of this issue see Julian Hartt, "Theological Investments in Story: Some Comments on Recent Developments and Some Proposals," responses by Stephen Crites, "A Respectful Reply to the Assertorical Theologian" and Stanley Hauerwas, "Why the Truth Demands Truthfulness: An Imperious Engagement with Hartt," and Hartt's response to the responses, "Reply to Crites and Hauerwas" in *Why Narrative? Readings in Narrative Theology*. Eds. Stanley Hauerwas and L. Gregory Jones (Grand Rapids, Mich.: Eerdmans, 1989), 279-319.

7. To the best of my knowledge, Beker has not expressed his reservations about narrative theology in print, but only in personal conversation.

8. That is not to suggest that the Bible is a seamless cloth of univocal meaning. Between the extremes represented, on the one hand, by those who would reduce the varied voices of the Bible

to a single message, such as some forms of scholasticism and in our time some forms of "salvation history," and, on the other hand, by those literary interpretations of the Bible that suggest we have only varied texts that have little or nothing to do with one another, a variety of gods but not diverse statements about God, there is a third possibility that amidst the Bible's diverse dramas there is a larger, unfolding story or drama about a single character. See Walter Brueggemann's helpful claim that "biblical faith as drama for our time and place is a way of reading that respects and takes full account of the text," in Brueggemann, *Texts Under Negotiation: The Bible and Postmodern Imagination* (Minneapolis: Fortress Press, 1993), 67.

9. For Beker's understanding of the relation between the terms eschatology and apocalyptic see Beker, *Paul's Apocalyptic Gospel*, 14.

10. For a discussion of the relation between Chris Beker's personal history and his affirmation of the importance of an apocalyptic gospel and its implications for Christian convictions about suffering and hope, see J. Christiaan Beker, *Suffering and Hope: The Biblical Vision and the Human Predicament* (Philadelphia: Fortress Press, 1987), esp. 9-12. The relation between Beker's personal history and his commitment to Pauline apocalyptic is spelled out in even greater detail in Ben C. Ollenburger, "Suffering and Hope: The Story Behind the Book" first published in *Theology Today*, vol. 44/3 (October, 1987), 350-59, and reprinted in J. C. Beker's *Suffering and Hope* (Grand Rapids, Mich.: Eerdmans, 1994), 1-16.

11. John Calvin, *Institutes of the Christian Religion*, ed. John T. McNeill, trans. Ford Lewis Battles, 2 vols. in "The Library of Christian Classics" (Philadelphia: Westminster Press, 1960), 1:37.

12. H. Richard Niebuhr, *The Meaning of Revelation* (New York: The Macmillan Company, 1962), 86. A major issue here is to what extent "narrative" entails "history," and what kind of history is meant. As psychoanalysis has shown us, remembered history is a reality regardless of whether it "happened."

13. Hence the appropriateness of Amos Wilder's claim that "The narrative mode is uniquely important in Christianity." Amos N. Wilder, *The Language of the Gospel: Early Christian Rhetoric* (New York and Evanston: Harper & Row, 1964), 64.

14. The other option would be to reconstruct the gospel on the basis of personal experience, an option that is explicitly proposed in some forms of feminist theology. For example, see Rosemary Ruether, *Sexism and God-Talk: Toward a Feminist Theology* (Beacon Press: Boston, 1983), 18-20.

15. Alasdair MacIntyre, *After Virtue: A Study in Moral Theory* (Notre Dame: University of Notre Dame Press, 1981), 203.

16. Ibid.

17. Alasdair MacIntyre, "Epistemological Crises, Dramatic Narrative, and the Philosophy of Science" in *Why Narrative?*, 140.

18. Ibid., 153.

19. Louis O. Mink, "History and Fiction as Modes of Comprehension" in *New Literary History* I (1970), 557-58. See also Louis O. Mink, "Narrative Form as a Cognitive Instrument" in *The Writing of History*, eds. R. H. Canary and H. Kozicki (Madison: University of Wisconsin Press, 1978). See also Hayden White, "The Value of Narrativity in the Representation of Reality" in *On Narrative*, ed. W. J. T. Mitchell (Chicago: University of Chicago Press, 1981), 1-24. In addition, see Paul Ricoeur's description of a "threefold mimesis" and his claim that "between the activity of narrating a story and the temporal character of human experience there exists a correlation that is not merely accidental but that presents a transcultural form of necessity" in Ricoeur, *Time and Narrative*, 3 vols., trans. Kathleen McLaughlin and David Pellauer (Chicago: The University of Chicago Press, 1984), 1:52. For a clear and concise study of the important debate about the "representational" nature of narrative, see David Carr, *Time, Narrative, and History* (Bloomington: Indiana University Press, 1986).

20. Stephen Crites, "The Narrative Quality of Experience" in *Why Narrative?*, 66.

21. Ibid., 76-77.

22. Ibid., 81.

23. Ibid., 69.

24. Ibid., 70.

25. Ibid., 71.

26. Ibid., 77. Italics mine.

27. Emil L. Fackenheim, *God's Presence in History: Jewish Affirmations and Philosophical Reflections* (New York: Harper & Row, 1970), 92.

28. MacIntyre, *After Virtue*, 202.

29. Not all NT scholars agree that Mark 13 is an apocalyptic text. For example see Dan O. Via, Jr., *Kerygma and Comedy in the New Testament: A Structuralist Approach to Hermeneutic* (Philadelphia: Fortress Press, 1975), 78-90.

30. Willi Marxsen, *Mark the Evangelist: Studies on the Redaction History of the Gospel*, trans. James Boyce, Donald Juel, William Poehlmann, with Roy A. Harrisville (Nashville: Abingdon Press, 1969), 183.

31. Norman Perrin, "Towards an Interpretation of the Gospel of Mark" in *Christology and a Modern Pilgrimage: A Discussion with Norman Perrin*, ed. Hans Dieter Betz (Missoula, Mont.: Society of Biblical Literature, 1971), 55.

32. Frank Kermode, *The Genesis of Secrecy: On the Interpretation of Narrative* (Cambridge, Mass.: Harvard University Press, 1979), 134.

33. For an excellent brief discussion of some of the major exegetical issues that surround Mark 13—such as historicity, date, purpose—see Adela Yarbro Collins, *The Beginning of the Gospel: Probings of Mark in Context* (Minneapolis: Fortress Press, 1992), 73-91.

34. Kermode, *The Genesis of Secrecy*, 127-28.

35. For a discussion of the relation between crisis, transition, and apocalypse see Frank Kermode, *The Sense of an Ending: Studies in the Theory of Fiction* (London: Oxford University Press, 1967).

36. Ched Myers, *Binding the Strong Man: A Political Reading of Mark's Story of Jesus* (Maryknoll, N.Y.: Orbis Books, 1988), 353.

37. That is not to suggest that what Jesus has to say about the Temple and Jerusalem is unimportant. See, for example, Elizabeth Struthers Malbon, *Narrative Space and Mythic Meaning in Mark* (San Francisco: Harper & Row, 1986), 30-34, 120-26, and Mary Ann Tolbert, *Sowing the Gospel: Mark's World in Literary-Historical Perspective* (Minneapolis: Fortress Press, 1989), 257-70.

38. MacIntyre, *After Virtue*, 202.

15. "Feminist" Theology and Biblical Interpretation

1. These issues pervade Beker's writings. As is well known, he proposes a model of "coherence and contingency" of scripture, inseparable from each other, as a way of dealing with these issues. This model is coupled with a model he describes as a "catalytic hermeneutic" that seeks to avoid both anachronistic literalism and modernistic rationalization of our own ideologies. See most recently and concisely his essay "The Authority of Scripture: Normative or Incidental?" *TToday* 49 (1992), 376-82.

2. See his *Suffering and Hope: The Biblical Vision and the Human Predicament* (Philadelphia: Fortress Press, 1987); also, B. Ollenburger, "Suffering and Hope: the Story Behind the Book," *TToday* 44 (1987), 350-59.

3. The word "feminist" is placed in quotation marks in the title of this essay to indicate that this adjective sometimes stands as a general descriptor related to advocacy for women but that in certain contexts it refers more narrowly to the work of white North Atlantic persons, with other descriptors being used for the work of other groups. See the body of this essay.

4. Letty M. Russell, *Church in the Round: Feminist Interpretation of the Church* (Louisville: Westminster/John Knox Press, 1993), 22. Note that Russell is offering her own definition as a white, North Atlantic woman. The significance of "womanist," "*mujerista*," and other theologies wishing to distinguish themselves from the term "feminist" is discussed later in this essay.

5. Androcentrism has scarcely been restricted to biblical studies. Until recently theorists attributed the development of language among human beings to "the coordination needed to hunt large animals (an all-male activity in conventional reconstructions)" and supposed that "consciousness itself emerged from the more complex mental functioning required to stalk game (another male preserve). Women, under these theories, were simply invisible. . . . " S. J. Gould, "The Invisible Woman," *Natural History* 102 (1993), 14.

6. C. Myers, *Discovering Eve: Ancient Israelite Women in Context* (New York: Oxford University Press, 1988), 24-45.

7. See for example E. Schüssler Fiorenza, *Bread Not Stone: The Challenge of Feminist Biblical Interpretation* (Boston: Beacon, 1984), 5.

8. For example, E. D. Gray, *Green Paradise Lost* (Wellesley, Mass.: Roundtable, 1979), 2-6.

9. "Feminist" theology is not just a Judeo-Christian enterprise. There are women who fit within the umbrella term feminism among the theological thinkers of Hinduism, Buddhism, Islam, and other world and folk religions. There are also a number of feminists who are trying to develop an alternative religious consciousness or conception of God. In particular, some feminist theologians

who began within the Judeo-Christian tradition have concluded that they cannot remain within it. They believe that the Judeo-Christian tradition is so intrinsically androcentric and patriarchal in perspective and structure that it cannot be reinterpreted so as to be compatible with the basic tenets of their "feminist" worldview. Best known and a pioneer among such feminists is Mary Daly (*Beyond God the Father: Toward a Philosophy of Women's Liberation* [Boston: Beacon, 1973]). The case has been argued more recently by Daphne Hampson, a former Anglican leader in the struggle for women's ordination (*Theology and Feminism* [Oxford: Basil Blackwell, 1990]).

10. Renita J. Weems suggests gaining greater access to African-American women's biblical interpretation by perusing "non-conventional" literature, such as publications of denominations and small religious presses. "Do You See What I See? Diversity in Interpretation," *Church and Society* 82 (1991), 29.

11. On the problem of generalizing white women's experience, see S. Thistlethwaite, *Sex, Race, and God: Christian Feminism in Black and White* (New York: Crossroad, 1991), 11-26.

12. Various lists of such biblical imagery are readily available. Among these is V. R. Mollenkott, *The Divine Feminine: The Biblical Imagery of God as Female* (New York: Crossroad, 1984). Trible provides a more specialized study of many of the OT examples in *God and the Rhetoric of Sexuality* (Philadelphia: Fortress Press, 1978), 31-59.

13. *Faith Looking Forward: The Hymns and Songs of Brian Wren* (Carol Stream, Ill.: Hope Publishing Co.), no. 3.

14. *Models of God: Theology for an Ecological Nuclear Age* (Philadelphia: Fortress Press, 1987), 91-174.

15. *Sex, Race, and God*, 109-20, esp. 117. See C. T. Gilkes, " 'Some Mother's Son, Some Father's Daughter': Gender and Biblical Language in Afro-Christian Worship Tradition," in *Shaping New Visions: Gender and Values in American Culture*, C. W. Atkinson et al. eds. (Ann Arbor: UMI Research Press, 1987).

16. *She Who Is: The Mystery of God in Feminist Theological Discourse* (New York: Crossroad, 1992), 61. For a broad discussion of the theme of experience in feminist theology, see Ann Carr, *Transforming Grace: Women's Experience and Christian Tradition* (San Francisco: Harper & Row, 1988), 117-33. See also L. Russell, *Household of Freedom: Authority in Feminist Theology* (Philadelphia: Westminster Press, 1987), 30-32.

17. *Bread Not Stone*, 13-14.

18. *All We're Meant to Be: Biblical Feminism for Today*, rev. ed. (Nashville: Abingdon Press, 1986), 31.

19. "The Bible and *Mujerista* Theology," in *Lift Every Voice: Constructing Christian Theologies from the Underside*, S. B. Thistlethwaite and M. Engels, eds. (San Francisco: HarperSanFrancisco, 1990), 261-68 and esp. 268 and n. 13, indicating her modeling of this view of the Bible upon E. S. Fiorenza's proposals in *Bread Not Stone*.

20. "Womanist Interpretations of the New Testament," *JFSR* 6 (1990), 42.

21. "Womanist Interpretations," 60-61.

22. *Household of Freedom*, 32-33.

23. *Toward an Asian Principle of Interpretation: A Filipino Women's Experience*, written for the EATWOT Asian Feminist Theology Meeting, Madras, India, Dec. 15–20, 1990 (Manila: Forum for Interdisciplinary Endeavors and Studies [FIDES] and Institute of Women Studies [IWS], 1991), 17. The general description by Chung Hyun Kyung of how Asian women do theology fits well with this concrete illustration from the Philippines. Chung emphasizes the starting point of "active listening to women's storytelling, especially those from the bottom stratum of Asian society." This leads to critical social analysis and to consideration of the Bible as part of theological reflection. In the Asian setting, however, women must take care to "free the Bible and its interpretation from its age-old captivity by patriarchy, colonialism, and Western cultural imperialism." *Struggle to Be the Sun Again: Introducing Asian Women's Theology* (Maryknoll, N.Y.: Orbis Books, 1990), 106-7. For further discussion of method from Asian settings, see *We Dare to Dream: Doing Theology as Asian Women*, V. Fabella MM and S. A. Lee Park, eds. (Maryknoll, N.Y.: Orbis Books, 1989), esp. Part Three.

24. *Toward an Asian Principle*, 18.

25. This point is made powerfully by bell hooks in *Ain't I a Woman: Black Women and Feminism* (Boston: South End, 1981), 136-42. See also Thistlethwaite, *Sex, Race, and God*, 11-26.

26. The practical value of working through particularities to an interest in commonalities, or to consideration of a dialectical relationship between points of unity and diversity among groups of many perspectives, was highlighted in personal conversation with Sr. Mary John Mananzan OSB, St. Scholastica College, Manila, February 1993. R. Weems speaks of the "commitment of African American

women to the survival of all peoples" as the meaning of a "womanist" perspective. ("African American Women and the Bible," in *Stony the Road We Trod*, ed. C. H. Felder [Minneapolis: Fortress Press, 1991] 70). The language sounds similar to Russell's description of feminism (see above), yet the emphasis is on the solidarity of a triply oppressed group (female, black, very often poor) with the least of the least throughout the globe in a way that is not possible for white women. First world white women need to heed Thistlethwaite's warning against glossing over cultural differences and seeking too soon for sisterhood or bonding across race and class lines (*Sex, Race, and God*, 125 and *passim*).

27. "Between Echo and Narcissus: The Role of the Bible in Feminist Theology," *Int* XLII (1988), 29.

28. "A Model for Bible Study in Context," in *Changing Contexts of Our Faith*, ed. L. M. Russell (Philadelphia: Fortress Press, 1985), 102-8.

29. *Church in the Round*, 27-36.

30. "Do You See What I See?" 28-32.

31. The Seoul group of the Presbyterian Church of Korea (PCK) Women Ministers' Association, May 1993. Arrangements for my participation in this Bible study were made by Choi Man Ja.

32. Judg 5:28-30.

33. "African American Women and the Bible," 67-68.

34. Participants were members of the Association of Women in Theology (theologically trained women) of the Visayas, with representatives from the areas of Iloilo, Cebu, and Dumaguete. The meeting in Dumaguete City was hosted by Rev. Renate Rose and chaired by Ms. Nhitz Guillergan.

35. Compare the interpretation by Sr. Helen Graham MM, a white North American Roman Catholic who has been living and working in the Philippines for about twenty-five years: "Separated, the two women are vulnerable to poverty and affliction, the lot of widows in patriarchal societies. . . . had they gone their separate ways [they] most probably would not have found well-being for themselves, nor brought blessing upon their contemporaries (let alone on generations yet to come)." From "Empowerment of Women for Peace," in *Woman and Religion*, ed. Sr. Mary John Mananzan, OSB (Manila: The Institute of Women's Studies, St. Scholastica College, 1988), 55-56.

36. These gatherings were arranged by Dr. Anna May Say Pa, Professor of OT and Assistant Principal of the Myanmar Institute of Theology.

37. A meeting of the Kansei Area Association of Women Doing Theology, chaired by its president, Dr. Akiko Yamashita of the NCC Study Center of Japanese Religions. The meeting opportunity was arranged by Mr. Tom Hastings.

38. A gathering of women (and a very few men) from across the Presbyterian Church of Taiwan, arranged by Rev. Shu-chen Chuang, head of the Women's Department of the PCT. Papers on Ruth were presented by Mrs. Susan Lu Hsu and Rev. Hsin-Hui Chen.

39. "Do You See What I See?," 29-30.

40. *Just a Sister Away: A Womanist Vision of Women's Relationships in the Bible* (San Diego: LuraMedia, 1988), 28.

41. "The Literary Characterization of Mothers and Sexual Politics in the Hebrew Bible," in *Feminist Perspectives on Biblical Scholarship*, ed. A. Y. Collins (Chico, Calif.: Scholars Press, 1985), 117-36, citation from 130.

42. *God and the Rhetoric of Sexuality* (Philadelphia: Fortress Press, 1978), 166-99. Trible also contributed the "Ruth" entry for the *Anchor Bible Dictionary*.

43. Ibid., 173. Trible's specific comparison is to the decision of Abraham to follow God's call (Genesis 12). Abraham has a promise, whereas Ruth has none.

44. Ibid., 195.

45. *Compromising Redemption: Relating Characters in the Book of Ruth* (Louisville, Ky.: Westminster/John Knox Press, 1990).

46. For discussion of these highlights of Fewell and Gunn's 140 monograph, see (in the order summarized in the paragraph), esp. 28, 98, 42-43, 91, 80-81, 105.

16. Biblical Theology and Social Ethics

1. See my *Violence and Nonviolence in South Africa* (Philadelphia: New Society Publishers, 1987), chapter 2 for an analysis of Jesus' teaching on nonviolence. On the question of method, Richard B. Hays has written an excellent piece, "Scripture-Shaped Community: The Problem of Method in New Testament Ethics," *Interpretation* 44 (January 1990), 29-37.

2. The potential of the Powers in the development of a Christian ethic has been most persistently explored by William Stringfellow in all his books; see especially *Free in Obedience* (New York: Seabury Press, 1964), and *An Ethic for Christians and Other Aliens in a Strange Land* (Waco, Tex.: Word Books, 1973). John Howard Yoder's *The Politics of Jesus* (Grand Rapids, Mich.: Eerdmans, 1972), 135-214, has an excellent treatment of the Powers, but they are not, as in Stringfellow, the framework of the entire study. Also of seminal importance is Hendrick Berkhof, *Christ and the Powers* (Scottdale, Pa.: Herald Press, 1962), and Heinrich Schlier, *Principalities and Powers in the New Testament* (New York: Herder & Herder, 1961). See also the important studies of Clinton Morrison, *The Powers That Be* (London: SCM Press, 1960); G. B. Caird, *Principalities and Powers* (Oxford: Clarendon Press, 1956); E. Gordon Rupp, *Principalities and Powers* (London: Epworth Press, 1952); G. H. C. MacGregor, "Principalities and Powers: The Cosmic Background of Paul's Thought," *New Testament Studies* 1 (1954), 17-28; James S. Stewart, "On a Neglected Emphasis in New Testament Theology," *Scottish Journal of Theology* 4 (1951), 292-301; W. A. Visser't Hooft, *The Kingship of Christ* (New York: Harper, 1948); A. H. van den Heuvel, *These Rebellious Powers* (New York: Friendship Press, 1965).

3. Walter Wink, *Naming the Powers* (Philadelphia: Fortress Press, 1984); *Unmasking the Powers* (Philadelphia: Fortress Press, 1986); and *Engaging the Powers* (Philadelphia: Fortress Press, forthcoming).

4. See *Unmasking the Powers*, chapter 3.

5. Ibid., chapter 4.

6. Author's translation. See *Naming the Powers*, 55-60 for a discussion of the translation difficulties.

7. René Girard, *Things Hidden Since the Foundation of the World* (Stanford: Stanford University Press, 1987), 209.

8. "The violence of the Cross mirrored [Paul's] own violence; in it he saw himself and what the law had made him, and he saw the whole human resistance to God," Robert G. Hamerton-Kelly, "Sacred Violence and the Curse of the Law (Gal 3:13), The Death of Christ as a Sacrificial Travesty," *New Testament Studies* 36 (1990), 102.

9. W. H. Auden, "The Chimeras," *Collected Shorter Poems* (London: Faber & Faber, 1950), 311.

10. Girard, *Things Hidden Since the Foundation of the World*, 214.

11. René Girard, *The Scapegoat* (Baltimore: Johns Hopkins University Press, 1986), 129.

12. Paul Tillich, *Systematic Theology* (Chicago: University of Chicago Press, 1951), 1:136. However, I cannot accept Tillich's statement that Jesus as the Christ is "the one who sacrifices what is merely 'Jesus' in him. The decisive trait in his picture is the continual self-surrender of Jesus who is Jesus to Jesus who is the Christ" (p. 134). We call Jesus the Christ, rather, because he was fully Jesus. I would prefer to say that Jesus sacrifices his ego to his Self, to use Jung's terms; sacrifices his socially conditioned self-understanding for the actual divine possibility latent in him through creation; sacrifices his belongingness to a fallen, alienated ethos, with all its penetrations into him through the process of socialization, to the authentic possibility of his existence as it came to expression through the creative promptings of the Spirit of God. It is this confluence, this actualization by an ego of its own self, which is what it means to become fully human, and which constellates in him the incarnate Christ.

13. Ibid., 134. This means that we are free to choose to follow or not to follow Jesus' traditions (wearing the phylactery, for instance—Matt 9:20); to choose to practice or not to practice his piety (Tillich refused to address God personally in prayer; others prefer a personal address); and to choose to follow or not to follow specific ethical advice (Jesus' teaching on divorce, for example, which was prompted in part at least by the ease with which wives were being put aside by their husbands in first century society, leaving many women no alternative for survival but prostitution).

14. Ephesians 1:20-22a NEB, modified, and using the reading in note d.

15. See *Naming the Powers*, 50-55 for the arguments justifying translating 1 Cor 15:24 as "neutralizing" rather than "destroying."

16. Bill Moyer, "The Movement Action Plan: A Strategic Framework Describing the Eight Stages of Successful Social Movements" (Movement for a New Society, 721 Shrader Street, San Francisco, Calif., 1986).

17. See Bill Kellerman, *Seasons of Faith and Conscience* (Maryknoll, N.Y.: Orbis Books, 1991).

LIST OF CONTRIBUTORS

Kathleen McVey: Joseph Ross Stevenson Professor of Church History, Princeton Theological Seminary

Jean-Loup Seban: Dean of the Chapel, Brussels, Belgium

Steven J. Kraftchick: Assistant Professor of New Testament, Candler School of Theology, Emory University

Ben C. Ollenburger: Professor of Biblical Studies, Associated Mennonite Biblical Seminary

Robert Morgan: Lecturer in New Testament, Linacre College, Oxford University

J. J. M. Roberts: William Henry Green Professor of Old Testament Literature, Princeton Theological Seminary

Bernhard W. Anderson: Professor of Old Testament Theology, Emeritus, Princeton Theological Seminary

Patrick D. Miller: Charles T. Haley Professor of Old Testament, Princeton Theological Seminary

Walter Brueggemann: William Marcellus McPheaters Professor of Old Testament, Columbia Theological Seminary

Kathleen M. O'Connor: Associate Professor of Old Testament, Columbia Theological Seminary

Hendrikus Boers: Professor of New Testament, Candler School of Theology, Emory University

Charles D. Myers, Jr.: Associate Professor of New Testament, Gettysburg College

James H. Charlesworth: George L. Collord Professor of New Testament Languages and Literature, Princeton Theological Seminary

George W. Stroup: Professor of Theology, Columbia Theological Seminary

Katharine Doob Sakenfeld: William Albright Eisenberger Professor of Old Testament Literature and Exegesis, Princeton Theological Seminary

Walter Wink: Auburn Professor of Biblical Interpretation, Auburn Seminary

Luke Timothy Johnson: Robert W. Woodruff Professor of New Testament and Christian Origins, Candler School of Theology, Emory University